THE
Return
OF THE
Rebel Angels

"Read this book! Timothy Wyllie's mammoth reconfiguration of humankind's imprinted perceptions rips apart concepts and questions, dissolving the mysterious shadow worlds and interlaced realms of science to brilliantly expose its reluctant but imminent surrender to strings of holographic universes he calls the Multiverse. Once reason is defeated the fun really starts as Wyllie's writing explodes joyously, using *The Urantia Book* as a cornerstone for comprehension of the past and all futures. Suddenly his proposition seems eminently plausible. Quite a mindblower . . . it's a delicious meal of mind and vision."

GENESIS BREYER P-ORRIDGE, AUTHOR OF
THEE PSYCHICK BIBLE AND *30 YEARS OF BEING CUT-UP*

"Timothy Wyllie presents a story as compelling as it is eloquent, while inviting you to travel with him beyond a planet too fragile to survive without divine assistance. The journey, unlike any you can imagine, is often uncomfortable, but companion angels are never far away. *The Return of the Rebel Angels* is a story you cannot put down once you begin reading."

JOAN LESLIE WOODRUFF,
THERAPIST, COUNSELOR, AND AUTHOR OF
POLAR BEARS IN THE KITCHEN

THE
Return
OF THE
Rebel Angels

THE URANTIA MYSTERIES AND
THE COMING OF THE LIGHT

TIMOTHY WYLLIE

Bear & Company
Rochester, Vermont • Toronto, Canada

Bear & Company
One Park Street
Rochester, Vermont 05767
www.BearandCompanyBooks.com

Bear & Company is a division of Inner Traditions International

Library of Congress Cataloging-in-Publication Data
Wyllie, Timothy, 1940–
   The return of the rebel angels : the Urantia mysteries and the coming of the light
/ Timothy Wyllie.
      p. cm.
   Includes bibliographical references and index.
   Summary: "Furthers the revelations of The Urantia Book, providing a beautiful
vision of our coming return to the Multiverse"—Provided by publisher.
   ISBN 978-1-59143-125-1 (pbk.) — ISBN 978-1-59143-945-5 (ebook)
   1. Spiritual life. 2. Angels—Miscellanea. 3. Extraterrestrial beings—
Miscellanea. 4. Wyllie, Timothy, 1940– 5. Urantia Book. I. Title.
   BF1999.W96 2011
   299—dc23

                                                                    2011023500

Printed and bound in the United States by Thomson-Shore

10 9 8 7 6 5 4 3 2 1

Text design by Virginia Scott Bowman and layout by Priscilla Baker
This book was typeset in Garamond Premier Pro with Baskerville, Copperplate,
and Myriad Pro used as display typefaces

To send correspondence to the author of this book, mail a first-class letter to
the author c/o Inner Traditions • Bear & Company, One Park Street, Rochester,
VT 05767, and we will forward the communication, or visit the author's website
www.timothywyllie.com.

Contents

Acknowledgments ix

PREFACE **Whispers of the Soul** xv

INTRODUCTION **The Apocalypse Is Canceled** 1

PART ONE

Travels with an Angel

1 **Travels Out of Body** 11
The Conference-in-Spirit, Out-of-Body Travels,
the Assassination of Anwar Sadat

2 **The Emergence of the Sacred** 54
The Unlikely Return of the Maitreya, Sumer,
Glastonbury, and the Magic of Sacred Landscape

3 **Glimpses of Reincarnational Threads** 93
The Path of Art, Passing the Powers, Sexual
Obsession, and Cathar Reincarnation

4 **The Re-enchantment of Sacred Landscape** 122
Shamanism, Dreamtime, Dragons, Ley Lines,
and the Reality of Thoughtforms

5 **Intimations of a New Vision** 150
Ancient Conflicts, Genetic Endowments, Spiritual
Alchemy, and Intimations of a New Reality

6 The Twilight of the Gods   182
The Delphic Oracle, Entheogenic Archaeology,
and the Twilight of the Gods

7 The Plight of the Rebel Midwayers   207
Cosmic Consciousness, Telepathic Influences,
and the Plight of the Rebel Midwayers

8 The Challenges of Empathy   225
Negative Thoughtforms, the Challenge of Empathy, and
the Return of the Beings of the Violet Flame

PART TWO

Life in the True Age

9 Re-enchanting the Planet   251
Nature Spirits, Working with Angels, Crystal
Geomantics, and the Returning Cathars

10 The Return of Quetzalcoatl   290
Altered States, Rascals, Floatation Tanks,
the Mayan Factor, and the Return of Quetzalcoatl

11 The Extraterrestrial Enigma   320
The ET Enigma, Djinn, Frequency-Domains, the
Holographic Multiverse, and Intraterrestrial Craft

12 The Angelic Conspiracy and the   349
Global Transformation
The Angelic Conspiracy, a Message from Zeta Reticuli,
and the Great Transformation

AFTERWORD **We're All Doomed to Be Perfect**   389

✠

APPENDIX A Some Speculative Scenarios on the Future
of the Human Race   402

APPENDIX B The Sacred Use of Entheogens, Power
Planets, and Sacred Chemistry   414

APPENDIX C The Spiritual Underpinnings of the
Multiverse as a Cosmic Hologram   418

APPENDIX D Three Unusual Personal Experiences
Suggesting Optimism   425

✠

Glossary   433

Notes   438

Recommended Reading   440

Index   447

About the Author   457

Note to the Reader
Regarding a Glossary of Terms

In this work the author has coined or provided specialized definitions of certain words that are derived from *The Urantia Book,* a key source text. A complete list of these terms and their meanings has been provided in the glossary at the back of this book for your ready reference.

Acknowledgments

I'd like to express my appreciation to all those named and unnamed courageous souls who participated in these explorations of the subtle realms. In particular, I'm thankful for the continuing presence in my life of Alma Daniel, P. R. D'or, Alexandra Manzi Fe, Christopher Castle, Urszula Bolimowska, Juno Atkin, and Andrew Ramer, all of whom played key parts in the developing story.

My mother, Diana Wyllie, and six other close friends—Carolina Ely, John C. Lilly, Lady Jaye Brewer P-Orridge, Raymond Bret Koch, Timothy Leary, and John Michell—died over the course of writing this book. Each one inspired me in his or her own way, and I wish them all well as they adventure on inward.

I want to thank Armand DiMele for finding A. S. J. Tessimond's poem *Day Dream;* Randy Trout for his futique friendship; Adam Parfrey for his hospitality and White Russians; Anthony and Jan Roberts for geomantic riffs; Robert Faust for our dangerous adventures together; Edward Mason for Thelemite insights; Roberta Quist for her delphinic ubiquity; Lifus for a magical mystery tour; Phillip Krapf for his courage and integrity; Peter Sterling for sharing his contact with the Zetas; the Parfit sisters for their Cathar heritage; Malachi McCormick for his humorous skepticism; Daniel Mator for his youthful wisdom; Francois Xavier for his depth of intuitive understanding; Rachel Garcia for her patient electronic support; Byron Belitsos for his probing questions; Yanni Posnakoff for his artistic commitment to angels; Premaratma for his tender caring; Robert Davis for his profound encouragement; Dimitri for his spiritual nobility;

David Field for reincarnational companionship; Elise Bailey for the story of her hybrid offspring; and to Jessie, my adorable Cathar reincarnate, wherever you are, my love and ancient resonance.

This is also a chance to express my gratitude openly to PaulMichael Waterman, who under the name of "Edward" was the light-trance medium responsible for the original 1981 angel transmissions that launched me off on this thirty-year interspecies journey. Although I quote from his angel transmissions as received and published in my first book, *Dolphins, ETs & Angels*, the continuing integrity of the information remains a credit to Paul's channeling clarity.

Editing inevitably improves a book, so my loving appreciation goes to Elianne Obadiah, the Writer's Midwife, for her sensitivity and wisdom in matters Urantian and for all her initial input in structuring this book. I've particularly enjoyed working with my Inner Traditions/Bear & Company editor, Anne Dillon. Her admirable intelligence encompassed and assimilated what has to be one of the more convoluted of angelic/human dramas and wove the depth of her understanding into the book in a delightfully graceful manner.

I'd also like to thank Jon Graham, acquisitions editor at Inner Traditions/Bear & Company, for his enthusiasm and for recognizing the value of this work. I also express my gratitude to all at Inner Traditions/ Bear & Company, including Managing Editor, Jeanie Levitan; the head of marketing, John Hayes; Virginia Scott Bowman; Priscilla Baker; Janet Jesso; and Manzanita Carpenter, all of whom I haven't met and yet who have supported, edited, proofread, designed, and marketed this book.

I'm happily grateful to my friend Kevin Sanders, who has rightly complained of the lack of an index in my previous books and boldly stepped forward to meet the challenge for this one.

A book such as this needs to be more than the whimsical ramblings of a heretical hermit, so over the years I've been fortunate to gather a small group I can rely on for honest feedback upon reading the manuscript; these include Kathe McCaffrey, Nikola Wittmer, Gordon Phinn, Rob Drexel, Yana Murphy, Roberta Quist, Nathan Guc, Juno Atkin, and Luna Olcott. I'm thankful for all their invaluable insights and encouragement.

When the veil between the worlds is finally drawn aside we will appreciate the part that angels play in all our lives. While this book is the result of my thirty-year interspecies explorations and any conceptual or speculative errors are mine, I've been continually grateful for the subtle guidance of my celestial friends: my companion angels, Joy and Beauty; Georgia, the watcher who works with me; and Zophiel, the angel who stands behind me as I write and gives me a jolt of pleasure when I get the words right.

All whom Moses called wise are represented as sojourners. Their souls are never colonists leaving heaven for a new home. Their way is to visit earthly nature as men who travel abroad to see and learn. So when they have stayed awhile in their bodies, and beheld through them all that sense and mortality have to show, they make their way back to the place from which they set out at first. To them the heavenly region, where their citizenship lies, is their native land: the earthly region, in which they became sojourners, is a foreign country.

PHILO, *ON THE UNCHANGEABLENESS OF GOD*

Whispers of
the Soul

Coming of age in the 1960s and growing up in London, it was all too conceivable to anyone with any imagination that an atomic holocaust seemed inevitable. By the late seventies, the global situation, if anything, was even more threatening. Yet, contrary to our '60s doomsday outlook, we hadn't destroyed ourselves thus far. Perhaps there was some hope after all. Was the planet transforming in front of our noses in ways we didn't understand? Were our heads so firmly stuck in the sand of our busy lives that we were missing what was *really* going on? Given the superpowers' belligerence, the devastating effect of atomic and hydrogen weapons, and Murphy's Law, our continuing survival seemed so counter-intuitive to me that it led me on a thirty-year exploration of why this might be so.

Thus it was that, in 1978, I started keeping notes for books I intended to write about my quest. I now have over seventy large black books filled with notes, essays, drawings, and photos, charting both significant personal changes and general changes on the planet since that time. This book, *The Return of the Rebel Angels,* is, like the first two in this series,* highly personal. For this reason I have also included a number of my

---

*The first two books of the series are *Dolphins, ETs & Angels,* Bear & Company, 1992, and *Adventures Among Spiritual Intelligences,* Wisdom Editions, 2001.

graphics—images that emerged as I sought to assimilate the spiritual impact of some of the adventures related herein.

During the course of my exploration, it was becoming sadly obvious that straight scientists in general had no real solutions for what was happening on the planet, so I felt more encouraged to follow the subtle whispers of my soul. I have become gradually aware over this three-decade journey that the frequency-domain we think of as consensus reality can be more constructively understood as a kindergarten. It's a domain in which we have the opportunity to explore the extremes of human behavior and belief systems, and to experience their consequences, positive or negative. It's not a "world that needs to be saved," it's a playpen created for individual souls to wake up within. It's a chance to choose love over fear, truth over lies, courage over timidity, forgiveness over resentment, and mercy over cruelty—individual by individual, moment by moment.

What we are witnessing now are the consequences of many tens of thousands of years of individual human choices, all converging at the same time, in what appears to be an irrevocable descent into a spiral of species extinction. There are so many impending disasters facing the human race at this point—many of them originally caused by the misuse of technology or its unintended consequences—that, in looking at the global situation from a purely human viewpoint, it can only get progressively worse.

However, this would be missing half the story. When our eyes are opened to the reality of a vast and populated Multiverse, inhabited by extraterrestrial entities not so dissimilar to us and organized from the subtle planes by countless celestial beings, the picture becomes very different indeed. We're no longer a cosmic accident, alone and shivering in the cosmic night and utterly dependent on our own devices to work our way out of a global situation that was rigged from the start. In the course of my travels and encounters I've also come to understand there are many of us who have chosen to incarnate at this crucial time in human history and also that we've been tirelessly trained for the tasks ahead.

Since I am writing from within a Judeo-Christian culture and using the symbols and cosmology of this tradition, I'm inclined to think of the coming transformation as focusing around the return of Christ Michael.* I use *The Urantia Book*'s name "Christ Michael" in my work since it accords the being we know as Jesus Christ, or Joshua ben Joseph, his formal Multiverse title. So, if I place more emphasis on the return of Christ Michael to the planet of his incarnation, it's because he's known to have promised it and because that is the spiritual form in which he'll most likely be recognized in the West. (See plate 1 of the color insert.)

In another culture the event might be perceived in terms of the return of Quetzalcoatl, the feathered serpent; or the appearance of the thirteenth Imam; or the Zoroastrian Saoshyant; or the final moments of the Kali Yuga. Many ancient indigenous cultures also point to this time as being the end of an era, holding prophecies that their most revered elders will return. Whether Maitreya or Messiah, and whenever this event *does* occur, of one thing I'm certain: every human being present on the planet—to the extent that they are able to integrate the truly mysterious into their lives—will have the chance to fully know and to fully understand what is happening.

When I was writing the first book in this series, about a quarter of the way through, I was given the choice by an angel who was helping me: either take dictation and channel the material directly from the angels, or work with the angels collaboratively to structure the narrative. Enjoying the challenge, I chose the latter and found I took easily to working cooperatively, allowing

---

*Christ Michael is one of seven hundred thousand Creator Sons, or Michaelsons who, with their female counterparts, the Mother Spirits, are the creative pairs responsible for sculpting the raw material of the Multiverse into smaller regions called Local Universes. There are one hundred thousand of these Local Universes in one Superuniverse. Of the seven Superuniverses, our Local Universe is located within the seventh. The Creator Son and Mother Spirit between them create the celestial beings within their own Local Universes. In the case of human beings—or mortals as they are more generally known on inhabited planets—they are responsible for the design and creation of our physical bodies, but as a cloak for the Indwelling Spirit of the Godhead. In each Local Universe the Creator Son is required to incarnate once on each of the seven levels of sentient beings within his Local Universe, the seventh of these incarnations being that of a mortal. In our Local Universe of ten million inhabited worlds, it was our extraordinary privilege to have hosted the seventh and final incarnation of our Michaelson in the form of Joshua ben Joseph, the one we know as Jesus Christ, on this humble sphere.

angelic wisdom to come through whenever required. With the second book this relationship deepened, and I could feel a palpably warm shiver in my auric field whenever Zophiel—one of the angels assigned to work with me, who was standing and looking over my shoulder while I worked— approved of something I had written.

The Return of the Rebel Angels, the third book in the series, focuses on some of the people I've encountered and the events in which I've participated over the past thirty years. All of these people, in different ways, have had their dealings with higher intelligence. Some are working with dolphins, others have had profound and complex extraterrestrial encounters, and yet others have pointed to long-term relationships with specific groups of non-human beings.

Among these beings are the midwayers, whom I later came to call the Beings of the Violet Flame (BVFs), to make a clear differentiation between their previous activities and their current manifestation. It's this group of beings—called midwayers because the spectrum of frequencies within which they exist lies between human and angel—who are closest to humans in vibrational frequency. All of them are working in the background to facilitate their part in the transformation of the planet. Since midwayers are posted to a planet for an extremely long time—some have served on this world continuously for half-a-million years—they could be considered to be the true planetary citizens.

And yet despite my understanding of *The Urantia Book* and my personal beliefs around it, I'm personally still no wiser as to what to expect on the winter solstice of 2012. At this point I trust my angels enough to understand that if I were supposed to know, I would have been told. What I *have* been permitted in glimpses over the years, however, has been reassuring and leads me to believe we are all in for the most wonderful surprise, however it manifests.

I don't believe this event is going to be the end of the world, although it will surely be the end of the world as we've known it. There'll be earthquakes and floods, wildfires and volcanic eruptions, as Earth seeks to balance herself, yet my intuition constantly reassures me the real transition will be "so gentle you'll barely notice it," as I've been told by an angel. Part of this "knowing" has led me to the intuitive conviction that humanity is not going to be able to survive without a lot of help from our "friends."

To know that it is love that permeates the Multiverse, to realize how profoundly each of us is cared for, to understand the purpose of life's adventure, to know the Indwelling God, to be aware of the significance of this seemingly insignificant little world, all this suggests that however and whenever this massive change in consciousness occurs, it is going to be of the most profound nature.

And I believe it will be remembered in the annals of the galactic universities as the time of the great transformation of planet Earth.

The Apocalypse
Is Canceled

Recently I read through an essay I wrote back in 1979, somewhat pretentiously titled "Some Speculative Scenarios on the Future of the Human Race."* One of the proposals in it suggested that the planet was facing a sixty-year window through which we have to pass if we are to avoid global self-destruction. I reckoned, fairly arbitrarily, that this window of opportunity started in 1960 and would remain open until 2020. I knew it would be a narrow and hazardous passage through which we'd have to negotiate. From what I'd seen of the human race, the outlook was not encouraging.

If it was a depressing prospect, there were also times when the light broke through.

One of these moments happened to me on a blustery afternoon in the fall of 1963 when the Cold War was heating up. Thousands of ICBMs in the United States and the Soviet Union were on hair-trigger alert, and American bombers circled endlessly, waiting for an order that would end civilized life on this planet. And even if there was no intention of starting a war, it wasn't a secret that one small error or a technological glitch could create an unstoppable conflagration.

Perhaps being born into a war oversensitized me to the horrifying possibilities, so walking along London's Wigmore Street in the drizzle on this day in 1963, weighed down with these thoughts and not looking

---

*This essay is included in this book as appendix A.

1

where I was going, I almost bumped into a youngish man striding toward me from the other direction. While we were doing the inevitable sidestepping routine, each gesturing the other through, he fixed me with a gaze from his remarkably blue eyes.

Seeming to pick the thoughts out of my head, he said with great certainty, "Don't be concerned. We can pick those rockets out of the sky just like that!" And he clicked his fingers loudly in front of my face, before sliding past me and disappearing into the crowd.

Wherever this conviction came from, I *knew* in my heart I'd just met my first extraterrestrial. It didn't seem a big deal, for some reason. I just knew it was true.

There was such an absolute confidence in his quiet voice. He picked up, telepathically I supposed, exactly what was concerning me at that very moment, so much so that his announcement seemed a perfectly natural extension of my own thoughts. I was also surprised, as I walked on, at how I *knew* so intuitively that the young man, who was dressed in a perfectly ordinary fashion, was an extraterrestrial. The encounter felt so easy—like passing on a message between old friends.

All very well, I might have thought at the time, yet there was a great deal more that could go wrong on the planet. At that time in the early 1960s, it was starting to become obvious that industrial materialism was slowly destroying the biosphere. While it was deeply encouraging to know at an early point in my life that the extraterrestrials had our best interests in mind, I also felt their intervention would, of necessity, have to be limited. Otherwise we'd be deprived of the lessons to be learned from our own efforts.

Yet, for me personally, this was the first time the possibility of some future extraterrestrial intervention entered my mind. In retrospect, this event, along with a couple of others, was the key that opened the door to what has become my lifetime interest in nonhuman intelligence.

In 1973 I had a near-death experience (NDE), which I described in some detail in *Dolphins, ETs & Angels*, the first book in this series. I hadn't used any entheogens for over eight years so I was fully conscious as the entire NDE unfolded with transcendent beauty and glorious lucidity. I was given the choice whether to return to my life or to continue. In choosing to return, despite the evident wonders of what lay ahead if I decided to continue, I was shown a choir of angels and then encountered (without realizing it at the time) my two companion angels. I was also healed in a technological device, which may have been extraterrestrial, before being returned to my body hail and healthy.

The NDE remains to this day the singularly most profound and spiritually all-encompassing experience of my life. In retrospect I can see how this event convinced me that life was a far deeper and more fascinating affair than I had previously imagined. While my brief encounter with the ET on Wigmore Street had been reassuring, my NDE revealed a profoundly deeper order of beauty and compassion. I also felt it was personally irrefutable evidence that my intuition was correct in positing forces at work behind the scrim of reality.

Once I was able to clear my commitments I settled down seriously to study and write about the transformative events I could feel happening beneath the surface of life.

As I threw myself whole-heartedly into this enterprise a series of synchronicities started appearing. These "meaningful coincidences" guided me to Florida and gave me the opportunity to swim with a pod of wild coastal dolphins and receive some insights into their lives and skills. Over the course of the next year I had two clear extraterrestrial experiences, including one in which I had the opportunity to question a young boy about Multiverse affairs. This occurred after two friends and myself had watched an unidentified saucer-shaped craft fly over Manhattan on Labor Day of 1981. The young boy, who'd also seen the craft passing overhead, must have fallen into a telepathic rapport with the extraterrestrial occupants, since the measured tone, the knowledge, and the certainty with which "he" answered my questions about Multiverse politics went far beyond that of even a mature human statesman.

This initiation into the reality of other intelligent species seemed to lead naturally to a series of long dialogues with a group of angels speaking though a light-trance medium by the name of Edward, in Toronto, Canada, in 1981. Edward was a sensitive who had been trained to induce and maintain a state of consciousness whereby angels could speak through him. Unlike full-trance mediums who need to leave their bodies for an entity to speak through them, Edward (as I do) chose to stay in his body while allowing his vocal chords to be used by the angels.

I describe what I learned both from the angels and from my encounter with the little ET telepathic mouthpiece in far more detail in the first book in this series. However, the nugget of the information, the reason the angels chose to communicate with us in Toronto, led us to understand that the Lucifer Rebellion, which took place 203,000 years ago and which so severely affected life on this and thirty-six other worlds, has finally been reconciled. This revolution among the angels who most directly care for us mortals has been directly responsible for the deplorable state of this world for almost as long as human history. The reconciliation of this rebellion, so the angels told us, would start a process by which the world will be transformed and uplifted over the course of our lifetimes.

Having been introduced to *The Urantia Book** while all this was happening, and having witnessed for myself that celestials are real creatures during my NDE, speaking with angels wasn't as startling as it might sound. *The Urantia Book* is also the best source I've come across for a deeper understanding of the dynamics of the Lucifer Rebellion. It should be kept in mind when reading this description that the celestial communicants describing the rebellion are speaking on behalf of the very authorities against whom Lucifer was rebelling and therefore need be forgiven for what are some thoroughly unforgiving attitudes.

One piece of guidance an angel passed along to our little group in Toronto that I took to heart was the assurance that anyone can make close and lasting contact with their companion (guardian) angels. She said we all have angels who attend us, whether we know it or not. With that I set out on a journey to discover if I could enter into a state of communication with my own companion angels. Two years of meditating, journaling, and constant reality-testing later, I found I was able to maintain a balanced state of consciousness in which I could hear my angels' voices, start to trust them, and then learn from them.

The reality of angels, which I would have scoffed at twenty years earlier, runs counter to so much contemporary thinking that it requires

---

The Urantia Book is a seminal book of channeled communiqués that discusses the Central and Superuniverses, our Local Universe, the History of Urantia (planet Earth), and the life and teachings of Christ. It was published in 1955. This unique book forms the context for many of the concepts developed in *this* book.

a profound shift in viewpoint. It takes patience and the courage to face aspects of the psyche we might prefer to ignore, but which turn out to be contributing to blocking the contact. That angels are here to help and guide us, without usurping our freedom of choice, no longer surprises me. I've been consciously working with angels for over twenty-five years now and have no doubt how helpful they've been to me and to those other individuals who are in touch with theirs.

This affinity with the angelic realms prompted me to write *Ask Your Angels* with Alma Daniel and Andrew Ramer. Published in 1992 as a manual describing what we had learned about angels and how to make contact with them, the book must have touched a nerve since it rapidly became an international bestseller and has gone into nine translations to date.

Writing after the financial meltdown of 2008, any objective assessment of the current state of the world has to admit the problems we saw coming in the '60s have reached a point at which they can't be solved in purely human terms. Greed in the marketplace and corruption in high places on the one hand and international terrorism and anarchy on the other increasingly appear as two undeniable faces of consumer capitalism. Environmental pollution and the burgeoning world population are only going to make the situation progressively untenable. It is as though we have simply used up the planet.

While it may be true we have ravaged the natural attributes of the planet, it also must be so that many technological species in a vast and inhabited Multiverse will have faced similar situations. The mess we have got ourselves into should be well understood by those whose function it is to steer primitive planets through their teething period: Earth can't be all that unique.

I've learned that this world, along with the handful of planets whose angelic overseers identified with the Lucifer Rebellion, is better regarded as a cosmic experiment. We have been quarantined and isolated from the rest of Multiverse affairs for more than two hundred thousand years, forced to try and work out planetary life without the benefit of knowing who we really are or our place in the Multiverse. In a Local Universe of ten million inhabited worlds, I believe some extraterrestrials refer to this world as being "the third to worse." In other words, the third to the most emotionally, psychically, and physically dense of the frequency-domains within our primary dimension. Arcturian ETs refer to this as being currently a third-density world that is moving up to a fourth-density.

Yet, dealing with this level of density allows those of us here to experience duality in its most extreme form. When we die and leave our physical vehicles, it is to move into another body vibrating within a slightly higher density, or frequency-domain. From my NDE I can vouch that this higher-frequency reality is every bit as solid to the senses as our present one, except it seems to have some magical attributes. During my NDE, I could float, for example, and a scene might transform in an eye-blink, reacting, it appeared, to the changing spiritual requirements of the moment.

Having spent time with various indigenous races, I respect their belief that Earth has died and been renewed four times and is about to enter its fifth epoch of death and transformation. Little is said or known about those species who inhabited this planet through these four previous transformations, so it's hard to predict what is going to happen to the human race in the coming singularity. In the event of widespread disaster, I have heard of a number of extraterrestrial races who are primed for a mass lift-off of human beings. And if there is physical death, there is no reason to fear it. Life continues, whether one believes it or not.

If the reconciliation of the Lucifer Rebellion, which emerged as the main revelation of my first book and which I will discuss again in this one, is indeed true, then we can reasonably speculate that the transformation of this planet will be surprisingly benign. After all, the turmoil created by the rebellion was a conflict between angels. Human beings were never involved. Humans were never to blame. Yet it is generations of humans who have suffered from this tragic isolation, deprived of our spiritual birthright, ignorant of angels and extraterrestrials, and left to find our spiritual purpose in a corrupted world. Earth is now considered by the extraterrestrials to be one of the most difficult of all of the planets to fall under rebel leadership.

So, my thinking goes, in what I've observed to be an eminently fair Multiverse, if humans weren't involved in initiating and participating in Lucifer's revolution and have had little chance over the centuries to right a situation not of their making, then surely humans can't be held solely responsible for the state of the planet.

In the light of this, I feel in my heart that the upcoming transformation will be both astonishing and profound, a reward perhaps for those many millennia of suffering. In support of this, and in spite of what appears to be a rapidly deteriorating global situation, whenever I have asked my angels about the forecasted Earth changes, they have assured me that the transformation will be more subtle and fluid than I might imagine. I take great hope from this.

Amid all the chaos and fear of these times, as I travel around I can feel there are two quite different streams of energy present on the planet that paradoxically appear to coexist. The most observable is, as acknowledged previously, the general deterioration of the environment: the irresponsibility, greed, and corruption we see daily on the twenty-four-hour news cycle, and most recently the fragility of the global financial systems.

However, as the planetary conditions get progressively worse, the opportunities for correct action also become more numerous. How we respond to the challenges will be the measure of each one of us. The angels are making themselves more available than ever, as I hope this book will demonstrate to anyone who has enough of an open heart and mind to be able to appreciate their counsel. Authentic crop circles continue to appear yearly, and an intelligent pattern is starting to emerge. Extraterrestrials persist in buzzing the skies and upsetting the status quo. With the Cold War over, it's been an encouraging affirmation of my chance meeting with the ET back on that rainy London street to hear of the reports now released by the military of UFOs hovering over ICBM silos and deactivating the weapons.

Given this, each of us as individuals faces constant daily choices:

Do we choose to fear or to love?

Do we grab for self-gain or support the greatest good?

Can we respond to unexpected situations with confidence and courage, or do we repeat the same tired old patterns of denial and timidity?

Can we greet the massive shift in consciousness soon upon us with enthusiastic understanding and the self-awareness to know that what might appear terrifying is, in fact, illusory? Or do we give up hope in the face of human incapacity to deal with the overwhelming issues threatening the world?

I don't buy the concept of the apocalypse. It appears the planet is too significant to our extraterrestrial brothers and sisters for that to be allowed to occur. All of the intuitive information that I'm receiving is pointing to some form of intervention, but until then life will doubtless get increasingly challenging for all of us, rich and poor alike, all over the globe.

Those of us who've chosen to incarnate at this time in history know in our hearts that we must welcome the coming events, not with fear, but with courage and the faith to know that ultimately we are in good hands.

PART ONE

Travels with an Angel

A Klee painting named "Angelus Novus" shows an angel looking as though he is about to move away from something he is fixedly contemplating. His eyes are staring, his mouth is open, his wings are spread. This is how one pictures the angel of history. His face is turned toward the past. Where we perceive a chain of events, he sees one single catastrophe which keeps piling wreckage upon wreckage and hurls it in front of his feet. The angel would like to stay, awaken the dead, and make whole what has been smashed. But a storm is blowing from Paradise; it has got caught in his wings with such violence that the angel can no longer close them. This storm irresistibly propels him into the future to which his back is turned, while the pile of debris before him grows skyward. This storm is what we call progress.

WALTER BENJAMIN,
ON THE CONCEPT OF HISTORY

1

Travels Out of Body

The Conference-in-Spirit, Out-of-Body Travels, the Assassination of Anwar Sadat

There are some advantages to being born in a war that don't become apparent until later on in life. A question that simplifies this issue is: Given the choice prior to incarnating, and knowing you were going to have to go through hell at some point, would you rather do it early in life or later on?

I'm sure there will be some who would choose to experience hell at the end of their lives, since they might think they will be better prepared for it after a lifetime of toil. But that was clearly not my choice. And a choice it was, although I didn't discover that either until many years later.

I was born in 1940 on the outskirts of London while the Battle of Britain was being fought in the air overhead. When the blitz heated up, my family moved to the small village of Cranbrook, about fifty miles from London, in the County of Kent. This turned out to be an unfortunate choice, since by my third birthday, the Germans were starting to launch their V-1 flying bombs at London. The village lay on a direct line between London and their launching sites across the English Channel. We called them doodlebugs, or buzz bombs, after the characteristic buzzing noise of their pulse-jet motors.

At first no one had any idea of what they were. I recalled being fascinated by them buzzing along, much lower than the aircraft I was used to seeing. And later, when we became more complacent about the flying bombs, I was able to sneak out and watch the British Spitfires diving down to match the buzz bomb's speed and trying to tip a doodlebug's wing so it would circle back from where it came.

Doodlebugs didn't remain a mystery for long.

Loaded with almost two thousand pounds of explosives and catapulted from sites on the other side of the English Channel, traveling low and fast, doodlebugs were utterly terrifying. They could be heard coming from miles away, and passing overhead at night (if we were lucky that night) they left a beautiful dragon's tail of fire.

But the worst of it was when their engines stopped. Suddenly there would be a penetrating silence as everyone in the village held their breath, followed by a high-pitched whistling, rapidly growing in volume and intensity, until a massive explosion shook all the houses. V-1s were marvelously ingenious machines, far ahead of anything the Allies possessed. Designed and developed for the German Luftwaffe at the infamous factory complex at Peenemünde, the V-1 can be thought of as the first weapon of a new paradigm of warfare. Although its pulse-jet propulsion meant it wasn't a true rocket—that's generally credited to the V-2—the doodlebug has led directly to the modern cruise missile.

Equipped with an early gyroscopic guidance system, the doodlebug's weakness lay in the difficulty in detecting when it had reached its target. This became particularly pointed for the villagers of Cranbrook. As the German scientists adjusted the V-1's unreliable odometer, the doodlebugs frequently fell short, landing in and around our village.

I don't want to belabor the agonies of a four-year-old shoved under the stairs or under a kitchen table, compressing himself into a tight little ball of terror. That is all I could remember up until recently, when one of the angels I work with mentioned in passing that she was the angel who drew me out of my child's body and held me in her arms, comforting me while the bombs exploded.

This answered a question that had bothered me for as long as I can remember. I'd never been able to understand why I have such a spotty and discontinuous memory of my childhood. I've realized since hearing the angel's statement that those early-childhood, out-of-body ventures in her arms may have allowed me a certain ease and familiarity in handling the subtle realms. I believe it is my hard-won facility with conscious dissociation (and reassociation) that has subsequently been of value to the angels.

Although I wasn't to know it for many years, those early childhood encounters with an angel shaped the direction of my life.

I had a fairly normal upper-middle-class English education: boarding school when I was seven, a scholarship to a public school (a private school) from twelve to sixteen, architecture studies in London, and my qualifying seven years later. From the little I recall it was an uneventful childhood in a country dulled by war, punctuated by varying lengths of time in the hell of an English public school.

Not only did my angel not make any reappearance of which I was aware, but I probably wouldn't have recognized her if she'd stood flapping her arms in front of me. By this time I'd become an arrogantly skeptical young man. I was widely read, far too bright for my own good, and had dismissed the whole God business as delusionary. And, as will sometimes happen to arrogant and skeptical young men, my head badly needed breaking open.

I can thank plant entheogens for that; morning glory seeds of two specific varieties were known to have psychoactive properties, and this was some years before they were made illegal. I described the trip that turned my hair white overnight in *Dolphins, ETs & Angels,* so here I will abbreviate it only to what I learned related to my subsequent interest in non-human intelligences.

The most significant vision was of a large black and gold snake, so utterly real that I could see, as it crawled toward me, the thick pile of the carpet separating under the weight of its body. It was when the snake reared up and thrust its body into my right eye, to coil in my stomach for an eternity before forcing itself out through my wide-open mouth, that I knew this was no mere hallucination. Neither could it have been "real," since I was lying on the floor in the bedroom of a London apartment—not a known habitat for large black and gold snakes.

Although terrifying in the moment, this incident reached so deep, was so ontologically puzzling, and provoked such a profound shift in my thinking that it set me off in an entirely different line of inquiry. My hardheaded cynicism was brutally demolished, and there was no chance of turning back. I had no way of understanding what had happened to me, only that it was terribly real. Twenty years later I met an advanced Indian yogini who surprised me by saying that what I'd gone through was an esoteric Kundalini Yoga initiation.

This process of shattering my previously held belief system resulted in a series of experiences that opened me up incrementally to a far deeper apprehension of the human potential. Two out-of-body experiences (OOBEs) demonstrated unequivocally that an aspect of me can travel free of my physical vehicle. I was accustomed to sleeping naked, and in one of the OOBEs I was snapped back into my physical body when, moving down a dark deserted street, I looked down in my "out-of-body" state and saw I was also naked. That moment of silly egoic embarrassment was enough to jerk me back into my physical body.

The inference from this is there are emotions appropriate to the physical vehicle, with its ego-driven needs and desires, that are not appropriate to the subtle energy bodies. It also gave me the chance to realize that when we leave our physical bodies, it's not merely as a point of light or some amorphous ghostly shape, but as a body that appears real and solid to its owner. Yet it is a body capable of transferring itself from place to place instantaneously.

All of this was extremely puzzling to a twenty-three-year-old novice.

In retrospect I've appreciated that my lifelong fascination with all things extraterrestrial was actually a thin cloaking for my repressed knowledge of angels. Even as a young man I intuitively *knew,* under my general skepticism, that some larger game was at play. I wasn't aware of the inner worlds, so I projected the feeling out onto extraterrestrials. This is not to say there aren't ETs or that they might not be intimately involved with our lives, merely that being open to the extraterrestrial presence was something I was more easily able to accept. And even that concept was regarded as somewhat bizarre back in England in the 1950s.

Kenneth Arnold's June 1947 sighting of nine "flying discs" over Mt. Shasta and the Roswell incident a month later might have caused a momentary flap in America before the U.S. military classified the Roswell crash. But the news didn't reach England for many years.

Yet, without knowing about either event happening in America, as long as I can remember I've been convinced there must be other intelligent life in the universe (as I then thought of it). To think otherwise seemed to me the height of human arrogance and shortsightedness. Then, when the air forces of all major nations, led by America, went into a collective program of denial about the existence of UFOs, it seemed to me obvious there must be a massive governmental cover-up going on. Being English and growing up in a country familiar with D-Notices (the press can be gagged at any time by the government on issuance of one of these D-notices), this didn't altogether surprise me—and certainly didn't discourage me from my belief. It seemed so obvious that extraterrestrials had to exist, that the official military and scientific denial merely illustrated how important the UFO issue must be to the governments of the world.

As for whether extraterrestrials have done more than flitting enigmatically around the skies of the planet, any open-minded review of human history and prehistory has to conclude other intelligent hands have been at work for a long time.

Of course, holding these views back in the 1960s was still tantamount to having a propeller twirling on my cap.

There were times, of course, when life could get weird without any prompting from me, as the next incident illustrates. I was alone and watching television one night in London. In the early 1960s programming finished at 11:00 P.M. Too lazy to get up and turn the TV off—this was well before the era of remotes—the screen soon became that familiar random blitz of electrons so beloved by stoners.

Gazing idly at the TV, tired but perfectly sober, I was suddenly jerked back into full wakefulness by what appeared to be happening on the screen. Not only was the electronic blitz rapidly resolving into discernible moving images, but the images also were drawn from my own life. This wasn't my brain trying to make sense of random patterns—I knew what *that* was like—since what I was looking at had quite as much clarity as a normal transmission.

It was for these reasons that I've long believed it was ETs who were responsible for getting to me through the TV. I recall nothing of what happened on the screen except that what was shown was terrifyingly honest and most likely a profound dressing-down for some of the poor choices

I'd made up to that point in my life. The next thing I was aware of was running in a panic full-tilt through London's Hyde Park to the house of a woman I believed was my spiritual teacher. I'd recently become involved with a mystery school and convinced myself she was the only person who could throw some light on what had happened.

Whether or not this woman truly understood what I was going though, she appeared not to be surprised I was having experiences like that, because she said she knew I was part of the Serpent People since she had first met me. I had no clue what she meant, but somehow it felt reassuring and I calmed down at being recognized—although recognized as what, I wasn't at all sure. Yes, I do have a natural affinity for snakes, and with a name like "Wyllie" perhaps I am somewhat cunning by nature. But—Serpent People? Whatever could that mean?

Some months later, I happened to meet Brinsley Le Poer Trench, the author of *The Sky People,* one of those books that tries to wrestle with the troubled origins of the human species from an extraterrestrial point of view. The story the author told of the Serpent People was starting to feel oddly familiar.

Although to this day I'm not much wiser about the Serpent People or my own identification with them, at the time the concept gave me a handle on what was happening to me. It also gave me a model to account for why I felt so different from most people. All my life I've felt alone, yet I can't recall ever being lonely. As an only child I've always been happy on my own, and my interests have invariably been slightly out of kilter with those of my contemporaries. Being identified with the Serpent People, delusionary or not, allowed me a deeper acceptance of feeling a perpetual outsider and shielded me through some troubled times ahead.

I spent the years between 1963 and 1978 as part of a spiritual community that started in England and then moved to America in the late '60s. I had the opportunity during that time to become the art director of *PROCESS* magazine, which has recently been recognized for its advanced graphics and its provocative and controversial choice of contents.

I've described my fifteen years living and working with the group in a recent book, *LOVE SEX FEAR DEATH: The Inside Story of The Process Church of the Final Judgment.* The experiences I had during that period functioned as an unparalleled training for many of the later events and encounters related here.

Having moved from England to live in America I find that one of the gifts of self-imposed exile tends to be a global viewpoint. Feeling neither English nor American, my attention inclines toward the larger perspective. The awareness of how fragile life is on this world was nurtured throughout the Cold War by the imminence of atomic devastation, which was rendered all the more real in my case by having been born in the Second World War. This, of course, was true for all of my generation, so the psychological reaction to the nuclear shadow was more extreme in England than in America. The British stoicism that had served so well in the past wars was starting to break down.

My generation was becoming increasingly skeptical of authority. And those in authority were starting to realize it. As schoolchildren in England, for example, we were never asked to believe that crouching down under our desks would ever save us from an atomic blast. We *knew* what bombs did! We'd seen the old guard get us into two world wars within thirty years; it was all too likely they'd stumble into a third. This realistic skepticism was the collective impulse behind the mass marches of the CND, the Campaign for Nuclear Disarmament, and much of the social unrest among the young in England in the 1960s.

After being harshly rejected by the public and demonized by the English newspapers for our attempts to tell the truth of what we, as the Process Church, saw happening around us—the hypocrisy, the fearmongering, and most of all the irresponsibility of those in charge—we'd had enough. They didn't want us, and we wanted nothing more to do with them. Turning our backs on the world, we sold all our worldly possessions, left England intending never to return, and attempted to create a new Utopian society on a deserted strip of coastline on the Yucatan peninsula.

It was inevitable we would have to return from our self-imposed exile and try to make our peace with the authorities. Utopias have a long history of failures. But we were never welcome back in England, and soon we set up in America, with communities in a half a dozen cities in the United States.

I was made director of the New York headquarters by the mid-1970s and spent three years organizing and mounting a series of public events—conferences and seminars on subjects designed to challenge contemporary beliefs. I gathered a small group of extraterrestrial contactees, people who'd had authentic encounters with ETs, including Betty Hill,* one of the earliest contactees to come forward with her husband Barney, so they could speak openly and honestly about their experiences. A conference on alternative medicine brought together the top practitioners of a variety of alternative treatments, as did another conference on alternative approaches to treating cancer.

I believe it was the success of these events that led two ancient Tibetan monks to our doors. The Tibetan diaspora was just kicking in, and they must have been feeling their way into America. Nechung Rinpoche and Draypal Rinpoche were both well over seventy, yet sparkling with life, their nut brown faces creased with smiles. The two conferences we arranged for them at our headquarters were extremely well received and contributed to Tibetan Buddhism taking root in America.

There were many more public events in those three years than I can list here, often three or four a week, month after month. It was exhilarating but also exhausting, for I never managed to lose the horrible sense of dread that no one would show up for them or that something would go terribly wrong. I felt tortured by it for hours and sometimes days before each event, regardless of how successful the previous conference had been.

After I left the group in December 1977 I resolved I would never put myself in that situation again. If I was ever going to mount another conference, I wasn't going to obsessively concern myself with filling the seats.

Well out of the community by this time, the Conference-in-Spirit on the full moon of October 12, 1981, was a very different affair. The concept came to me in the spring of that year as a result of explorations I'd been doing into out-of-body travel.

I'd had a few spontaneous OOBEs over the course of my life, as I imag-

---

*Betty and Barney Hill's contact experience is best described in John Fuller's book *The Interrupted Journey*, Berkley Books, 1974.

ine is true of most people. Using entheogens I also had a number of more controllable out-of-body flights, which showed me that with directed intention this was a facility that could be developed. So the concept of holding a conference in which participants could meet in an out-of-body state was appealing on many levels. It would be a noble experiment that pushed the envelope of conventional thinking; it would be fascinating to see the responses of the participants; and, of course, there was always the outside possibility that is just might work. It just might be feasible for a group of advanced souls to gather together to exchange information while out of their bodies. I reasoned that in all likelihood most of us do something very much like this when we're in certain dream states. Could this be emulated deliberately in full consciousness?

Most of all, however, organizing an out-of-body conference meant I didn't need to worry myself into a frantic state prior to it happening. The conference was an experiment—maybe it'll work, maybe not. I had no emotional investment in the result. And no seats to fill.

Working with a small group of friends, we compiled a list of all the most progressive, open-minded, concerned, and adventurous people we could think of, before culling the list down to two hundred invitees, the maximum number we agreed as optimum. A glance at the list shows how broad a spectrum our choices covered, though it shouldn't in any way be considered complete. Almost all the people chosen were from the Western world, most you will have heard of, a few not, many are dead by now, and the handful of unfamiliar names will likely be our little group, not shy to include our names among the famous, the gifted, and the erudite.

My companion Melinda, with whom I was developing the project, felt it important we should create the conference anonymously. This was not to be an ego trip. Naturally, the half-dozen people we were working with knew who was behind it, but we decided to structure the invitation so that any one of the invitees could have been be the person making this unusual conference happen. This led us to produce it under the banner of the Future Studies Research Group, a somewhat enigmatic think tank with an address in Manhattan.

This was before we had ready access to the Internet, so the job of looking up all those addresses fell to my tireless companion. Melinda patiently combed all available sources for the personal residences of the men and women, many of whom clearly preferred to be hard to find, until we had all two hundred.

It was, perhaps, a little cheeky simply sending the invitation out to the invitees without any preamble. And we did receive one angry letter back from an eminent physicist to that effect when we sent out a follow-up questionnaire. But we reckoned while some of the invitees would *get* it and be charmed and excited about the concept, there would always be others who thought it absurd or who forgot all about it as soon as they'd seen the invitation.

With this in mind, we needed to make the invitation we'd be sending out to our two hundred invitees as striking as possible. I found a specialized ten-inch-by-ten-inch, good-quality envelope I could get in a small quantity and started designing an oversize invitation that would both grab the attention and get across that it was a serious endeavor. I also wanted the invitation to stand up on its own so it wouldn't be overlooked, or forgotten, sitting on a counter or a mantelpiece.

It soon became obvious that we would need to specify a location that would act as a "locus focus" for the etheric gathering, and the Queen's Chamber in the Great Pyramid of Cheops at Giza felt an obvious place to do it. This choice led naturally to the need to provide a visual aid for those who were going to use focused meditation as a means of leaving their bodies.

Melinda dug up an arcane way of dividing human activities and aspirations into twelve broad categories, which I was then able to draw and letter as a twelve-petalled flower, with the image of the pyramid as the central point of focus. The Queen's Chamber was delineated as a small, white rectangle. The timing of the event was possibly of less importance than it would be with a conventional conference, because time appears to be less relevant in the higher frequency-domains. So, we settled on a midpoint, 2200 GMT on Monday, October 12, 1981, and requested in the invitation that people simply take a few hours, or a day, off, but to center their efforts around the suggested midpoint. Since many of the names and addresses of the invitees were from different places on the planet, Melinda drew an elegant world map with all the time zones indicated.

We decided between us to focus on the theme, "FUTURE ALTER-NATIVES: As Exercises in Reality Creation," since one of my particular interests at the time was how the future might be molded through acts of the creative imagination. As the planning and design process progressed it became obvious we needed to provide some more information on the purposes of the conference. Just because I, and a few friends, were exploring out-of-body travel, that didn't mean it was familiar to all our invitees.

In a serious Helvetica italic typeface, reversed white out of the overall indigo blue of the invitation, I wrote:

Many issues can be resolved if we know what we want. When we decide what we want, form it and give it substance in our imaginations, our experience suggests that such projections can become reality.

The theme of this Conference-in-Spirit is Future Alternatives, with special reference to the quality of life on this planet. To avoid getting bogged down in short term issues we recommend making two key assumptions, those of space migration and unlimited energy resources.

Given these factors, how would each of us wish to see our race functioning on this planet? What systems of social coordination could be beneficial? How can the distribution of power and resources work to the benefit of the race and our beautiful Earth as a whole? How can belief systems be nurturing in principle and flourish free of bigotry? How might our contentiousness as a race be creatively channeled? And the other pressing questions facing us on this planet. . . .

For those who wish to participate we have provided a visual cypher in the form of a mandala, in which key words suggest the main areas of human affairs. You may find it helpful to take these key words or, of course, key concepts or words of your own and, over the period of the conference, consider or meditate on them.

Allow yourselves to move down the 'thought lines' into the future and visualize as fully as possible the reality in which you are participating. . . .

Needless to say, if you wish others to join us in this experiment, loved ones, colleagues or friends, their presence will be very welcome.

The Future Studies Research Group

ALAIN RESNAIS • ALAIN ROBBE-GRILLET • ALBERT HOFMANN • ALBERTO VILLARDO • ALEX TANOUS • ALISON GARDNER • ALLA RAHKA • ALLEN GINSBERG • ANDRE REDATUS • ANDREW WEIL • ANN MEDLOCK • ANVAR SADAT • ANDY WARHOL • ARMAND DIMELE • ARNOLD FORSTER • ARTHUR KOESTLER • BARRY ROSSINOFF • BILL CLEESE • BILL APPLE • BOB DYLAN • BOB MONROE • BOB SCHWARTZ • BOB THIBODEAU • BOBBY FAUST • BRANDO CRESPI • BRIAN ALDISS • BRIAN ENO • BUCKMINSTER FULLER • BUNA • BONEWITZ • BUSY PALE • CARL SIMONTON • CARLOS CASTANEDA • CARSE CHAMBERS • CHEECH MARIN • CHERI QUINCEY • CHRISTEL GARRICK • CHRIS CASTLE • CHUCK NORRIS • CLAUDIO NARANJO • COLIN WILSON • DALAI LAMA • DAN MALAMUD • DAVID BOHM • DAVID BOWIE • DEAN LATIMER • DIANA ROSS • DIANA WYLIE • DIETER MITTLESTEN-SCHEID • DORIS LESSING • DOUGLAS HOFSTADTER • EARL HUBBARD • EDGAR MITCHELL • ELIZABETH KUBLER-ROSS • ELIZABETH TURNER • EMMA CHRISTENSEN • EUGENE DOLGOFF • FRANCOIS TRUFFAUT • FRANK HERBERT • FRANK WILHOIT • FRED HOYLE • FREDERICK DODES • FREEMAN DYSON • FRITJOF CAPRA • GEORGE CLINTON • GEORGE HARRISON • GEORGE LUCAS • GEORGIA O'KEEFE • GERARD O'NEILL • GORDON WASSON • HANS VAN KEHRBERG • HARLAN ELLISON • HEBERT KAHN • HERBERT FILL • HILDA BROWN • HIRINI MATUNGA • HUNTER THOMPSON • IDRIES SHAH • INGO SWANN • ISAAC ASIMOV • JACQUES COUSTEAU • JACQUES SANDULESCU • JAMES ROBERTS KAHN • JAMES WEBB • JAMI FOURNE • JEAN HOUSTON • JEAN WILLEY • JEANETTE LARVA-KUBENA • JEAN-MICHEL SARRE • JERRY BROWN • JERRY POURNELLE • JID KRISHNAMURTI • JOAN CARROLL • JIM HARRIS • JIM LOVELOCK • JOE HALDEMAN • JOHN CAGE • JOHN CLIETT • JOHN EISEN • JOHN GRIBBIN • JOHN LILLY • JON MICHEL • JON PIERRAKOS • JOHN SCUDDER • JOHN WHITE • JONATHAN HERBERT • JOHN CLETT • JOSEPH CHILTON-PEARCE • JOYCE PETSCHER • JULIAN JAYNES • KARL PRIBRAM • KATHERINE HEPBURN • KATHY KEETON • KEN KESEY • KENNETH RING • KIYOSHI KUROMIYA • LARRY NIVEN • LAURA HUXLEY • LAWRENCE LESHAN • LEE ROY LONGENBACH • LEWIS THOMAS • LUCILLE KAHN • LYALL WATSON • LYNN SCHROEDER • MALACHI McCORMICK • MARCIA MOORE • MARGE KING • MARILYN FERGUSON • MICHAEL WEISE • MICK JAGGER • MOTHER TERESA • MUKTANANDA • NATHAN GUC • NICK ASHFORD • NORMAN BISHOP • O.J. SIMPSON • OLGA WORRALL • PAOLO SOLERI • PAT CARRINGTON • PAUL SIMON • PETER O'TOOLE • PETER RALPH BPHL • RALPH METZNER • PHILLIP DICK • PHILLIPE DRUILLET • PREM DAS • PRINCESS DOR • RAY BRADBURY • RAM DASS • J. SATER • ROBERT ANTON WILSON • ROBERT A. BRETTOCH • RAYMOND MOODY • RICHARD DAWKINS • RICHARD PRYOR • RICHARD SCHULTES • RONALD LAING • ROY MASON • RUSSELL TARG • SAI BABA • SAMUEL BECKETT • SAMUEL DELANEY • SIMON VINKENOOG • SOEN SA NIM • SPENCER HOLST • STAN DEOF • STAN LEE • STANLEY KUBRICK • STANLEY KRIPPNER • STEFANIE POWERS • STUART TROY • SUE TENNANT • TARTHANG TULKU • THOMAS CHONG • THOMAS SZASZ • TIM SCULLY • TIMOTHY LEARY • URSULA LEGUIN • VALERIE SIMPSON • WALTER DI MARIA • WALTER HOUSTON-CLARK • WERNER ERHARD • WILLIAM BURROUGHS • YOKO ONO

We are happy to announce that there will be a Conference held on Monday October 12 1981

The theme for the day is

FUTURE ALTERNATIVES as exercises in reality creation

The two hundred invitees are requested to attend in spirit only

• location •
The Queens Chamber in the Great Pyramid of Cheops at Giza, Egypt

Many issues can be resolved if we know what we want. When we decide what we want, form it and give it substance in our imaginations, our experience suggests that such projections can become reality.

The theme of this Conference-in-Spirit is Future Alternatives, with special reference to the quality of life on this planet. To avoid getting bogged down in short term issues we recommend making two key assumptions, those of space migration and unlimited energy resources.

Given these factors, how would each of us wish to see our race functioning on this planet? What systems of social co-ordination could be beneficial? How can the distribution of power and resources work to the benefit of the race

and our beautiful Earth as a whole? How can belief systems be nurturing in principle and flourish free of bigotry? How might our contentiousness as a race be creatively channelled? And the other pressing questions facing us on this planet....

For those who wish to participate we have provided a visual cypher in the form of a mandala, in which key words suggest the main areas of human affairs.

In the center is a drawing of the Great Pyramid of Cheops at Giza. We have chosen the Queens Chamber (shown white) as the site of the Conference to provide a focus for visualization.

You may find it helpful to take these key words or, of course, key concepts or words of your own and, over the period of the Conference, consider or meditate on them. Allow yourselves to move down the 'thought lines' into the future and visualize as fully as possible the reality in which you are participating.

We ask of you only that you take Monday, October 12 off from your normal activity, relax and make yourselves comfortable. To simplify the timing, the midpoint of the Conference will be 2200 GMT on Monday, October 12.

Needless to say, if you wish others to join us in this experiment, loved ones, colleagues or friends, their presence will be very welcome.
—The Future Studies Research Group—

Fig. 1.1. The invitation to the Conference-in-Spirit, held on Monday, October 12, 1981

Fig. 1.2. The "locus focus" for the Conference-in-Spirit

✦

In my experience, when a project springs from the heart and the people involved do it without any thought of personal gain, small miracles frequently accompany its development. I'm now aware of the help we receive from our angels when we're involved in something they support, but when we were planning the conference I didn't know the part angels play in our lives. I just thought it was synchronicity and took it that we were on the right track.

Danny Faust, the owner of a large New York printing outfit, and the father of Robert Faust, one of the friends who collaborated on the project, volunteered to print the invitation at a fraction of the cost. He was delighted to be involved and did a handsome job, although I suspect he might have had his tongue firmly in his cheek. The invitations went out promptly six weeks before October 12, and a postcard reminder a month later. Now all we had to do was sit and wait for the day. But, of course, we couldn't do that. The alternative was far too tempting.

I think it was Melinda who first suggested we should actually go to Egypt for the conference. It had never entered my mind; I'd been so focused on the out-of-body side of things I hadn't considered where I'd want to be during the conference. Anywhere I could close my eyes and relax would have been just fine with me. Melinda's parents at that time lived in a small coastal town in Israel, so it seemed a good idea to visit them first and then go on to Egypt overland, crossing over the Suez Canal to get to Cairo. I'd never met the parents or been to Israel before and they'd been hoping we'd visit, so it all fell neatly together. (See plate 2.)

We arrived in Israel in early October, me with one of those rotten colds made only more wheezy by the frigid, recycled air of the long plane ride and the light drizzle when we stepped out of Tel Aviv airport.

It took a day to kick my cold, cosseted by my companion's very Jewish mother, chugging down her homemade chicken soup while tucked in the guest room of their high-rise apartment on the cliffs overlooking the Mediterranean.

Netanya lies about fifty miles north of Tel Aviv and is obviously a new town, built since 1948. It was a bland place, with rows of identical, blisteringly white apartment blocks marching in rows perpendicular to the coast, coming to an abrupt full stop at the edge of town. When we ventured out we found the streets unexpectedly filled with people, mostly young and trailing children, lots and lots of children. Everyone appeared intensely interested in us, stopping their boulevard conversations in midsentence to stare unabashedly at these two creatures from another reality.

Popping into a supermarket we witnessed what we later discovered was a local joke: elderly women, generally well-covered in black shawls, a couple in this case, standing stock-still and staring unblinking at the rows of produce, hypnotized by the multiplicity of choices. Recent immigrants from the U.S.S.R., we were told. I could identify with the poor women. When I left the community, after fifteen years of not having to do any shopping—I had other tasks—I, too, found myself baffled in a modern supermarket, unable to decide which of twenty cereals I wanted.

I'd hoped to catch a glimpse of dolphins as we scrambled down the cliff and walked along the deserted, sandy beach. One look at the water, however, confirmed it was filthy with the accumulated tar and grunge of the entire Mediterranean washing up on these shores. Not something that would attract dolphins.

My health restored, Melinda and I set off early on the morning of October 6, driving north to get the feel of the country. Since it was my first time in Israel Melinda's parents, intensely proud of their land, insisted I see as much as possible in the short time before we left for Cairo. A clear, cloudless sky arced overhead as we drove north toward Mount Tabor. It was the dry season so the mountain, technically a *horst,* appeared to rise abruptly out of the patchwork quilt of dusty, arid fields, like a boil on the bum of history. And its history lies thick on the land of this country: the strategic importance of Mount Tabor, with its panoramic view over the surrounding plain, would have been obvious to the earliest tribes.

Reaching the top of Tabor we found it crowned by not one, but two Christian churches: an Eastern Orthodox temple and a horribly fake-looking Roman Catholic church, built in 1924 and designed to look impressive, yet ending up more like a Miami Beach hotel. Taxis buzzed like flies around the gates of the church, disgorging well-dressed worshippers who had modestly left their Audis and Mercs at the base of the mountain.

Yet for all the appearance of religiosity, there was the stench of death about the place, which mixed uneasily with the pall of incense billowing from both churches. It was a windless day, and the heavily scented smoke hung low, swirling like a fog with our movements. Thinking that the two sects were battling for control of our noses we quickly retreated to an isolated ridge, a rocky aerie overlooking the plain almost two thousand feet below us.

Whether it was Mount Hermon or here on Mount Tabor that the transfiguration of Jesus took place, he is said to have climbed to the mountain's top when he was nine years old, with his father. Both churches continue to flourish from the streams of pilgrims after the somewhat arbitrary decision by a fourth-century priest to claim that Tabor was indeed the true site of Christ's transfiguration. Yet, it was not a peaceful place.

At Melinda's suggestion I ran back to the car for the gold-leafed crystal spur that I've found in the past so mysteriously useful in balancing energetically turbulent sites. I perched the crystal rod on a flat rock in front of us. It glistened and seemed to shiver in the bright sunlight. We meditated together, perched on a crumbling fourth-century abutment—a relic of the original Byzantine church—with a liturgical choral chant echoing out of the church far behind us. Soon I felt the weight of the past, the cloying incense and somber chanting, dropping away in our cleansing meditation.

Glad to get away, we skittered down the steeply turning mountain road, heading for the Sea of Galilee, some twenty-five miles farther inland. My ears popped as we dropped lower and lower into the earth to reach the slate blue lake, six hundred feet below sea level. The air grew steadily more humid and dense, with a whiff of sulfur from the spas once frequented by arthritic Roman limbs. The lake itself looked healthy enough, although evidently somewhat low since it was the dry season. Both Israel and Jordan draw water off it, and with increasing population demands I feared for its future.

It was around 4:00 P.M., after we'd spent some time in Capharneum, a small ruined village at the northern tip of the lake, that I started feeling unaccountably emotional. It couldn't have been the village. It was an archaeological travesty: carved stonework, broken Corinthian capitals, splinters of plinths, fractions of fluted columns, and assorted archaic bric-a-brac from countless eras, all piled up behind signs that could be read in six languages. One such slaphappy sign informed us that a particular jumble of rubble was "Saint Peter's House."

My feeling of profound sadness continued as we climbed out of the compressive atmosphere of a two-hundred-meter dive, into the soft beauty of the golden hour. And indeed it was true. This time each day brings the purest and sweetest light of a declining October sun, flooding across the arid landscape to irradiate the world, for a few fleeting moments, with the hues of the finest amber.

During the long climb we'd overtaken three army flatbed trucks laden with tarp-covered tanks being moved to some new crisis. I surprised myself by leaning out the window and shouting encouragement at the smiling soldiers. As we struggled past I noticed ten feet of fabric trailing behind one of the trucks and signaled at the driver that his load was becoming untied. Moments later, looking back down the hairpin bends, I saw he'd stopped and was tucking the fabric back under the tank.

Possibly because I was so emotionally tender, I was oddly moved by the driver's taking seriously what must have been a challenging gesture to interpret correctly. And the smiles of the young soldiers were spontaneous and warm. As someone who has always sympathized with the cause of the Palestinian Arabs—after all, my German shepherd was called Ishmael—it did me good to see the warmth and decency of these Israeli soldiers.

We stopped the car sometime later when I became overwhelmed with tears. Admittedly I do weep easily, but invariably from joy, not sadness. These were heaving sobs of misery and despair. I cried freely as images from the centuries of tragic conflict between these two great races, karmically shackled to one another as surely as fractious conjoined twins, flickered across my eidetic screen.

Yet, as I wept, I simultaneously knew the emotions weren't mine; something deeper was going on—perhaps the wave of feeling that had originally triggered my perplexing emotional outburst.

It was only when we got back to Netanya that we heard that Anwar Sadat, the president of Egypt and an invitee to the Conference-in-Spirit, had been assassinated earlier that afternoon.

The next evening Yom Kippur slid over the land in a sweeping swathe of silence. Everything stopped. No traffic. No TV or radio. No industry. No noise whatsoever. In a few minutes we magically switched from living in the latter part of the industrialized twentieth century to hundreds of years in the future, when all manufacture takes place silently, when travel is simple teleportation, when all is heard are the sounds of the birds and the happy squeals of children.

The assassination delayed our departure for Cairo since the borders were closed. With a couple of days to spare it would have been foolish to not have gone to Jerusalem. We arrived midmorning in the city, traveling on the small-gauge railway that rises up out of the well-irrigated orange groves and cotton fields of central Israel into the Judaean mountains, finally winding into the white-on-white city of the ages. Catching a cab into the old town we fell to discussing what we understood about Jerusalem. We knew from *The Urantia Book* that it had originally been called Salem in the time of Melchizedek, circa 2000 BCE.

Received mediumistically in a variety of ways in Chicago during the early part of the twentieth century, *The Urantia Book* is a collection of 196 closely reasoned papers written by a variety of celestials, angels, and midwayers (more about them later) and transmitted directly through the agency of an anonymous sleeping man, who apparently was quite indifferent when awake to what he was receiving while asleep. Over the three decades it took for the book to be compiled, from the little that is known, a number of different modes of transmission were used. The papers, once they were transmitted, were then subjected to a thorough examination by a group of seventy solid Chicago citizens. Once they'd made their notes, their modifications would then appear when the paper was next transmitted from the celestial author.

Much of what I have learned of the doings of the Multiverse has been derived from this book. For all intents and purposes, it appears to be the administration document of a governing body of celestial beings discussing the nature of the Multiverse that (according to the book) comprises seven vast Superuniverses, each of which contains one hundred thousand Local Universes. Every Local Universe has its own Creator Son (ours is Christ Michael or Jesus Christ) and Divine Mother, who are the creator beings of their domain. Each Local Universe contains ten million inhabited planets.*

---

*These Local Universes are further broken down into a series of administrative strata, of which a Local System is the smallest political unit. Each Local System contains one thousand inhabited or to be inhabited planets, and each has its own System Sovereign (ours was Lucifer) appointed to govern the System, as each planet, in turn, has a Planetary Prince (ours was Prince Caligastia), who govern his particular world.

Thirty years after first reading *The Urantia Book,* I still regard it as the most reliable source of information about both extraterrestrial and celestial activities. It is broken down into four parts devoted to the following subjects: the Central and Superuniverses, the Local Universe, the history of Urantia (their name for this planet), and the life and teachings of Jesus Christ. (For a definition of terms common to both *The Urantia Book* and this book, please refer to the glossary on page 433.)

The Urantia Book takes a little getting into since its language is dense and somewhat archaic, but if you stay with it you may find, as I did, that the papers resonate with the authentic voices of an altogether different intelligence. Those who may be cautious of embarking on its over two thousand weighty pages, but whose intuition leads them to explore the deeper currents of life, are recommended to make up their own minds as to the authenticity of the narrative. Until that time I can only assure the reader that in the many years I've been exploring the book and applying its revealed wisdom to my life, I have not yet found it anything but what it claims to be.

After discussing what we knew about Jerusalem, our conversation turned to Melchizedek. Although he only makes a brief appearance in the Bible—as an ally of Abraham—*The Urantia Book* is far more forthcoming about this enigmatic priest. The communicants (of *The Urantia Book*) called him Machiventa Melchizedek, and according to them, he was in fact a high angel, one of the Melchizedek Brotherhood, who are the great teaching angels of the Multiverse. He appeared outside the tent of a group of nomads around nineteen hundred years before Christ, announcing that he was a "servant of the Most High." Over the ninety-four years he spent in this incarnation, "long before his material body had begun to disintegrate," the book coyly tells us, his impact spread over the face of the globe. He created the most important teaching center of his era at Salem and sent missionaries and envoys all over the world.

His specific mission, so we're told, was essentially to bring the experiential reality of One God to the planet as a preparation for the coming of the Christ some two thousand years later. There is a reference to Machiventa Melchizedek in the Dead Sea Scrolls, one that talks of him as a Divine Being. Hebrews titled him El Elyon, and certain Gnostic scripts even place Melchizedek on a par with Jesus Christ.

Central to Machiventa Melchizedek's teachings was the concept of the Covenant. We know of this Covenant and its suggested relationship with the rainbow mainly through a reference in the Bible, but *The Urantia Book* lays it out with a much starker reality.

At a time when thoughts of divinity were invariably accompanied by fear, retribution, and animal or human sacrifice, the concept that an individual could be saved through faith alone was revolutionary. Agree to *believe* in God's promises and follow His instructions, so Machiventa Melchizedek told a startled Abraham, and God agrees to do *everything else!* The offer was apparently good for all time. This promise would be depicted in art and iconography down through the ages by the symbol of the rainbow, which represented God's Covenant to humanity.

Nobody had ever conceived of this idea of the Covenant of Faith before, and we are told that Abraham, when he was presented with it, found it as radical as anybody would—until he tested it out for himself. The antinomian idea of salvation through faith alone was almost too advanced for the times. However, the impact of its truth and simplicity, together with its implicit monotheism, was carried across the face of the civilized world by Machiventa Melchizedek's missionaries—thus paving the way for Christ Michael some two millennia later.

Melinda, knowledgeable in the ways of Jewish learning, told me how scholars have struggled over the generations to fit Machiventa Melchizedek into some ancient bloodline, identifying him, as do the Mormons, with Shem, son of Noah. When I suggested that he might have been some sort of an angel, Melinda responded by laughing and saying that if he *had been* an angel, he would have come and gone and wouldn't have left much of a trail. Yet, this Melchizedek was present in his ageless physical body on the planet for over ninety years before he left as mysteriously as he has appeared. An unarguable presence and a profound and lasting influence, Machiventa Melchizedek has given scholars through the centuries a perennial puzzle about which to endlessly argue.

The cab dropped us off in the Old Town, the "place of spiritual polarity," *The Urantia Book* calls it, explaining that Jerusalem is the location out of which most of the planetary etheric comings and goings are sourced. All very well, but the narrow streets themselves were inundated with hordes of tourists, as well as the multitudes celebrating both Muslim and Jewish Holy weeks.

This wasn't the Jerusalem I'd hoped to see. Trying to get out of the crowd we wended our way higher up through progressively narrower cobbled lanes. We were joined for a few minutes by a Christian fellow who couldn't stop talking about the fourteen stations of the cross: what a death-orientated religion Christianity has become! We both shuddered with relief when he went on his way.

Further into the warren of tiny lanes the sound of Arabic music beguiled us into a little adobe storefront, no bigger than twelve feet square, in which a commanding middle-aged Arab was playing exquisitely on a Bedu rabaka. Invited to sit and eat with him, a plate of salad and hummus seemingly magically appearing from the dark depths, we were treated to a speech in halting English and many suggestive gestures, promoting his secret formula for sexual potency: a glass of olive oil every day, especially while making love, he added with a roguish grin. He claimed to be "the best fuck in the Middle East" and pulled out a sheath of dog-eared letters to prove it.

Uncle Kamel was an irresistible salesman. Fortunately his taste in knickknacks was as funky as his conversation, so we were able to find an appropriately idiosyncratic gift for the parents.

I had a dream that night in which there was a message not to tell the Arabs or the Egyptian authorities about our Conference-in-Spirit. There was an implication they might see it as working with the devil, or the CIA.

The radio announced the borders to Egypt were still closed, so Saturday left us with another day in Israel. The country is so small that a trip to the Dead Sea, on the eastern border of the country, takes only a couple of hours. Soon, we were dropping into the depths of the earth, as we had with the Sea of Galilee, this time down over twelve hundred feet—and we could feel it! The hills lining the sea were arid, leached of color and moisture, and yet as we followed the road alongside the shore, the trapped heat, exaggerated by the slight change in pressure, made us both sweat profusely.

Jordanian tanks lay burned out by the roadside, toasted sculptures of war, rusting against the sandstone ramparts, while the mountains of

Jordan on the opposite shore floated ominously on top of a misty blue cloud of evaporation that hung like a shroud in the intense heat. Passing deserted mud villages, some huts occupied, most not, the dense heat overwhelmed us, and we turned into a "Bathing Center." It was crowded with Arabs, many still tentative at the dubious habit of bathing, picking their way tentatively around the garbage and rocks on the sandy beach, one hand hoisting up the robe, the other dripping with melting ice cream.

We undressed in natty little geodesic domes made of wattle and split reeds, which, of course, were gender segregated, before making our way through a teeming, noisy mob to the gently lapping waves.

The salinity of the water is every bit as curious as people make out. It's a unique experience, not exactly comfortable and certainly idiotic to look at. Feet stick up at one end, the head bobs unnaturally high in the water at the other. Looking across the sea, the unrippled surface is broken only by these oddly paired lumps. In the shallows fully dressed Arab women paddle, giggling and squealing, flicking water at one another and trying to control their little boys' joyful rampages. The little girls, like their mothers, are all fully dressed. Their robes float in the water around their waists, so they appear, in an irony likely missed on them, as the stamen, the male organ, of large water lilies.

Afterward, as we sat watching the Arab families returning from the sea, it was impossible not to notice that in family after family it was the mature women who controlled their families, including their men, by taking the roles of victim/manipulator. They complained and whined, some of them blaming their kids, some their men, as they limped their lumpy overweight bodies, still wrapped in black robes, now damp and sparkling with salt crystals, back up to the bathing huts. The men ignored them, talking only among themselves.

Small sample though it was, I wondered whether it was a valid insight into the emotional machinations of the average Arab household and whether or not, as my companion suggested, this emotionally immature behavior was one of the unrecognized products of centuries of suppressed female power.

It was later that afternoon when we heard over the car radio the Israeli/Egyptian border would be open any day now, perhaps even the very next day. It was already the weekend, and the conference was in another country on Monday. Time was getting tight, and this unexpected delay was grinding on our nerves. We hurried back to Netanya, arguing with each other over the slightest matter, to spend a last evening with the parents before setting off early next morning for the Egyptian border.

When we stepped off the bus at the Suez Canal crossing and joined the mob milling around, it was to find the border had only been opened a few hours ago. A container ship towered over us, seeming to glide over the desert itself. As we shuffled forward I could see the soldiers and border guards were jumpy, moving a little too abruptly, eyes darting like lizards under their caps. The Israeli guides, shepherding their flocks of tourists through immigration, picked up the tension immediately and, adequately trained in paranoia, barked orders at their charges, herding them all the more like sheep.

The tellers in the border Change Bureau were all soldiers, suave with neat, rich mustaches and paradoxically friendly eyes. We wondered if they were relieved at Sadat's passing, since Hosni Mubarak's name was on everyone's lips. Perhaps the dead president wasn't as popular in Egypt as he was respected by the international community. A person of Sadat's intellectual sweep and personal courage makes life a little scary for the average citizen. Here was a man, after all, who had pledged to do at least one truly extraordinary act each year. Not just govern well, not necessarily balance the budget, but to do something that would change the world for the better.

Sadat had apparently become a changed person in the years since he and Hafez al-Assad of Syria launched their ill-considered surprise attack on Israel that led to the 1973 Yom Kippur war. After being heralded as a hero by his countrymen and the Arab community for the military successes of the first few days, he went on four years later, in November 1977, to evoke their fury when he became the first Arab leader to officially visit Israel and meet with Prime Minister Begin. Two years later there was the Egyptian-Israeli Peace Treaty, which must have galvanized Sadat's radical opposition, the core of it in his own military intelligence agency.

Having been informed of the assassination plot earlier in 1981, Sadat arrested and jailed over fifteen hundred people, intellectuals, high-ranking clergy, and many Jihad members. Yet they missed one cell, the one that assassinated him months later. Surely, that he was killed on October 6, the very same day of the year that he initiated his attack on Israel in 1973, had to be more than a coincidence, but I've found no expressed explanation for the timing.

On the way to our hotel our taxi driver was chortling at Sadat's boldness when we asked him about the Soviets having been thrown out. It was one of Sadat's acts that pleased almost everyone in Egypt. "Because the Russians had no style," our driver shouted back over his shoulder amid a cacophony of car horns, "They were rotten tourists!"

Threading our way through dusty, crowded streets our taxi reached the Mena House Hotel, a few miles outside Cairo and very close to the pyramids. Although evidently a luxury hotel, we'd chosen it for its proximity to the pyramids. Since the assassination had frightened away the tourists, we were given a generous deal and had the hotel pretty much to ourselves.

After our taxi driver's enthusiastic support of Sadat and his sadness at the president's death, as if to illustrate the complexity of the country, the plump and jovial owner of the small restaurant we visited our first evening in Cairo referred to Sadat as "the devil himself." And he claimed to have been a Sadat supporter for years! In the recent purge of Islamists a number of senior Copts had been swept up, and this had both disgusted our host and opened his eyes.

Back at Mena House Hotel, eating alone under high-ceilinged relics of British colonialism, we encountered another aspect of the Egyptian personality; the perfect waiter. He glides silently among polished brass tables, long dangling chains of carved olive wood and glass cabochon sway as he passes, his reflection flickering from mirror to mirror, his eyes search for a tourist who is self-confident enough to appreciate his considerable aplomb. Our waiter served us with such a dignified deference, every gesture practiced and passed down over the generations, treating us as if we were Osiris and Isis returned for a night of revelry.

This is not a militaristic nation. In over seven thousand years they've never seriously invaded anyone, and their defeats in the wars against Israel since 1948 merely go toward confirming this. They are traders, artisans, and dreamers, and most of all they are the keepers of one of most ancient and enigmatic of the world's civilizations.

It was on the bus in Cairo that we fell to talking with an Arab professor at the American University in the city. He had a sweet face, which was unexpectedly familiar to me. I've come to accept this odd sense of familiarity and rapport with certain strangers met by chance as being a reincarnational affair, and I fold easily into the deeper connection. I never knew the professor's name, but he turned out to have an articulate view of the Arab side of the Israeli conflict.

Sitting next to the cracked window of the crowded bus, Melinda on the seat next to him and me leaning over from the bench in front, the professor kept his voice low as he said, "The Arabs have no picture of the cohesive historicity of the Jewish people. They see them as a band of adventurers who occupied Jerusalem in ancient times for a mere one hundred and fifty years."

I couldn't help noticing that as a passionate Arab, he'd put himself outside the statement by the use of that "they."

Interrupting him, I asked him how he accounted for the presence of Machiventa Melchizedek a couple of thousand years earlier, who had set up his headquarters in Salem, (later, Jerusalem, as we know). Being a contemporary and mentor of Abraham, Machiventa Melchizedek is regarded as a seminal Jewish prophet; didn't that give the Jewish people a fair claim on Palestine?

The professor pointed out that in Machiventa Melchizedek's time the Middle East had many tribes, some nomadic, almost all warlike, worshipping a multitude of gods and practicing blood sacrifice; it wouldn't be accurate to say that Machiventa Melchizedek taught only to the tribe that became the Hebrews. Abraham, the professor reminded me, is regarded as a forefather of both Arabs and Jews.

He wasn't to be diverted and went on dismissing the Jewish claims. "They were just derelicts, rebels, and assorted riffraff who tried to throw the indigenous Canaanites out of Palestine, build their temple, and claim Palestine as their Holy Land." His cultured voice rose a little in repressed anger when he continued. I had no desire to break his flow.

"And then it happened all over again after the Second World War, by another bunch of outcasts, this time northern European Jews. This made it even worse for the Palestinians: the Jews had a natural hatred of them because the Arabs had aligned with Hitler's Germany."

I hadn't realized this particular dynamic before, but of course it would account for some of the horrors reported to have been committed by the Jewish settlers as they poured into the country. "It's for all these reasons," he said, leaning toward us, his voice more emphatic, "that the Arabs totally reject the Zionist claim of Palestine being the Jewish Holy Land."

The bus clattered on, black smoke streaming from its exhaust as we sat in thoughtful silence. Knowing it was a difficult subject I chose my words carefully.

"I have read, and been told by Jewish people," I glanced at my girl-friend, whose parents had been firm on this subject, "that when the Jewish settlers arrived after the war, the Palestinian Arabs were told to leave by their religious leaders. . . ."

This time the professor interrupted me, his elegant face flushed with anger. "That's complete nonsense! It's Israeli propaganda, pure and straight. Of course it might have happened a few times when the Palestinian vil-lagers were utterly desperate. But in far more cases they had their villages destroyed. Their lands and houses were razed to the ground; olive trees were destroyed, their women and children were terrorized, all by roving gangs of Zionist extremists. Having destroyed their villages, the Zionists' then told the villagers they could stay on if they wanted. Great choices!"

I appreciated how intractable the situation has become. If it was true, and the Arabs were savagely forced out of their homes and land, was the Israeli government *ever* going to admit it? If false, and they really were deceived by their leaders, were the Palestinian Arabs *ever* going to let go of the prime justification for their claim of return?

The professor seemed to be quietly stewing in his seat against the window. A scatter of pebbles suddenly hit the bus. A window somewhere behind us was hit, causing the professor's head to duck down. The bright sunlight, muted by the filth on the window, sparkled in the starburst crazing of previous stones hurled. Before he sat up straight again I could see the kids, pointing and shouting with pleasure, refracted in the cracked glass. In the bus there was some nervous laughter and a few claps. Then, belching black smoke, we accelerated out of range.

I wanted to bring his attention back to what we were talking about and for him to bring his analysis more up-to-date.

"And now?" I asked. "Is the situation for Arabs in Israel any better?"

He flinched when I said "Israel" and quickly corrected me.

"Israel!" he said contemptuously. "Palestine! It's called Palestine!" He was working up a head of anger, and I hoped he wasn't going to direct it at us. But he quickly got control of himself and prepared to get off at the next stop. A traffic jam jerked the bus to a sudden halt, and the professor collapsed back into his seat with a grunt of frustration. We smiled at him in sympathy, and he leaned over again, speaking quietly and clearly trying to suppress his anger.

"Did you realize when you were in Palestine that the Arabs are not allowed to vote? They have no land or water rights! They're treated worse than second-class citizens!"

The bus lurched forward again, and the professor hauled himself to his feet before turning to us and delivering his final statement.

"The Arabs have been in Palestine for a thousand years. Now they're living in occupied territory! How would *you* like that?"

With that he shuffled his way up the gangway and disappeared into the dusty streets.

Melinda, who was quiet for most of this exchange, reminded me that Arafat and the PLO were currently calling for a secular state, neither Islamic nor Zionist, with full separation of church and state. It sounded good in theory, but we wondered whether the extremists on both sides of the fence would ever go along with it.

The bus jolted to a halt outside the Mena House Hotel. It was early evening, and as we gazed back at Cairo, the broad brown smudge of pollution swathing the city was now turning blood red in the setting sun. Cairo looked like hell, painted by Turner. I wondered what it boded for the conference the next day.

On Monday, October 12, the day of the conference, I sat down with my journal to take stock of the situation.

We were both exhausted after the intensity of the last week, our shock at Sadat's killing having to be set aside as we needed to stay as upbeat as possible, constantly bolstering our hopes we'd be let in the country in time for the event into which we'd put so much time and energy. My cold made a comeback, and Melinda soon caught a mild version. For all the positive synchronicities that accompanied the conference's planning stages, this last week had been a trial.

As I wrote that morning, the pyramids visible through the windows of our magnificent suite, I recalled a mantra that popped into my mind in Peru, a few years earlier, and under not dissimilar circumstances; "the more the magic, the more the stuff" is how the insight came to me. I take it to mean the more magical an event or project is, the greater are the challenges in realizing it. Here were both of us, after months of work culminating in this one special day, wheezing and coughing and erupting in one fight after another. This is not how we thought it was going to be.

We had already decided not to try to get into the Queen's Chamber. It felt unnecessarily intrusive, and we didn't want any of the focus to be on us. I made no note of whether we fasted that day, but I expect we did. We wanted to approach the occasion with a clear head. We drew long baths and relaxed, trying to ignore our sneezing and spluttering. Then, dragging an elegant table over to the window, I set up my crystal spur so there was a direct alignment with the rising moon, the apex of the Great Pyramid, and the invitation, propped up with all the invitees names facing me. Thus the pyramid on the invitation faced the Great Pyramid of Cheops in an unintentional symmetry that pleased me.

At 6:00 P.M. we settled down to meditate and start the conference. We had no particular plan or ritual, feeling we'd know spontaneously what to do in the moment. The only premeditated decision we'd made was to throw ourselves wholeheartedly into the conference, as we had with the preparation. If we had any doubts we would simply put them aside for the duration. There would always be time for that later.

A small gust of wind through the open window blew the invitation gently onto my lap. I felt the natural world was with us. I knew what I needed to do. I quietly called in each of the two hundred invitees (and their friends) by name, taking a few minutes to tune in and get the feel of each of them before we both thanked them all for attending. We introduced people where appropriate and suggested favorable seating arrangements. The list was so broad and eclectic that many people there were anxious to meet others for the first time.

I made a note at the time that almost all the invitees were present. The few that weren't there said they would be by later. Jerry Brown, I recall because of his courtesy, had some emergency business at the state capitol. For some we sang their songs, such as "Georgia" for Ms. O'Keefe;

others we thanked for their contributions to humanity, and yet others we greeted as friends or companions.

This introductory period lasted for several hours, and as darkness fell with tropical suddenness we lit two candles, placing one between where we sat and the invitation. The other candle I carefully lined up with my crystal rod so that the flame, gathered and focused by the crystal, projected a throbbing circle of light on the image of the pyramid on a second carefully placed invitation. We agreed previously it would be unlikely we'd be able to record the Conference-in-Spirit with conventional technology. My gold-leafed crystal spur came to me under such propitious circumstances, I felt confident on some level it was recording what was occurring on the subtle energy levels.

This silent little magical alignment burned its way through the next few hours as we meditated together. I recalled nothing of this period after emerging from the meditation, which I took as a good sign. I must have been in a deeply altered state of consciousness, because I certainly wasn't asleep. At 11:00 P.M., the moon, coming into its fullness, moved into the precise alignment we'd set up, hovering at the very peak of the Great Pyramid, to complete our magical conjunction.

I read aloud through all the words on the twelve segments of the mandala on the back of the invitation. As I completed this I found myself almost overwhelmed with a sense of gratitude and blessings, and I shifted into an even deeper state of cosmic consciousness. I saw for a moment what we had accomplished and that it was good. We had done our bit, and the consequences were now in other hands. It had been an act of faith. Ridiculous to some, a noble experiment to others. And great fun for us.

After midnight we considered our work around the conference complete. We dressed and made our way through marble corridors into the glittering opulence of the hotel's Colonial British dining room and broke our fast with a simple and delicious vegetarian meal. The waiters, as reverential as ever, glided and sidled around us, polishing glasses, pouring wine, flicking imaginary bread crumbs off the fine white tablecloth and shyly smiling at us whenever we caught their eyes.

Perhaps it was something in the way the waiters were treating us, as if we were royalty, that suddenly brought forth a memory from my earlier meditation. The memory stream started when I was shown a culture in which the rulers were believed to be gods, and they considered and felt themselves to be gods. The manner in which the waiters were treating us reminded me of what I'd experienced in the meditation.

After opening my heart chakra, I'd found myself overlit by what I can only call a "god-king reality." I experienced myself as a god-king, with profound and complex responsibilities to my people. I felt myself permeated and surrounded by all the organic life on the planet. I was It, and It was Me. I knew in those moments, seeming to last forever, that the pharaohs—the god-kings of antiquity—were wholly responsible for their peoples' well-being. I knew the meaning of the stars and the rising and falling of the Nile. I felt the adoration of my people and knew their concerns in my own body.

In my contemplation of the Egyptian god-kings, I didn't experience that they actually were gods, although they might well have thought of themselves as such. So, if they weren't gods and unless they were merely mythic figures, who or what could they have been?

Contemporary rationalistic thinking finds it convenient to dismiss the gods and goddesses as superstitious delusions or as psychological archetypes. Others believe that these god-kings were extraterrestrials; there was talk of the Russians finding the mummified body of a small extraterrestrial in a secret tomb close to the pyramids. While ETs may well have had some localized presence on the planet in ancient times— Atlantis and Lemuria were both reputed to be in part extraterrestrial colonies—I doubt whether they would have wanted to mix with human beings, let alone rule over them.

My attention was then drawn to the midwayers, the small group of beings that *The Urantia Book* tells us have a primary concern with material life on this planet. They are invisible to the human eye, yet can manifest in this physical reality when a situation is significant enough to require their help. Indeed, midwayers feel very responsible for all of life on the planet.

The midwayers came into being over five hundred thousand years ago, when our Planetary Prince Caligastia and his Deputy Prince Daligastia, together with a staff of one hundred "off-planet" supermortal volunteers, came to Earth on a specific mission to uplift humanity and start the civilizing process. The supermortal volunteers, who were effectively immortal at that stage, began mating with each other to produce, over time, the fifty thousand of these angels we call midwayers, who then became invaluable assistants to Prince Caligastia. It is due to their off-planet genetics that midwayers possess their rather unusual attributes. They are immortal and are normally imperceptible to human senses and yet can manifest and affect physical reality. They say their interventions are relatively infrequent and demand considerable energy from a number of them remaining in their dimension to facilitate the appearance of one of them in *this* dimension.

Eons of time passed. Then, roughly a quarter of a million years ago, the high angel Lucifer was appointed System Sovereign (of *our* System), and in this new capacity, he was responsible for overseeing the welfare of the evolution of the mortals in our System of one thousand planets. More time passed, but all was not well. Lucifer, apparently, was not happy with how he was being permitted to rule, with the result being that roughly 203,000 years ago, Lucifer and *his* assistant Satan fomented a revolution, with Lucifer leading the charge.

According to *The Urantia Book,* Lucifer and Satan (Lucifer's main assistant) came to believe that an elaborate conspiracy had been concocted by the Creator Sons of the Local Universes to promote the existence of a fictitious unseen divinity, which the Creator Sons then used as a control device to manipulate the orders of celestials and angels within their creations. Having announced the existence of this conspiracy, Lucifer demanded more autonomy for all beings and for System Sovereigns and Planetary Princes to follow their own approaches for accelerating the spiritual development of their mortal charges.

The revolutionaries quickly gained followers, and the rebellion spread rapidly to affect thirty-seven planets in this System, with Urantia, our planet Earth, being one of them. Choice was given to the many angels involved with supervising System activities as to whether to join the rebel faction. (I will be discussing the curious destiny of those angels who aligned themselves with Lucifer in the afterword.)

Lucifer's charge—that too much attention was being given to ascending mortals—appeared to ring true to a large number of angels, as well as the thirty-seven pairs of administrative angels, the Planetary Princes and their assistants who were responsible for the orderly progression of mortal (human) beings on their worlds.

The revolution was effectively suppressed by the administration authorities and recast as a heinous rebellion, its immediate consequence being the removal of Lucifer and Satan from their posts in the System. Yet paradoxically, the thirty-seven planetary administrations who had aligned with the rebel faction were turned over to the Planetary Princes of those worlds to apply the Lucifer doctrine. So, in a way, Lucifer got what he wanted—with one disastrous and possibly unanticipated exception. Presumably to prevent the rebellion from spreading, our entire System of planets, including the thirty-seven worlds falling to Lucifer, was isolated and quarantined, essentially cutting us off from the rest of the Multiverse affairs.*

At the time of the Lucifer Rebellion, the vast majority of the fifty thousand midway angels on Earth—over forty thousand of them—aligned themselves with Lucifer and Satan. They were destined to remain on our planet until the time of Christ, when, according to *The Urantia Book,* it was one of Christ's occulted functions to remove them. It is a brief reference, and no further details are given in the book as to where the rebel midwayers were taken. However, with the removal of these 40,119 rebel midwayers, a mere 9,881 loyalist midwayers remained here to fulfill the tasks of five times their number.

As a result of all of this, in contrast to a normal planet (one not quarantined), on which angelic companions and the presence of helpful midwayers and extraterrestrials must be commonplace knowledge, we Earthlings have slumbered in our corner of a populated Multiverse, unaware of who we are and how we got this way. Having been quarantined and isolated from normal extraterrestrial activity for the long 203,000 years since the rebellion, we first lost touch with, and then forgot entirely, our rightful place in the populated Multiverse. Given this, we were bound to evolve as a troubled species. Our world is one of the few planets that, due to

---

*One of the results of the quarantine was to cut off certain incoming cosmic rays, which had helped to sustain the staff's immortality over the centuries. When the staff finally all died they left behind their original offspring, the midwayers, whose immortality was *not* dependent on the cosmic rays. As it dawned on the members of the Prince's staff that they were going to physically die, Caligastia encouraged them to interbreed with as many indigenous humans as possible as a way of maintaining his influence through controlling their bloodlines.

the Lucifer Rebellion, have been thrown off their normal patterns of development.

This disquieting situation, this planetary quarantine, has persisted for a little over the last two hundred thousand years, only to have finally been adjudicated, in my understanding, in the early 1980s. As a result, the planetary quarantine has been lifted, enabling the rest of the Multiverse to make more legitimate contact with us. More recently what we are witnessing is the return of the rebel midway angels, who are now coming back to assist us in the coming transformation of our world.

As angels, midwayers are undying, which is why I think of them as true planetary citizens. Existing in a frequency-domain just the other side of the veil, they are, as implied earlier, invisible to the human eye and yet, under certain conditions, are able to interact with our material reality. When they are created on a world, they remain on it as aides, guides, and emergency workers until the planet is settled in light and life. This is their genesis and their true nature, but by the time that recorded history rolled around the rebel midwayers were becoming self-serving and cynical, caring for humans merely as playthings in their power games. (I will be discussing some of these delinquencies in ensuing chapters of this book.)

It should also be noted that it was as a response to a petition from the loyalist midwayers on this planet that *The Urantia Book* was assembled. By the end of the nineteenth century, although there was upsurge of interest in psychism and spirituality all over the Western world, the midwayers realized that there was a desperate need for authentic and accurate cosmological, historical, and spiritual information. In fact, this massive infusion of spiritual knowledge is rightfully our heritage, which would have become embedded in the religious and social mores of the global population had it not been for the interruption created by the Lucifer Rebellion.

When we examine the Bible, in Genesis 6:1–4 and Numbers 13:32–33, we find a mention of the Nephilim. They appear again in more detail in the *Book of Enoch,* in which they are named as the fallen angels who mated with human females. Biblical scholars in general are undecided as to exactly who the Nephilim were. Were they a race of giants, as some suggest? Others believe they were the progeny of the descendants of Seth, mixing with those of Cain. One aspect appears to be fairly definitive: unlike midwayers, the Nephilim were physical material beings.

One reference to the Nephilim that might point to a more extra-terrestrial origin: the word *Nephila* in the Aramaic culture referred specifically to the constellation of Orion. Having spent time with a Walk-In* from Orion I've come to understand that Orion is one of the seven star systems with more advanced cultures than ours that maintain vested interests in *this* planet. As can be easily verified, there are many features of the Great Pyramid at Giza and its alignment with the other two pyramids that directly reflect the Orion constellation.

There is an intriguing clue in *The Ra Material*, the extensive channeled transcripts from an extraterrestrial source named Ra, received and collated by Don Elkins, James Allen McCarty, and Carla Rueckert. In it Orion and its very mortal inhabitants are talked of as one of the races flying UFOs in Earth's atmosphere. Ra paints an Orion/human close encounter as an unpleasant experience, since in the case of the Orion ETs, they appear more interested in bending more "negatively-oriented" humans to their will. Here we see how, in this arena, like tends to attract like: "The most typical approach of Orion entities (Walk-ins) is to choose what might called a weaker-minded (human) entity (so) that it might suggest a greater amount of Orion philosophy to be disseminated."[1]

In Ra's cosmology he contrasts the fundamental motives of what he calls the "Confederation" with those of Orion. The Confederation are clearly the good guys here, and fortunately for this planet they appear to be in the vast majority. The basic contrast Ra outlines is that of service to others as opposed to serving the self.

Since the first approach is serving the Creator in others and the Orion way is serving the Creator in the self, both obviously end up by serving the Creator. What this fundamental disparity in philosophy produces is the necessary creative tension between different planetary cultures, which

---

*A Walk-In is generally an extraterrestrial entity who, by prior incarnational agreement, takes over a human body just prior its demise (most often a premature death), allowing the original occupant to move along, and then uses the body for a (hopefully) higher purpose. Walk-Ins are rare, and I assume they are an emergency response to the increasingly critical state of our world.

in turn furnishes the challenges and choices all beings need to grow in wisdom and spirit.

Turning back to our broader discussion, whomever the Biblical Nephilim might have been, and supported by Enoch's reference to their size, their brutality, and their sexual hunger, we can conclude they were evidently material enough to have children with humans. This suggests that the Nephilim were most likely a trace record of the prince's staff and their exceptionally long-lived progeny. While the Nephilim may have been the *forebears* of the god-kings, the characteristics described in the Egyptian texts gives no prominence to those features of the ancient divinities, their immortality and invisibility, you'd expect to be featured had they been midwayers.

Although *The Urantia Book* doesn't explicitly state it, given the lack of other candidates, I propose that the gods and goddesses of the ancient pantheons were almost certainly midwayers.

As for the god-kings, possibly in the early days of prehistory they may have been drawn from the progeny of the prince's staff who, the book tells us, did indeed procreate with humans after the planetary quarantine sealed their fate. While the Egyptian gods and goddesses were most likely midwayers in the lack of other contenders, the Egyptian god-kings, despite their superior genetic heritage, were all too mortal.

Yet, since this pharaonic line of ancestry descending from the prince's staff would have possessed a far wider field of knowledge than humans, those early god-kings would have appeared very much like gods to primitive mortals. If the pharaohs of recorded history were of this heritage, they would have been so depleted by that time, all they could do was to try to emulate their remarkable ancestors. This would certainly go toward explaining their obsession with immortality and the after-death realms, as well as their custom of procreating within the royal bloodline.

It was with these speculations that we finished our dinner. Moonlight was streaming in through the high windows, and we could see the Great Pyramid glowing in the silver light.

The walk from the Mena House Hotel to the base of the Great Pyramid was farther than it appears, the vast size of the pyramid deceiving the eye. It was also a long hill, this evening lined by heavily armed troops. The moon was so large every detail of the landscape stood out, and we could see the soldiers' eyes following us as we plodded up the deserted road.

Around a bend we came to a barrier across the road and a gaggle of soldiers with machine guns, smoking and talking between themselves. As we came to the barrier an officer detached himself from the group, walked toward us gesturing, and said in cultured English, "Reasonable people would not walk near the Great Pyramid at this time of night!"

I replied that we were *not* reasonable people. There was a surprised pause before he roared with laughter, and ordering his troops to lift the barrier he ushered us through, saying, "In that case it is fine for you to proceed."

We heard the laughter of his troops while he told them what I'd said echoing behind us as we got closer to the pyramid. Since we had arrived in Cairo so close to the conference, we hadn't yet visited the massive structures, even in daylight.

As we drew nearer I realized I was quite unprepared for the pure size and bulk of the Great Pyramid. I was used to seeing modern skyscrapers that architects strive to make light and airy, barely floating on the ground, yet here was a structure as high as any skyscraper and so unashamedly planted on the Earth as to appear in the moonlight to grow out of the desert sands.

Some wild dogs must have picked up our scent, and they started baying. A light wind, warm and sweet smelling, ruffled our hair. The massive size of the pyramid, bathed in a steely light, loomed over us as we got closer. Although the broad platform on which the structure sat seemed deserted, shadows that might have been people, or might have been tricks of the moonlight, flickered in the darkness around the base.

Energized by all the excitement of the conference my first thought was to climb to the top. My companion was somewhat less enthusiastic, but gamely climbed with me up to the sixth horizontal line of the colossal slabs of stone. It was not an easy climb, each individual limestone block as tall as Melinda, both of us scrabbling for purchase on the smooth surface of the blocks and dragging ourselves up to the next layer.

When we reached the sixth level she quite reasonably refused to go any farther. At the time, however, I didn't think it was at all reasonable. I had quite a head of steam going by now, and I was obsessed with getting to the top. And if I was going, she was going too. She declined again. I began to get angry and shouted at her that we weren't reasonable people, remember?!

Now, Melinda is a feisty woman, known as a girl to have wielded a large knife while chasing a hated stepfather around a kitchen table, and she wasn't about to take any nonsense from me. The nervous tension and the mutual bickering of the last week we'd been able to push aside for the duration of the conference now erupted into a dreadful row.

Ah! The male ego! Consumed by my anger I accused her of ruining the most important moment of my life, of always ruining my peak moments . . . and so it went; my companion was every bit as furious with me by this time, both of us throwing insults, dragging up old scores, shouting at one another . . . until finally, when I saw her pick up a stone to throw at me I grabbed her firmly by the waist, bent her over my knee, and gave her an angry spanking.

This was not in character for me. I've never done it before, or since. I would never even have thought about it unless Melinda's mother hadn't taken me aside one afternoon in Netanya and told me if I ever needed to spank her daughter I had her permission. I don't recall the context of this surprising remark, but she clearly didn't have any illusions about her daughter's refractory nature.

Yet, in a sense, it did work.

As the first light of dawn crept over us, the full absurdity of the situation struck us both simultaneously, and we started laughing uproariously. How could we be so stupid? Here we were, at this wonderful moment in our lives, and we were behaving like angry and foolish children. On this night of nights! What on earth was going on?

It was after we clambered down to the base and were quietly watching the dawn light redden the sky that Melinda reminded me of what we were talking about as we'd walked up the road toward the pyramid. Still riding the energy of the conference we decided as we set off for our walk that we wanted to understand the basis of conflict on our contentious little planet. What is it that perpetuates the belligerence? Is there something so fundamental, so deeply embedded in the human experience, so commonplace and readily experienced, that we have collectively overlooked it as the basic source of conflict?

The face of the Great Pyramid was turning from pink to a deep red, and the distant sounds of Cairo waking up floated in the clear morning air.

Although it was Melinda who said it first, we both must have thought it at the same time, because we starting roaring with laughter again.

"Of course! Of course!" She squeezed out tears of laughter that ran down her cheeks, "We've just acted it out. It has to be the conflict between men and women, doesn't it?"

It seemed too simplistic at first, yet as we came to talk about it we started realizing how basic is the antagonism between the sexes. Loving relationships, it seemed to us, are the arenas in which individuals can work out their own troublesome issues. We're all bent out of shape to one extent or another by our childhoods, and these influences, often traumatic, will surface as we mature. The emotional security provided by a loving relationship will often be exactly the situation that permits these repressed personal demons to appear.

The most obvious manifestation of emotional or psychological damage in childhood, if it isn't dealt with and the trauma released, will be the compulsion to project the issue out onto the other. This dynamic is well understood by psychologists, but doesn't seem to have filtered down to the general public yet.

If there is authentic love and trust in the relationship, then the projection can be recognized as such and withdrawn. By owning the projection, it can be examined and the repressed thoughtform (the demon) can be released.

The smell of baking bread drifted up from the desert below us, and we could see people starting to move around, lighting small fires and shouting at their children.

"What about cultures like this one in which women are suppressed and have no rights?" I wondered, as a bullying male voice echoed up from one of the Beduin tents.

"Until they accept their women as equals they won't be peaceful cultures," my companion stated flatly.

"But cultures like ours, we believe in the equality of women, and we're just as aggressive and belligerent, aren't we?"

"Just because we've legislated equal rights doesn't mean men suddenly treat women that much better. Perhaps it's a little fairer in offices, but that doesn't mean it's really seeped into the average relationship."

A camel belched and gurgled somewhere behind us.

"Happy men and women who love and trust one another don't make wars," Melinda announced with some finality, and we set off back to the hotel for some sleep.

Returning to New York and settling back into the rhythm of our lives, input on the conference started coming in from our friends who'd been involved. This raised an issue we'd put aside until after the conference was over. Should we ask for feedback from the invitees, and if so, how can we go about it while remaining anonymous?

I wasn't enthusiastic about the idea of revealing who we were. We'd conceived the project as an art piece and a spiritual experiment. We both felt the Conference-in-Spirit ought to stand on its own, a Zen gesture with its own touch of mystery. What the other attendees had experienced was, for Melinda and me anyway, of less importance than carrying the initial concept to its fulfillment. It was enough that we'd laid the groundwork.

However, since we created the conference in the name of the Future Studies Research Group, the majority of our little group prevailed and out went cards asking if invitees wished to receive a questionnaire. A satisfying number answered in detail the questions we posed, and while we never collated the results, I'm including a few of the reactions and comments here. In some cases they mentioned their names and wanted to know who was behind the conference, but most people appeared to appreciate the anonymity of it. Respecting this, I'm not including names with the comments.

From Michigan: "Around 3:00 P.M. I experienced that my vegetable/flower garden transformed into the Holy Grail and that all of us at the conference (were) in the Grail Cup simultaneously. I experienced a spiritually nourishing sense of community and sharing."

From San Francisco, California: "The idea of 'inner' conferences, located in specific external time/space location, is a good one. How about tying it in to specific traditional celebrations, Christmas, Wesak, Solstice, Equinoxes, etc."

From Richmond, Virginia: "I feel that the conference was an opportunity to join with others in the search for new directions in human evolution and motivation. During the conference I saw more clearly the conditions that brought us here and the directions ahead. . . .

"Technology can provide us with the means to satisfy our need for food, water and protection from the elements. Although we haven't achieved this for all people, it is possible. Beyond these mortal motives we have a need to discover our individual creative selves and to communicate that discovery to others.

"Technology is an amplifier of human motives. Our instincts have directed intelligence toward physical survival and now our consciousness must turn the power of technology toward liberating individuals from institutions of control-for-profit. Such institutions are obsolete in the world of spiritual motives. The institutions of the future will encourage, develop, reward, and support individual creativity and communication with emphasis on self-knowledge. Participation in the creative process is the one thing that we have in common with the Almighty."

From San Francisco, California: "Image of a gold scepter of light rising upward, then radiating Maypole style to all parts of Earth. Experience of awakening; Strong sense of healing; scepter changed to winged caduceus."

From Oxford, England: "I realized that the core of the sun is spinning faster than its surface layers (figures being something like three and twenty-five days), and that this ratio applies also to Saturn. This was previously unknown.

"Any opportunity to bring nearer to consciousness the forces of Kundalini, the collective unconscious, and the collective superconscious (which I believe still to be in the process of formation) is greatly to be welcomed.

"Choosing a subterranean rendezvous has its dangers for weaker psyches. I would suggest in future Macchu Picchu, or maybe the Great Lamasery in Lhasa, Tibet; height is always to be preferred to depth, since this is where the psyche must go in both personal and evolutionary significances.

"I propose that the conference was a success in terms of psychic power-building and in greater awareness that temporality is a staircase which we can—however fumblingly—learn to ascend and descend. I am disconcerted to find that as one approaches in fear and trembling the shadowy world of the Spirit, one is aware that one of the laws there prevailing is a law of godlike laughter—a laughter to which mankind cannot yet aspire."

From Denver, Colorado: "Whether or not there was an actual spiritual focalization at Egypt, or anywhere else, there seemed to be a spiritual unification in the sense that through the conference there was knowledge of participation of the other conferees. This served to give a feeling of group effort, and therefore more value to the experience.

"The conference acted as a catalyst for personal action. These significant conceptions and resolutions emerged: 1) The sense of world unity and progress being a task undertaken by a team scattered hither and yon, nevertheless, working together. 2) This team's work is unified by a superteam—those spirit intelligences and agencies assisting us. 3) That I have something personal to contribute to this endeavor. 4) That there is nothing better on Earth I would rather do. 5) That I resolve to try to do it."

From San Francisco, California: "I had a transcendental experience in my understanding of the computer as it relates to education/communication. It is a realm I have avoided—and now I know what I will be able to contribute to the field. The insights I experienced that day are directing me into a new dimension."

From Hove, England: "The blue space-like surface of the conference invitation functioned as a perfect field for the harmonious geometry of the 'flower.' I realized that the radiating patterns on ancient artifacts do not express radiation, but are radiation itself.

"At the center point of the conference there was a huge build-up of the attentiveness—I could feel more and more participants tuning in their energies. The general level seemed to move through several barriers previously considered the limit.

"The strange circumstances of Sadat's death seems to have occurred specifically to bring our attention directly from any idea of abstracting the life/death dynamic, to a direct contact with the basics of (the) Earth. The arbitrary manifests in a specific surreal moment."

From London: "After 9:30 P.M. a certain calmness and peace prevailed; approaching 10:00 P.M. all external visuals were dropped, the atmosphere became at once completely still and totally vibrant. Over the midpoint, there was an overwhelming vibration of peace (the word in mind was PEACE) seemed to well through me and out of the top of my head. I was extremely high in a state unique in my experience, but resembling a totally controllable acid trip. The power of the moment was total and lasted until well after midnight. It was wonderful."

From Berkeley, California: "I perceived the potential of an education in group decision-making as a means of education for democracy, and for exploration and research institutes interested in therapeutically-assisted decision-making groups. I understood better the role of education, as an alternative to power, in bringing about a desirable future."

From San Francisco, California: "I felt an upsurge of optimism, not quite an out-of-body experience, but an out-of-ego experience; a sense of unity with people on all continents; a visualization of different racial types, all striving for peace.

"I think we are about to jump to a new level of coherence; not just cooperation, but an increased awareness of previously unconscious species-goals—what we are here to do."

We were encouraged by a number of the respondents to make our Conference-in-Spirit the first in a series, yet it never felt quite right. We'd always conceived of the event as a single magical act. If other people took it up and ran with it, so much the better. Besides, organizing and funding the conference consumed many months of our lives. We could get away with being anonymous once, but if we were to develop Conferences-in-Spirit, we would have to come out from behind the curtain.

The conference was never really meant to be about finding solutions to the world's problems; it was created simply to provide an arena in which people could think about and visualize a positive future. To my knowledge such an event hasn't been repeated, yet the past three decades have seen the growing popularity of large group meditations with specific intentions.

We knew it was a fairly advanced concept, pushing the boundary of accepted belief, and it would be dismissed by some as absurd or impossible. It's likely a person needs to have some experience in conscious out-of-body travel to understand the potential of spiritual reality creation.

We'd thought merely to pop the idea of out-of-body collaborative work into the world mind. On a personal level, we wanted to show we were willing to collaborate with higher intelligences, with angels or any interested extraterrestrials who might have tuned in.

It soon appeared both species had plans for us. With no idea of what awaited us I traveled to London a few weeks later to visit my mother, Melinda having arranged to join me a few days later.

2

The Emergence
of the Sacred

The Unlikely Return of the Maitreya, Sumer, Glastonbury, and the Magic of Sacred Landscape

The Maitreya is back. He's here working quietly for the good of humanity. There was even some talk of his living and teaching in the Brick Lane area of London's East End. Apparently his flock included Hindu, Muslim, Buddhist, and Christian believers. His message was universal. He will reveal himself. The time is right.

So the rumors went that spring in 1982. I'd seen one or two of the full-page advertisements that English artist Benjamin Creme had been placing in some of the major newspapers. Creme claimed openly to be telepathically in contact with the Maitreya. Creme was told the Maitreya would be making himself known on worldwide television over the weekend of May 22 and 23 of that very year. Not only would we, the waiting public, be able to see the Maitreya, but he also would be speaking to us simultaneously, each in his or her *own* language.

That was how certain Ben Creme was. He was staking his reputation on it, and he had himself a fine old time going around telling everybody about the great day approaching. Publishing books. Going on TV. Giving news conferences. But, unless I missed it, and May 1982 has long since come and gone, Mr. Creme doesn't have his Maitreya quite yet.

Benjamin Creme wasn't in the country when I phoned; he was giving a lecture in Holland. It was late September in 1983, and I was in London and on my way to Glastonbury to pay my respects to one of the most potent sacred sites in England. The thought to contact Benjamin Creme popped out from Diana, my ever-curious mother, always happy to be on some trail. She'd read about Creme's pronouncements in the English newspapers and in spite of her agnosticism couldn't wait to meet a Maitreya.

A lady answered the phone. She didn't introduce herself, but from the intimacy with which she spoke of "Ben" she was either loving wife or bewitched acolyte. It was difficult to decide which—or possibly both. She confirmed what I had supposed, namely that the Maitreya had not manifested himself as Ben Creme was predicting, either on worldwide television or anywhere else for that matter.

We immediately hit a cloud of confusion. I'd assumed this "speaking to each in their own language" on the TV appearance would be—if it was to be—some sort of supernatural zapping into the satellite circuits, possibly even angelically assisted. In essence, a self-evident miracle. I'd imagined something of that order would jolt everybody out of their complacency. But, it appeared from what the woman was telling me it wasn't the Maitreya's plan at all. He was going to do it by calling all of the world's press together and having them print his words in every language.

And what had happened? I asked.

Apparently, the press couldn't find the Maitreya. She told me two or three people had indeed come forward to claim the post, but in Ben's opinion, they certainly weren't all-powerful, all-knowing entities, and Ben had disqualified one of them because he was too short!

Great heaven! I thought, has it turned into a Maitreya contest? I wondered to myself how Benjamin Creme really fit into all this. Ringmaster? Judge? Perhaps the Maitreya himself in disguise? Who would want the job anyway? All that publicity, never a moment to yourself. Make-up for television. He'd be sealed away in a little box before he even started his mission.

This time it looks like it is going to be different. I doubt if anyone knows what is really going to happen, but all the signs seem to be pointing to a collective consciousness, perhaps more along the lines of a group messiah. It would surely be too easy if some omniscient, omnipotent, godlike figure walked onto the world stage and took over—even if there are times when any one of us might call passionately for just such an intervention.

"But, Ben feels sure the Maitreya will make himself known when we're all ready for him," Creme's companion was rattling innocently on. "Ben thinks the press didn't get behind it. They weren't interested enough!"

Well, *there's* a surprise! I wondered if any of Ben's people had ever dealt with the press. I asked about the Pakistani whom I read about while I was still in New York, one of those who'd declared himself as Maitreya. She hastily assured me there'd been two men who had come forward. Fortunately, it sounded like the Pakistani man had stepped down so at least that simplified my quest. All she could tell me was the other man lived and worked in the Brick Lane area of Bethnall Green, among the Asian communities that have settled there.

"But doesn't the Maitreya of Mr. Creme's transmissions also work in that community?" I asked, confused again.

"Yes, well . . . ," she said, uncertain, "it just can't be the same man because Ben says the Maitreya came from the Himalayas and only arrived here in 1976." The "impostor" had apparently moved here from Sri Lanka in the mid-1960s.

I was most intrigued to meet a man whom someone else thought it necessary to denounce for *not* being the Maitraya. So next day my mother, still fascinated, and I set off in her little Renault deep into the heart of the Brick Lane area.

We left off the car on a deserted side street and plodded down the interminably long Brick Lane, fighting the wind as a drizzling rain blew into our faces. Torn posters advertising Pakistani movies flapped in the gutter. Dilapidated shops sold a variety of heavily scented sweetmeats, the smells combining in our noses with the indefinable odor of old mattresses. It was an unloved place. Disenchanted people leaving their lands and roots to settle, for who knows what real reason, in a miserable London slum.

The Muslim dynamic, too, had taken its toll. "By crediting Allah with all, the people have allowed too little joy into their own lives," an Egyptian friend had told me in quite another context, and it seemed this dispirited quality spread to the atmosphere through Brick Lane like smog.

A startling modern structure loomed out of the gathering mists. We were drawn into its courtyard, the mirrored surfaces of its shiny curtain walls reflecting myriad images of us walking, first caved in, then out, then elongated, then dwarf-plump out of an arcade. We whirled through the revolving doors to be told by a nice-girl receptionist that it was a local Truman Brewery.

Ironic that, my mother joked, the devil alcohol bedecked in such silvery splendor amid the teetotalling Muslims of this Asian colony. But neither the receptionist nor any of the other more likely looking prospects we asked on the streets knew where the Maitreya lived. Some had difficulty with the word itself, some scuttled off, and the others just shook their heads in mystery. The nice-girl receptionist had smiled with a tolerance reserved for nuns and the mentally retarded and had suggested we should ask in an Indian restaurant.

Nothing vaguely psychic was happening. No buzzing sounds. Our feet weren't being led. . . . But, of course, in a way, they were. Looking up, right in front of us, we both saw a tiny police station. Flat-topped, two windows and a door.

"When in doubt, always ask a policeman," my mother intoned, and in we went.

"Er, 'scuse me, officer." I notice my voice falls into a slight Jagger-cockney accent when I'm talking to English cops, although it must have been an obvious affectation to the bland-faced young fuzz smiling across the counter at us. "Remember all that Messiah stuff a few months back?" Merriment simmered in his eyes for a moment.

"Ho yus," he says, straight out of Gilbert and Sullivan and putting me on, I suspect, something dreadful. "Wha' ever happened to all tha'? Lived down this way, din' he? Back in May, warn' it?" He turned to his mate for confirmation.

"We 'ad the press darn 'ere an' everyfing. Over on Commercial Street, warn't it?"

My mother squeezed in between all the questions. "But how would you know if it was the Messiah?"

The rosser's mate, head reeling from the larf of it all and not quite believing the setup, stammered, "'Cos 'e'd 'ave 'oles in 'is 'ands!" and started the slow heave of a pub-laugh. Midway he caught my recoil of pain and decently choked it back into more wonderings.

"May 22, or were it the 23rd? Suddenly the papers were all over the place. Lasted abart a week, din' it?" A dreamy look came over his honest, open face at the thought of the Messiah, right there, on his beat. "Wouldn' it 'ave been wonderful," he mused. "Now, wouldn' it 'ave been luvly?"

And that was all they knew, apart from the Maitreya's address, which they recalled as being 75 Commercial Street.

Number 75 was a dump. As we climbed the dark, rubbish-strewn stairs I was wondering if this were ever the place to find a Messiah. I opened the second-floor door to see a crammed sweatshop, full of clicking, whirring machines and bright-eyed Pakistani lads. One detached himself from his machine.

"I'm looking for the Maitreya. I'm told he lives here." He didn't understand me at first, and then when I said "holy man" his face lit up.

"Oh! Sadu, Baba. He not here now. Back seven o'clock."

I gave him my phone number and asked him if the Maitreya would call me back after nine o'clock that evening.

It was 10:00 P.M. that same evening, and I had all but forgotten about the Maitreya's call. The woebegone surroundings of the afternoon seemed an unlikely place to find such an august being, but then, sure enough, the phone bleated away in its strident English dissonance.

"Could I speak to Timothy . . ." He couldn't read my writing. But, at least, he could speak English! I had a moment of disequilibrium. What *does* one say to a Maitreya?

However, after a few formalities—luckily it was he who did most of the talking—his story spilled out in a bubbling, singsong rush.

"My name is Premaratma. People around here call me Sadu, Baba, many names. . . ." He said he was born in Sri Lanka in 1926 and came to England in 1966. Then, obviously taking his courage into his hands, he told me he'd known he was the Maitreya for the past thirty years. He'd been told so by holy men in Sri Lanka, but hadn't understood exactly what it meant at the time. All these many years later, when he came across Benjamin Creme's pronouncements, it had started him wondering. After all, he *did* work in the Brick Lane area. And there weren't any other Maitreyas working the Lane, and he'd know if there were, wouldn't he?

He told me he'd sat quiet for a couple of years after first reading about Creme's announcement. He'd literally stumbled over the newspaper advert on a sidewalk, a synchronicity clearly not lost on him. He confessed he'd gone through tremendous worries and had only summoned the confidence to announce himself when the press had descended on the lane that week of May 23.

Some of the articles, he blurted out proudly, had reached all of two or three million people. I couldn't tell if he felt that these numbers constituted enough people to claim it as a worldwide phenomenon.

I was starting to feel sorry for the guy. He was so evidently happy I'd called, that I'd taken some notice, so open and enthusiastic, and so lacking in any of the sort of gnosis I might have imagined in a Maitreya, that I could see why Creme might have thought Premaratma was not his man.

Whatever had happened? What had gone awry? Could there really be more holy men in Brick Lane who think of themselves as Maitreyas?

"There's much that Mr. Creme doesn't know . . . ," Premaratma was tailing off. He wanted to meet us, he said, even that he'd been waiting for us. "There's so much to tell you."

We agreed on a time the next weekend, after Melinda arrived from New York, and arranged, the three of us, to meet outside 75 Commercial Street. We would find out just how much Premaratma had to tell us in a few days time.

Sometimes the paranoia sets in. Not that I'm crazy, or ever really have been, but I have some harsh early imprints from war that have taken most of a lifetime to resolve and to fully release.

In 1982 I was still very much of a beginner in deciphering what these temporary fits of high anxiety were all about, and I'd just come across the shamanic idea of a "ring of demons surrounding a sacred place." So when "the voices" began to whisper of cosmic plots for my soul and my friends would start looking particularly menacing, rather than giving over to the panic and fear, I gradually began to understand that I was merely going through a transition; I was passing through the ring of demons that so thoughtfully protect the sacred places of peace beyond.

I had left London for the south coast the day after talking to the Maitreya, anxious to be getting into the next stage of my pilgrimage: Glastonbury and the enormous zodiacal figures supposedly carved from the very landscape itself.

So there we were in Brighton, my cousin Christopher and I, sharing sacred mushrooms and catching up on all the news since we'd last seen each other. We've been close for as long as we can remember, and that's what really helped when the demons appeared. Suddenly, everything he said took on a new and threatening tone; his words all had three or four deeper meanings, each more ominous than the others in their consequences. He didn't quite grow horns as others have in previous encounters with this manifestation, but all the gloating malevolence of the demonic was there.

Oh! No! I thought in a panic. *My cousin is in on the plot, too!*

It was only then, when I realized the full absurdity of it, this man whom I'd known all my life conspiring against me, that I was able to let go of the fear and love him through all the horror. The monstrousness fell away like a tired, stupid suit of old clothes. We were through the ring of demons and into an entirely new space of communion.

The next day blew howling off-sea winds with squalling gusts of rain. We walked along the tan, stone beach, laughing and calling to the Elementals. The sea broke massively against the shingle, and clouds of spray hung in the air like smoke from late-evening campfires. As I waded through the shifting pebbles, the storm drove into my unprotected right ear, setting up a hurricane in its minute ecosystem. My head throbbed and roared with the storm and the sea, a cacophony that didn't settle down until later, in my cousin's studio as we sat listening to Chris's friend Mitchell's unhappy story.

I'd never met Mitchell before, but within minutes, with an openness quite uncharacteristic of the English, he was telling us about his brother-in-law, who had taken to seeing devils jumping in and out of dogs. The man was a born-again Christian, a native of Japan, who had been working and living in Canada. The dogs had finally caught up with him over there, and he'd sailed back to England in a complete mess. Now the craziness had started all over again, and the family didn't know which way to turn. He seemed perfectly normal most of the time, but these diabolical visions would suddenly overpower him.

It was all rather familiar. I thought of myself the night before, becoming convinced my dear cousin Chris was a demonic entity. The thought came to me that these demonic visions would be better thought of as holding patterns or as ceilings of psychic activity, which can keep us held in their thrall until either we summon the courage to move through to the other side or the overall situation itself takes a forward step. The answer that was reaffirmed for me last night was not to get lost in the fear, but to stay loving and openhearted throughout the encounter.

Clearly Mitchell's brother-in-law was suffering from some form of mental illness, and there was nothing much I could say to alleviate that. I tried telling Mitchell my understanding that demons were thought-forms, which can be dissolved with a blast of love from the heart. In my attempt to clarify this concept and after talking this through for a while, I merely suggested that Mitchell assure his brother-in-law that in reality the demons were merely angels in disguise. Being a spiritual man himself, this seemed to appeal to Mitchell, and he quite appreciated the righteous simplicity of the observation.

It was a perfect drive to Glastonbury, through King Arthur's adopted country. And, after all, around here, what wasn't perfect? The atmosphere has a peculiar density, as if history itself is freeze-dried and packed into every square foot.

A broad sunset broke over the day's storm clouds, unveiling a wildly mottled landscape with the sun, bright red and huge in the sky, slicing in through the trees. Chris played his clarinet, happily cross-legged on the front seat, as I drove fast down the winding one-car lanes.

It was late evening when we came across Glastonbury, almost unexpectedly. The tor loomed darkly up to our right-hand side, a conical blot of darkness against the night sky. We'd taken our chances on bed-and-breakfast places, deliberately not phoning ahead, rather trusting in angelic guidance to place us where we needed to be. We checked out a couple of B&Bs that turned out to be full up, a clear sign, we reckoned, that the evening was intended to be more personal. Chris remembered that his friend, the writer Tony Roberts, lived just outside town, so off we were again, along night-scented lanes, to root Tony and his wife out of a quiet evening at home.

They greeted us effusively, happy, it seemed, for the diversion that travelers bring. And they were a magnificent couple. They'd been together fifteen years and danced a very fine dance. Tony, at forty-two, was large, loud, and forceful. He had a wonderful mind with an encyclopedic knowledge of Earth lore, and Glastonbury in particular. A voluminous author and self-styled anarchist geo-mythologist, he talked at top speed, top volume, and yet listened and heard every word you'd say. He seemed to enjoy everybody talking at once and worked the conversation like a jazzman, swaying and moving to the ever-changing rhythms.

Jan, Tony's wife, was just as strong, stronger, perhaps, in the way that women are. With an excellent intuition, she could *feel* the earth energies, and it was obvious what a deep sensitivity she brought to their investigations. It seemed to me she carried that special breed of calm I've always associated with the Egyptian goddess Hathor, and she clearly held the whole madcap pace together with an unobtrusive, yet firm, hand.

The talk sped through an update on all the subjects that mutually interested us.

"Have you heard their new line on UFOs?" Tony shouted at me from across the room. "They're all getting behind Carl Jung and dismissing them as projections of our minds!" He was pulling books out of the floor-to-ceiling shelves and throwing them at me.

"Silly asses!" He hefted a particularly heavy tome on UFOs at me. "Wait till *they* get abducted. Let them try to explain *that* away as a men-

408 848 8622

tal projection!" Then it was full speed on to the gathering of the clans in Glastonbury. More and more people were finding their way to this special little town, drawn by something they couldn't quite explain.

It is generally acknowledged as more than a myth that Joseph of Arimathea arrived here with a small band of believers shortly after the crucifixion of Christ. They were well received by the resident druids and given land on which they built the first church in England.

Without question, both Glastonbury Tor and Chalice Well, a spring at the foot of the tor that runs red with iron and has never been known to dry up, were sacred to the old gods for thousands of years before the arrival of Christianity. And like many places that have been held sacred for a very long time, Glastonbury also carries its own measure of woe. Modern pilgrims, often neophytes embarking on their first spiritual vision quests, find themselves caught up in the tidal psychic stresses of the place. Their own darker, repressed emotions will frequently rise to the surface in unfortunate displays of spiritual ambition or unexplainable depths of despair.

Then there was the Glastonbury Zodiac itself, with all of the mystery surrounding it. Early in the twentieth century, with the advent of detailed maps and aerial photography, Katharine Maltwood, a student of Arthurian mysteries and the grail legend, discovered what appeared to be a vast terrestrial zodiac, some thirty miles in circumference, geomantically shaped from natural features of the land. The zodiacal figures, sometimes two or three miles long, are delineated by rivers, streams, hills, earthworks, old roads, and footpaths. All these figures tally precisely with the appropriate star systems in the sky above them.

Tony suggested that both mystically and physically the earth has been molded to conform to the harmonies of terrestrial and celestial energy patterns. And what was especially strange about all this was the fact that these vast figures, and their grand design, only become clearly visible from a height of many thousands of feet. Since an aerial perspective would have been essential to the planning of the logistics of the scheme, Tony maintained that they must have had some pretty remarkable forms of spiritual technology to accomplish all that was here.

The date of this supreme creation of antiquity is unclear. While Mrs. Maltwood's researches led her to believe that 2700 BCE may have been the approximate date of the zodiac, Tony was inclined to push the timing back to the Atlantean era of about 10,000 BCE, while mentioning other colleagues who related the work to the great Dendarah Zodiac in Egypt and placed the date at around 7000 to 8000 BCE.

However ancient are the astrological forms created in the landscape, what we do know with some degree of certainty is around 2000 BCE a race of astronomer-priests came to Glastonbury and erected various standing stones and earthworks within the precincts of what Tony calls the "Zodiac's hallowed ground."

More recent studies by Professor Alexander Thom, who Tony reckoned was the foremost living expert on megalithic geometry, have shown that the people of 2000 BCE were quite capable of creating complex structures in earth and stone that reflected precise astronomical, mathematical, and geometrical knowledge. By examining the Glastonbury landscape, Professor Thom has reached the conclusion it was laid out to form a lunar observatory in which eclipses could be predicted with great accuracy.

Whether or not you accept these curious findings, you only have to travel with an open heart in and among the hills and wooded valleys of Somerset to *feel* the presence of these ancient sculpted forms.

As we talked I knew there was a key in this place. A part of the supreme puzzle lay here waiting to reveal itself. As we decode the puzzle we will find ourselves drawn together, each with our own unique part of the grand mosaic, discovering as we close in that all the pieces we carry fit together to make a wondrous new whole: the co-creation of the New Reality: a vast collaboration of humans, angels, nature spirits, cetaceans, and extraterrestrials.

We all nodded silently, sitting around the roaring fire, as rapture-quiet music filled the space between the sounds. We all saw this vision together while the consciousness of our group-soul swelled happily and broke like a wave of revelation around us. Enough had been said and seen, and beds were beckoning. We slept soundly that night, cradled in the crook of an immense geomantic arm, at ease in the hallowed ground of the Glastonbury Zodiac.

The previous evening our hosts had referred to a new discovery in the Gemini figure: twin streams of clear water had been found spurting from a rock. Within a few inches from where the streams emerged they came together to form a single bubbling rivulet. As Jan had pointed out, in the symbolic life this intertwining of divine and human is represented by the Christ figure, who could be seen outlined between the two hills of the Gemini twins.

The spring was the destination we had in mind as we set out from Tony and Jan's house under a damp, overhung, autumn sky. Rapidly scudding clouds, heavy with water, soon broke into gusty showers, darkening and mystifying still further the deep greens of the trees and hillocks. Never had the earth felt to me so much a living being, and we such transient little creatures scrabbling across her soft, green back. Geomantic montage or not, something undeniably powerful has been claiming this land for countless millennia.

It was during the adventures described in this book that I first became aware that a midwayer angel was accompanying Melinda and me. We'd named him Mich—pronounced "Meesh"—and he appeared to smooth our way and guide us into the situations he wanted us to experience. Neither of us could see Mich with our physical eyes, but we sensed he was male, and we could feel his presence, hear him from time to time, and observe the results of his fruitful guidance. Although I wasn't always aware of Mich's company, I've no doubt his hand was behind many of the key events narrated in this book.*

---

*I'd had a previous experience with midwayers, although I didn't realize it at the time. It remained one of those mysterious events I assumed occurred occasionally in everyone's life. I was eighteen years old and driving with a girlfriend on an English country road in my recently bought, secondhand Citroën Deux Chevaux. Another car banged into us, sending us careening off the road, turning our little car over and over; we eventually landed upside down and crushed flat in a field. I came back to consciousness some moments later to find Jennifer and myself completely unhurt and laid out neatly on either side of the wrecked car, its wheels still spinning. Now, anyone who remembers the Deux Chevaux will probably recall the two side front windows. Each window was ingeniously split by a horizontal hinge about halfway down, so the top pane was fixed while the bottom half was free to flap open on the hinge. Thus, the opening part of the window was no bigger than about ten inches high. Yet here were Jennifer and I, without a scratch on us and somehow lofted out through those improbably tiny windows. It was only recently, since I've come to know my angels better, that they informed me that it was a couple of midwayers who had spirited us out of the crashing car. Thus it's clear that the midwayers are evidently quite capable of interacting with material reality if a situation merits it.

✤

Although cousin Chris and I left excitedly to look for the Gemini spring, Mich (whom I was enjoying visualizing sitting on top of the car's roof, the rain streaming through his light body) evidently had other plans for us. The Church of St. Andrew in the village of Compton Bishop loomed out of the squalling rain, compact and beckoning, standing in a felt-green graveyard. Next to the thirteenth-century church's stone stiffness swayed a majestically yielding yew tree, which must have been well over one thousand years old.

The door unlatched easily. We went into a simple, whitewashed space. As we made our way over uneven flagstones to the altar, our voices echoed from the high, vaulted roof and rumbled back to us, now entwined with the sounds of the storm building up all around the church.

We stared up at the stained glass panel showing a liberated Christ bestowing peace on a world while watched over by a benign Trinity, together with a fourth figure who could perhaps be representing the emerging Supreme Deity. While I'm sure there's a more accepted doctrinal explanation for this enigmatic fourth figure, it amused me to imagine what feat of sacred prescience might have led the window's creator to include it.

The thick stone walls muffled the storm for a moment so the cool silence of the church interior suddenly became tangible, and yes, audible, too.

Both being musicians, Chris and I have the same thought at the same time. The acoustics are perfect. Turning, we dash back out into the storm for our instruments. Then, sitting cross-legged in front of the stern altar, we play for the Spirit.

Starting slow and tentative, we find each other among the slashing of the driven leaves and the drumming of rain on venerable stones. We coil and twist, dancing a dance of sounds, building in tension, now slackening into a melodic relaxation while the storm seems to respond in its own sweet way. In my mind's eye, I see the angels of the churches as entranced as we are by the soaring cadences, pitching and dipping in a revelry quite their own.

Such music, the sounds of imagination and freedom, has seldom, if ever, been heard in this somber place. Chris's clarinet lofted high, reedy parabolas over the thrumming of my guitar: the pipes of Pan were accepted at last, welcomed even, by the stultifying rigidity of old and hardened ways.

We played for a long time, making sure the deed was done. In some manner we didn't understand we both felt empowered by this intuitive opening, and in feeling this, we also sensed we had in turn empowered the church in ways, perhaps, that the angels had intimated back in Toronto at the beginning of my journey.

After peaking amid the dark rafters, the music died into a long silence. The storm outside momentarily subsided, stilled apparently by the once-blasphemous joy of free, unfettered sound. Then, after a long and seemingly appreciative moment, all nature joined together in a leaf-slapping, rain-splatting, wind-roaring howl of applause.

We sat quietly together in one of the pews. The music was touching a deep place in both of us. We feel at one with nature; words between us aren't needed.

I find myself slipping into a deep hypnagogic state, images coursing and flickering around me. I'm seeing a series of hints and clues to the destiny that will raise us all, in that company with our small and gifted planet, into the presence of higher beings. I know in these sculpted hills there is a vital link in the unfolding saga of the cosmic drama that is overtaking each of one us.

I see Leviathan, the cosmic snake, devouring everything so it can be made anew. I see Ouroboros encircling the planet, trapping the stench of a polluted noosphere; ever recycling, reshaping, renewing; now opening her great mouth, her body reforming into an ever-widening new spiral of Multiverse potential.

I see the Rainbow Serpent, the wisest of creatures and bearer of godly knowledge, now redeemed and seeing her most treasured hopes lived out.

I see dragons, fiercesome and misunderstood, yet loving and protective of the woman who befriends them.

As I sit here on the old wood pew, my guitar set aside, I sense in my heart that there is a connection between these visions that I need to know and understand.

The images start again: It's as though I'm being shown a trail start-ing in the inconceivable past and floating through the eons. I catch a flickering glimpse of an entity, of an unmanifest "something," a sin-gularity even, from which this ancient energy extends into the present moment.

Had something profound in me been activated by the stained-glass image of the fourth figure? Was it my bemused invocation of the Supreme that created this powerful sense of *presence*? This is a particular quality of being, a certain laissez-faire wisdom, an ease and casual humor I'm learn-ing to associate with this elusive deity.

The impressions faded, leaving me feeling extraordinarily charged, almost overwhelmed by this massive macrocosmic hit. When I had my original adventures with dolphins back in Florida during the previous year, I knew I was opening myself up to contact with other intelligences. I had an encounter with an ET mouthpiece, and later I talked with angels. Now here I was in Glastonbury being touched by the most subtle yet tan-gible presence I'd yet experienced. I *knew* in those illuminated moments that this being in some way stretched down through cosmic history itself, rippling out from the Central Universe in an expanding wave of intel-ligence and high humor.

These were just powerful *feelings* I was experiencing at the time, feel-ings that I've only been able to start putting into still-inadequate words as I've come to experience and learn more about the Supreme.

Back in 1982 I was a novice. I was getting sensitized to these subtle feelings and yet had no way of understanding them or explaining them to myself. My books have become a way of making sense of what is being revealed to me over the years. Acquiring knowledge, after all, needs to be incremental to have any lasting value.

Later that same afternoon, with the elements somewhat settling, Chris and I intuitively positioned ourselves on either side of the ninety-foot-tall monumental column built in memory of Admiral Sir Samuel Hood. This proud stone erection stood alone on the crest of a hill overlooking Glastonbury plain and was clearly sited in some magical relationship with the tor, which rose like a soft, green breast from the marshes five miles away.

The supernatural quality of the surroundings was beginning to cavort with our creative imaginations. We both looked across the plain, through the swirling mists and vapors, and saw with a new clarity that these physical landmarks were nodal points in a vast geomantic matrix. In those moments, the landscape became for us one integrated whole, threaded with dragon lines and places of power.

Our coming here in this widely opened state of consciousness was having its effects. A reciprocal relationship was developing between the land and us. We both felt simultaneously a palpable new charge from the earth energies in the matrix, and as we stood there transfixed, I *knew* we ourselves were acting as some form of human terminal for a far-wider-ranging piece of angelic activity.

As if in confirmation of these unseen involvements, our prayer for a clear sunset in which to climb the tor itself was answered in the most direct way. From the moment we put the request out there, as Admiral Hood's column and the two of us stood with the squalls gusting all around us, the unlikely skies started clearing. Blue spots were appearing, small and wispy at first, then gaining hold and filling the sky until the gray monsters were left leering at us from over the hilly horizon.

We picked up our third in a chance meeting, and by this time I was starting to see a synchronous pattern emerging. It was in the village of Street, a few miles from Glastonbury, as we were returning to the tor for our sunset vigil. He was standing reading the notice board in the village's old meeting place, Crispin Hall, when, on an intuition, I approached him. Tall, loose, with a long, thin, bony face, Lifus introduced himself as an artist and a musician. He told us he'd put together the major underground group in the area and modestly admitted to having accrued something of a cult following.

Lifus summoned up a key to the great hall while we fetched our instruments in from the car and settled down to share some music and a pipe of peace in among the ghosts of generations of town elders. I had the impression of stepping briefly into someone else's dream as it seemed we'd arrived at a key moment in the life of Lifus. As a result of doing a man a good turn, Lifus had missed his connection and was, when we arrived, musing on the advisability of ever doing favors at all. Then we had shown up, with money for gas and a little something for his head, and here he was mumbling on in happy disbelief at all the coincidences.

Chris and I, always delighted to be on time, of course were more interested in the unlikely groupings that emerged as we were going through this dance. A unit of three people seems to be required for specific modulations of Earth energies, although at that time none of us had any idea of what lay in store for us. Three, as in an equilateral triangle, is a balanced and stable form, unlikely to buckle under the assorted telluric energies that can pour through when working with the power of the earth.

Later, as the last reservations dropped away, Lifus showed himself for the young magician he was. He told us he'd been approached, twice now, by the chief of the English Order of Templars and asked to participate in their inner workings. Clearly nobody's willing messiah, he'd sent the aging primate scuttling back to his musty books and secret signs.

"I've got more power in my little finger than you have in your entire group," Lifus retorted to the second approach, and had proved it by matching wits and incantations with the *grand fromage* for a whole day. Apparently the old lad had emerged exhausted and muttering defeat. It all sounded a little like a Vincent Price movie, but I could feel it wasn't an empty boast. Lifus was simply accounting for his spiritual pedigree in the best manner he knew how.

I'd met this dance before, particularly in the guru circuit. Those of the Old Power, with their traditions and fear-filled dogmas, approach the young expecting them to leap at the opportunity to possess all that "secret knowledge," just as they themselves must have done all those years ago, as had the generations before *them*.

The young changelings, however, recipients of the *baraka* of who and what they are—their courage and the demons they've faced—are bound in their honesty to reject the magical traditions of the Old Ways. So the cycle of revivification goes. A Krishnamurti, for example, casts off the messianic mantle designed for him by Madame Blavatsky and her Theosophist chums, and emerges a truth-sayer, a stronger and more effective teacher for resisting the temptation to become someone else's messiah.

With us, I was happy to see, Lifus felt no sort of unease and threw his spirit in with our group-soul for whatever adventure lay ahead.

The three of us arrived at Glastonbury Tor about an hour before sunset, tucking our car into the side of the small lane running at the foot of the surprisingly steep, green slopes. Like many of England's places of power, it has been largely left unspoiled by fences and commercial interests.

The tor itself is another of the region's mysteries. Its conical form rises about five hundred feet above the surrounding fenland. Until perhaps a thousand years ago, the marshes were tidal, which would have created the dramatic effect of thrusting the tor up out of a sea of glass. It's for this reason that the name Glastonbury is thought to have been derived from the old British words *Yns-witrin,* meaning "Isle of Glass."

The sharply angled sides of the hill are shaped into a series of seven rounded steps, not unlike the step pyramid at Saqquara, in Egypt. This is thought to be the legacy of the geomancers who created the whole zodiacal pattern millennia before. According to Celtic mythology the entrance to the land of the dead, known as Avalon, was always a high hill surrounded by water. The hill is also linked to *Caer Sidh,* fairies' glass mountain or spiral castle, where the supernatural powers inherent in the etheric realms met the natural energies blended from terrestrial and cosmic interaction.

As the three of us started up the wet incline a small figure some fifty feet above us turned to wave and beckon us on. There was something indefinably strange about him. Him? I couldn't be at all sure, and when he turned and resumed his own climbing, it was with a curious, rolling, almost monkey-like gait.

My feet were slipping on the long wet grass, and I dismissed the odd sight, thinking to myself that his rolling walk must be the way to climb a tor. Then, about halfway up, with the sun well down and hidden behind the other side of the hill, the figure appeared again, ahead and above us, short, squat, and dark against the blue sky. He beckoned once more and then disappeared behind one of the spiral crests.

We went on climbing. It felt astonishingly easy. No cramps or stiff limbs slowed us down, and I imagined the angels swirling all around us, uplifting our spirits and levitating us in their enthusiasm.

I was first over the top, immediately breathtaken by the sight of the old tower against the low sun, red-golden beams scintillating through the open, pointed arches of its base. We walked around the top of the tor, looking down at the 360° panorama. The great zodiac was spread out for us, outlined in hedgerows and hills, in ancient watercourses and stands of trees.

Lifus was the first to break the windy silence. "We're alone up here!"

There was a quiet surprise in his voice, and I knew then he had also glimpsed the squat, beckoning figure . . . who was now nowhere to be seen, in a place impossible to hide. All of us quickly scanned the slopes of the hill, but there was no sign whatsoever of our curious guide. This apparition remained a minor mystery, however, when set against the majesty of a perfect sunset.

We clambered inside the tower itself, open at the top some eighty feet above our heads, a square hole of azure blue with a hint of stars glistening through. This structure is all that remains of the fourteenth-century church built for Saint Michael. The previous church, dating back to the twelfth century, had been completely destroyed by an earthquake, an unusual enough event in England.

After meditating quietly together in the last beams of light, we reached for our instruments and played for the beauty of the place, for the gathering invisible multitudes whom we could *feel* there, even if we couldn't see them. Then we were soaring around each other in a triple-braided helix—up, around, and out of the top of the tower—each of us supremely happy to be alive and of service to a cause so vast that we knew in our hearts we saw but one veiled fraction of its full implications.

Our music fell silent with the final falling of the sun behind the distant hills.

Lifus spoke again. "One of the closely guarded Templar secrets of the tor is that it's built on top of a far older stone circle. And that's actually the source of its great power . . ." And I saw my cousin, with many of the megalithic stone circles of northern Europe under his belt, nodding in agreement.

"Here's another of their secrets." Lifus's dark eyes were glimmering in occult amusement. "They say that King Arthur used to come up here, spread out his prayer mat, and meditate in the evening sun."

We fell silent again, contemplating the impact of these historical patterns as we stood, our instruments behind us, our arms outstretched and heads gazing up at the square hole of sky. Through the lavender mist swirling in the tower we could see gray clouds smeared with rain scudding across the opening high above us.

In that moment we felt overlit by higher powers as we stood, the three of us triangulated in the center of this most central of places. I felt as though the stone tower was dissolving around me. I knew powerful energies were pouring through us; I was feeling them in my body, a rapid electrical tingling . . . and then it was over. Brief, but quite distinct, the feeling rippled through our bodies and then was gone, leaving us roaring with spontaneous laughter.

A young couple wandered up the tower, climbing over the rail to join us in looking up. He said his name was Michael in reply to our introductions. He was tall and seemed quiet inside, yet he had the look of a well-dressed pirate, with heavy, dark sideburns on a face as long and as dark as Lifus's.

"Are you a man of the spirit, Michael?" I felt the question drawn out of me. It wasn't what I usually asked first.

"No." His reply was flat and even.

"You will be. You will be." I found myself saying, "It'll happen to you when you least expect it!" We all laughed together, catching one another's eyes. I could see that inside he understood. For a long moment, the five of us stood, forming a living pentacle in the very center of the square tower.

It was so elusive, this magic. While the energies were definitely there and I *felt* them in the ground of my being, the feelings were also extremely subtle. I didn't think we would have been ready for the unexpected ritual had we not had our day of pilgrimage. I *knew* in those moments of transcendence that the Spirit fell over all five of us, each to the extent that he or she was aware of it. This was real, and not the cant of tradition-bound rhetoric or the manipulation of power-hungry sorcerers. This was an energy that was both massively powerful and infinitely tender at the same time.

When it felt to us as though the transmission was completed we glided down the still-wet grass, invoking angelic guidance for our sliding feet amid our laughter and amazement that we hadn't yet fallen flat on our faces. We were off, apparently, to the healing stone. Lifus knew where it was and had added, in his best, most authoritative, mystical manner, hamming it for our benefit, "They say when the right person comes along the stone can be lifted by mental power alone."

The prize, as usual in these epics, lies beneath the stone. He rolled his dark eyes as if to suggest that we might be the right people. We were not.

At the base of the tor we stopped to drink the spring water bubbling from a small pipe in the rock face. This was Blood Spring, where Joseph of Arimathea was said to have hidden the cup from the Last Supper. Giving some basis for the legend, the water did taste strongly of minerals and carried the sharp tang of metal. Behind us there was an opening in the rock on the other side of the lane. Chalice Hill Well was built deep into the earth, a large, five-sided masonry structure, immensely old and possibly even the work of the same geomancers who had erected the megalithic stones.

Human sacrifices had been carried out in that dark, sodden chamber. They were willing offerings in another time's dream, placed inside the underground reservoir at the summer solstice, the sluices opened by the hand of a priest or priestess until the victim drowned. Although I found out this unpleasant detail later, I sensed something of this sort from the solemnity and sadness of the chants that were drawn out of the three of us as we hunkered down in the dripping damp at the heart of the hill. A long dirge in a minor key gathered together the disparate emanations of our watery dungeon, slowly changing to a more joy-filled chanting as the energies rose into an echoing crescendo.

As we emerged from the well out into the gloaming, there was Michael again, standing in the lane, openmouthed that he should have seen us again, so soon.

"You must know a faster way down than I do." His face seemed puzzled.

"We do, Michael, we do!" The double meanings hung in the air as we all laughed together.

We found the healing stone as light was failing. The stone turned out to be twin stones instead. Both were deeply buried, and it was clear from their size that they must have been part of the original stone circle. An arrowed benchmark had been carved into the surface of one of the stones, and it pointed straight out over the small town below us, now starting to come alight in the dusk. Lifus told us that over the centuries many miracles have been attributed to these stones, as has also been the case with Chalice Hill Well, healings still ascribed by the locals to the old gods.

On intuition I placed my gold-covered quartz crystal rod on one of the healing stones, aligning it with the etched arrow.

The design for the crystal wand had come to me in a dream a few months earlier, together with the clue that the device may facilitate telepathy. I found what I saw in the dream a week later in a New York lapidary shop: a clear, crystal quartz spur about five inches long. Melinda had then gold-leafed its smooth exterior to produce what appeared to be an alien artifact; a device that no amount of retro-engineering would ever quite decipher.

Needless to say, there were no hummings or whirrings, no levitations, no apparent magical effects at all. Nor did any of us feel like putting any particular energy into raising the stone; if anything dramatic was going to happen, then it was going to be without any huffing and puffing from us.

Yet, as the three of us sat silently around the healing stones, the dawning of a deeper realization did well up in me. I followed with my eyes the direction that my crystal rod was pointing, looking at the curved back of the hills curling around the base of the tor. Streetlights and the warmer glow of house lights outlined the forms in the land below, until it appeared for all the world as if we were perched on the back of a vast green creature whose body and great tail stretched away from under us into the gathering darkness. There was such a sense of familiarity to the form itself. I'd seen it before, perhaps in a dream, with the same massive head and body and its immense, elongated tail. Was this the deeper secret? The secret behind the secret? Is this what may lie stretched out beneath this enchanted place?

A night breeze rustled the leaves in the trees beneath us. In the silence of twilight I felt an ancient pattern coming slowly into focus. The fleeting connection with that unknown chthonic presence I'd experienced earlier in the church was present here too, in this vast sculpted landscape. I felt sure then there was another far deeper matrix swirling beneath consensus reality, constantly pouring energy and information through to us. I was getting a telepathic nudge from the etheric realms. With this intuitive understanding came the sense that I was an inseparable part of some ancient undertaking.

These feelings were all so tentative, so wonderfully strange and yet so close to my fondest hopes, that I could have easily brushed the whole affair aside as a mere figment of my imagination. And yet, I asked myself, how else would a telepathic presence make contact with me, but *through* my imagination?

I've come to think of my imagination not simply as a clean slate on which I can project my hopes and fears but also as a window through which energy and information can be back-projected.

The three of us ran joyfully back down the tor, this time in almost total darkness. We were hurling ourselves down, fast and without a care, the angels guiding our footsteps safely through the mud and sheep shit.

Chris and I parted company with Lifus at the base of the hill, agreeing we'd all try to meet again at the next spring equinox. We'd talked about the need for a new form of ceremony without ritual, perhaps more of a party, with dancing to the music of the stones, a reforming of the old ways into the new and supreme shapes of our own times.

We sped out of the Glastonbury Zodiac in our small car, curving through the lanes outlining the great figure of Sagittarius. Tony Roberts warned us the zodiac tended to lay claim to her own and that engine trouble often halted those who had fallen entranced by the magic of the place.

Mich, however, proved up to the task of getting us out without any such problems, and we left the area with the palpable sense of passing through an air lock.

Premaratma was waiting outside of 75 Commercial Street when Melinda, newly landed from New York, and I arrived that next Sunday afternoon.

It was unmistakably him; he was small, pleasantly plump, with sweet delicate features that broke into a broad smile of recognition. His wide-set, gray/blue eyes twinkled amid all the scrunchy crinkles. The skin on his face and hands had a yin-softness, yet his grip, when we shook hands, was far stronger than I would have expected.

As he led us upstairs I was able to see he'd wound his hair up into a bulbous spiral, which lay like a soft beret on the tilt of his head. He ushered us through the family sweatshop (not *his* family, he told me) into a tiny office at the rear. The back wall was one entire factory window from the sill up, with some individual segments opened up to let through the rays of an autumn English sun, filling the space with gold.

It was in those first few moments, as we twisted and turned around each other in the tiny space, Baba showing us to our places amid what were presumably his few worldly possessions, that we all knew something special was happening. As soft as a whisper, the Spirit fell over the three of us, allowing a far deeper level of contact to occur, one that seemed comfortably beyond our rational grasp. It was clear that the three of us felt a connection made and our spiritual minds were joining together in a new way.

I felt that I was fully there, and yet in a state of witnessing, of a detached wonderment that allows for a deeper resonance with the Indwelling Divine Presence and is not a matter for intellects or words. The richness of the moment passed, and we all settled into our spots to hear Baba's story. He'd been born in Sri Lanka to an honored and illustrious family. They were proud and independent, people of the land. In what was to become a clue to the whole unfortunate affair, Baba told us his great-grandfather had also been known as the Maitreya of his people. According to Baba's researches and the family tradition, the old man was known to have fomented enough righteous indignation in the passive populace to secure nationwide land reforms—the great land reforms of the 1840s. (I felt that somehow I should have heard of them.)

The family were staunchly spiritual folk possessing a cultivated acquaintance with the inner life born of the interactions of two world religions, Hinduism and Buddhism, meeting and blossoming on their doorstep. C. W. Leadbeater, one of the foremost spiritual forces of the past one hundred years, also attended his father's guru. In fact, that was one of the reasons why Theosophy was drawn to Sri Lanka in the first place.

"Madame Blavatsky," Baba told us, "had a vision while she was sitting in Green Park, I think it was, in London. Apparently a beautiful young Indian guide appeared to her in a cloud of light and told her the answer to her quest lay in Lanka." There was no hint of family aggrandizement in Baba's telling of his tale; he was simply laying it out as he saw it.

Then: Baba's childhood. He'd always been spiritually inclined, he told us, and devoted his life from an early age to his religious studies. On two separate occasions he'd been informed, under rather remarkable conditions, that he indeed *was* the Maitreya. In one of these situations, the Sadu in question fairly leaped at him, bowling him over backwards in the certitude and energy with which he'd pronounced young Baba as the Maitreya.

Both these incidents happened when Baba was a child, and he told us that, in a curious way, neither encounter had really registered on him, although he recalled thinking them strange at the time. He had other matters to take care of. After all, he was still a kid. Baba had all but forgotten these two events when a *Los Angeles Times* article fell in to his hands. It described one of Benjamin Creme's press conferences. And there it was in black and white: "The Maitreya—living and working in Brick Lane."

Brick Lane!

He explained that this was already two years in the past, around 1980, after he'd been in England for about seventeen years. He had moved around the country until he was drawn to work in this predominantly Asian community. Now, he said proudly, he was accepted by everybody. Muslims, Hindus, and Buddhists all regarded him as a holy man, and he moved freely among the otherwise dissenting groups.

He hadn't pursued the Creme situation, finding that information would just show up at the right time. He pointed to a pile of newspapers and magazines that, together with some religious books, lay on the floor beside my folding metal chair. Every so often Baba would reach over and scrabble through the pile, although I did notice he kept them neatly in chronological sequence. I dreaded being read the whole lot.

"So what actually happened on that weekend of May 22 and 23, when the Maitreya was supposed to have announced himself?" I asked him.

Before he could answer, Melinda, fresh off the redeye from the States and exhausted, asked if he would mind if she took a quick nap. Clearly unfamiliar with such relaxed American informality, yet quite unfazed by it, Baba offered his sleeping mat and solicitously unwrapped a new blanket for her. Celibate surely, for all or most of his life, Baba was discreetly attentive while obviously unaccustomed to the ways of women. There was something of the feminine about the caring way he settled my companion down for her catnap.

Speaking quietly, he went on telling me how he'd watched the journalists that weekend scouring the streets for the Maitreya they'd been told by Creme was waiting for them. But, of course, it wasn't going to be as easy as that. First, the young Pakistani I'd read about, a self-styled representative of the government in exile (even Baba had to wonder what *that* might have meant) had stepped up and claimed the title.

Benjamin Creme had chosen to meet the Pakistani man at a local Brick Lane teashop, and in one of those odd synchronicities that pepper Baba's tale, he, Premaratma, happened to be walking by the teashop at the time. Baba recognized Creme from his photo in the newspapers, went in, and sitting down, joined in their discussion. The Pakistani lad hadn't put on a very good show, in Baba's account, since within a short time at the table he'd recanted his Maitreya bit and asked to become Baba's disciple. Baba hadn't told either of them about his being the Maitreya at this meeting; that was to come after some young Americans arrived in his life some weeks later.

The world press never did find the Maitreya, or Baba for that matter. But, in among all this excitement, it sounded like some canny young American searchers, alerted by Ben Creme's advertised pronouncements, had been sniffing around. One, said Baba, kept being led to his door. Every trail, apparently, had taken the American there, and he'd become personally convinced, and persuaded his friends, that Premaratma was indeed *the* Maitreya.

Baba himself had remained distinctly ambivalent; it hadn't felt seemly for him to make such a claim. If it was so, Baba told me, it would become known gradually in the normal course of events, then so be it. From his hesitation I could see he must have felt he was stepping into someone else's dream.

The Americans were insistent, so he told them his story. Benjamin Creme had subsequently heard about this, and not associating Premaratma with the small, modest man with whom he'd had tea a few days earlier, organized an important radio interview with his newly found Messiah. After all those many years of announcing the Maitreya's imminent return,

Creme must have really thought he had his man at last. I can only imagine Mr. Creme's mood upon arriving at the radio station and recognizing Premaratma. The interview did not go well: Baba, shuffling through his pile of newspapers while explaining his ancestry in halting, softly spoken English, could not have made good radio. Baba tried his best to answer Creme's questions, but I could tell from the rhythms of Baba's speech that they weren't the rhythms of a fast-moving radio show. He was also unnerved by realizing from the start of the interview that Creme had already rejected him.

Benjamin Creme, who has never actually met this Maitreya of his, having only received what he believes are telepathic messages, must have needed to vent his frustration, because it was right there on the radio that the self-appointed Messiah-maker busted poor Baba's chops. And the reason given? Premaratma was too short to be the Maitreya! *Too short!*

Baba, of course, by this time was utterly bewildered. He'd done all they wanted, against his better judgment, and Creme dismissed him as being too short—an impostor, no less!

Did that make him any less the Maitreya? he wondered. *He* knew perfectly well there wasn't anyone else in the Brick Lane area who had any such notions of Maitreya-hood. Yet Creme was continuing to insist that *his* Maitreya was well known in the Asian community and that he gave numerous public meetings.

Perhaps Mr. Creme's insistence on a taller Maitreya demonstrates one of the problems with channeled or telepathically received information. Timing. The information might be accurate, but the timing is always up for grabs. In Creme's case this timing gap seems rather overextended. Allowing that his messages were authentic, as I write in 2010, no Maitreya, short or tall, has yet emerged to my knowledge.

It's possible Ben Creme is simply another spiritual huckster, with a vested interest in keeping his fictitious Maitreya safely tucked out of sight. The man certainly appeared to enjoy traveling around the world in a remarkably well-cut white suit; I saw him dressed like an icon of spirituality, giving a lecture some years later in New York. He continued to make his progressively unlikely predictions for the Maitreya's imminent arrival, as he was forced equally to make up reasons for his Maitreya's continuing reticence.

I'd heard nothing of Benjamin Creme for some years, so, wanting to bring myself up to date for this book and with the advantage of the Internet, I confirmed that his Maitreya still hasn't declared himself, which has predictably made Creme a figure of fun in the English press. Yet as I scrolled through Wikipedia I found to my surprise an unexpected insight attributed to Mr. Creme. Apparently he'd created a small controversy in England when he was alleged to have made some positive remarks about Lucifer. In clarifying himself he explained he wasn't endorsing the devil, merely pointing out a misinterpretation of terms.

Evidently agreeing with Alice Bailey, Creme quotes her as saying, "Lucifer is the name of a great Angel, not an upstart in heaven who revolted against God and was put down into the nether regions as the devil. This is a complete misinterpretation. Lucifer means light, and comes from the Latin *lux*, *lucis*, meaning light. It is the name of the Angel who ensouls the human kingdom. . . ."[1]

This statement, with its truths, its half-truths, and its justifications, reveals perhaps more about Benjamin Creme than it does about Lucifer.

Once Premaratma had told us his story and Melinda—her dark hair still tousled from sleep—was awake and sitting cross-legged on the mat, we were able to explore each other's ideas on more substantial issues. For Baba, cosmic consciousness was the central point and aim of Buddhism. In his wide experience no other teaching outlined so clearly the path and the pitfalls involved in acquiring an ongoing relationship with the inner divinity.

In response to my question about the lack of a personal God in Buddhism, he said that it was cosmic consciousness that brought a real awareness of God. He then surprised me, since I didn't know that Buddhists acknowledged a personal God, by saying that only after attaining cosmic consciousness was it possible to have any real depth of understanding of a personal God.

Baba saw this as humankind's greatest adventure: first to acquire cosmic consciousness and then, further inward, to know and love the Atman, the divine inner spark of God living within each of us.

I got a glimpse from this unusual explanation as to why Premaratma is considered a holy man by three great religions, each with its own quite different vision of divinity. The gentle ease with which he slipped from the impersonal transcendence of cosmic consciousness to the personal immanence of the Atman came from a deep inner wisdom. Buddhists are recognized for their striving for cosmic consciousness, Muslims are included for their worshipful personal relationship with Allah, and the followers of Hinduism for their recognition of the individual Atman.

It's always been a puzzle to me as to why such a vociferous disagreement should exist between those believing in a transcendent impersonal God and those who are sure their God is a personal one. In my panentheistic view, God is both transcendent *and* immanent. How we relate to God has more to do with personal preference and where we are in our own spiritual growth. Both experiences of God are accessible to sincere seekers; both are credible, and neither one contradicts the other.

The use of the word *god* has become so freighted with different meanings over the centuries, as it has been appropriated by an assortment of religions, cults, and shysters, that I feel it necessary to explain as fully as possible what I mean by God.

In principle, it's more than simple. God, as I *experience* It, is everything, manifest and unmanifest, seen and unseen. How could God be anything else? And, if God is everything, then God is all things. To put a heretical spin on Paul's Biblical admonition, "What is *not* God?"

Having totally rejected any belief in God until my twenties, it was having the undeniable *experience* of God that so profoundly turned me around. I'm no theologian, but a quick scan of Wikipedia suggests my viewpoint is closest to panentheism, which it defines as, "A belief system which posits that God exists and interpenetrates every part of nature, and timelessly extends beyond as well. Panentheism is distinguished from pantheism, which holds that God is synonymous with the material universe. . . . In panentheism, God is not necessarily viewed as the creator or demiurge, but the eternal animating force behind the universe, with the universe as nothing more than the manifest part of God. The cosmos exists within God, who in turn 'pervades' or 'is in' the cosmos. While pantheism asserts that God and the universe are coextensive, panentheism claims that God is greater than the universe and that the universe is contained within God."[2]

I was intrigued to see that a number of North American native peoples, including the Cree, Iroquois, Huron, and Navajo, as well as some others were, and still are, panentheistic, in that their conception of God as the great mystery is both immanent in creation and transcendent of it.

I'm suggesting here that panentheism emerges from the direct personal experience of God, rather than from the dictates of someone else's dogmatic belief system. And since God can be *experienced,* much depends on the personality quirks and characteristics of the person doing the *experiencing.* People will have the experience of knowing God entirely dependent on their ability to expand their capacity to engage with the Divine experience.

On one level it's purely a matter of preference. Some people prefer a personal God to whom they can talk, some divide God into a Trinity, while still others prefer an impersonal God of pure energy. Since within the panentheistic understanding God is everything, all these different viewpoints are perfectly compatible. On a deeper reincarnational level, I believe all of us are working steadily toward a progressively fuller knowledge of God. It's what lures us on, whether we know it or not.

The Urantia Book maintains that human beings are predisposed to worship, that we contain spiritual circuitry connecting us with a deep need to worship. In a degraded form this can manifest as hero worship and personality cults, and in the very broadest sense, this spirit of worship can make itself felt in whatever or whomever a person loves more than anything or anyone else.

A man might say he "believes in the God of his religion," yet what he loves beyond all else is money, or security, or the market; then one of these will be his God—or, at least that aspect of God he is capable of worshipping. An atheist might claim not to believe in God, yet spends his life devoted to and "worshipping" rational thought or the Darwinian paradigm. We do appear to be hardwired to worship *something.*

Clearly this "worship circuit" is a double-edged sword. At its finest it allows us a direct connection with the Creator, yet it can also take us deep into our obsessions and addictions. While for some the object of worship is alcohol, or sex, or rock and roll, each of us chooses which image of God satisfies our need to worship. It could be Jesus Christ, Allah, a sacred grove of trees, Brahma, or the impersonal self. Clearly there are also different consequences to worshipping these different representations of God: some feed the soul and expand the consciousness, some seek to control and punish.

Without knowing God through direct experience, we can easily become prone to fall into other peoples' belief systems. Most of us raised in the West and subject to early Judeo-Christian religious dogma are presented with an angry, punitive God, somewhat mitigated by its later Christian makeover. Yet, that representation of Jehovah as God—if Jehovah wasn't merely a particularly megalomaniacal midwayer—is so obviously an amalgamation of disowned human emotions projected out onto an imagined deity that it's hard to take seriously. Many of us as adolescents rejected that concept of God along with the religions that promote such nonsense. It simply didn't *feel* right. From that point on it's almost entirely a matter of whether an individual has a direct personal experience of God as to whether he or she chooses to delve deeper into the great mystery.

When a Richard Dawkins or a Christopher Hitchens congratulates himself on how he saw through the "God myth" and rejected God along with religion at a young age, what he is really exhibiting is his lack of profound spiritual experience. Such an important decision made at that young age could barely be considered emotionally or spiritually mature, however mentally gifted a person believes himself to be.

This elementary error can lead to the silliest of beliefs.

Claiming, for example, that so many of the wars and violent acts in human history result from religious differences, while unfortunately true, never takes into account humanity's fearful and violent animal nature. Sad though it is, some humans have always fought to dominate others, and they will use religion, or nationalism, or racial superiority—anything that works to whip up the emotions of the people—to accomplish their ambitions. If Soviet Russia is an example of an atheist state, then religion can hardly be held responsible for the millions killed.

Rejecting the *concept* of God because of the horrors committed in religion's name, or because as an atheist one "doesn't feel the need for a God," merely speaks to a sore lack of transcendent or mystical experiences. In our materialistic culture, with its emphasis on consumerism and trivia, the experience of oneness with God can be easily derided as the result of brain chemistry or religious delusion.

Yet, I don't believe anyone fortunate enough to have had an authentic *experience* of God, either through grace, or a transcendent NDE, or, for example, by taking a powerful entheogen like psilocybin or 5-MeO-DMT, would be able to dismiss his or her encounter with the Divine quite so facilely.

Since God is everything and God's spirit permeates all things, it is inevitable that each human will love and worship some aspect or facet of God. It is my understanding that as mortal beings the underlying theme of our many lifetimes is a progressively deeper experiential *realization* of the nature of God.

The sun slewed in through the commercial metal windows. Motes of dust disturbed from the stack of newspapers eddied and swirled, defining the sunbeams as they bathed us all in the afternoon light. In the silence, the lines of the past met in Baba; the rhythms of generations of God-realization joined and centered in this small, delicate man, in this nothing little back room.

In those moments he talked as the Maitreya.

In singsong Pali, the original spoken language of the Buddha, Baba chanted the eight *sudras,* the teachings the Buddha gave immediately after receiving enlightenment. The echoing melody of the words had a power to them, a loving wisdom that communicated itself quite beyond whatever the words may have actually meant.

Translating them for us, Baba dedicated each sudra to the three of our activities ahead, separately or together. In Pali again, he invoked the devas, especially the Old Ones, the Energy Beings who hold together the physical fabric of the solar system and the planets. We, in turn, asked our angelic friends, whom we imagined coursing happily around the entire encounter, to bless the Maitreya Premaratma with their joyous presence.

Then, among that host of supermortal beings, the three of us broke bread together, Baba offering pieces of apple he carefully cut into slices with his soft, brown hands. As we sat in the golden silence, I *knew* that the Supreme Being, the vast, collective entity that is starting to overlight so many on our world, had taken another deliciously casual forward step.

We rose to leave in the calmness between us. Baba silently knelt down to kiss our shoes. We both shuffled our democratic feet at the gesture.

"Good Lord!" I said, embarrassed. "Is this all part of it? Is kissing feet part of the deal?"

Baba smiled, taken aback by my frankness, and assured us it was just the way of his people.

"Well, here's one from the ways of our people . . ." Melinda chuckled softly and gave Baba the biggest hug he'd probably ever received. His little arms dangled by his waist in surprise, his hands twitching yet unable to quite make the reciprocal shapes.

Then we all three broke into fits of happy laughter.

Before I left London I gave Benjamin Creme another call. This time he was in. He had nothing new to add to his story, insisting it was all the media's fault: they didn't discover the Maitreya because they were not sufficiently interested. He claimed his man was still lying doggo waiting for his time to emerge.

I probed Creme a little on the collective messiah concept, but he would have nothing of it, reasserting that the Maitreya, literally an omniscient and omnipotent being, as Ben constantly predicted, would soon be making his personal appearance. I felt like the young policeman back there on Brick Lane. "Well, that would be lovely, but don't you think it would be a bit boring if some superhuman personality just stepped in and sorted it all out for us?"

Benjamin Creme didn't have an answer for that one.

In the final analysis, however, Creme has centered a lot of public awareness on the coming of an important spiritual being and has raised a great deal of passionate interest in these overtly messianic times. He has been, in all likelihood, playing a different and vastly more complex role in the unfolding of the master plan than even he might have imagined. After all, Creme has become something of a collecting point for a whole host of spirit-orientated people. But, then again, perhaps he did know more than he was saying, since he ended the conversation with a phrase he had reiterated a couple of times in the course of our talk.

"I'm sure Baba is a very nice man," Creme said, "but he's no more the Maitreya than you or me."

✣

As I write, three decades after Melinda and I spent time with Premaratma, the Maitreya of Brick Lane, and still with no sign of Ben Creme's man, I'm inclined to think Creme might be at least half right. As his quoted opinion of Lucifer was half right—he knew enough to identify Lucifer correctly, but not enough to know it was Lucifer who fomented the rebellion—so also might he be right about an imminent arrival and wrong about the personality involved.

If Creme remains convinced his Maitreya lives and works in Brick Lane, while it's clear there's no evidence for this, might he possibly be picking up telepathically on something that *does* appear to be occurring? Could he be really predicting the long-delayed arrival of the Magisterial Son? And for this I need to turn back to *The Urantia Book*.

A Magisterial Son, they tell us, is a high celestial being who, with a large staff, appears as a mortal of the realm on a world when it reaches a certain level of development. We would have most likely received a Magisterial Son by now if it weren't for the incarnation of Michael as Jesus Christ, which has thrown the timing of the arrival of the Magisterial Mission up for grabs.

In the great plan of uplifting the material and spiritual well-being of the inhabited worlds of the Multiverse, missions such as that of the previously mentioned one of Prince Caligastia and his staff are regular events. These missions differ in purpose from the earliest, which tend to focus on the material and social welfare of early humans, to the more recent, which are devoted to spiritual matters. The Magisterial Mission is primarily one of assessment and judgment, and its arrival on a world signifies a major turning point in that world's social and spiritual development. All these celestial missions are carefully planned, and under normal circumstances they occur in an orderly sequence. But, as we well know by now, conditions on this planet have been far from normal since the Lucifer Rebellion nearly 203,000 years ago.

In addition to this, we have the fortunate complication of the incarnation of Christ Michael, the Creator Son of this Local Universe, who chose to live his seventh and final incarnation as Jesus Christ on this humble world, the impact of which continues to resonate in the world mind to this day.

Exceptional spirits have regularly made their appearance over the course of human history: Lao-tze, Machiventa Melchizedek, Teresa of Avila, Confucius, Siddhartha Gautama, Moses, Plato, Raphael, Hildegard of Bingen, Attila, Gandhi, Mohammed, and Leonado da Vinci, among others, and each has made his or her lasting impression. However, *The Urantia Book* echoes Christian belief in emphasizing the overriding significance of Christ Michael's incarnation as Jesus Christ.

Christ's brief life appears to be of a different order of importance entirely, which if this planet was the one chosen out of many millions for Michael's mortal incarnation, makes us most privileged to be living here. In fact, we are told in the book that Michael's exemplary life was of far more significance and interest to those on other planets within his vast domain than it has been accorded on this contentious world. Those observing from other worlds would have known perfectly well who Jesus Christ really was.

Like many people who had to submit as children to the image of Jesus promoted by organized Christianity, I'd lost any interest in him, along with the religions promoting him. I'd spent many years railing against organized religion and the misery and violence perpetrated in Christ's name. The concept of Jesus "dying for my sins" never felt right to me, nor did the demand that Jesus be worshipped as God ever feel natural to me. I had too many negative attitudes, and looking around at the state of Christianity, with all its hypocrisy and priestcraft, had done nothing to change my opinion.

It was only my experiences with entheogens in my twenties—which brought me face-to-face with a transcendent Divinity and formed a personal basis for all my subsequent spiritual exploration—that had opened my heart. With this firm sense of knowing God in my heart, I felt I didn't need an intermediary. But, of course, it isn't an either/or choice. I'd rejected Jesus Christ for the dreadful things done in his name before I was mature enough to know this was the way of the world.

So it was somewhat humbling to come across Jesus Christ in *The Urantia Book,* a book I'd already established for myself as authentic, and to see that he had been written about in such real and exalted terms.

Before I launch into a discussion about Jesus, however, I would like to provide a broader context by way of outlining the nature of the cosmology conveyed in *The Urantia Book* (which is covered in greater detail in appendix C).

According to the communicants of the book, the original Creation is called the Central Universe. From this springs the material Universes of Time and Space, which comprise seven Superuniverses and four Outer Space Levels.

As for the Creator itself, they tell us it consists of three aspects (the Father, the Mother/Son, and the Holy Spirit). It is not unlike the Christian Trinity, but with one significant feature that differs from the Trinity. The Eternal Son, the second person of the Urantia Trinity, is actually two beings in one and is called the Mother/Son. This identification was lost as Christianity, in its early days, became progressively more patriarchal.

The three aspects of the Trinity reside in the Central Universe, while the Creator Sons (the Michaelsons—our Jesus Christ) and their accompanying Mother Spirits (seven hundred thousand of each) modulate the energy emanating from the Central Universe to create the matter (lifeforms) that exists in each Local Universe.

These Creator Sons are gods in their own right. They are not the creator gods of our souls, but as stated above, they do modulate the building blocks of their Local Universes. As well as creating the realms of the celestials, they create the conditions in which our souls can inhabit material vehicles. After we shuck off our physical bodies we are given the opportunity to ascend through the many levels of the Local Universe, to ultimately travel to the heart of the great Central Universe itself.

Christ Michael, the Creator Son of our Local Universe of Nebadon, is, so we are told by the angels dictating *The Urantia Book* with their customary numerical precision, numbered 611,121 in a Master Universe currently sporting a total of seven hundred thousand Creator Sons; there is one Creator Son per Local Universe. The Multiverse is quite a sizable affair when we remember that a single Local Universe is made up of ten million inhabited planets.

The Urantia Book also maintains that, as with Christ Michael, every

Creator Son in each of the hundreds of thousands of Local Universes is required to incarnate on each of the seven primary levels of his created domain, with a human incarnation being the final one. There are many details of this that aren't relevant here, but I've no reason to doubt the book's communicants when they emphasize the significance of Michael's incarnation as an event of vital interest to the rest of his observing Local Universe.

Here we come back to the exceptional conditions we find on *this* planet. Under normal circumstances in other Local Universes, there might be one or many magisterial missions. As we know, each Creator Son rules over ten million inhabited planets, however, he incarnates as a mortal on only one of these. Because of this, the Magisterial Sons represent the Creator Son on those 9,999,999 worlds where the Creator Son does not incarnate. Our world has never seen a magisterial mission, but the communicants of *The Urantia Book* believe it could any day now.

What do we know about this Magisterial Son and his mission? Well, as the name suggests, the Magisterial Sons are the high magistrates of the inner realms. They operate under the authority of the Creator Son and are drawn from an order of celestials called the Avonals, who hail from the Central Universe. Although a high celestial being, the Magisterial Son manifests as an adult human being, while the seventy Avonals who accompany the mission aid and support him from the subtle energy realms.

The Magisterial Son is no shrinking violet, but a world-figure who will be immediately recognized for who he is and the authority he carries. There'll be no crucifying or killing him, this guy won't be so easily disposed of, and for all of us he'll be bringing the inevitable days of judgment. The Magisterial Son's arrival, together with his seventy invisible Avonals, marks the true end of a dispensation, and his judgments—and yes, there will be judgments—are intended to clear the way for a new era.

Could this Magisterial Son be the Maitreya whose daily appearance Benjamin Creme has been promoting with such opportunistic enthusiasm for these last thirty-five years? They certainly share many of the attributes consistent with a high spiritual personage, and both no doubt come in glory to some and the opposite of that to those deserving others.

✠

The imminent arrival of the Magisterial Son is also being advanced in quite a different quarter by a group of readers of *The Urantia Book* who've gathered over the last decade into what they've called the Teaching Mission, as a subset of the larger, worldwide community of readers.

The Teaching Mission was formed after the spontaneous and unexpected emergence of a group of discarnate teachers who spoke through some of the more mediumistically adroit individuals among the groups who meet to discuss the book. Along with a wealth of material communicated over the years, there have been increasing references to the Magisterial Son, culminating over the last few years in telepathic messages from the Magisterial Son himself.

I've had only peripheral contact with the Teaching Mission over the years since, in many ways, we are working in the same territory. Telepathic communication with discarnate intelligences is extremely challenging for the channels and for those giving credence to the information received. When there is no objective way of establishing the coherence and truth of a transmitted message, everything depends on the intuition, on how it *feels* in the light of one's spiritual intelligence. Which, in turn, will depend on how well-developed one's intuition is.

Personally I find it more productive and reliable in this most tenuous of human activities to remain independent. In this way I can compare my data with the information received in the Teaching Mission's transmissions.

One of the more unpalatable pieces of data being advanced in the Magisterial Son transmissions, for example, concerns a massive reduction of Earth's population, stating for example, "Your population will be reduced worldwide by a third to two-thirds." Apparently this will be achieved by some form of biological apocalypse that will affect people of all races and nations. Predicted to occur within the next twenty to thirty years (though probably sooner), this die-off is spoken of as a necessary clearing away of the many encumbrances of the previous age.

This is a complex and disturbing reality, with many aspects, both positive and negative. For a fuller analysis of the material that the Teaching Mission is receiving from and about Monjoronson, the Magisterial Son, I recommend the reader to the recent essay *The Call to Co-Create: The Omega Project, Radical Wisdom, and the Magisterial Mission* by Byron Belitsos.[3]

I should emphasize this mass die-off is a considerably more sanguinary prediction than anything I've been shown personally, and given the current state of the world perhaps not wholly unjustified. We should also remember that all predictions and prophecies are inherently unreliable and are subject to change by all manner of forces of which we have no idea.

If the singularity that so many are anticipating—from those expecting a Maitreya or a Messiah to those believing in the Hopi prophesies or the implications of finality of the Mayan calendar—turns out to be a collective intuition as to the arrival of the Magisterial Son, then however difficult global conditions become there will be clear and undeniable evidence in the person of the Magisterial Son that we are truly part of a vast and caring inhabited Multiverse.

Simply knowing this one truth will irrevocably change life on this world forever.

3

Glimpses of Reincarnational Threads

The Path of Art, Passing the Powers, Sexual Obsession, and Cathar Reincarnation

Raymond Bret Koch is showing us his most recent drawing. It's of a drooping, eighteenth-century flintlock pistol, bent like one of Dali's clocks into a plumply swollen but flaccid phallus. A small sprig of pubic hair curls out from the region of the pistol's hammer.

It is a raw image and so unexpected that I found myself laughing out loud, partly in appreciation, but reflexively too, as the image elbowed its way into my psyche. Melinda and I had arrived earlier that evening, after a channel crossing and three French trains. Following a scrumptious and welcoming dinner we sat around the open fire in the central hall of this fine old Normandy house. The books and drawings came out. Our host was keen to show us the trail he'd been following in the course of a long life.

Ray is a compact, forceful man, eighty-two years old and as sharp a shaman as could be found in a Western setting. Bright blue eyes shone out from a deeply creased tanned face. A flurry of white hair capped a large head dominated by an imperial nose and well-formed French lips. He spoke halting English, frequently looking to my bilingual companion for the right word. They knew each other well. Melinda had studied with Ray some years earlier, knew him and his wife, Lora, very well, and respected the old man as a serious occultist as well as an extremely proficient painter.

Having been a committed artist all his life, he's managed to hold on tenaciously to his integrity through the many bitter times of the twentieth century. Ray shows us his first published book as a commercial artist, a 1929 large-format edition illustrating a whole series of different wild animals, each apparently content in its own carefully painted habitat. It looks like a sensitively put-together endangered species campaign—until we arrive at the second half of the book. Here, the animals' skins and hides are magically transformed into the coats and wraps of a less ecologically sensitive era.

Ray, perhaps pre-capitulating our generation's more sensitive awareness, had painted the condemned animals with such a soft sweetness and appeal that it couldn't have been a very effective selling tool for the furrier who, no doubt, originally commissioned the work.

While we peer in fascination at his work, Ray is hopping up and down from the big armchair to get this book or that drawing. Lora is also bustling around, clearing the dinner plates away, happy, apparently, from her smile, to see Ray excited again. As Melinda and I constantly shift our positions to better see the illustrations under the light, I notice an odd thing. Although I knew from our conversation over dinner Ray spoke adequate English, he was almost completely quiet while he showed us his life's work. He seemed to be demonstrating something to us that he didn't want to put into words.

That Ray was an occult master I knew from what Melinda told me about his life, and besides, the atmosphere in his house felt steeped in mystery. Leather-bound books on mysticism, philosophy, alchemy, psychology, and medicine ringed the walls of his study. His own oil paintings, all done in the latter period of his life, stared down at us from around the walls of the great hall and off up the stairs, to fill every inch of wall space in the old house. I knew they hung there virtually unseen and completely unexhibited.

Ray evidently has no need for public acclaim. There is a directness and a brilliance to his work. Most of the paintings are rooted in surrealism and rendered with a near photographic exactitude. Yet the images, unlike those of photographic realism, are always wholly unexpected. They are never those likely to be seen in everyday life. Sensuous young women appear again and again, invariably painted with some bizarre twist involving danger, all exquisitely carried out, and the paintings appear to be trying to reveal some of the layers of darkness in the psyche of the Goddess.

Ray's paintings are intensely personal, and I can see why he might have held them back from public view for so long. However, he is a fine artist, quite unrecognized in his own time, whose work will be discovered at some point and no doubt provoke and delight future generations.

I'm thinking along these lines while Ray is showing us some of his earlier and more commercial productions: a French encyclopedia in which the insects, reptiles, and small animals are breathtakingly crafted in early airbrush, some so carefully done as to be indistinguishable from photos. Next, it's book after book of the most superbly rendered anatomical illustrations—kidneys, eyeballs, brains, livers, spleens, and all the other assorted wetware of biological systems, from medical textbooks to still more encyclopedias.

He tells us that his interest in the human body had taken him to China, to live there and learn the endless subtleties of oriental medicine. Now he ministers to an increasing number of the local folk in northern France, popping his needles in along those unaccustomed peasant meridians.

His later art certainly reflects Ray's love affair with the human body, particularly those of beautiful young women. While a sadness often colors his individual paintings, Ray's personal dream vision, with its dark, intense edges, cuts across any possibility of sentimentality. There is so much symbolic reverberation in each element of a painting that the nude figures, always placed in the foreground, seem to recede into a token existence as mere symbols themselves. It is this ambivalence, this tension between the real and the dreamed, and the almost pornographic dehumanization of the female form that give his work such discomforting power.

Ray is infatuated with youth. He willingly admitted as much some days later, and yet the paintings, with their intense symbolic overlays, suggest a rather more complicated story. It seems women have become largely objects for him. The female wisdom, the occult sensitivity, the deep awareness of cycles and rhythms, have all become transposed into the realm of symbols, as if the mystery of life itself has become lost in all the mystery surrounding it.

However, he is open about this quirk. He says he knows that an uncomfortable gap exists between his idealized vision of Woman and the flesh-and-blood reality of the actual women in his life. When I come to know him better and hear more of his life's story it becomes obvious that this scar goes particularly deep, back to a mother who didn't much care for her artist son, and certainly made no effort to understand him. He speaks of early imprints garnered at unwittingly brutal moments, which have continued to send their obsessional programs echoing down through the long years of his life.

As if to underscore this ambiguity, his wife Lora is a highly sensitive and intuitive woman who is both a fine artist in her own right and a naturally occult astrologer. She is some twenty-five years younger than Ray and, on the outside, all bustle, high energy, and efficiency, but it clearly hides a much deeper and more personal sense of loss. Like so many other talented women of her generation, Lora elected to squelch her own vision and instead run an artist's home, hoping to live through her man. It never really works though, as sacrifices like Lora's demonstrate; something inside turns off, and a woman can be left with precious little of her own.

The warmth of their welcome, however, was profound and genuine, their hospitality, thoughtful and generous. Yet, there was considerably more going on under the surface. We could all feel it. Somehow we *knew* each other, as though we'd been through this before. When we initially arrived, both Melinda and I remarked on the strong sense of coming home. The moment we drove through the old metal gates, up the winding gravel driveway, through pine trees and past dark lawns, a pervasive atmosphere of peace tinged with mystery settled over us. Heaven knows! It almost lulled me to sleep.

During dinner we talked about some of the weightier current affairs topics and were happy to find a remarkable level of agreement in spite of our generational differences. Ray, as an artist and magician, kept returning to the language of dreams and poetry and the pivotal role of the visionary in the management of human affairs. He evidently understood the hidden impact people of the spirit can have on the nature of the reality of their times.

In spite of holding this broad philosophical view, both Ray and Lora claimed they were worried about the ongoing international tension, that the warlike rhetoric exchanged between Russia and America could only lead to ultimate devastation. Ronald Reagan had just been elected president, and the Europeans, not fooled by an actor for one minute, could see he was a puppet of the arms industry, as well as being fundamentalist Christian enough to welcome the coming Armageddon. They were feeling they had every right to be concerned.

We weren't about to argue the political realities or the personalities of those involved, since the mention of Armageddon brought up another line of thought. In my stilted French, until my companion came to my rescue, I tried to explain how a growing number of us have been told, in very direct terms, that there was nothing to fear; indeed, rather to the contrary, we were about to enter what was to be a golden age on this little planet of ours. Yes, there might be some hiccups along the way, but essentially we were in good hands.

They both brightened upon hearing this and seemed to grasp immediately that what we were talking about were changes on other, deeper levels of reality, which were in the process of filtering through to us. Ray wanted an example of what we were talking about.

"Well, a friend of ours in New York, Ruth, a young woman . . ."

"How old?" Ray interrupted.

"Maybe thirty-five. Very down to earth, though. Not the sort of person you'd think would hear voices. Ruth was in her shower one morning in the fall of 1980." Melinda, who knew the story, was nodding her head in confirmation of the date. "And she heard this loud clear voice speaking directly to her. It was as distinct as a radio, she told us. The voice had simply said, 'Armageddon has been canceled. Tell all you meet.'"

Ruth had said the impact was so powerful, the voice so direct and clear, she very nearly collapsed. Too stable to dismiss such an apparition as a mere psychological aberration, she'd started passing on the message to those to whom she was drawn. In doing this she discovered what many of us were finding out, that we were all getting approximately the same information, although expressed in different ways. And we agreed between us that this revelatory insight seemed to be coming available since the fall of the previous year, 1979.

When this date was mentioned, Lora and Ray looked at each other in surprise. Apparently it was just about then that life for them had taken a decidedly better turn.

We talked more about this line of thought, giving examples from our own lives and discussing what we had been through recently with the angels while we were in Toronto. After two weeks of daily conversations with angels, our small group had been told that the conflict among the angels, the Lucifer Rebellion, was well on its way to being finally resolved.

Ray appeared to be familiar with the fact of the Lucifer Rebellion and its many ramifications over the last two hundred millennia. The concept that this upheaval has finally been put to rest must have stretched his reality somewhat since he returned again and again to ask whether we were sure about this.

Looking back on this conversation, it is hard to imagine now the degree to which most of us were convinced a world apocalypse was imminent. Growing up through the fifties and sixties, I realized recently how few of my generation had ever made plans for the future, because we didn't think we had a future. It must have been even more difficult for Ray, who'd lived through the entire century only to see it ending in nihilism and despair. I knew the old man was pondering this matter throughout the rest of the evening, although it was only when the evening was ending and we were heading off to our rooms that he asked me, "Do you know this to be true in your heart?"

"Yes!" I replied, as certain of this as I was of anything. I knew that he heard me.

Day follows day behind the high, stone walls. The final heat of summer seems to gather and focus itself on that small patch of land. The garden buzzes with the last-minute activity of insects, before rain and frost arrives and freezes their little thoraxes off. The estate seems endless and is carefully tended into a continuity of differing experiences. We walk from one microenvironment to another. A grotto. A stream. A well. Stone figures stand, half hidden behind blankets of rhododendron. Magical rocks are set into the ground. The sound of water is everywhere.

We were becoming entranced. Something inside me was calling. I couldn't quite make out what was going on, but I knew I was connected to Ray in some deep yet still unacknowledged manner. During the evenings we were getting to know each other better, in front of a roaring fire that was set generously against the new cool of the autumn nights, and under the enigmatic smiles of two large, smoke-darkened wood angels hanging from the black beams overhead.

Ray was unquestionably a master, although, of course, no such claims would ever be made. The moves he took toward us rippled with deeper meanings. I started to appreciate just how much he was a repository for the Old Ways, for the secrecy and silence surrounding the Mysteries. Ray, like sages through the ages who have sought to protect the Truth from the ravages of mammon, preferred to talk in parables, stories drawn from his own life's experience and that illustrated his own patchwork quilt of a spiritual lineage.

He told us he'd been staying in San Francisco in 1934, hanging out with the rich set, an artist among the brash merchant barons of the day. His host was a button king, Ray remembered, who was later ruined by the invention of the zip fastener. They'd set off for Tahiti on the button king's yacht, five of them, with all of a twenty-seven-person crew.

"Those were the days. . . ," Ray rolled his eyes, half amused and half still genuinely impressed. But alas, they were a thick crowd and played bridge continuously, a game that bored poor Ray out of his wits. Fortunately, they had their four for bridge so he was able to spend time sketching, away from the madness. Fortunate too, because Ray was posing as wealthy while, in fact, he was completely impoverished and living on his wits. The last thing he needed to do was to lose at bridge.

Shortly before they reached Tahiti the button king fell ill. Ray wasn't surprised, considering the vast excesses of opium and hashish consumed around the table. He recalled the button king as being as green as the sea. Naturally this ailment left a hole in the table that Ray couldn't very well refuse to occupy, trapped as he was on a small floating platform in the middle of the Pacific, posing as something he definitely was not.

Whether due to the other players' stonedness, an amazing run of luck, or some occult native cunning, Ray just kept on winning. He didn't lose a game that night.

Tahiti was horrible, a complete failure. Needing to get the button king to a doctor, they docked in the face of a typhoon, just making it ashore in time. Even after that excitement, all the others wanted to do was to keep on playing bridge, desperately trying to win their money back. They played without stopping for the next two days. And still Ray won.

The interpersonal situation, by this time, was growing increasingly tense. Ray was embarrassed. He hadn't wanted to play cards in the first place; his role was of an artist, perhaps even a rich artist, who was somewhat abstracted and inept when it came to money. He found himself being exposed in a way he'd least expected. Since he was playing dumb he'd no real idea, amid all the comings and goings and the slapping and flapping of cards, of just how much money was changing hands. He told us he hadn't even really appreciated or paid much attention to the stakes. Having no money of his own when he went into the game, Ray had no idea how much he'd won.

With their host, the button king, doctored and at least sufficiently cured to be raring to get back into the game (*he* hadn't lost any money yet to Ray), they set off again, this time for Bali. Well before they arrived, the other four, including the now much-subdued button maestro, had had quite enough of Ray. He clearly couldn't stay on board and continue to win astonishingly large sums of money. Neither could they stop playing bridge.

Ray was unceremoniously dumped onto another island. After the totting up was finished, the button king and his friends, at least being honorable in their debts, handed him an enormous envelope, stuffed with over a million francs in large bills. In the embarrassed, stunned silence Ray felt suddenly sick to his stomach. The thought that so consumed him was what might have happened to him had he lost.

Ray never saw Bali. The plutocrats sailed on without him, leaving him still sickened, in a hospital tended by Dutch nuns, He had been dropped off like some sort of Jonah.

A few weeks later, during his long journey home, Ray reached Calcutta. While walking the streets after a brief disembarkment, an

Indian *sadhu* ran up to him, insisting they take tea together. After a long silence, the holy man announced, "There's somebody in the South of India who is waiting to see you." And he gave Ray the whereabouts of a small village.

Thus was Ray faced with one of the crucial decisions of his young life. The boat to France, to home, sailed in a few hours, and this near-naked holy man was insisting he was expected by who knew who, or what, waiting for him over one thousand miles away. Once he made the decision, Ray told us, all his anxieties and indecision lifted, and he arrived at what turned out to be the ashram of Ramana Maharshi some days later.

Something was definitely afoot because the moment Ray entered all the disciples surrounding the Master quickly faded into the woodwork, leaving the two of them alone together. Ray remembered that the Master was chanting, as he always did; he hadn't talked in fifteen years.

Ray sat down. He told us he felt impelled to do so, almost as if he'd become hypnotized. The first day was hell with the chant going crazily round and round in Ray's head. He felt rooted to the spot. The singing seemed to be working directly on his main motor zones. On the second day he experienced an inner opening. He started to hear with his heart. After that, Ray and Ramana Maharshi became the closest of friends, and the two of them settled into a longstanding telepathic relationship.

It appeared the Master knew exactly who Ray was and bestowed on him the new name of Rayananda.

As I listened to this saga I wondered if what was really going on between the two men was that Ramana Maharshi was preparing to transfer his spiritual power over to this unlikely European. I would have asked Ray about this directly, but I knew by this time he was so secretive that even if it were true he would never want to make that claim. But there again, perhaps it was simply another example of the movement of Eastern metaphysical systems into the Western mind. Having deluged India for so many hundreds of years with our materialism, it seemed the least the holy men of the subcontinent could do in return.

Apparently, the closeness of contact continued on until the Master's death several years later. On the night Ramana Maharshi died, he came to Ray in a dream and gave him a white lily as they walked together on a beach. When Ray and his wife of the time woke up in the morning there was sand in the bed and two white lily petals on the pillow between them.

One afternoon, two days after Ray had talked about his connection with Ramana Maharshi, Melinda and I went for a long walk in the wooded grounds of the estate. We cut through the orchard, with fallen apples and pears already turning brown on the ground. A long hedge of apple trees, trained French-style to grow low and stumpy, was trimmed neatly in a line, approximately at the height of a sheep's mouth. We passed some sheep later, out in a meadow, looking fat and self-satisfied with their applefest. Then we continued on through the dense scrummage of trees, farther and farther into the woods.

All of a sudden we came across a curious structure sitting by itself in a clearing in the forest. It appeared to be a small temple with a bell-shaped dome. The wall was circular and continuous, made from the local flint embedded in beige-colored mortar. A smooth, sweeping, diagonal curve in the wall suggested a staircase inside, which must have wound down to a sunken room below ground level. The door was fastened with two well-oiled modern locks.

We walked around the carefully tended structure a couple of times before noticing a small arched window set up under the eaves. A twisted iron bar was cemented firmly in front of the window, a simple stained glass circle within which we could see seven stars. A metal ridge spiraled up the bar like a single lonely serpent on the staff of Hermes.

A powerful sense of psychic presence imbued the whole place.

I broached the subject of the chapel in the woods later that evening. I was tentative to ask about it because it was so obviously a secret. I should have known Ray better. He skillfully deflected the issue with a mumbled, "I speak about matters as they arise within me." And that was the last we heard about it. The temple was going to have to be a puzzle to which we would have to find our own answers.

The first clue, however, was not long in coming.

After dinner that same evening the talk turned to the Cathar "heresy." It was a name I'd heard associated with some sort of Manichean dualism, but I knew little more than that. A brief history of the Cathars, as relayed by Ray, gave us a glimpse into a very different world and a period in history that would turn out to be pivotal in the movement of the Spirit through Western religious thought.

The Cathars were founded in the Balkans in the tenth century and flourished in most southern European countries through to the mid-thirteenth century. Like most other tributaries of a more ancient dualism, Cathar doctrines were both ill understood and harshly suppressed by the Church of Rome.

Cathars were certainly extremists—religious libertarians, we might be calling them today. Cathars believed that only celestial and spiritual entities were created by God. Jesus Christ, for example, in their belief system, was believed not to have had a physical body. It was Satan who created matter, and the Cathars associated matter with sin. Human beings have a twin nature, and salvation lies in liberation from the physical influences of matter. Predictably enough, the Cathars were great self-mortificants, practicing flagellation and fasting with a gusto special even to those sanguinary times. Procreation was frowned on too; the Cathars saw it as an extension of the physical, and why give Satan any more bodies to work through?

Toward the beginning of the thirteenth century, Pope Innocent (Ha!) the Third launched a crusade against the so-called Cathar heresy. Anxious as ever to grab land, the French nobility needed little encouragement to fight a war of extermination. It was so atrociously bloody that even the pope became troubled, though not enough, apparently, to keep the Inquisition, created originally to deal with the Cathar heretics, from murdering any survivors.

Finally, in 1243, two hundred and ten of the last remaining Cathars holed up in the mountain fortress of Le Chateau de Montsegur in the south of France. The siege lasted a full nine months, until the Cathars put an end to it by burning themselves alive. (This I later found wasn't entirely true, but I understood why Ray might want to believe it.) The Cathars were burned alive; after surrendering to save the lives of their lay followers the Cathar Parfaits were said to have gone willingly to their deaths, refusing to renounce their faith. But this was no act of intentional suicide; this was a mass burning at the hands of the French nobles bribed by promises of Cathar land.

As he was finishing his description of the Cathars' short and unfortunate history, Ray produced two picture postcards of the fortress of Montsegur. It took me a moment to see the association, but there it was. One of the views of the mountaintop structure appeared identical in form, allowing for Montsegur's present state of partial ruin, to the little chapel we stumbled on in the woods.

My mind was whirling. Was I starting to delude myself? Was I just making up connections that weren't really there? I knew that vital secret knowledge was coded into many of the Gnostic belief systems, that these dualistic "heresies" often yielded valuable information about Lucifer, Satan, Caligastia, and the rebel angels. Had I come across someone who could help me read between the lines? Someone who could help point me in the right direction for answers to some of the insistent questions that were accumulating since our sessions with the angels in Toronto?

And the Cathars themselves? If we lay aside their extremism and their sexual choices, they espoused values not so very different from those held by many of us today. They lived extremely conscious lives and would certainly be regarded as enlightened were they still around.

I was starting to see Ray in another light, too. I already appreciated he was a carrier and transmitter of Western alchemical thought; he'd shown us a large eighteenth-century wooden box in which he kept his legal papers. Each face of the box had been painted carefully by him with alchemical symbols. He slyly admitted the gold he was cooking up would be the favorable resolution to an estate settlement currently buried in the nigredo of bureaucratic inertia.

Ray was also clearly acting as a coordinator of Eastern knowledge; his dedication to Chinese medicine and his meetings with Ramana Maharshi demonstrated that. Now I was being made aware of the possibility of an even deeper underlying connection with the Cathars, probably the last group of people who, within a Christian context, believed the world we inhabit is a subcreation of the larger whole. It is a concept that prepares us for the revelations contained in *The Urantia Book* concerning the impact of the Lucifer Rebellion on planetary life.

While the Cathars were unlikely to have known about the Lucifer Rebellion, they certainly had no doubt Satan was running the show on this world. In casting Satan as "creating matter" they may be pointing to a more subtle concept: that the world as we experience it—with our senses—is a subset of the real world, created at the time of the rebellion for Lucifer and Satan to put their revolutionary theories into practice.

This is an extremely nuanced concept. Whether it's thought of as the *maya* of the Vedic philosophers or the *alternate reality* of a contemporary physicist, mystics and sensitives of all ages and cultures have spoken about this magnificent reality existing somehow behind the reality we apprehend with our senses.

So, where is this line of Cathar thought taking us?

The Cathars' centerpiece was their conviction that Satan created matter; this included the world and all the physical beings on it. Some centuries earlier, many of the Gnostics had claimed much the same thing, maintaining that Yaldabaoth, the eldest son of the goddess Pistis Sophia, created the world in a fit of pique. Other Gnostics arrived at much the same conclusion, having placed their sentiments behind the enigmatic serpent in the garden. They suggest a more likely interpretation of the Garden of Eden story was that the serpent (whoever or whatever that energy was) may well have been attempting to free humanity from the fetters of an authoritarian deity.

What is common to almost all dualistic beliefs is their attempt to explain a simple paradox: if the Creator God is a God of love, just how could the world have become such a disastrously rotten place? What might have gone wrong to explain the apparent imbalance toward evil? The question is as relevant these days as it was when the Gnostics first posed it.

With the transmission of *The Urantia Book* we now have a clearer idea of how these confusions may have arisen. What the communicants of *The Urantia Book* tell us is that, while the universe and matter itself, as well as the spirit beings within the universe, are all ultimately emanations of God, our small system of inhabited planets has fallen under the sway of over forty thousand rebel midway angels. The Lucifer Rebellion occurred far earlier than recorded history, so the debilitating consequences of this profound upheaval on life on this world have steadily accumulated over the centuries. By the time the ancients were recording their thoughts it must have seemed to many of them that the entire fabric of the planet was the direct fruit of evil—a reasonable misconception based on the information they had available to them.

Yet many of these dualistic-minded groups also inspired tremendous loyalty and a host of martyrs to their causes. What was the truth in their underlying train of belief that made the Cathars, in particular, so threatening to the Church of Rome? They were clearly picking up on something.

The Urantia Book is invaluable for exploring the deeper causes of many of the planet's conflicts and confusions. Since the book includes a detailed history of this planet from its formation to the original seeding of life and its relationship to the angelic entities at the center of this cosmic drama, it helps us to trace many of the planetary ills back to their source.

Among other things *The Urantia Book* tells us that we are not the only ones in the universal family. The realization of this has been a long, slow process, and with the current depth of denial of the scientific, military, and political authorities, it appears each of us has to work this out for ourselves.

The extraterrestrials certainly do not appear to be making themselves known to the political leaders of the nations, and none has yet landed its craft on the White House lawn and announced itself. The meeting reputed to have taken place between President Eisenhower and a small group of extraterrestrials in 1954 was one of the few formal encounters attempted, and the results were inconsequential. It's thought that Eisenhower believed it was too soon for the world to know about extraterrestrials, and the ETs informed him they would be back.

As I write this in 2010, it looks like they have returned, and it seems that they are now more interested in contacting regular people. Only a week ago, for example, I received a report from a friend of mine, the harpist Peter Sterling, who had found himself drawn into a Zeta Reticulan space ship. I include what the Zetas passed along to Peter in chapter 12.

We can derive from Peter's encounter that contact now is more a matter of the heart and concerns each of us individually. As each of us opens, first to the possibility, then with further understanding, to the actuality of being part of a vast and teeming Multiverse, so too will our planet become aware of the presence of angels and other high spirit beings, who are presently returning to the Earth in large numbers to assist us.

As this occurs, so also will start the massive and fascinating adventure—a true collaboration of extraterrestrials, humans, and angels—one that will literally transmute, in an act of cosmic alchemy, the spiritual state of this world.

What then might be the role of the rebel midway angels in the coming transformation of this planet? They might well have quite a different view of how life is turning out on this world. Since they were created here half a million years ago and have spent the majority of their time here ever since, perhaps to them, *we* are the visitors—humans who live out our four score and ten and then move on to other levels. On the other hand, the midwayers, created as functional beings, are posted for very long (by our standards) periods on the planets of their assignments.

The Urantia Book tells us these midway angels were extremely helpful to Caligastia and his staff, becoming the intelligence arm of the mission, and because they could interact with physical matter, they were also able to aid unsuspecting human beings in all sorts of surprising and delightful ways.

The small city the staff built as their headquarters, now under the waters of the Persian Gulf, served as the center of learning. Although Earth was regarded as a difficult planet and there had been occasional murmurs of discontent, life for the Prince's staff proceeded in an orderly fashion in the gradual social and spiritual upliftment of the planetary population.

As mentioned earlier, the staff and the midway angels had been present on the planet for over a quarter of a million years when the revolution erupted. Lucifer had his own ideas about administering his domain, with an emphasis on accelerating the glacial pace of spiritual development of the mortals in his charge. As we know, the administration responded, not by overtly fighting with the rebels, but by appearing to give Lucifer what he wanted. These were not quite the radical changes he was demanding, but at least a free hand in overseeing those planets whose Planetary Princes sided with him. I suspect it was the administration's decision to quarantine this entire System of planets, containing the rebellion and cutting the planets off from the everyday business of the Multiverse, that must have most concerned Lucifer, Satan, and

Princes Caligastia and Daligastia. Thus this world became part of an unusual cosmic experiment.

Prince Caligastia, in this account, pledged his support to Lucifer at the System level, and suddenly, every spiritual entity on this planet capable of understanding what was going on was faced with what must have been an agonizing dilemma: whether to remain loyal to the long-established methods of the Multiverse—those who sent the prince and his staff here in the first place—or to team up with Caligastia and the rebel agenda. Of the fifty thousand existing midwayers (*The Urantia Book* is precise with numbers), they tell us that 40,119 midwayers chose to side with Caligastia.

We know that the revolution was mainly concerned with a call for greater freedoms for all beings, and as might be surmised, this can be a particularly ticklish issue in the matter of Multiverse governance. This factor becomes even thornier at the intersection of human and angelic endeavors. In other words, the lower the order of angels and as they became progressively more into contact with mortals, the more likely they were to have sided with Lucifer against their administrative superiors. It is only then, apparently, when the angels working in a Local System have to deal with mortal beings, that the freedom of choice available to all mortals is most strongly contrasted to the theocratic inflexibility of the celestial realms.

This must be a perennial issue, and it may give us a clue to something about the nature of the revolution that is not focused on in *The Urantia Book*. In fact, the book presents a curiously incomplete description of this epic, dwelling mainly on the disruption caused by Lucifer's actions. The book's communicants paint the Lucifer Rebellion in the very harshest terms, as though the revolution among the angels was the most terrible crime imaginable, and yet they also tell us there have been *three* previous rebellions in our Local Universe. So it's clear such acts of revolution by high angels were not completely unknown.

I have to assume that Lucifer and Satan, as well-trained System administrators, must have been aware of these previous revolutions, but I don't think that Lucifer and Prince Caligastia and his deputy Prince Daligastia, or any of the other Planetary Princes aligned with the rebels, really expected that their System of planets would be placed under a quarantine. I doubt if they anticipated being left completely on their own to develop their own systems of social order (or disorder) for themselves, free, presumably, from the constant presence (and advice) of their older brothers and sisters.

With the privilege of being able to take the longer view, I suggest that such angelic revolutions, however distressing they are for those subject to them in the moment, may well turn out to be the most reliable way of introducing change or novelty into a bureaucratically rigid administration.

Take a moment to imagine the plight of the beings based on the planet—the two princes, Caligastia and Daligastia, their staff of one hundred, the fifty thousand midwayers, and all the administrative and observer angels who accompany the Prince's mission living here for over two hundred thousand years in what must have been a kind of a golden age—a period that lasted up until the rebellion. They were here on a noble mission to help the indigenous peoples of the planet move along their righteous evolutionary trail, and it sounds like the angels were thoroughly enjoying their mission. Although we would understand the indigenous human beings of the time to be fairly primitive, what with slightly smaller brains and some genetic traits that would drop away over time, they were not so very different than we are today.

Much is made in *The Urantia Book* about the closeness of the links formed by the prince's staff and the immortal midwayers with their loyal human friends, and the depth of the affection felt between the two groups. The arrival of these off-planet workers, plus the presence of the midwayers, must have created an indelible impression on the indigenous life-forms over the thousands upon thousands of years that they labored here together.

Then, there would have come a day when they heard about Lucifer's revolution on the Local System HQ planet. The two Planetary Princes signed onto the rebel cause without much need for persuasion. So, for the first time in their long lives, each one of the staff and all those fifty thousand midwayers would have had to make an impossibly hard decision: to align themselves with Lucifer, the two princes, and the rebel faction and risk everything or to remain loyal to the Multiverse Administration. Most of them will likely have had only minimal information to make their choice and no doubt preferred to put their faith in their immediate supe-riors and the decisions made by them. They may well not have known all the possible consequences of following the rebel faction.

However, whether the prince's staff knew it or not, the resulting isola-tion and the quarantining of the world, which effectively cut this planet off from the normal cosmic influences a world such as ours might enjoy, also spelled death for them. Their immortality relied on their consump-tion of a fruit of a certain off-planet shrub, which was deliberately shipped in for this purpose. The biochemical reaction between this plant and the incoming cosmic rays—the very rays that were cut off by the adminis-tration and which I discussed earlier—was what maintained the staff's state of deathlessness. Isolate one side of the equation, and the other side became useless.

In this way, of these once magnificent superbeings who had toiled for over two hundred millennia to help uplift and civilize the native peo-ples, forty of the prince's staff stayed loyal to the administration and all but one were promptly shipped back to Local System HQ, while sixty of them chose to follow Prince Caligastia and Lucifer. It was these sixty who remained on the planet and, remembered as the Nephilim, mated with humans and created the ancient ruling bloodlines before they died what can only be the most unpleasant of deaths.

This left their deathless midwayer offspring, all fifty thousand of them, here on the planet, the vast majority of them in the rebel camp, under the leadership of a Planetary Prince who would become progres-sively more unhinged as the millennia passed.

Now, from a purely human point of view, sharing a planet with beings who just go on living and living endlessly must have caused a stir sooner or later. What would humans have thought of the presence of midwayers, invisible to the human eye, yet quite capable of making an impact within our level of physical existence? Whatever might they have been capable of manifesting? Where can we find evidence of midwayers in action?

Take Jehovah, for example. Or, perhaps it was *the* Jehovah, the English writer Brinsley Le Poer Trench suggests in an intuitive leap in his book, *The Sky People.* I suggest Le Poer Trench may well be correct in this sup-position, since by proposing the Jehovah as a plurality, he introduces the far greater possibility that there were a multiplicity of gods. Why else would one of Jehovah's demands be a prohibition on worshipping any other god?

According to the Urantia document, which expands on the biblical references of this period, Jehovah started out as a mere volcano god. As the spirit of Mount Horeb, Jehovah was presumably only meaningful to the small tribe of Bedouins who lived in that vicinity. This would have started prior to the arrival of Machiventa Melchizedek, his missionary school in Salem, and his contract with Abraham, and would have been what formed the fertile soil for the resultant flowering of Jewish monotheism. However, material science and common sense, too, suggest that volcanoes do not have spirits as such, or certainly not ones capable of the feats attributed to the biblical Jehovah. Also, from the various descriptions of the qualities of this "god," we derive a very different picture of the deity than that of the loving and ever-present personality of the Indwelling God.

Might it not be much more likely that Jehovah, or *the* Jehovah, and indeed most of the gods of that era, were in reality midway angels, either those of the small cadre loyal to administration governance or of the much larger group sympathetic to Caligastia's cause? Is this how they tried to maintain their planetary regime?

What about Ba'al, Odin, Ahuru Mazda, Zeus, Set, and all the others? Most contemporary thinking tends to dismiss the beliefs of the ancients as fantastical or mythical, yet clearly something was going on that was real and powerful enough to deeply influence large groups of people over long periods of time. In this materialistic age it's hard to comprehend what the appearance of one of these midway angels right in the midst of a busy life might have on any one of us.

Any examination of the Greek, Nordic, Egyptian, or early Roman mythologies suggests that the "gods" possessed a wide range of extreme emotions: they could be cruel, vain, self-indulgent, arbitrary, grandiose, vindictive, often foolish, rarely wise, but sometimes clever. These are not the attributes of the God of our hearts; they are the kind of darker emotions that seem to be our strange privilege to experience as human beings. These are the emotions of the autocrat, the authoritarian, the petty dictator, and the paranoid personality.

Could it have been that with the pervasive influence of free will inherent in the Lucifer Manifesto—the central statement of the rebellion—the midway angels fell unwittingly into the pit of human emotional extremes? Might the rebels' call for unbridled freedom have deteriorated into the sort of self-indulgence and emotional games we find in the Greek, Sumerian, or Nordic legends? From what we now know about the psychology of the authoritarian personality—the damaging effects of early abandonment and the subsequent self-hatred projected out onto others—might it not be their own abandonment that these midwayers were acting out when we read about them in the myths of the past?

If this is so, then the mythologies of the ancients are alive with the recorded stories of this group of midwayers and their continuing attempts to control their human wards. The Gnostics, the Manicheans, and later the Albigensians and the Cathars, did they retain some knowledge of these ancient events stored in their rich spiritual traditions? Will they allow us, if we can gain access to their esoteric knowledge, a crucial glimpse into that long and hidden period of planetary history?

The Urantia Book tells us almost nothing about the activities of Lucifer, Satan, and Caligastia subsequent to the rebellion. It was also such a long time ago that apart from the enigmatic ruins of cities long sunk beneath the ocean, we have no records of these events. The burning of the Library of Alexandria would have destroyed the last vestiges of a memory. A few hints are dropped in *The Urantia Book,* Caligastia, for instance, is pointed to as being the most identified with "the devil" in many of the world's belief systems. But on the whole, the book concentrates, as one might expect of an administration's report, on the doings of those who remained loyal to the administration hierarchy.

This leaves us with a period of a little over two hundred thousand years in which Caligastia, his staff of sixty off-planet beings, and 40,119 immortal, invisible, and from a normal planetary perspective, thoroughly superhuman entities must have wielded an immense influence over the affairs of humankind.

What as a race, I wonder, did we learn from the Caligastia regime during those long millennia? Did they just fool about, seeking power for their own ends, as is implied in much of *The Urantia Book*? If, as I have come to understand, the rebellion was actually permitted to occur at the highest levels, might not Caligastia and his crowd been up to something of real value in the grand scheme of things? More pointedly, what might they have had of value to teach us, in this Multiverse where nothing is wasted, to help us negotiate these transformative times?

It is now, at this crucial point in the transmutation of humankind, that the old knowledge and the new vision need to coalesce, need to reform into a deeper pattern of understanding, discernible to the eyes of the Spirit. It is this pattern, this drawing together of events and visions from across time itself that allows an integrity and a coherence to the most magnificent miracle of all, the eventual bringing into manifestation of the Kingdom of Heaven here on good old planet Earth.

These, then, were my thoughts at the time, tentative and syncretic, and I found myself a little nervous that I was getting in over my head, messing with some thoroughly undesirable entities. However, I was encouraged by the obvious courtesy of my encounter with Lucifer, described in the first book in this series, so I resolved to be open to all that Ray was showing us.

I certainly wasn't in sympathy with Lucifer and Satan. We all are living with the unpleasant results of their rash decisions, but it was difficult for me to believe they were quite as iniquitous as some the Urantia communicants were making out. There are always at least two sides to every issue, and the way the rebels are presented in the book is so totally weighted toward the negative as to make the thoughtful reader question the harsh and unforgiving attitudes being expressed.

I also needed to remind myself that in all my inner work I've never encountered an entity that I cannot relate to by employing love and courage. The quest that had started back in Florida with the telepathic possibilities of dolphins had rapidly led Melinda and me on a winding path through a whole host of nonhuman interactions. Extraterrestrials made themselves known to us both. Then, the angelic kingdom broke through in its own way, and soon a whole bevy of celestial personalities were springing to life.

What had started for me as merely speculative—since I thought of myself as something of a skeptic with a prove-it-to-me attitude—was progressively becoming an experiential reality. My Multiverse view was progressively broadening, and it was as entertaining as it was increasingly spiritual.

The sweetness and beauty of the old Normandy house, the quietly articulate and artistic ways of out host and hostess, the introduction of the midwayers into our midst, and what appeared to be a call from them for further and deeper understanding were growing all-encompassing. I was becoming bewitched, and deeper psychic energies were pulling at me. I felt as if I were falling, without really wanting to, into a mellow trance.

Consciously I was well primed. The experience that Lifus had had with the Knights Templar bigwig—relayed to me only weeks earlier— forewarned me as to the true state of the old European shamans, but on the deeper levels of perception I was entirely unprepared for the subtlety of the psychic crosscurrents.

On the surface, I should emphasize, all was wonderful, and very genu- inely so; our hosts were both delighted to see Melinda back after so many years, and there was a lot to share. That was the plane on which the whole encounter was being conducted. Ray was imparting his knowledge to us in a manner that suggested a linkup of some sort was occurring.

The first few days were filled with him showing us paintings, occult objects, and writings relevant to whatever subject was under discussion. At one point he gave me a French edition of *The Gospel According to St. Thomas* to study—those strange and tricksterish but somehow familiar series of the sayings of Jesus, which must have proved too puzzling to include in the Bible.

It felt like he was putting us, in some magical way, directly in touch with those who had carried the *baraka* for their age. Ray had been, for example, Jean Cocteau's closest ally, using his knowledge of Chinese medicine to help the poet through his difficult last days. The fact that Cocteau died in Ray's arms did not strike me as being out of the ordinary when he mentioned it. Some years later, when I read in Baigent, Leigh, and Lincoln's *Holy Blood, Holy Grail* that Jean Cocteau was one of the Grand Masters of the Prieure de Sion and no one knew to whom the poet had passed on the leadership, I thought again of Ray. I knew how the lineage of many of these ancient soci- eties was passed on at the moment of the death of the Master. I wondered if I'd spent all that time in Normandy with the Grand Master of the most secret of all secret societies?

Ray's stories of the period between the two major European wars of the twentieth century painted a graphic picture of a very different world from the one in which we live today. There was an unselfconscious pride about the faces of those who stared out at us from the photos Ray produced of that period. It was a vision of a people with little self-doubt, far too certain of themselves—for better or for worse—all with a glint of determination in their eyes, sadly unaware of the ravages of another war so soon to come. Underneath the joie de vivre, the apparent bonhomie, lay a staring contradiction. They were the royalty of this era of the twentieth century, the kingdom of the communication industry of the 1930s, the opinion setters, the manipulators, all with their self-interest thrust out in front of them. They were standing tall because they stood on the heads and shoulders of the people. Achievers perhaps, but at what a cost!

I could appreciate from the photos the massive leap in consciousness we've made as a species over the period of the two world wars and since. The process can be thought of as nothing less than a vast democratization of knowledge. Information spread like a healthy virus throughout the world, carried first by soldiers, then by tourists and television, and now by the even more efficient means of the Internet. In spite of the continuing imbalance between rich and poor, the twentieth century saw the most rapid and broadest based process of equalization the planet has ever seen.

All this was evidently being taken into account within the subtle sharing and the transfer of power I felt was taking place between us. My eyes were being opened to the Old Ways, good and bad. Ray must have repeated five times, in five different stories, the moral: Be Yourself. It was absolutely central to his whole approach to life and to those spirits of his generation, fighting, as they were, the excruciating weight of materialism and social conformity.

I found myself getting sucked into it all. The beauty of the place; the creative urges it summoned forth; the secret thoughts that seemed to emerge spontaneously; Ray's persuasive, gentle ways and his skill and knowledge. I wanted to stay and stay and stay.

Meanwhile, I was getting sicker and sicker! My lungs were filling with phlegm, and my head was aching in sniffling, blurry-eyed, nose-pouring agony, with my bones hurting and joints creaking.

The psychic crosscurrents were having their day.

✣

On the first evening together Ray had spoken eloquently about dreams. As an artist he knew their value. He had sought to find out, like Lao-tze, which was the dream and which the waking. He understood, deep down, the power of dreams to influence and shape reality.

He had asked me to keep a sharp eye on the dreams I would be having while I was staying with him. God bless him for that because it was the dreams that led me to see the more hidden dynamics of the situation. Those first three nights I dreamed, but remembered nothing. Then, on the fourth night I had a dream in remarkably vivid color. I noted at the time:

> In an unknown city. In a taxi. I look out of the window and see a solitary girl, naked and on a horse. It is a sweet sight. We catch eyes amiably and she looks away, concentrating on turning the horse around. In front of her I see a whole cavalcade of naked men and women on horses. Mostly women. Just in front of me a horse falls, dumping a bare hairy man gently on the ground. It's funny to watch—his attempts to look dignified and somehow not naked.
>
> Our cab slowly passes the procession. It's a comical sight because everybody is taking themselves so seriously (I think in my dream: like the sexual philosophy column in a seamy magazine). As we get to the front, I realize there are progressively less naked people among the riders. I wind down the window and yell provocatively at them, pulling their dignified legs, "There are naked girls at the back!" to some consternation and ambivalence. I see an old friend dressed as a clochard and riding in a cart. He winks at me. The dream then shifted: I'm going down into the subway with my companion when I'm called back to a small glassed-in shop window done up like a torture chamber. Arched windows with phony looking black instruments on the walls. I think it is a masquerade performed as a centerpiece for the cavalcade. There are three or four of us watching from outside. We are very close. One of the torturers straddles the backs of the kneeling victims, tapping them each in turn with the tip of his ax, not hurting them at all. He is wearing dirty baggy pants,

which fill the small arched window when he has worked his way backward along the line of kneeling figures. As he moves out of the way I see another ax man over to the right. Then I see a television camera pointed directly at me. I make joke faces, exaggerated horror and disgust, playing into the absurd activity that I take to be some kind of S & M club. A commotion starts and I turn to leave. The victims are angry and let down when they see the TV is more interested in my silly reactions than in their melodramatics.

Then, tickets bought for the subway, a young black girl asks me aggressively why I had reacted like that; wasn't I being prudish about it? "Possibly," I say, walking back to where she is sitting, "but they are taking something very sacred and holy and making a farce out of it." I turn again to the subway entrance and then wake up.

Having dutifully written the dream down, I lay awake pondering its meaning. Its richness of detail led me into seeing the dream as an amusing and pointed symbolic comment on the excesses of libertine sexuality. Whichever way I turned it in my mind, however, I kept coming back to the thought that it was not exclusively my dream. The naked women were those in the paintings all around the great hall. They were redolent of Ray's adulation and love of youth and of the female body. Yet, for all his fascination—and perhaps because of it—his surrealism consistently objectified the nude female figure, turning it into a chattel merely to be possessed. Under his artist's love of beauty lay what I was coming to understand was a far deeper ambivalence toward women. I felt my final remark in the dream was as much directed at Ray as toward the girl who had asked the question.

Despite these thoughts about our host, as I lay there I found myself getting swept more and more into Ray's trip. It was at this point that the desire to stay welled up with the most persuasion. I felt challenged, even, to stay on there with Ray and let Melinda journey on. Our plans to travel south suddenly seemed to be largely those of my companion. I felt manipulated, my own self-certainty crumbling and my autonomy of decision waning in the light of Ray's stern admonition to Be Myself. Meanwhile my physical condition was falling to pieces, the speed of the deterioration playing directly into my desire to stay . . .

My physical state! Ah! A vague memory scratched away inside the back of my head as I lay there torn and uncomfortable with the rain splashing off the moonlit trees outside. I'd let Ray adjust my spine, hadn't I? Just two days ago, and I'd completely forgotten about it. He did his acupressure on points on my hands and elbows. Had his ministrations brought on this illness, I wondered? In spite of my bout of flu on our recent trip to Israel and Egypt, I'm extremely seldom ill.

It was not a happy thought. I had grown to love the old man, with his mysterious and magical ways. But hadn't Ray himself advised me on more than a few occasions to give full credence to everything that came into my mind? Nothing is false or untrue, he'd said; all that we think must come from somewhere.

Could this have been the hint? He told me to trust the slightest and most delicate intuition. I pushed the thought aside. I didn't want to give any energy to the belief that consciously, or unconsciously, he might have brought on my illness. The day after the dream was living hell. I could barely walk—retching, sneezing, wheezing, coughing my way through the rain from the guest quarters to the main house.

Ray seemed delighted at our decision to stay on, yet, in spite of that, something felt indefinably wrong. Both Ray and I knew it. The balance of our relationship had changed in some way, and neither of us liked it. I wondered if I was blowing it. Here he was trying to get something intensely valuable across to me and I'd just bought into the irrelevancies and my vision was clouding up. In the silent, almost telepathic bond set up between us I felt Ray was having these thoughts, too. We couldn't hold each other's eyes that whole day.

In the late evening the atmosphere started lifting. We'd all evidently had enough of the morbid shadow hanging over the house and were laughing at the fact that the more ill I became, the younger and better Ray looked. We sat up late around the fire, the three of us. Lora had gone to bed. We were staring into the flames in the large fireplace. I was softly playing the guitar. Our souls had quieted, perhaps by the music, and the air was still after the earlier storms, when suddenly a heavy cast-iron oil lamp hanging beside the fire began swinging all by itself in small but deliberate circles. We knew, without speaking, it was a sign of the presences settling over and around us.

In that silence, another more soulful Ray emerged. Saddened by the lack of real love in his life and his relentless pursuit of youth and beauty, he was showing us in his tried and graceful way the shortcomings of his most dearly held code. A lifetime of Being Himself had taken its toll. It had all but discouraged him from truly giving himself in love to another being. Now, in his old age, he was telling us that he understood this. He was demonstrating the truth of this in the most powerful way he knew how. I could see he was doing us the greatest service. By opening his heart with such courage and love, and allowing us to see the ravages of the "selfish path," he affirmed for us our awareness of being part of a far larger network.

Melinda, always very much her own woman, and I had talked about this before, agreeing there is a logical progression in first loving and being oneself; this then allows one to love another person openly and freely, which can lead to the far more challenging act of love, that of loving all beings. After all, in this vast living matrix of the emerging Supreme, where exactly does the one of us stop and the others start?

I had another dream that night, as clear and vivid as the night before. Ray's hand was in this, I knew. I felt he was opening up the dream world for me in some mysterious way, that a linking through dreams was starting to occur.

I noted in my journal:

I am wandering around the grounds of a new house still in the process of being built. Behind the house runs a broad river. Soon I am ankle-deep in mud and walking along the bank. I see bubbles and movement in the water. It's a river dolphin and seeing it starts off an ecstatic physical gasping in my heart. I am filled with joy. By the time the dolphin swims past me I am up to my armpits in water. After swimming back to the bank I walk to the house, wet, but very happy.

A group of beautiful young carousers passes me. We look at each other briefly without too much interest.

I woke up with one of those odd convictions the dream was actually happening on a parallel reality. At the same time, I was almost overwhelmed by a feeling of deep and confirmatory joy.

I was still feeling this when I fell asleep again and tumbled into the same dream, picking up where I had left off. The house turned out to belong to the singer Rod Stewart, and the three of us, Melinda, the singer, and I, settled in for a long and happy exchange. I finally felt back with friends, no longer having to hurdle the forty-year age gap and negotiate the social intricacies of the situation.

In the dream there was an understanding between the three of us that needed no testing—a contact based on innate trust and an instinctive mutual understanding. It was direct and unquestionable. Intuitively I was aware this was the drawing power of the Supreme matrix, which united all of us of like mind and heart. When I awoke from this dream I knew I had to leave the Normandy house. The task, whatever it was, had been completed. With that I experienced a tremendous surge of love pass through me and onto Ray. For all his scorpionic ways, I knew he'd made the transaction as straightforward as he could.

Sure enough, when I saw him the next morning, the joining of our eyes told us both the mission had been accomplished.

The remaining day was soft and loving. Throughout, a light rain fell like a shadow, gently urging us south toward the sun, the sea, and possibly some dolphins. Ray, emotionally open now in a way we hadn't seen before, moped around, sad we were leaving, yet never looking better. He took the morning to make quick pencil drawings of each of us in preparation for oil paintings he was planning. The work had for me a new delicacy of awareness and understanding without the surface sheen that mannered and lessened the impact of some of his other portraits. He'd cut well below the masks this time. The breakthrough we'd all felt the previous evening was manifesting through his art. It shone bright and clear through the drawings.

At eighty-two years of age Ray had finally given himself in love. He'd fully shared with us who and what he was and what he'd become. It hadn't been what he thought was needed or required, nor was it by the imposition of his considerable will, nor indeed by the wielding of any of his wide range of skills. Yet he'd shared with us the most complex and valuable gift of all—the essence of his life's experience.

I could see he knew in his heart the treasure would be well revered; it showed through in his love and his gentle solicitude. That he was strengthened by the giving was clear from the drawings and from his face. The battles won and lost were on the more subtle levels, in dreams and in the personal world of our hearts, with only the faintest ripple, a distant echo of their power, permeating through to everyday consciousness.

On this note, we shook hands, hugged, and kissed one another on both cheeks, happily sure we would see each other again.

4

The Re-enchantment of Sacred Landscape

Shamanism, Dreamtime, Dragons, Ley Lines, and the Reality of Thoughtforms

The angels back in Toronto warned us France would be difficult. Although they'd word-played with Paris and Paradise, they also emphasized that this conflation wasn't currently the case. Angels aren't known for their irony, so perhaps they were warning us in their own way of just how extreme we'd find the sense of forlorn sadness in the city.

Melinda knew Paris well, having lived much of her childhood in France. I'd been to the city about ten times, many years earlier. Yet neither of us was quite prepared for the power of the psychic onslaught. I certainly had my memories: of roll-necked *flics* hustling a seventeen-year-old into jail for merely being in the wrong place at the wrong time, jammed sixty into a cell meant for six; of the marks of the wire grill pressing into my flesh—they lasted for days. At another time: as a young traveler, out of money, sleeping under the bridges of the Seine and waking with my fellow *clochards* to see a phalanx of gendarmes sweeping down over the cobblestones toward us.

One can tell a lot about a city—or a nation, for that matter—by its police force. *Les Inspecteurs,* decked out in their absurd hats and standing outside the reception for the Dalai Lama that first evening in Paris, were not very different from my memories.

In London, I'd asked a policeman where the Maitreya lived, and he'd told me amid good-natured joshing. Here in Paris, the hard, official eyes of the many gendarmes were cruising the crowd for anything glimmering of provocation. French socialism was overtly supportive of China, and the government evidently did not want any unpleasantness from Tibetan Buddhist sympathizers at an evening dedicated to world peace.

We hadn't known about the Dalai Lama's reception when we arrived in Paris. The news had popped up—probably Mich's handiwork, we thought at the time—in the form of a small handbill staring up at us from the floor of the packed subway train, surrounded by the evening push of tired, disconsolate Parisians.

The sadness really came through in the Metro: unhappy faces, isolated and drooping in their own separate vacancies. It was well nigh impossible to get a smile out of any of them. The girls were slick and polished, fashion pictures of studied self-concern. The men seemed abrupt and hyperaware of their personal boundaries—neat, trim, and oblivious to my catching-of-eyes and fatuously misplaced efforts to get some fun into the subway. Regardless, my attempts at camaraderie served to keep us amused, hovering as we were on the brink of the general psychic gloom.

Out of the Metro now, we hurried through the gathering twilight and wound past buildings still pocked with bullet holes. The gloom washed over me for a moment, bringing with it the horrors of the Nazi occupation; of times filled with impossible decisions; of collaboration out of fear, or meanness, or avarice; of brother turning against brother; of families split, divided, falling to pieces. . . . I chased the images away. To the extent the angels had given us any guidelines for this journey, they'd told us firmly it was not our business to hold with these old thoughtforms. The difficulty with this is that I seem to need to entertain negative thoughtforms prior to releasing them. If I lose awareness at that critical juncture I can find myself pulled under by the emotional groundswell of the group-mind.

The more I can think of old thoughtforms as information resources, however, the easier it is to discern what can be learned from them prior to letting them go. Thoughtforms invariably have information for us. Considering them in this manner, as quasi-real beings bringing news from the group-mind, encourages a detachment with which to handle what can often be powerfully upsetting emotional barrages.

It was not altogether surprising then that, for us, the Evening of World Peace turned out to be a nonevent. Granted we arrived late. There were already several thousand people milling around outside who hadn't been able to make it in. It was starting to pour with rain, and there was a thoroughly strange atmosphere in the air. Cold, wet, and frustrated at not getting into the hall, people weren't sure what to do next.

Melinda suggested with a rueful laugh that the odd atmosphere we'd both commented on was probably all these Buddhists wandering around strenuously trying to suppress their irritation and maintain their equanimity.

Standing on a raised part of the sidewalk at the back we could see lightning flashes strobing across the crowd and bouncing off the shiny sheen of the top of black umbrellas. Thunder mixed sporadically with the background roar of Paris traffic. For an evening of world peace the event seemed to have a tinge of the apocalyptic.

Inside the hall, we heard later, the Dalai Lama and the leaders of a number of other religious denominations had joined together for a prayer of peace. They symbolized this by all lighting a central candle while holding up their own candles as spokes on a wheel.

Outside, the cobblestones were gleaming in the light of street lamps. The worst of the thunderstorm had passed over, and the mood of the crowd was lifting. No one was quite ready to leave. Some young bucks from among the by-now more amiable crowd were attempting to scale a monumental wall to the side of the locked doors. They were threading their way up the ornamental stonework to the mezzanine some fifty feet above their heads. It was a hard and slippery climb with the rain threatening to slide them off the sheer stone facade. Intermittent cheers of encouragement arose from the crowd; it seemed wonderful to us to witness all this effort going into such an evening. They'd come to see the High Lama, and *merde alors,* they were *going* to see him!

But, in another disappointment somehow symbolic of the first phase of the evening, the mezzanine doors, too, were locked. As this journey was progressing, my appreciation of the synchronicities that were leading us on was noticeably deepening. Seldom was any effort ever wasted or squandered. If Mich guided us to be there, outside the hall with the damp crowd, then there was likely to be a good reason for standing so unceremoniously in the drizzle.

Pondering this issue while the drips trickled down my neck, I thought, rather grandly, perhaps I might be carrying some special energy garnered at Glastonbury, or possibly as a result of my psychic battles with the old shaman in Normandy, or perhaps we were there simply to absorb the saintly vibes emanating from the conference . . .

I could have saved myself the trouble.

At the end of my ruminative gaze was quite clearly one of reasons we were there. What I saw pulled me out of my reverie with a tingle of recognition. The crowd had started to thin out. About six yards away a young man dressed completely in white was standing talking to a small group of friends. It all seemed very natural and normal, except the young man was glowing. He was discernibly pulsating with a faint golden-white light.

I'd no idea whether this glow was obvious to others, or indeed how the effect was being produced. It didn't look as if any of his circle of friends were paying the glow any attention, if they'd even seen it. I started toward him. Halfway across the intervening distance, we caught each other's eyes. It seemed to me that a quizzical look flickered over his face before he settled into recognition. It must have been he assumed by my confident stride that he knew me. Yet, I was just curious about the odd glow, which continued to be quite evident and didn't diminish as I approached him.

We shook hands and said our *bon soirs*. There was a moment. Something passed between us, but it was so fleeting, so ephemeral, that I don't want to exaggerate it in retrospect. Whatever it was that occurred, I felt complete with the exchange and turned to leave, his friends more surprised than he appeared to be by this brief interlude.

As I made my way out from the circle of people I saw, over on the other side of the square, another gentle glow. And then another. Over the course of the evening I must have seen half a dozen people, men and women, who possessed what I can only describe as a distinct emanation, a glow that was being made perceptible to me and who knows who else?

I made sure I greeted them all, realizing as I did so that this event, at least from my point of view, could not have been better orchestrated. Whatever might be happening inside the hall I had no idea, but out here in the rain I was able to touch, and be touched by, men and women who I knew intuitively were part of the gathering wave of higher consciousness sweeping the planet. Maybe they were guided, too, for whatever their own personal reasons, to be outside the hall that evening. I thought of them as the spiritual nobility of Paris, not those inside seeking the limelight by rubbing up against the holy men, but the ones content to stand outside, modestly waiting their turn.

Sometime during the second day in the city the sadness and the meanness got to us. The downward drag we were feeling just became too much trouble to continue to ward off. At that point I knew I needed to go with the mood, even though I realized it was going to be hellish.

Coming back from the event the night before, the magic had continued, and the light entrancement in which I found myself persisted well into the Metro. I'd grinned happily at all the long faces, chattering to them in my mind until they, too, started smiling and talking to each other.

At one of the stations we hissed to a stop right in front of a motley group of French kids in multicolored punk haircuts. They were lounging on the Metro's raspberry-hewed plastic seats, eking away their evening, glum gum-chewing faces idly watching the train. Somehow I must have caught their collective eye. All ten of them locked onto me at the same time, and I felt a sudden charge of excitement, almost of exhilaration, flood my body, already overstimulated by the evening's activities. It took a moment to pull myself together, and when I did the doors were closing. I winked at them all once, slowly and rather theatrically. They went crazy. They clapped and waved, getting up to dance and shout after us as the train drew out of the station.

However, the sense of elation passed by the time we reached our hotel in Montmartre. It was a fleapit, something we had overlooked when checking in earlier. And yet we both felt we'd been guided to this particular place. The room was barely big enough for the bed and appeared even smaller and more wretchedly cramped by virtue of a strident, yellow and brown, leafy wallpaper pressing in on us from all sides.

We spent a fitful night shivering and scratching in the premature cold snap that followed the storm, the hotel too surprised by the sudden drop in temperature, or simply too cheap, to turn on the heat. It was a strange place for Mich to deposit us, we agreed, and yet it certainly succeeded in introducing us to the underlying feeling of the city in a most palpable way. After all, the angels had told us back in Toronto we would find bitterness and belligerence in Paris. An appropriate climate, they'd said, for the brewing and simmering of conflict.

The rest of the morning was spent on the edge of our nerves, snapping and bickering at one another. The troubled city had grabbed us by the necks and was shaking us. Somehow knowing this allowed us to gradually climb out of the murk and find a spiritual meeting place in which we could formulate a plan. We found that we both wanted to get to the center of it all, and in this case the center had to be the Cathedral of Notre Dame.

The French, over the centuries, have become a peculiarly centralized people. Maybe that is why the thought sprung so readily to mind. Have a look at their town planning, or their railway maps, to appreciate how everything radiates out from the middle. Paris was no different. There was a center of power radiating out from the old Cathedral of Notre Dame. I'd felt it before on my travels in the city, and it was no secret to Melinda.

What I found myself mildly resenting was having to go to what I thought of as primarily a tourist trap, a cathedral in which it was hard to believe the spiritual energy hadn't been dissipated by those millions of visitors, pilgrims, and tourists, over the hundreds of years of its long life. Once I set foot in the glorious structure, my doubts faded away. Its height and sheer size did much to absorb the constant flow of twittering tourists. The cathedral worked just as its architect and builders must have originally intended because my head jerked back in astonishment. My gaze swept heavenward, up to the jeweled glass windows set in the flanking walls. It was the oldest spatial trick in sacred architecture, and it still worked like a charm.

I sat down in awe and happiness, bewitched by the sparkling mandala of one of the rose windows; the deep purples and reds—colors never to be duplicated because the old formulas have long been lost—glimmered and glinted, shimmering in the backlight of a watery sun.

Here was a more balanced place, I felt, as I settled into a light meditation. Within a few moments, however, I found I was experiencing something very different. A much deeper emanation of power seemed to be flowing from somewhere *under* the cathedral. It was as though a massively large motor was purring way off the lowest limit of human hearing and I was sensing only its highest and faintest frequencies.

I turned to Melinda and found she was experiencing much the same thing. First it was the extraordinary glowing people from last night's rain-sodden gathering, and now there was this deep throbbing.

Had Glastonbury sensitized our perceptions in some way? I knew from experience that power places radiated an energy all their own—I'd felt it previously in Peru and Egypt, to say nothing of my more recent episode on the Glastonbury Tor—yet I had surely never perceived such a strong current of telluric energy with any of my purely *physical senses*.

As I sat there in my reverie, my experiences with the earth energies started to link up and form a coherent pattern. I was feeling, and now even hearing, that the Cathedral of Notre Dame was built over a far more ancient place of power. The Île de la Cité, on which the cathedral squats, is a natural island that divides the Seine for nearly a mile and must have always been a place of security and relative peace. I knew, too, this spot had played an important role in prerecorded history and was part of a much larger geomantic creation, spanning all of France with a web of ley lines and dragon paths. Stone circles, similar to the one on which the tower at the top of Glastonbury Tor was built, can be found over the whole of northwestern France, and Brittany in particular.

Many of these geomantic factors I'd learned from Tony Roberts, as well as from my cousin, Christopher Castle. They, along with a growing number of unorthodox archaeologists and artists, are pointing to what they see as evidence for the onetime existence of extremely advanced and spiritually adept civilizations.

These were folk who apparently regarded Earth as a living organism, far more alive and vibrant than much of our contemporary scientific thought will allow. They knew the planet was girded with a matrix of lines of power and understood how to tend and balance those energies. From what researchers such as John Michell have pieced together, these ancient civilizations appreciated that the fertility and well-being of the land depended, in some manner, on the interaction of one's "personality" with ley lines and places of power. They *knew* the Earth's meridians needed their human care and attention. This is the knowledge that has filtered down through history and is recorded in the stone circles and the dragon lines, the dikes, mounds, and earthworks, in all the myriad ways by which the ancients sought to balance the topography of heaven and earth.

It felt good to me to be able to think of Earth as a living being. To think of Gaia, of Urantia, of Doris Lessing's poor, sick Rohanda, as a wonderful, pulsating entity, constantly adjusting and modifying herself to her own complex rhythms and necessities. Any off-planet intelligence would have surely understood this and may well have passed on ways of servicing the old darling to the locals. Thus the ancients, with their Earth magic, would have known ways to tickle out of her the finest harvests and the richest yields.

Whether true or not in the objective sense of a proven issue, it was a splendid picture and carried a playfulness and a vitality about it I'd come to recognize from my adventures among spiritual intelligences. If there is one single thing I've learned in the course of these years of exploration, it's that the Multiverse is a great deal more alive than I'd any previous idea of.

The Urantia Book talks about other entities in the Multiverse, living beings who possess qualities we might well perceive as technological: Transport Seraphim, Energy Beings, Living Chronometers, Reflective Spirits, and Recording Angels.* The contactee Oscar Magocsi, whom I'd met in Canada, had little doubt that the UFO that picked him up was a sentient biological entity. And, of course, there are the dolphins. Immense intelligences, beautiful, wise creatures, patiently working out their destinies. Through all this, a sense of personality seemed to be revealing itself, a feeling of friendliness and trust. It did not seem at all unreasonable to me that the planet itself would have been considered a goddess by the ancients, who themselves most likely carried trace memories of earlier times still, when the visitors from the stars came and worked among their people.

Sitting there in the flickering sacred space I found my thoughts turning to the Universe Broadcast Circuits. These are the lines of communication that *The Urantia Book* tells us connect all inhabited worlds throughout the Multiverse into one vast integrated communication system. The only

---

*Generally of the Cherubim Order, Recording Angels record everything of spiritual value (good and bad) over the course of a mortal's life—to be played back as needed in the life review after death.

exception to this vast network are worlds such as ours, which have been placed under quarantine.

Then, the night of the vernal equinox of 1982 came back to me. On that night, Melinda and I had been standing on a little bridge on Paradise Island in the Bahamas when we heard three distinct waves sweeping under us and up onto the dolphins beyond. I remembered my powerful conviction that the circuits indeed were opening at long last. I barely knew what I was saying at the time, the words were streaming out of me, uncensored by rational thought.

It was only later we discovered that Edward, the channel in Toronto who had reintroduced me so personally to the angels, received his only contact to that date from Christ Michael, at the very time I was being overlit by such an overwhelming certainty the circuits were opening.

Bringing myself back to where I was sitting in Notre Dame, I wondered whether this long, slow, pulsation of energy I was feeling coming from deep under the cathedral was in some way associated with the circuits opening. I'd no real idea what the Universe Broadcast Circuits were or how they would actually manifest if they were opening. Would some people hear and feel the energy, and others not? Would the circuits open all over the world or in specific places?

The regularity of the vibrations precluded the possibility I was hearing passing Metro subway trains. No, this was something quite different. I wasn't even sure I was sensing the pulsating energy on a physical level, yet Melinda appeared to be feeling it too. Putting my doubts aside and remembering Ray's advice to trust my subtle feelings, I wondered if there was something I personally needed to understand from what I was experiencing.

Sitting on the hard wood pew I let myself sink into the reverberations. A few minutes later I found I could no longer discern the limits of my body. I dissolved into the energy and yet didn't lose my sense of self. It was during this time that the pictures rising to the surface of my consciousness showed me that during this transformative period on the planet, the profound realignments taking place will once again require personalities to activate the ancient circuitry with their presence.

The Multiverse is, after all, a surprisingly personal place.

✠

Getting up from the pew after our brief meditation, with these thoughts in mind, Melinda spotted a small wooden door tucked away behind one of the massive columns. There were no tourists around so we started up the long, circular, stone staircase to reach, after twelve minutes of hard climbing, the top of one of the great towers. The main roof of the cathedral lay some seventy feet beneath us, surrounded by parapets capped with staring gargoyles—frozen thoughtforms, clutching the ledges with their crumbling stone talons. Paris spread around us in every shade of gray.

Once again, I felt touched by the Spirit. I was utterly alive, at the center of something I only barely comprehended. Spontaneously, we both threw our voices up into the spiritual winds in a call for the rapid transmutation of the negative energies we'd been feeling since the previous evening and that we felt were permeating the city.

We offered our prayers of gratitude aloud to Christ Michael and to all the angels: to the angels of the churches, for caring for the great cathedral and the generations of sincere worshippers, and to the angels of progress, whom we imagined might have had a hand in those strange vibrations. We asked for their help in spreading the good news of the final settlement of the rebellion over the power circuits of this land.

Still calling into the winds, we turned a corner, and there, only feet away from us was a single angel, soaring up on a pinnacle of stone from the roof far below. Seeing this apparition, shining white against the grey of the clouds, seemed to us a silent confirmation of the celestial cooperation for which we asked.

Sure enough, and appreciating the synchronicity of it, we watched the skies clearing before we were granted a most beautiful sunset.

Later, with spirits much lighter, we settled into enjoying what was peace loving and good about the city. We walked around the Left Bank, picked through the bookstands, admired the jewel-like shops with their elegant windows, and ended up in a small bistro. It was there we met and fell into conversation with a man by the name of François Xavier. He was glowing too, although more with enthusiasm than the palpable luminosity of the previous evening's encounters.

We *recognized* each other immediately, with that odd sense of familiarity that appears to come with this spiritual territory. But by this time I'd started to see a pattern emerging from these evidently "chance" meetings. I thought it started with the dolphins; it was then we found ourselves first patched into what I'd come to think of as the Network of Light.

Back in Toronto, a few months before setting out on this trip, the angels told us that we had a specific function to fulfill as we made our way down through Europe. "There has been given to you information which would be of an enlightening nature to many," Beatea, a seraphim of the order of the Angels of Enlightenment, had replied to our questions through Edward, the light-trance channel. The angel claimed our sharing the information about the termination of the Lucifer Rebellion would consolidate much within what she'd called "the Great Network."

This certainly held true for François Xavier, although I felt much of what we were able to pass on to him acted more as a confirmation to something he already knew was true. In spite of evidently not having a sufficiently broad Multiverse context within which to fully appreciate the unfolding events, he asked many of the right questions. His conviction that knowledge was always and ever presently available from the inner realms must have been a valuable ally in helping to open his consciousness.

He told us he'd learned this from some extraterrestrials back in Switzerland in the early '70s. He'd been involved in three notable UFO sightings while working with a contact group, and they'd been able to establish contact with a number of ET sources. As in so many of these cases, nothing significant came of it in terms of the communication breakthrough for which the group had hoped, but it did leave François Xavier a changed man.

Within the depth of feelings stirred up by our brief and unexpected meeting, I became aware of something of the predicament in which many of the more thoughtful among our generation find themselves. François, for example, sensed he has a function and clearly knew through personal experience a planetary linkup was taking place, but that was as far as he had been able to go on rational grounds, using purely mental reasoning. Yet, many of these areas are not easily talked about, let alone proven to be true by consensus wisdom. They require the ingredient of faith in order to come together into a meaningful montage. And, as François Xavier agreed, faith is certainly helped by the spontaneous corroboration of like-hearted people.

I had the feeling, too, that by telling him of the rebellion and its recent adjudication, with all its wonderful possibilities, Melinda and I were talking in some way we didn't understand to those other glows of light we had encountered the night before. I was sure the news would get through one way or another. The message of planetary transformation, given to us by the angels back in Toronto, struck a deep chord of recognition in François. It was a spiritual communiqué a tired, old, strife-torn country badly needed.

Melinda and I awoke in a couchette, a small and comfortable sleeping compartment on the late train from Paris, to dawn spilling over a wild landscape. It was a beautiful part of France, easygoing and unspoiled. Although the stone houses were invariably dilapidated, they folded back into the rock-strewn countryside with an unplanned neatness.

By Toulon it was evident the best was over. Then it was Frejus, Cap d'Antibes, and by Cannes, it was a tragedy. The beauty of the Mediterranean shoreline was buried completely beneath humanity's worst excesses. The cheapest, the most banal, the most commonplace apologies for architecture, erected in haste for doubtless wholly avaricious motives, visually shattered the rocky inlets and quiet golden beaches.

Cars, small this time and unlike the hand-me-down American monsters we encountered in Egypt but spouting the same gray bursts of cheap gasoline fumes, jostled each other in the early morning rush. It looked like everybody was out for themselves without the slightest awareness of what they were leaving for the future. After getting off the train at Nice and negotiating the whirl of the traffic, we settled into our hotel room. I found myself once more utterly exhausted, even though I'd slept a restful night in the couchette. I realized later I must have been called on by the inner realms because I proceeded to have one of the most revealing in my sequence of lucid dreams to that point.

I recorded upon waking up:

Melinda and I are at an informal party. The atmosphere is delightful. A number of people we know as public figures come to introduce themselves. Then, there arrives a Major-General, formal and stiff and looking unsure of where he finds himself.

Following the army come three prelates from the Holy Roman Church, all rather small men, like overgrown dwarves. They skitter and tumble, laughing all the time. They fall over themselves with mirth at the prickly general's attempts to introduce himself.

I take one of the clergymen aside and I suddenly feel very emotional. He tells me that 25 to 30 percent of the Catholic Church, plus Jesus Christ, of course, he adds while grinning hugely, are now "with us." I become even more emotional and through my rapture I manage to blurt "You've no idea what it's been like thinking that they've been corrupt through and through."

The prelate on my left puts his hand on my shoulder in comfort. I turn to meet the others, feeling confident and happy again. I notice that everyone is relating to one another in a particularly kind and respectful way.

I emerged from the dream with an overwhelming intuitive sense this was how it was going to be done from now on. Meetings and encounters with those we are unlikely to run into in everyday life will be facilitated through the dream world.

The meaning of the dream must have touched a nerve because as I finished writing it down, I recalled many years ago my atheist mother shamefacedly telling me as a baby she had me baptized in the Roman Catholic religion—in order to placate *her* mother!

This small act of hypocrisy wasn't revealed until I was well into my thirties, but it helped clarify for me my long-held visceral aversion for the Catholic Church. The rebel in me was never able to stomach the false certitude with which the Pope and so many priests make their autocratic pronouncements about subjects in which they have no personal experience. I also found the opulence displayed by the Church so counter to Jesus Christ's every admonition as to be completely absurd, if it wasn't so sad and insulting for the impecunious believers. And this was only the tip of an iceberg of my distaste. In my atheist days I could get filled with righteous anger about the horrors perpetrated by the Roman Church over the centuries.

As I write now, in 2010, in the midst of the clergy sex-abuse scandal, much of what made me so instinctively uncomfortable with the ways of the Church is now coming to light. What is becoming evident is the Holy Roman Church has long been due for a radical self-assessment, if it isn't too late for that, and what we might be witnessing is the crumbling of the entire edifice.

Although the Papal Prophecies attributed to twelfth-century Irish Bishop Saint Malachy have an uncertain pedigree and, like all prophecy, can be open to interpretation, it's oddly significant the pope following the current pope, Benedict XVI, is predicted to be the last. Named Petrus Romanus, the final pope is described in the English translation in Wikipedia as follows: "During the final persecution of the Holy Roman Church, the seat will be occupied by Peter the Roman, who will feed his sheep in many tribulations: and when these things are finished, the city of seven hills will be destroyed, and the formidable Judge will judge His people. The End."

I might well have continued with my angry judgments about the Catholic Church had it not been for the lucidity of my dream of the cavorting clergymen. I found it interesting it was the dream that softened the harshness of my criticism and not my rational mind. After all, here is this strange state of consciousness that everybody experiences and about which almost nothing is known. We spend a third of our lives asleep, much of that time presumably dreaming, yet we probably know more about the planet Mars than we do about what really happens when we dream. As a culture we appear to have written off dreaming as mere mental downtime; we've pushed it aside, perhaps with the exception of the analyst's couch, as a valid tool for understanding ourselves, our world, and our universe.

Are we far more influenced by our dreams than we have any way of knowing? And as a corollary to that, is it possible our dreamworld is also an arena in which we can interact with other intelligences and with the dead, as well as astral thoughtforms? Could this confusion be one of the reasons most objective studies of dreaming produce such inconclusive results? And there is so little agreement between the experts as to what might be the actual function of dreams.

The beliefs of the ancients gave much more credence to the reality of the dreamworld, and perhaps for good reason. Interaction between human beings and angels has traditionally been in the province of dreams—Jacob, his ladder, and his wrestling match with the angel being probably the best-known example. Dreams figure prominently in ancient Egyptian life, as they do in almost all ancient religious and spiritual traditions. The Greeks had temples dedicated to the healing that can be accomplished through dreaming.

There are statements in *The Urantia Book* to the effect the dreamworld can also be used as an arena for training "contact personnel" in what the Urantia communicants call the personnel's "deep minds." This must mean certain people are being trained for the tasks ahead on levels well beneath their conscious knowledge—a spymaster's delight, I would imagine. With these thoughts very much in mind I determined to keep an even sharper eye on my dreams as this journey opened out.

Now it was time to explore Nice.

We'd grown used to, perhaps even a little complacent about, the ease with which we were making all our connections. Trains, planes, taxis, and hotels were all there exactly at the point we needed them. Was this what it meant to be shepherded around by the angels? Yet, it was a full twenty minutes before a bus arrived at the roadside shelter. I'd been coughing and swearing at the oversized trucks rumbling past us and turning fine old buildings to rubble with their deep mechanical vibrations. It was as though we were dumped there to get a glimpse into the dark side of life in fin-de-siècle Provence.

Frankly, the bus ride could have been in New Jersey. The city of Nice, alert presumably to its responsibilities toward tourist dollars, had drawn a five-floor limit on its inner city buildings. But this scarcely applied to the outlying areas. The result was a mishmash of white, half-finished buildings towering over vacant lots and crumbling (those trucks again) once-gracious houses. The single difference from the chaos of New Jersey or New York kept us from the depth of despair—there was virtually no trash. The worst devastation merely seemed to be automobiles in various stages of rusty decay and disintegration.

We headed first for the Old Town, ravaged but still holding up somehow on bandy little legs. The Château, an old castle set high up on the hill that separated the urban sprawl from the original fishing port, drew us toward it in a way we've started to recognize as angelic nudging. It was quite clearly the main power spot in town and appeared unchanged from the way Melinda had remembered it from her frequent visits there as a child.

Compared to the aching legs of the Notre Dame climb a few days earlier, we ascended in stately form indeed, a clanking elevator depositing us onto an overhanging turret, the city shining golden and suddenly beautiful beneath us. The sky opened up after some midday clouds, and sunbeams were slicing through the dark, flat cloudbank in a fan of pastel light. Jesus rays we called them, joyfully admiring their pre-Raphaelite beauty.

The grounds of the Château were woefully higgledy-piggledy, as might be expected of a castle destroyed and rebuilt on the same spot so many times by history's conquerors. I would imagine that the Phoenicians, the first in recorded history to settle here, would be about halfway up a cross-section through the gnarled, old foundations. The town, nuzzling around a natural harbor, would have always needed protection from some man's army.

Stone dolphins, who had grinned at us from half a dozen Paris monuments, now breached and blew from every cluster of mosaics we encountered. We'd seen nothing of them in the flesh since our adventures with the captive dolphins at the Britannia Beach Hotel on Paradise Island, and that was more than four months ago. Yet, there was a continuing sense the path on which I felt they'd set us was leading somewhere. All we were expected to do was to follow our hearts' desires as much as we could, take note of the signs and synchronicities—the footsteps of the invisible world—and simply *be* in any situation in which we found ourselves, with as much presence and consciousness as we could muster.

We climbed slowly, swinging from one side of the hill where all we could see was the smog and dirt of the modern urban mess below, to then zag to the other side of the hill for a refreshing view of the time-sculpted old harbor and its attendant stone cottages. This duality seemed to be an appropriate metaphor for our voyage through Europe. So it was barely surprising when we found, set into the paving of a turreted platform overlooking the port, a beautifully executed mosaic, a tribute to Ulysses. And of course, two dolphins were happily bobbing in one corner.

The late-afternoon sun, after riffing with some clouds, cut through again and bathed in a soft glow the sepia roofs and neat, pastel-colored houses that stepped up the scrubby hills. It was certainly sweet, but somehow it was not enough. The devas put on a fine old show for us, the golden early-evening sun stroking the ancient stonework, yet there was no doubt the place was lacking in Spirit.

The piazza at the top of the hill turned us back west into the setting sun. Oddly, the small square was named after that macho old philosopher, Friedrich Nietzsche, and I could imagine him sitting out there eating his sandwiches with the bratwurst sticking in his great walrus mustache. "God is dead," he'd boldly announced, to be largely misunderstood by both atheists and religionists.

Water from a natural spring cascaded from under the stones of the piazza and tumbled down through small pools hewn into the rock walls of the fortress, to end up in an open storm water sewer at its base.

An Air France 747, trailing plumes of blackened kerosene, banked sharply—so close we could almost reach out and touch it—before it began its steep descent. It appeared enormous and absurdly out of scale with the town below, and it plumped heavily onto Nice's pocket handkerchief airport.

Unnerved, we skittered down the uneven steps, past niches sheltering the ever-present Virgin, into doglegged streets that appeared as though they'd never seen a tourist. As we came into a square three young men passed in front of us laughing and talking. With dark clouds masking the late afternoon sun, we could see the man in the middle was unmistakably glowing. He and I winked at one another to more laughter and general happiness.

Melinda and I agreed it must have been this brief and rather unrevealing encounter with another of these glowing people that drew us to this part of town, because it certainly wasn't the Nice Cathedral. We saw it first looking down from the Château, its golden dome sparkling extravagantly against the earth tones of the surrounding buildings. Inside, however, it did not check out. Like the town itself it lacked Spirit—just gilded junk and dark, ill-lit paintings of pain and sadness. Whatever the reason we'd come to Provence, it certainly wasn't to be found in Nice or its depressing cathedral.

The angels back in Toronto had suggested we visualize the environment, especially the landscape, as we would like to see it. France, they emphasized, was particularly in need of this treatment; the angels made it sound like the country's arteries had hardened and they needed a bit of spiritual terra-surgery.

The visualizations proved difficult to hold onto, however, until Melinda, with her artistic perspective, realized we could incorporate this factor into our drawings and paintings. Then it became a more straightforward affair, since we could simply leave out what we didn't want to include in the new vision. There was a sense, too, as we sat together drawing on a small hill overlooking Nice, of tending to the earth as our early ancestors must have done with their magical ways.

When we did subsequently travel back into the hills of Provence Mich saw to it we were guided to the small town of Vence. Although sitting in some of the most beautiful hills in the world, the permeating debris of the last half-century now surrounded the ancient walled town. In the center of that stood Vence Cathedral—one of the first built in France.

Now, this *was* a spiritually charged place; we both felt it immediately when we entered. It had a simplicity totally lacking in the ornate splendor of the more flamboyant churches and was completely different in atmosphere to the dingy, blood-racked edifice we'd left behind us in Nice. Neither was it that large for a cathedral.

The stained glass windows, although remarkably restrained for their time, made up—in clear, direct symbolism—for what they lacked in technical skill. One sidewall was covered in a mosaic tribute to the birth of Moses by the Jewish artist Marc Chagall. Its soft, poetic elegance—an echo, perhaps, of the grace of the stained glass windows—carried the seed of a subtle interfaith rapport. The infant Moses, pictured recumbent in his floating basket, could easily be seen as the child Jesus lying in a manger.

It was a church's church, and we both felt a delicious sense of happiness emanating from its angels. After we were in there for a while soaking up the atmosphere, Melinda beckoned me over to a small chapel set off well to the side of the nave of the cathedral. The moment I stepped into it there was no doubt the main source of power appeared once again to be emanating from beneath the floor of the chapel. I felt intimations of the same flooding roar I'd experienced in Notre Dame, and this time it appeared to be accompanied by the subtlest of golden glows.

But there was more, which I wasn't able to see until I fully entered the chapel. I found myself in what seemed to be a perfect cube, clearly designed by the cathedral's architect to be a sacred space. More surprising to me, however, were the proportions of the chapel and the Gothic pointed arches that supported the roof. If they were not identical, then they were of déjà-vu similarity to those of the chamber buried deep under Glastonbury Tor to which we had been led by Lifus only a few weeks earlier. It was as if Mich were pulling on my sleeve with invisible fingers. There was something here he wanted me to take note of, something he wanted me to discover for myself.

I settled down into a meditation, quietening myself and attempting to open up to the subtle feelings I sensed radiating from beneath the chapel. As in Glastonbury, while playing music with my cousin Chris in the Church of St. Andrew, I had the impression of an enormous dormant power, a sleeping giant that lay somehow just beyond the limits of my senses, biding its time, waiting perhaps for a chance to reveal itself again as once it had.

It was sometime later, when we were examining the cathedral in more detail, that we stumbled on what may be a clue to those restless energies. It lay embedded in one of the thickest columns that supported the main roof.

The builders had preserved a single carved stone from the original structure that was erected in the mid-sixth century and then destroyed in a Saracen raid in the 720s. Yet the stone, with its unusual bas-relief, must have been far older since the motif suggested a delightfully playful vision of a dragon, uncoiled, relaxed, and smiling happily. There was no hint of judgment in the image, no tempting of an innocent Eve and Adam, neither was the dragon being trampled underfoot by some macho knight on horseback. It seemed to issue from another age altogether, in which dragons and serpents were not looked on with such fanatic disfavor.

Well before the Christian era began serpent energy was already starting to fall into disrepute. Apollo's mythic victory over Python, the primordial serpent and creation of Hera, was itself an echo of a far older story
from the great days of Sumeria in which Marduk fought and destroyed
Tiamat, who was depicted as a great serpent.

As I looked at the sculpted stone set into the column of the Vence
Cathedral I had the inner conviction I was gazing up at a dim memory
of another time when the cosmic serpent was a more generally accepted
entity, blessing the fertile Earth with its happy, rebellious presence.

This was not the case in the Church of St. Paul, which overlooked the
village of St. Paul de Vence, a few kilometers away from the larger town
of Vence. In its time the village must have been a beauty, with its diminu-
tive houses straddling a ridged promontory running down to the coastal
plain. Tiny, twisting, cobbled passages separated the houses, which were
surrounded by a steep rock wall, protecting them not only from attack,
but also, perhaps in some fortuitous future memory, from the ravages of
the automobile to come.

Unlike much of the crass urban development on the coast, the village
elders of St. Paul de Vence had evidently taken another option. They'd
turned the beautiful old village into a tourist trap, selling chic, glossy,
impressionist rip-offs in among the many preparations derived from local
herbs and flowers.

If I might have been tempted to rail against this crude commercial-
ism, personally preferring the dilapidated naturalness of a less opportunistic approach, I only needed to remind myself that in the past two decades
virtually all the menfolk had left the village, trudging off to the cities to
sweat out a living in the factories. Yet inevitably, as a result of the villagers' collective decision to go tourist, the place felt tired and diminished.
Any power the village might once have possessed had been walked off by
the steady stream of visitors.

The Church of St. Paul, for example, built on the highest point in
the town, was a horror. Though larger, darker, and more ornate than the
cathedral we had just left, it had nothing of that superb structure's grace
and intensity. It was as though Mich might have planned this as a contrast. In Vence Cathedral, we were presented with the best of the Old
Power, revered and uncorrupted; and yet here in the Church of St. Paul

was all the hypocrisy born of an authoritarian religion and nurtured by manipulative priests for their own ends.

A few old women, apparently kneeling in prayer, jerked around, scowling at the sounds of our steps on the slick tiled floor. I turned to leave. I couldn't stand the atmosphere. And there, dominating the large stained glass window at the end of the nave, was a triumphant St. Michael skewering a dragon on the end of his spear. Although Python, Leviathan, and most of the other assorted serpents and dragons of our ancestors' nightmares had bit the dust well before the Christian era, the early church fathers evidently found it useful to encourage fear and hatred to be directed at the serpent and dragon as devil figures.

The idea of the devil as adversary is an ancient one. The adversary wasn't thought of as punitive, and there was no relationship with hellfire and damnation. Later, however, the concept of the devil as being the lord of hell, waiting to tear sinners apart with his red-hot pincers, became a useful device of priestcraft—a simple way of terrifying their superstitious flocks into exploitable submission.

I felt sick to my stomach at the sudden cruelty of the image. That a religion of love should have built its symbolism and iconography on such a love of violence has always seemed to me to be a hideous travesty. Christ Michael, in his lifetime as Jesus, according to *The Urantia Book*, made the situation clear. The perfidious Caligastia notwithstanding, there was never any creature like the common concept of the devil, no cosmic entity opposed to God and desiring pain and eternal horror for the human race. How could Christ Michael's message of loving our enemies have become distorted into this unhappy carnage? It was such a marked difference from the joyful dragon carved onto the stone that we had spotted earlier in the cathedral. Surely this remains one of the saddest distortions of the Roman Church.

In reality negativity and evil persist only in so far as we choose to involve ourselves with them. Until such a time, they exist merely as a potential. As for the fruits of evil, they are surely self-destructive enough for the evildoers and their coteries without having to include the presence of a fictitious devil.

The belligerence born from the tradition of killing your enemies rather than loving them, or indeed outwitting them, has become deeply ingrained in the Judeo-Christian mentality. Since the deeper truth, most recently articulated by the comic stripster, Pogo, as, "We have met the enemy and he is us," cuts to the core of the issue, it isn't difficult to see that the path of violence must invariably lead to acts of schizophrenic self-mutilation.

The attenuating influences of this great deceit had clearly taken their toll in the France we were being shown: in the long, sad faces in Paris; in people's ambivalence toward America and all she had come to represent; in the constant political strife down through the centuries; and in the unresolved feuds that still tear families apart. All the deceits and double standards of the country were making more sense to me and starting to fit into a pattern.

In those moments of immediate and personal distress, and as I stared up at the image of St. Michael and the dragon, still inwardly reeling from its cruelty, I was able to see France as the historical center of the expanding tendrils of European value systems. I could feel their influence spreading first through Catholicism, then through trade and art, and later from the instigation and support of the great social revolutions of the past three hundred years.

Old and tired as the country felt to us, the nation's influence was still a presence on the world stage. I experienced this as a subtle yet insistent pulsation in my power chakra, as though the entire country were struggling to rise to the collective fourth chakra of the heart. I understood then why the angels had stressed the need for change in this particular country. The seeds for the coming transformation were already well established in France. All that was required of us was to be fully present and to react openly and honestly in all the situations into which we were guided. We were asked in some cases simply to witness what was happening and only to participate to the extent that we were intuitively drawn to do so.

I *knew* in my heart that we were being used by the angels, and it was from them I had the sense information was being transmitted out along the expanding lines of power to animate the rest of Europe. Though it may come across as grandiose, it didn't feel self-important at the time. In a situation like this we were simply being channels for energies we barely understood.

By the time we left St. Paul de Vence I was spent. Exhausted. Yet as we wound our way down the sinuous road back to Nice, I felt I was starting to catch on to some of the ways in which the angels work. I understood through the experiences we were having that we were being shown the deeper undertones of Provence, and perhaps of France in general.

Back in our hotel room I settled into a meditation. I knew what I had to do. After I grounded myself and worked through my chakras, cleansing and releasing any psychic debris I might have picked up during the day, I centered myself in my third chakra, the power chakra. This is where I was experiencing the turbulence from earlier in St. Paul de Vence. After releasing any personal conflicts in or around the chakra I visualized it as an expanding sphere radiating out to cover all of France. After I had this as a firm mental image I visualized moving the energy up from the power chakra to my heart—in my creative imagination drawing up the rest of France into the kingdom of the heart.

I came out of the meditation to find Melinda quietly finishing a drawing out on the balcony, with a magnificent, wide, rose and lilac sunset spread out across the sky behind her, rendering her virtually translucent in the crepuscular light.

It was all so casual, this angelic guidance. No great lights in the sky, no signs and portents. We needed simply to follow our hearts' preferences and we would be in the right place at the right time. Our invisible guides were taking us through a whole range of encounters designed, presumably, to key specific patterns of their own and, from our point of view, to unlock some of the suppressed old forms. The angels never fed us too much at once, always allowing us as complete an exploration of a particular approach as we needed before tripping us off into another set of experiences.

We were led to the next part of the puzzle in, of all places, the Municipal Museum of Nice. The sign on the side of the painting assured us that it was St. Michael killing another hapless dragon, yet . . . there was something rather different about the way the creature was depicted.

By now I was finding these constant references to dragon slaying both discouraging and unpleasantly preoccupying. Even the revelatory charge I felt in the cathedral in Vence only lifted my spirits momentarily. Surrounded by these images I was beginning to despair about the hold this symbol was continuing to have on contemporary society, locked as we've been into the buildup of weapons and ongoing paranoia.

As individuals we have allowed ourselves to be persuaded we are powerless to do anything about the proliferation of violent solutions in the world around us. I believe if we are able to trace the sources of socialized violence and our seeming knee-jerk willingness to go along with it, then perhaps we can move toward lifting the negative hold such aggression has on the planetary consciousness. With this in mind there was a central ingredient in the dragon/serpent drama that was not fitting into place.

Whether or not dragons, or creatures that people called dragons, ever actually existed has not yet been established by fossil records. Perhaps they were always creatures of dreams, used to scare children into line. Yet, clearly the disturbing power of the dragon as a symbol, originating in the distant past, still retained its vitality well into the dawning of the Common Era. The Roman Church merely inherited the symbol—probably empowered by the book of Revelation—and used it for their own purposes.

What was keeping the symbol fueled and potent all these years? Chinese cosmology is replete with dragons, and they are considered in a much more positive light than they are in the Western world. They are deemed to be a blessing, in fact.

What has kept our Western way of thinking so locked into the fierce aspects of dragons? And how could two cultures perceive the same entity, symbol or not, in such profoundly different ways and for so many thousands of years?

I was writing the first draft of these adventures in the relative sanctuary of our apartment in Israel overlooking the Mediterranean. As I reached the segment above, both Melinda and I became aware of a pervasive and disturbing change in the psychic atmosphere in the apartment. The more I focused on the issue of evil and my attempts to describe the dragon-slaying icon we'd stumbled on in Nice's museum, the unhappier and more distraught we were both becoming.

It was all the more odd since the fifteenth-century altarpiece, as I have suggested, portrayed the dragon in a rather unconventional manner. The artist had shown the rare sensibility to paint the recipient of St. Michael's anger not as a figurative dragon this time, but as a monster that could only have emerged from a nightmare. Gone were the wings and the sinuous body, and in their place was something infinitely more sinister and unpleasant. This was a creature that had never known the world of three dimensions, the everyday reality we all share. This monster was something quite different, and my intuition told me there was a clue here as to what might have been really going on.

If this wasn't a depiction of something considered real then the image must have emerged from the human imagination. Could it then be a thoughtform?

Thoughtforms will be familiar to clairvoyants and students of metaphysics. They are purely mental phenomena brought into being as quasi-lifeforms in the astral realms by the creative power of human emotions. Greed, anger, fear, love, jealousy, hatred—all these emotions can generate, or feed, thoughtforms. These entities exist both in the astral, as conglomerations of emotionally driven thought-material, and in the everyday cut and thrust of our lives.

Who hasn't, for example, while mildly jealous in some small matter, become suddenly consumed by the green-eyed monster? Or, when initially in love, hasn't become unreasonably consumed by it?

A sensitive clairvoyant, or a skilled shaman, will likely be able to perceive astral daggers being thrown about when people are furious with each other. They will tell you that these emotionally driven thoughtforms can become impacted in the subtle energy bodies of human beings. Further, these fear-impacted thoughtforms, if not consciously released, will drop into the material vehicle and result in physical disease.

If history is examined through this lens it becomes clear that thoughtforms have played a significant role in both the personal lives of individuals and in the waves of irrational violence that sweep through every culture from time to time. Particularly intrusive thoughtforms can become symbolized into the monsters of our collective imagination—the devils that bedevil the unfortunate schizophrenic as well as the demons that appear in eighteenth-century scientist and mystic Emanuel Swedenborg's elaborate cosmology.

Has the dragon of Western Christian symbology, for no good reason, become falsely identified with the devil?

This question opened up a stream of concepts in which I could see something of the confusions and manipulations that have entangled the poor old dragon in such a web of negative imaginings. Aided, no doubt, by the Genesis Garden of Eden story, with all its blame and stormy curses, Pauline Christianity supplanted and suppressed paganism by placing its leaden boot firmly on the back of the serpent, a prime pagan symbol. Then, by linking the serpent/dragon with demonic thought-forms, the religious propagandists of the past sought to discredit paganism by association.

The dragon and the serpent, I reckoned, have no more to do with evil than anybody, or anything, else. They become the objects of projected blame in a Christian belief system, in which the leaders encourage delusions like "the devil" and "hell" in order to control their flocks through fear.

Most worthwhile spiritual traditions warn about thoughtforms as manifestations of the human creative imagination without really knowing why, or how, they come about. I can only imagine that thoughtforms are somehow a product of the human beings' unique function as the co-creators of future worlds. Thoughtforms may act as quasi-lifeforms through which we might learn to master our mental and emotional bodies—rehearsals, perhaps, for destinies to come.

As human negativity creates and powers negative thoughtforms, so also this holds true for positive thoughtforms. True love, beauty, goodness, honesty, and altruism are all thoughtforms too, but they tend not to be the ones that trouble us.

Whatever the reason for the existence of thoughtforms, it is generally stressed in metaphysical traditions that these denizens of the astral regions need to be acknowledged, but not dwelled on. Students of Tantric Buddhism, for example, are warned not to become entranced by *siddhis,* the supernatural or magical powers acquired as a result of persistent practice. Positive or negative, thoughtforms are generally considered a distraction from the true spiritual path.

And here I was, dwelling on the most negative thoughtforms possible: considering whether they needed a more detailed explanation, reasoning that any explorer of the inner worlds is bound to come up against them from time to time so it's worth describing them, and wondering whether the reader will know what I am talking about.

Possibly at that time thoughtforms weren't totally real to me, or more likely I needed some palpable evidence of their existence. Whatever the reason, negative thoughtforms arrived, magnetized by the intensity of my mental activity. I must have opened myself by focusing my attention on them since they just moved in and started to wreak havoc with my life.

All the doubts that any writer must feel from time to time welled up in me, far stronger and more discouragingly virulent than I'd ever felt before, or since. Pacing around the small room, I couldn't sit still . . . I would get up . . . then sit down again, just as suddenly. Staring vacantly out over the blue sea, seagulls circling, my thoughts tearing at me with indecision, I felt the full brunt of a negative thoughtform careening around and through me.

When I could stand it no longer I went through to the next room, which Melinda had set up as a studio, to find her as distraught as I'd become. I looked at the canvas on which she was working, and there, in the middle of an elegant landscape, was a dirty purple, amorphous blob. She was certainly a skilled enough painter not to have allowed this to happen under normal circumstances. Neither did she have any idea of how the blob formed as she'd turned away from the painting when she'd started feeling the psychic tremors. We wondered if the thoughtform could have manifested itself through the fluid medium of the pigments.

I realized in those moments, as we both stared in sadness at the ruined landscape, what a complete fool I had been—how thoroughly trapped I'd become in my own misconceptions. I could see how desperately I wanted to rescue something from the past. I needed to believe there was some retrievable goodness in these old forms, and I'd got the idea into my head somehow that I was required to examine and assimilate the Old Power. I saw how I had started poking around in forms that are best left well enough alone. I knew that all thoughtforms, both negative and positive, thrive on the energies put into them by the human imagination. Equally, they will starve and drop away when ignored.

I trust I found out once and for all, to my own satisfaction, that no good can come from prodding the monsters to see if they have any positive features. If this was so then I could truly hear the angels when they tell us, "All things have been made new," and accept that the old forms have indeed passed away.

I saw that my duty and my joy was to give power and life to the new forms. The New Vision. The coming of the True Age. There are enough true, beautiful, and good thoughtforms buzzing around in the human creative imagination to occupy all of us for many lifetimes—no need any longer to give one jot of energy to what is negative or death oriented.

A simple task faces each of us: to identify with what is loving and to allow what is fear driven to fall away. This recognition, repeated in more and more hearts, will surely be enough to release us from the hold these negative thoughtforms once may have had over us.

5

Intimations of a New Vision

Ancient Conflicts, Genetic Endowments,
Spiritual Alchemy, and Intimations
of a New Reality

After the tumult and emotional stresses and strains of our journey through France, Provence ended up managing to give us a fine and righteous sendoff.

We'd been drawn back into the mountains again for a day or two of good fresh air in preparation for the drive down through the Alps into northern Italy. Stopping off at the small village of Valdeblore La Roche, high on the French side of the mountains, we joked together at the idea of being given some time off by Mich. We wondered if angels ever got time off.

And a time of joy and relaxation it turned out to be. Happy to be out of the cities we'd been visiting, we climbed La Roche, the immense, jutting crag after which the village was named. We pulled our way up through juniper and rose hip, passing through minute meadows echoing with the colors of mountain flowers, blossoms that grew with such care and apparent loving attention as to make it immediately clear life here has a delicately precious side. No doubt in spring the mountainsides flood with colors and scents, but even in early fall at these altitudes, we could feel in the slight chill of the air the hints of a bitter winter ahead.

Perched on the very top of La Roche, we painted and made our drawings, soaking up the visual richness of the valley and feeling as though we were the gods of this abandoned place, reveling together in its growing wildness. Occasional sounds floated up, accentuating the lonely silence. A church bell. The faint call of a child. The stuttering putter of a powered bicycle. And, because the quality of silence is modulated by what disturbs it, everything felt good and natural, at one with the golden beauty surrounding us.

The mountains, humped together like sleeping animals, welled up from the zigzagging gorges below in every tone of gray and green, the colors of their flanks merging and flattening against the lowering sun.

A family of swallows came to check us out, circling, sailing, swooping, hovering for long moments like fluttering Nijinskys poised for inspection and perhaps relishing, as we were, our mutual pleasure and harmony. Then, there were the gnats. As if all nature had come out for us, a swarm of these tiny flying creatures, their wings glinting red in the final glow of the sun, surprisingly left us entirely alone, playing only feet from where we sat, yet well out over the edge of the precipice. The mountainside fell steeply away to the valley floor hundreds of feet below.

In the calm I found myself able to focus on a single gnat, following its progress through easy looping double and triple spirals. Gradually, as my eyes grew tired from the concentration, I saw all their individual little flight paths resolved down into one great spiraling ever-changing mass, as if in demonstration of that most basic formula of life, the DNA double helix.

The apparent significance of this observation, the quiet beauty of the evening, and the pure sense of rightness to everything around us seemed to lead us irrevocably into a state of consciousness in which all is one, with no boundaries separating us, either from each other or from the quiet majesty surrounding us.

It was a state of mind we were to look back at gratefully more than once as we pottered along in our small French rental car through the grime of industrial northern Italy. The weather had started to break. Our last sun-filled day on La Roche felt like something of a miraculous hole in the gathering thunder and rain clouds. By the time we got to Turin, already dark and soggy with pollution, the downpour was catching up with us.

I felt I should be welcoming the first rain we'd seen since Paris, but instead the dismal atmosphere of the place and the constant drizzle bore down on our spirits. No amount of nifty creative visualizations could alleviate the depression brought on by the ugliness of it all. Somehow it was even worse than pure ugliness—worse because it felt like the desecration of a place that was once beautiful. Some of the fine old buildings still stood, surrounded by the tasteless compromises made between ancient grandeur and the more recent excesses of junk materialism.

As if to demonstrate this ambivalence, we couldn't help noticing how many advertising gimmicks, slogans, and billboards featured the use of an apple. As we walked in the rain through downtown Turin, luminescent signs, ruddy with temptation, winked and blinked from shop windows, propositioning us with one insalubrious offer after another.

Although urban Italians would doubtless claim to have thrown off most of the shackles of Mother Church, to the canny outsider it would appear as though the advertising industry is continuing to find it profitable to exploit the religious guilt and shame still snuck down there among the new licentiousness.

There was a lightness about the people, though, in spite of the conditions, a happy contrast, we agreed, with the cold, dulled stares of most of those we'd seen in France. A surprising number of them looked at us with quick, open smiles, skittish even, before retreating back into embarrassment. It seemed to us there was something of the eye of the spirit here, but it felt layered under centuries of disillusionment.

The city of Parma, when we got there, turned out to be a much more enlivening experience. Smaller than Turin and far less anesthetized by industry, it too combines some of the contradictions that give Italy its oddly schizophrenic atmosphere. Ancient cobbled streets came alive with little shops set into sixteenth-century brocade facades, yet selling the most elegant of modern light fixtures. Gone was the willful abundance of Turin, of stores piled high with the dumped excesses of the multinationals. The objects we saw presented here in Parma were simpler, often exquisite, and invariably displayed with pride.

Following an intuition, once we settled into our small hotel, we set out to go to the octagonal Battistero, which had taken my attention as we drove into the city. A remarkably tall, many-faceted cylinder of a building, it stood strangely on its own just next to the cathedral. The way the odd structure caught my eye had me craning out of the car window—even when we were well past it. I had the strongest feeling Mich wanted us to have a closer look.

Entering the twelfth-century structure brought on a moment of quiet exhilaration. I've noticed multisided symmetrical spaces often have that stilling impact. As in the Cathedral of Notre Dame, I found my eyes drawn upward, this time to the segmented mandala glowing in the cupola over one hundred feet above our heads. I wanted to get directly to the center of the marble-paved floor, but a large carved stone basin had been already placed at the point of focus of all this energy.

I was beginning to feel this energy in my body without quite knowing what was happening to me. I must have completely lost contact with Melinda because at that point I had no idea where she was or what she was doing.

Perhaps it was lucky for me that I couldn't stand in the very center since the large bowl forced me into a circular movement, walking round and round with my head tilted right back, gazing, fixated almost, on the apostolic mandala way up in the dome above. As I circled around I found myself prompted to start a slow whirl, as a dervish might, spinning on my own axis while continuing to move around the bowl. Gradually I spun faster and faster. After a few moments the paintings on the sixteen side-panels were flickering hypnotically in the corners of my upturned eyes.

I am soon in a light trance state, and as I relax into it I find myself drawn up into the great mechanism of the place. I say mechanism because that more accurately describes the sense I'm having. The place is far more than it appears to be on the surface. It feels more like a massive mechanistic contraption than any kind of building.

I sense myself being drawn up toward the top of the dome. The next thing I'm aware of is being hurled out, almost literally, along tendrils of energy, over the surrounding landscape, to fall as fine as gossamer thread over the hearts of the people.

It sounds fanciful now, as I am trying to describe it, but as I was whirling around that sacred space the experience was quite real. I *knew* then, with all my subtle senses, I was in a place of power. Possibly the Battistero was itself built over the far more ancient sacred remains of progressively earlier cultures. It was hard to believe the creators of a place like this wouldn't have known what they were doing—if only on an intuitive level.

As I'm spinning, my eyes firmly fixed on the dome, I know with a revelatory clarity the Battistero functions as a projection center, a broadcast station if you like. The labor and craft, and most of all the love put into the painting of the high walls and the domed ceiling, are even now impressing themselves into the lines of power radiating out from the center of the mechanism.

The Middle Ages may not have had access to television as a behavior modification device, but I wondered, in those moments, whether they might not have inherited the rudiments of a far more intriguing method of modulating the thoughts and feelings of their populations.

As this comes to me I feel a new softness and pliability wash over me while I whirl quietly around the darkening space. Nothing is coming through now, and I'm content merely to enjoy the effects of the expanding energies.

Too soon the guard came back in and, probably somewhat perplexed by my antics, was shuffling his feet, anxious to close for the night. I was left deeply heartened. I felt a new presence had entered the spiritual balance wheel, one that was to stay with us throughout our travels through Italy.

The next day in Parma I decided to wander wherever my legs would take me. Melinda had interests of her own that didn't concern me, so that allowed the time to follow my own intuition in seeing if I could get to the bottom of this new presence I'd started sensing the previous evening.

Tilted houses skewed over narrow streets, warm now in the sunlight. Panel trucks swept past me as carriages must have over those very same cobbles centuries earlier. I passed the Battistero and decided I would come back to it later. I found I'd no desire to see the cathedral; it was a pompous looking place, and my feet were leading me somewhere else anyway.

Off to the side of the main piazza was a much smaller and less ornamental church. I popped inside, more to see what was there than drawn by any stronger feeling, and sure enough, here was another poor dragon being berated, this time by a group of angels surrounding a youthful St. John. The saint appeared to be making an attempt, with quill and a stack of leatherbound books, to capture the highlights of his frightful vision. After what I'd been through in France this magnificent painting seemed to contain a message of somewhat humorous sympathy. I wondered if it was a sign I was on the right track.

Penetrating deeper into the maze of tiny streets, this time my legs were drawing me to a far older structure. The building appeared definitely pre-Renaissance, broken and busted by time. Finding an entrance, I made my way through the garbage and the fallen detritus to feel an immediate sense of holiness and presence, in spite of the church's dilapidated state.

The church must have been a simple yet magnificent place in its time, the timber beam roof soaring overhead and the burn-blackened rafters slowly being repaired by artisans of an almost-forgotten craft. The darkened strips of plaster work had long-since discarded their images, with one sole exception: a pair of fading angelic eyes, which seemed to follow my progress as I picked my way up the main aisle through the rubble. Except for the pigeons constantly swooping from side to side of the high, pocked walls, I was completely alone.

The spacious aisle led me to the main semicircular apse, with its vaulted and domed roof. The stonework stood, grizzled by smoke, while the altar had all but disappeared under rubbish. Dust hung in the air, swirling and defining the narrow beams of sunlight pouring through the gashes in the walls.

I turned away from the altar to survey the full length of the church only to find, looking down at me from the only remaining portion of a fresco, the likeness of God the Father, arms crossed and fully complete in himself. Evidently the images of saints and angels could fall off the walls, but the Father was staying put. I wondered if the Italians appreciated the implications.

After meditating in the space for a while I set off again, winding back past the unattractive cathedral. This time my feet led me in through a small side door. I could see why immediately, as the door creaked shut behind me: a full orchestra was set up and was evidently rehearsing for an upcoming concert.

I sat down, bathing in the sound. Cadences swam in the voluptuous space, swirling and twisting around me, sounds now complementing, now following each other, winding around the main theme. My heart opened as I sat there. I heard distinctly within the music another music, echoing and turning like the implication of an altogether different melody entirely, lodging in the spaces between the sounds themselves.

I must have sat there entranced for at least an hour before I swayed out of the cathedral, my head still full of music, and found myself once again drawn over to the Battistero only yards away. I thought the guard would probably recognize the crazy whirling man of the night before, now reeling to a different beat, but if he did he was courteous enough not to show it and stood aside dutifully as I went in.

This time the Battistero was filled with light. There was a life and a vigor it had lacked in the darkening shadows of the previous evening. Shafts of thin sunlight pierced through the space like the holes in Swiss cheese. In their glow I could now finally see the main fresco, which previously I hadn't even discerned as I was whirling around the floor. The image was of a woman, her arms raised in supplication. Behind her, two figures appeared locked in combat.

No prizes for guessing the contenders.

Yet there was a fundamental difference in this painting; something else entirely was being suggested. The introduction of the woman into the confrontation between dragon and knight completely changed the dynamic. For a start, whatever was she doing there? Most Christian traditions would have it that a St. George or a St. Michael—according to local legend—is rescuing the woman from the dragon and presumably from a fate worse than death. Given the male-dominated overtones of the last few thousand years, St. Whoever first dispatches the dragon and then carries off the woman. But, frankly, that doesn't *feel* quite right to me. There are other traditions that portray dragons as having a profound respect for the feminine principle. Besides, there's too much of the propagandist's hand evident in the rescue motif for it to sit well with me.

Since I find myself to be a "metal dragon" in Chinese astrology perhaps I have a bias for what I think is an altogether more plausible story: The woman and the dragon have been hanging out together. Not only do they share a mutual interest in matters of fertility, but I've no doubt the woman also enjoys the touch of danger an average dragon brings into her life. Then, along comes the man, misunderstanding the situation entirely—perhaps even misinterpreting the woman's squeals of delight—and before you know it, knight and dragon are once again at each others' throats.

Although the main fresco obviously could be read in different ways, it seemed to me the woman in the painting was showing every sign of pleading with the pair to stop their tomfoolery; she was acting as the peacemaker between civilized man, you could say, and the dark demands of his animal nature.

It came to me then it was just this sense of feminine balance I felt in the Battistero the previous evening, to which I'd been unable to put a name. Could it have been just this powerful yet yielding equilibrium that the Battistero has been projecting all these years? In the midst of a religious tradition that had come to see women as chattel, had the ingenious artist managed to sneak in a rather more developed understanding?

As I sat quietly in that now-golden space I found myself pondering the way so many of the major religious traditions have not only denigrated women, but in some cases have even considered them as the root cause of evil. Whatever the reasons they may have given themselves, Judeo-Christian and Islamic systems of thought appear to have been particularly prone to this delusion.

This is particularly sad in the case of Christianity since Jesus Christ taught and emphasized a complete parity between the sexes and evidently continually surprised those around him with his steadfastly fair treatment of women and his easy rapport with them. *Everybody* is a child of God, Jesus had said, and it was no coincidence it was Mary Magdalene who insisted, in the face of considerable scorn from the disciples, that she was the first to have seen the resurrected Christ.

Yet, this spirit of fairness has got lost in the shuffle. St. Paul, by some accounts still smarting from an earlier rejection by a woman, went along with contemporary standards for the poor treatment of women. This virtually ensured that women would be written off in subsequent religious texts as second-class citizens.

Whether or not it is true that there have been periods in the development of the human species when women dominated men—when the matriarchy was all-powerful—it's clear that through the course of recorded history, with few exceptions, men have used their physical strength and organizational skills to subjugate women. This tendency seems to be present in the "lost tribes" that continue to surface in New Guinea and every bit as much in the tension continuing today in the kitchens and workplaces of the most civilized of nations. It seems to be part of the human condition.

Perhaps we will not know whether this battle between the sexes, which has so colored our history, is endemic to the human species until we have a chance to learn more about the social development of intelligent species on other planets. Do other extraterrestrial races have harmony between the sexes (if they have sexes)? Will we discover that as a species we are painfully retarded in the way we treat one another across the gender divide? Or are the very differences between the sexes part of a masterful arrangement in which all of us, men and women, get the chance to experience the concept of *otherness*? Might our journey through the Multiverse of Spirit, discovering more and more of the myriad forms God chooses to take, start with an appreciation of the differences between women and men?

Gazing up at the fresco I realized there was something of the truth of the old alchemists in it. Their "pearl of very great value" has always stood as a metaphor for the resultant state of consciousness that comes from resolving the profound polarities in the human mind. Mightn't this also be extended to the successful resolution of the differences between a man and a woman in a loving union? And wasn't this the underlying message of the painting? The dynamic between the three figures clearly suggested a recognition that men and women (and even dragons) are parity partners in the art of living. Here it was—going out on Renaissance television!

As one who can often identify more easily with dragons than with men or women, I'm preconditioned, perhaps, to see the female element as the redeemer in the painting. Here was Woman, the much ignored Mother Spirit, who supports and nurtures everything in the Multiverse and who is not, therefore, prepared to throw aside the life and vitality of the dragon. She would rather see mortals transmute, through love, the opposing elements in their natures into the true gold of the Spirit.

In my reverie, our journey through Europe was taking on yet another shade. By this time, I'd no doubt we were being guided—shepherded even—through what we thought of as the Old Ways. We were here to witness firsthand the results of the decisions made in the past—their consequences, intended and unintended, and the rhythms they have followed down through history. Here, in this magnificent place, I saw we were being asked to respond to these cultures with the fullness of an open heart.

I realized, with this insight, I'd been having some harsh judgments directed at what I felt were some of the profoundly corrupting aspects of the Old Ways. I felt myself face-to-face with much of what the Cathars found so repugnant about Roman Catholicism: the social cost of the sumptuous grandeur of their churches, the misogyny and manipulation, all the corruption that convinced the Cathars that the Roman Church had fallen into the hands of the Demiurge.

If we were being asked to merely witness and respond with an open heart, I knew I needed to release the bitter feelings as they came to the surface. This is not to excuse the many wrongs done in Christ's name, because people are going to be people however holy they claim to be. Melinda, wiser than me, likes to pose the fair question (never considered by the Dawkins/Hitchens brand of atheism) as to what history might have been like, given the belligerent nature of human beings, without the (slightly) restraining hand of the Church.

Rather than dwelling on all the iniquity, I reminded myself to simply observe and release whatever negativity arose to the surface. I knew if I did this in good faith, then in some mysterious way, note would be taken. Whatever was felt to be sound would be extracted and become part of the crystalline insights that the angels in Toronto had talked of as shaping and modulating the coming True Age.

Writing this some time later I find myself slightly embarrassed once again at the seeming grandiosity of this concept. Yet, as I stood and whirled once more under the echoing cupola, it was very real to me that we were being allowed to have an impact on the waveforms of these ancient, sacred places. By changing and moving us, the Spirit of the land was itself being transformed.

I knew in my altered state that the groundswell shift in conscious-ness, which directly resulted from the final reconciliation of the Lucifer Rebellion, was indeed starting to take hold. It was this movement toward freedom and reconciliation, though I didn't know it then as I spun around in my small circles, that would soon blossom into such events as the fall of Soviet communism, peace in Ireland, the collapse of apartheid, and the reunification of Germany.

The intuition I had concerning the pervasive sense of feminine receptivity in the psychic and spiritual atmosphere of Parma was gently confirmed for me when Melinda returned from her morning's visit to the Lombardi Museum. That's where *her* feet had taken her.

Awaiting her there was a ten-foot-tall portrait of the Empress Marie-Louise, who was by all accounts Parma's most remarkable doyenne. She ruled her city-state with grace and wisdom through the singularly unset-tled time in the early nineteenth century when Napoleon Bonaparte was ravaging much of the rest of Europe. What struck Melinda most, however, was the *wholeness* of the woman. The empress lived an incred-ibly full and long life and was much loved for who she was and what she accomplished—a noblewoman of true nobility.

In addition to her social and political savvy the empress was evidently a skillful watercolorist of beguiling sincerity. Among her paintings in this most demanding of media was a night scene—the *Hours of the Moon*—that contained such a spirit of meditative tranquility that it was impos-sible not to see a highly original mind at work. Moonlight is known to be desperately challenging to paint in any medium, yet here was this exqui-site small masterpiece, its shadows awash with silver-blue radiance.

Nearby stood her watercolor box, a small and eminently portable chest, barely changed in design over the centuries, with drawers opened slightly to show the cakes of pigment, each neatly named and placed with a measured sensitivity. Her needlework yarns, gathered with all the aware-ness of a woman who could have had anything she wanted, were laid out with the symmetry of a rainbow. A diary lay open at an entry. Her neat hand translated read, "Some writer wrote that the person who brings a blade of grass where there is none does more for the world than all the politicians put together."

So this was all part of the soft and yielding atmosphere flooding over us in the town of Parma, and how appropriate that it so intimately concerned artistic integrity. The angels told us in Toronto that we would find the strongest devotion to Spirit within the arts—the human activity probably least affected by the negative outworking of the Lucifer Rebellion. This was what Parma was reflecting to our rejoicing hearts. It has proudly kept the balance between the creative and receptive principles, and as a direct consequence, the city feels to this day to be an enlivening and soul-filling community.

We had to go to Ravenna to catch the more complex web of harmonic undertones of this essentially soft and benign culture. The city was felt to have much the same atmosphere of receptivity as Parma, so we happily settled into its voluptuous folds.

Ravenna lies on Italy's east coast, somewhat south of Venice, at the mouth of the charmingly named River Po. Known to be one of the oldest continuously inhabited towns in Europe, Ravenna was already doing thriving business by the time recorded history came along. Its closeness to the sea seemed to foster the easygoing ambiance we'd encountered in other port towns.

Sure enough, here too, in Ravenna, we found the spiritual imprint of three other prominent women of grace and creativity: the fourth-century Empress Theodora, the Empress Galla Placidia, and Emperor Theodoric's daughter, the Empress Analasuntha—in whose reign was created surely one of the great wonders of the creative spirit, the Basilica of San Vitale. It drew us like thirsty travelers to water.

We found the basilica's exterior to be oddly commonplace—after all, this was built in the fifth century, before the Mother Church had fallen into decorative decadence—and it contrasted soberly with the famous mosaics we knew were inside. The symbolism was direct and incisive: Seek the inner truth.

After our long walk through the rapidly warming streets, entering the basilica was as if we had dived deep underwater: it was that cool and blissfully disorientating. The main space still retained a massive presence, although evidently largely reconstructed. Nothing interrupted the spatial experience, no fonts or sarcophagi. Unlike the impulse to gaze upward upon entering a Gothic cathedral, it was the smooth beauty of the inlaid marble floor that first caught my eye, its many different hues and striations sometimes reversed, one against the other, like so many Rorschach cards.

Three hundred feet over us hung another cupola, this time incongruously decorated with enormous oversized figures. Yet, once again, the architects chose an octagonal structure, and like Parma's Battistero, this particular form seemed to exert an almost irresistible upsurging of the spirit.

Lost in my thoughts and surprised at the palpable uplift of energy, I returned to myself and found Melinda already sitting in one of the side chapels. I wandered over and sat next to her, still dazed by the considerable energies coursing through the main body of the church. It was a few moments before I was able to look up. When I did, it was to see one of the most beautiful works of the heart and spirit this world has ever seen.

In this cool, contained setting, the mosaics of San Vitale glow with a soft luminosity, full of light and humor and as fresh as the days they were laid fifteen hundred years ago.

Such infinite patience and care had gone into the making of the mosaics; many of the tiny glazed squares were set at slight angles to the plane of the work so the raised edges could glisten in the candlelight. There was a love of nature everywhere evident in the prancing of the many small animals and the blossoming of the flowers surrounding the central figures. The figures themselves, both of whom were portrayed as startlingly young and forceful, seemed to come alive with a casual grace that bore witness to a very real spirituality on the part of subject and artist alike.

Facing us and reflecting down onto our upturned faces was an exquisite garden scene depicting the images of Abel and Machiventa Melchizedek, each making their offerings in their elegantly laced sandals. Significantly, while Abel is sacrificing a lamb, Melchizedek is offering up bread. Although there has been much fruitless speculation by the church authorities as to why they have been shown together, in choosing to portray Melchizedek, the artist has contributed to the remarkably few representations in sacred art of that redoubtable and mysterious old magus.

Knowing this might have primed me for the next illuminating discovery, for there, set in a rainbow circle in the middle of the triumphal arch of the chapel and formed in exquisitely colored mosaic chips, was the strong and forceful image of Christ Michael as Jesus. Around him danced two pairs of dolphins, green, fat, and full of I-told-you-sos.

Could this have been where the dolphin trail was leading us, to the Master himself?

Well, why not? I thought, as I stood there captivated at the way it all seemed to be coming together. I recalled the little-known Naboteans, builders of rose-red Petra and surely one of the most retiring cultures in history. They existed for only five or six centuries, straddling the life of Christ, and functioned as the caravaners of the great trade routes threading their way across the ancient world. They left us no literature, no philosophy, no law, and no religion. They adopted the dolphin as their central symbol, and I wondered whether they, too, had found that the consciousness of these magnificent beings led irrevocably to a deeper knowledge of God.

When this trail started with our tentative explorations of delphinic intelligence, it was in the spirit of poetic inquiry. I approached the investigation with an open heart and mind, with no expectations as to where the journey would take me. I'd had the experience of *knowing* God, but as mentioned earlier, I'd never been able to open my heart to Jesus Christ in the same way, so I had shunted the whole issue aside and got on with my life.

The dolphins, I was now realizing, had other intentions.

I'd held out on reading *The Urantia Book* for three years after originally receiving it in 1977. This turns out to be not unusual among those who do get into studying the book. As mentioned earlier, it makes for a formidable challenge in that it is relentlessly long, with a precision and density to the language and a complexity of sentence structure born of another intelligence altogether. I suspect that a large proportion of the half a million copies sold since its initial publication in 1955 serve as doorstops, to be read, hopefully, by later generations of inquiring minds.

Yet there must be currently many thousands of people all over the world who have become convinced the book is authentically what it says it is—a massive slew of information transmitted from the subtle realms to a small planet very much in need of accurate spiritual knowledge.

As a trained architect I have a pragmatic side to my nature, and the idea of a document actually transmitted from the angels was initially hard for me to accept. However, having seen and experienced angels in the course of my near-death experience back in 1973, this allowed me to suspend disbelief long enough to get a good feel for the angelic voice.

I'd been reading the book seriously for a few hours a day—not just dipping in—for about nine months before I was staring up at those magnificent mosaics of the Basilica of San Vitale. By this time I was starting to form a new feeling for Jesus Christ. I found *The Urantia Book* presented a wholly different portrait of this being, yet one that resonated in my heart. It just plain *felt* right.

For me this tangible sense of Jesus began when I read the final part of the four parts into which the massive book is divided. This is *The Life and Teachings of Jesus,* as told by the midway angels who accompanied him. And what wonderful insights into the Master's life this elevated viewpoint provides!

Whether or not this can be considered an authentic viewpoint—and it's wise to be skeptical in these matters and reality test as much as possible—it was soon obvious to me the various Urantia communicants have distinctly nonhuman authorial voices. I've read a great deal in my life, widely and in many different disciplines. I've absorbed, to the best of my ability, most of the world's major belief systems and cosmologies. Yet it became clear to me very quickly that, in *The Urantia Book,* I was encountering a different *order* of intelligence entirely. Not necessarily a higher intelligence, just very different, with a far wider frame of reference.

Although there are many different voices in the book—some high celestial beings, the Chief of Archangels, the Chief of Seraphim, a few of the Melchizedek Brotherhood, and a number of midwayers, to mention only some of the more readily recognizable titles—they all speak with an intelligence unclouded by purely human concerns and possessing the clarity of authentic knowledge. No other book I know has quite its tone and resonance.

John Ballou Newbrough's 1882 book *Oahspe: The New Bible,* received through automatic writing and claiming to contain "new revelations" from "the Embassadors of the angel hosts of heaven prepared and revealed unto man in the name of Jehovih [*sic*] . . ." attempts to emulate biblical words and phrasing.[1] And yet it entirely lacks the linguistic rigor and conceptual lucidity of *The Urantia Book*. James J. Hurtak's *The Book of Knowledge: The Keys of Enoch* purports to be received knowledge from a visitation from Enoch, but has a fearful tone that is all too human.

Without wanting to overstate my case for *The Urantia Book* I can only encourage intrigued readers to pick up a copy—which I believe is now available broken down into the four separate books—or dust off their copies, or retrieve them from garage or attic, and see for yourselves. The authorial voice (by whichever communicant has dictated the particular paper—there are 196 such papers, many by different celestial personalities), invariably carries with it a natural assurance unlikely to have been encountered before.

The various communicants are never shrill or preachy, but appear simply to lay out the facts as they know them to be. They can sometimes be a little tendentious and every once in a while, even a trifle petulant. They are occasionally tedious, with their species' mind-numbing enthusiasm for names and numbers. Yet, in a paradoxical way, these very frailties give the nonhuman communicants more credence in my eyes; it is reassuring to know that angels have their idiosyncrasies too!

The attentive reader will also spot occasions when the angels evidently have difficulty with the limitations of the English language. Many words had to be created to describe situations, beliefs, and entities about which we have no previous knowledge. In the light of this, the writers clearly do their best to communicate profound universal concepts as simply as they can.

It was here in this strange, otherworldly book that I found a wholly new and different personality in Joshua ben Joseph, the Jesus they describe in such fascinating detail. Far from the cloying sentimentality of much of contemporary Christian iconography, I found Christ Michael a Creator Being in his own right, who chose to incarnate in the body of Joshua, son of Joseph, the carpenter of Nazareth. I could *feel* the reality of Joshua the man in my heart.

This new sense of Jesus finally dissolved the issue that had troubled me for so long and distorted my view of Christ—the insistence of Christians on the ultimate divinity of Jesus. It had never rung true to me. Always having an interest in astronomy, I knew how boundless the Multiverse is. It just felt too much of an unlikely coincidence that the second personality of the Trinity would appear in person on this one little planet among the many billions upon billions it was obvious were out there. *The Urantia Book* confirmed this by explaining the historical Joshua ben Joseph was the human vehicle for the "bestowal" of Christ Michael, the Creator Son of *this* Local Universe. Since there are, according to the book, seven hundred thousand of these Local Universes, there are the same number of Creator Sons.

Jesus himself never required that people worship him. He always directed them toward the Father God, of whom he maintained, and he'd include himself, we are all children. But, equally, because Michael is the Creator Son of this Local Universe, it's inevitable that the mortals within his domain, whether they are Gautama Buddha, Muhammad, or Lao-tze, will pass through the Christ as we continue our Universe's career from the Local to the Central Universe.

Such is the reality *The Urantia Book* presents.

The Creator Sons, each paired with the Holy Mother Spirit of their Local Universe, between them modulate the energies pouring out from the Central Universe. Each pair creates the angelic personalities within their domain, and when a planet is ready for organic life, it is a particular group of angels, the Life Carriers, who seed that world with the biological ingredients of life.

This seeding took place on Earth 550 million years ago, simultaneously in three different locations. Bays with sheltered, shallow water were selected for these three marine-life implantations and designated as "the central or Eurasian-African, the eastern or Australasian, and the western, embracing Greenland and the Americas." An intriguing aspect of the Life Carriers' work is that once they have seeded a world, they essentially step back from the evolutionary process and are instructed not to interfere with it while life is developing.

The Urantia Book maintains every tenth planet is designated experimental, and the Life Carriers are able to modify and tweak what they have learned on previous worlds. As a "decimal world" this holds true for Earth.

A small, but aggravating, postscript to the Life Carriers' work on this world is a slightly rueful admission—not quite an apology—from the Life Carriers regarding the excess of parasitic bacteria we find here. They tell us that they had been concerned about "the reversion of certain primitive plant life to the prechlorophyll levels of parasitic bacteria on such an extensive and unexpected scale."[2]

They say it was their "greatest disappointment" and go on to explain, "This eventuality in plant-life evolution caused many distressful diseases in the higher mammals, particularly in the more vulnerable human species."[3] When this unfortunate evolutionary reversion took place, the Life Carriers responsible "somewhat discounted the difficulties involved . . ."[4] that a subsequent genetic upliftment would compensate by producing a blended race, who'd be almost immune to bacteriological and viral diseases.

This anticipated infusion, known as violet blood, was intended to uplift the genetic endowment of the human species some thirty-eight thousand years ago. Sadly, like other off-planet missions, this too failed due to the turbulence and confusion resulting from the Lucifer Rebellion and the planetary quarantine. Thus, it was onto this dark, confused, and warlike world that Christ Michael chose to make his seventh and final bestowal in the very mortal body of Joshua ben Joseph. It was not destined to be an easy life. Joshua's intense interest in everybody and everything, his sense of humor, and the fact he loved to play the harp, yet had to sell it to help support the family after his father died, revealed the more personal side of Jesus.

The book allows us insight into many of these fascinating details: a boat he created as a fisherman, a design that continues to be used to this day; his difficulties and personal problems and the way he coped with them; his complex and deteriorating relationship with his mother and all the plans she had made for him; his respect for women and his fairness in his ways with them. All these were issues I could identify with and have had to deal with myself in my own way.

There is a charming story of being approached when Joshua was nineteen years old by Rebecca, the beautiful young seventeen-year-old daughter of a wealthy local merchant, who'd fallen in love with him. The girl's father was enthusiastic about a potential marriage and thoroughly supported his daughter's choice in the face of Mary's opposition. Joshua's mother had always been convinced that he was a child of destiny and had her own ambitions for him. More important to her at this stage, I imagine, was her family's reliance on Joshua for an income after the death of her husband.

At nineteen, Joshua sounds very much his own man, so I don't think it was purely maternal pressure that caused him to decline the proposal, although we're told he used the requirements of his family as the reason. By this time he knew he would need to keep himself free to do "his Father's will" and pointed out to Rebecca in the kindest and most gentle way that it really wouldn't be fair on her.

Naturally she was heartbroken, but he must have turned her down with such tender grace that she remained in love with him and was among the women gathered at his crucifixion.

There was something extremely touching about this incident. For any healthy nineteen-year-old man, a beautiful girl offering a lifetime of married bliss would be a challenging temptation. That Joshua knew his mind so clearly at that age and was able to handle the situation with such elegance gave me a deep insight into his personality.

It was an incremental opening for me, and as I read deeper into the text, I began to *feel* the truth that this profoundly significant personality had indeed lived the life of an regular person, tackling the ordinary crises and problems confronting all humans to differing degrees. His personality was coming alive for me. His teachings, presented in some detail by the spiritual entities commissioned to transmit the book, were now ringing true in my heart.

Having had the *experience* of God in its *impersonal* form earlier in my life, I realized I was being opened up to a far more *personal* relationship with the Deity. Similar to Hinduism and the Vedas' teaching of the Atman, or Indwelling Divine Spirit, Jesus affirmed that all mortal beings contain a fragment of the Father God. It's in this way each of us potentially can come to know the Father and not simply have to take someone else's word for what some distant and uncaring deity is demanding of us.

Although I'd felt intimations of this presence inside me during the course of my life, it was through reading *The Urantia Book* that my Divine Indwelling Spirit has become a firm reality. I've come to understand the angels when they say it's this Indwelling Spirit they attend and serve because they can perceive what we so often cannot: that each of us alive on the planet and inhabiting a human body contains the Spirit of the Creator God.

There, in the Basilica of San Vitale, as I stared up at the glowing mosaics, I found I'd arrived at a masterful intersection of three of the main currents in my life, each one supportive of and dovetailing into the others in such a way as to show me a brief vision of future possibilities.

I *saw* that as we sensitize our thoughts and feelings in the course of our spiritual journeys, the Spirit of Christ Michael will become an increasingly present reality for more and more of us. His presence in our minds, and the growing realization of the Indwelling Spirit of God the Father, will move us rapidly and irrevocably to the dawning of a new epoch for the planet. This represents the pinnacle of achievement for an inhabited planet, a time the angels describe as the era of light and life.

I *saw* the dolphins, with a longer history and finer senses than ours, delighting in doing the bidding of the Planetary Seraphic Government and waiting patiently for the time when they can work cooperatively with members of our species to enjoy the vast resources of their underwater world. I *saw* in those superb mosaics prescient hints of how more and more of us will turn to the sanctuary of creative endeavor as the beauty and goodness of the Art Spirit spreads across the world.

As we become more spiritually open and welcoming toward the "other" so will we move more into alignment with the rest of the Multiverse, spirit beings and extraterrestrials alike. It is a Multiverse of relationships, and everybody "out there" is waiting and anxious to help us negotiate this difficult transitional period.

The answer, I saw as I still gazed up at the mosaics, lay squarely with us and with our decisions in the light of the new information available to us. Melchizedek's covenant still holds true, if we have the nerve to work with it. Simplistic though it may sound to our cynical age, all we are required to do is to *believe* in the presence and goodness of God, with all that this implies, and God agrees to do the rest.

The act of faith is the key.

Set in the grounds of the basilica is the tomb of Galla Placidia, although some will argue whether it is really hers. The mosaics, over a century older than those of nearby San Vitale, glowed with a beauty that struck me even more forcefully than those we had just seen in the basilica.

Perhaps it was the smallness of the building, and the inescapable intimacy it engendered, that produced the exquisite ambiance; it was one of those few perfect marriages of art and architecture.

As the small wooden door creaked shut behind us we both let out gasps, involuntary in-drawings of breath that immediately transported me back to a primal state of wonderment. The sunlight, filtering through finely wrought alabaster windows set high in the walls, was golden-white and almost tangible in its density. In this rock-cool chamber the mosaics reflected the texture of soft cushions, filled with animal and floral forms. Mandalas of snowflakes hung overhead, framing the easygoing scenes of pastoral spirituality.

There was nothing of the macabre here. I could sense these images were the personal visions and dreams of a superbly creative spirit. It came to me that this gentle, more encompassing, feminine energy was radiating out from the tiny mausoleum every bit as much as those powerful *yang* energies projected from the Battistero in Parma.

A rather different scenario developed sometime after emerging from the glories of the architecture and mosaics of San Vitale and the small tomb, yet there turned out to be a connection, too. Great art, while good for tourism and doubtless wonderful to possess and cherish, has to be very trying to live alongside, as I was soon to see for myself.

Right now, for us anyway, great art was acting as a powerful spiritual enhancement, and we both agreed we were finding ourselves surprisingly open and psychically receptive as we made our way through the dusty streets. Wanting to spend some time quietly digesting the subtle resonance of these two moving experiences, we found a small park, greenery parched by a long summer, and a bench happily positioned so I could see, and therefore could draw, the roofline of the Nueno Baptistry, which rose grandly over the trees at the far end of the square.

Melinda wandered off on her own, leaving me, warm in the sunlight, sketching away. I can often think more clearly when I'm drawing, but this wasn't to be one of those occasions. After a while, I emerged from my creative trance to become aware of a commotion going on under the trees away to my right. A group of young adolescents, boys and girls, were giggling and carrying on. I tried to get back into my drawing as their manic enthusiasm didn't seem to be anything to do with me, but before long it turned into shouting and overloud laughter. Then I saw the sparkle of a glass syringe reflecting light against the gloom under the trees. From what I could make of what was going on, it seemed they were doing speed; they seemed completely unconcerned about being observed and were unabashedly drawing attention to themselves.

It was a depressing sight concerning about a dozen kids coming and going over the course of half an hour. At one point, the main lad—he couldn't have been more than sixteen—swayed over to where I sat, idly shading in the trees on my sketch. He was completely out of it, his eyes flickering white under limp lids, so I imagined in his case he'd been doing heroin. Slumping next to me on the bench, he watched me drawing while we shared a cigarette together.

I could sense his intelligence, but mostly his boredom. I suppose he felt in his own way he was taking a stand of courageous defiance in the face of the old and fearful ways. In his commitment to getting high he'd been able to reject, in his own mind anyway, the phony security and materialistic values of his parents' generation. He felt he had broken free. Yet, he told me he knew the drugs were turning on him, that they were starting to get him nowhere. But at least they were better than what he clearly thought of as the interminable density of the past.

He was young and a rebel, and already he was a natural leader. If he was going to survive the down-drag of the path he'd chosen he would need to be a formidable presence. As he watched me sketching with an intense fascination I wished silently that some aspect of this shared experience would take root in him. At a key point in his life I hoped he'd remember these quiet moments in Needle Park and make a decision that might change his life for the better.

Will I ever learn! For all the wonder and magic of the mosaics and, for that matter, feeling filled with the Spirit, I still did not see it coming. Maybe it started with the young druggie—it was a sobering enough contact yet—in retrospect I'm inclined to suspect it was Mich who wished us to experience the dark underside of the lightness and charm of Italy.

A growing rumble of dissatisfaction set in. Everything started grinding on our nerves; the strident screech of traffic—previously muffled by the mellow haze—now bored its way into our bodies. Even the pollution seemed exhausted, hanging low and limp over the parched, stifling streets.

My mood turned dark and vicious as we walked across the Piazza del Popolo. Threading our way through hundreds of old men, gathered in their groups, endlessly palavering, gesturing, posturing, talking about nothing, filling the air—the psychic space—with the dulled weight of the past, I appreciated all the more what the young junkie was up against. I felt how the old ways were clogging the channels of inspiration and pulling energy off the young—the rightful bearers of the New Vision.

There was something in the undercurrents of the belief system here that was squashing the unique specialness of every individual. I glimpsed it in the rapidly repressed glimmers of spirit recognition among those few I encountered who were willing to meet my eyes, tucked away beneath what seemed to be an almost slavish devotion to fashion among the young women of the town.

Returning to our hotel I found myself falling back into the overbearing vortex of the past. The notes I was writing up were becoming increasingly acerbic and rejecting. I tried all the releasing techniques I knew to get out from under the awful weight of the past, including rejecting it as the cause of all our current problems. True as this might have been, there was no working the negative energy out of my system. I just needed to sit tight and feel the full suffocating psychic weight of all that had happened over the thousands and thousands of years of continued habitation.

This trying atmosphere stayed with us as we journeyed south, down Italy and toward the Gargano Promontory, which is the area of geology's Apulia Platform that sticks out like a spur on the heel of Italy. Melinda and I alternately grunted or spat at one another and then, at other times, found ourselves adopting what seemed a ridiculously over-formal stiffness. I was soon to discover this was one of the standard ways of repressing emotional turmoil in this part of the world. It was this insight that fortunately broke through the gray cloud of mediocrity hanging over us, and it came in a suitably casual manner—changing money in a bank.

Traveling down Italy's east coast amid rolling, arid fields of obsessively neatly planted olive trees and trim stone walls, we could see the tiny plots of land that lay divided and subdivided over the generations—my portion, your portion. The visual regimentation and the implied smallness of thought the countryside created in us only served to pound our more subtle perceptions into a dulled uniformity.

We'd arrived in Manfredonia, a small town tucked into where the southern coast of the promontory meets the country's shoreline, and were still a day's drive from the port of Brindisi, our destination. To add to a general feeling of dejection we'd been waiting for almost an hour in a bank, hostage to the endless bureaucracy of provincial bank clerks, with their slow hands and pencil-licking precision.

Gradually we crawled to the front of the line and watched the little squares getting laboriously filled in with our particulars—our passport numbers and all the other clutter of personal identity. This was then laboriously transferred to yet another piece of paper in an illegible spider scrawl before we were passed over to the cashier, who sat behind another desk only a few feet away, for the next process.

Here was a somewhat different story. The young clerk had 1930's film star good looks and not only knew it, but clearly considered himself on his way up in the world. I watched him juggle the forms and paperwork of half a dozen people who were trying to attract his attention. A stocky man in dark glasses and checking in a fat wad of large bills got beckoned to the front soon enough. An apparent friend of the clerk who arrived late in the turmoil went through fast. The remainder, mainly old peasant folk, shuffled their feet and prodded the air uselessly with their crumpled notes.

The Ronald Coleman smile and the gold teeth flashed endlessly on as the clerk continued three conversations at full volume simultaneously. An old man who was at the front of the line, right there at the clerk's desk all through this performance, had his papers whisked away from him and buried at the back of the cashier's sheaf—like a crooked croupier. I saw the old man recoil at the obvious insult. There was no turning away from what we were both watching: the sad power play of small town pecking orders, of young against old, town against country, modern against ancient, all the underlying social machismo of the truly powerless.

I caught a blast, too, of the rigid formality with which the insulted old man held his seething anger at bay. I knew I was seeing a microcosmic interchange in action, a fragment of which must happen here day after day, year after year—endless bickering, the controlling and the controlled—a concise example of the holding pattern this culture uses to block the free movement of the spirit over the land.

In that moment of illumination we slid from the depressive thought-form's grasp.

Spending the rest of the day in the grounds of Manfredonia's sole pride and joy, the Castello, we were able to recuperate somewhat from the psychic bruising we'd undergone since we left Ravenna. In the sun and the sweetness of well-kept gardens, with an azure sea quietly lapping at the base of the castle, some of the many strands of our trail through Italy were starting to draw closer together.

This castle in Manfredonia had been built by the crusaders, and it was from here that they had set off for the Middle East and the licensed murder of the Saracen hordes. Sure enough, carved into a stone panel and set into one of the bland, sloping walls of the Castello, was yet another depiction of Saint Michael skewering the inevitable dragon. I assumed this image was a symbol of one of the fundamental justifications behind whatever the crusaders thought they were doing, so far from their homes in England and France.

Up to this point I'd been hanging loose on trying to braid the various threads of our experience, preferring merely to record what had taken place and to allow its impact to play on our psyches. In spite of the bloodthirsty carving on the wall behind us, we observed how the harshness of so much of the sacred symbolism we came across in France was giving away to the softer and more receptive ways of the female principle. It seemed perfectly natural, as we sat warming ourselves in the sun, to find our thoughts turning toward the general state of relationships and the imbalances that still exist between men and women in virtually all cultures on the face of the planet.

That we were stalking the Old Power mainly in its male aspect we both knew from the moment we touched foot in Europe. As we moved steadily south from England we made a point of regularly checking into this Old Power and allowing it to psychically permeate us—to feel out its strengths and weaknesses.

The strengths of the Old Power are evident. In spite of the inequities that still exist between rich and poor, we've seen two thousand years of the most rapid cultural evolution the planet has seen in millennia. There are more opportunities for more people, a democratization of energy and information, and a greater expression for freedom of choice than would ever had been considered possible in the past.

There's no doubt, all being taken into account, we have become a kinder and wiser species for it. Yet it's been at a great cost. The suffering resultant from the mechanization of war merely in the previous century has been a horrific reminder of how violent conditions can get, and these wars were on the global stage.

Did it have to be that bad? Did we need it to be that bad? And if we did, and there is no denying the historical facts of an Auschwitz or a Gulag, do we really want or need that depth of horror to continue?

What has been at the root of all this belligerence, of all the harm and unhappiness? Is there a deep-seated psychological disturbance, a pathology that has instigated and fostered the continual enmity on our planet, on dear old Mother Gaia? For all the domineering and power mongering, the territory-grabbing blood lust, the genocidal racial hatreds, and the individual conflicts and cruelties, we felt there had to be some supremely simple underlying cause to all this trouble and strife. We also knew it had to include us all, since for any fundamental transformation of consciousness on this planet, every sentient being would need to be involved.

Possibly the very size and complexity of the problem was making us overlook what was obvious. In a fair and benign Multiverse, there also had to be something each one of us could do individually to help remedy the situation.

When we had posed this very same question at the Conference-in-Spirit at the great pyramid at Giza, the answer we finally received was indeed supremely simple. The issue, as we were to experience it, lay fairly and squarely between men and women: the proverbial battle of the sexes, which runs like a great current through all the cultures and societies of humankind.

It might seem simplistic, or sophomoric even, to try to pin down so much of humanity's ills to a single cause, and clearly there are many dynamics and motives involved in any course of action. It would be truer to say that much destructive action and negative thinking, while not necessarily springing directly from the conflict between the sexes, can certainly be alleviated, or entirely removed, by someone who has been able to establish a fair and peer-based relationship with someone of the opposite sex.

I am not talking here about homosexual relationships, which I'm sure have their own particular stresses and strains, but the vast bulk of humanity, who in our matings and marriages confront in our personal relationships what is an essentially alien species. Which of us hasn't looked at a partner and wondered, along with John Gray, the writer of *Men Are from Mars, Women Are from Venus,* whatever planet did he or she come from?

While this approach is a metaphor, it wouldn't surprise me one little bit if, in the last analysis, women and men, in their spiritual and psychological makeup, turn out to have been drawn from two quite different species. If one of the intentions of our current lifetime is spiritual growth and this frequency-domain is a training school for ascending souls, clearly our loving relationships are important parts of the curriculum.

Men and women in every culture and civilization in the history of the planet have needed to form male/female relationships in order to perpetuate the human race. This is an obvious commonality all humans have shared throughout the ages. Every one of us has to deal with the issues that emerge when men and women, with their very different emotional systems and approaches to life, come into intimate contact with one another.

If each of us in the privacy of our own heart's relationships with the opposite sex cannot resolve our differences and come to treat each other as equal partners in life's adventure, how can we ever expect an entire planet of such individuals to do so?

The enmity generated in the minds of unhappy and unloving people, as in almost everybody during moments of depression or negative thinking, gets carried out psychically into the mainstream of life. This poisons the way we interact with the world, ultimately compounding to fuel the interminable conflicts we see daily in different parts of the world.

Of course, the reverse is also true. The gift of a loving relationship can become the opportunity to discover the unique differences between female and male principles. In welcoming and understanding "otherness" each of us receives an essential training before going out and encountering extraterrestrials, angels, and a teeming, inhabited Multiverse. In a very down-to-earth way, this love also spreads out to help heal the troubles of the world, thus moving us toward reversing the old situation.

The depth and simplicity of this approach, plus its obvious and immediate applicability, opened our hearts to a new line of comprehension as we sat there in the afternoon sunlight. Every exploration we were undertaking seemed to lead to the inevitable conclusion that we were all participating in a key period in the evolution of spiritual intelligence. We sensed subtle moves were afoot that can only be described as a quantum leap in consciousness. (See appendix B.)

This is now more generally accepted by those sensitive to such signs and revelations. However, these are still early days, and it is hard to imagine how this radical shift in consciousness will be implemented across such widely diverse cultural barriers.

The truth is that we are *all* involved. The planetary transformation is not something that is happening *to* us, as much as something that is happening *through* us. The angels were clear about this back in Toronto. They also confirmed what we'd previously been silently pondering, that the wonder in which we have the privilege of participating was no less than the emergence of the Supreme Being in the hearts and actions of all beings involved with the changes to come. This recognition gave us some essential insights into the nature of the personality of this enigmatic fourth aspect of the Deity.

The little we know—or can even comprehend—about this entity suggests it's an evolving Deity. Unlike the Trinity in the Central Universe, who are eternal, having no beginning and no end (the angels suggest this is a bit of a stretch for our limited intelligences), the Supreme comes into being within the *experiential reality* of all the universes and in the lives of the creatures within them. It is a form of Divinity, created by the Trinity, fed by personal experience, and manifesting through every sentient being in their overall creation.

Since the Supreme is experiential, it can obviously be *experienced.* And if it can be experienced, then in all probability it's what many of us have been experiencing these last few years. On those rare occasions when my body simply dissolves into the Light there is a moment when I feel identified with everything and everybody simultaneously.

I believe the states of cosmic consciousness now becoming available—the development of the Network of Light and the appearance of the spiritual nobility of whom I have written in previous books, and indeed much of the advanced dreaming that is now taking place—are all a direct result of an opening within humanity of the Supreme circuits.

The angels in Toronto spoke of a shared activity, of a "something" that has been happening to them as well, of new mandates and actions that allow a much closer liaison between them and their mortal charges. Perhaps this was why our small group of friends in Canada was able to talk to them so freely at the start of this adventure. The whole affair, as described by the angels, rang with enjoyment and an exhilarating cooperation between different types and orders of beings.

This is another sign, I feel, of the Supreme in motion.

So it was with the pair of us, concerned as any lovers might be in the most central part of our lives with what seemed to be happening to us. We were discovering, piece by piece, event by event, the unlimited potential that can result from the union of female and male principles triangulated with a shared love of God. We were getting to experience directly the changes in consciousness emerging from a magical union, and we assumed there must be many others who were encountering this same spiritual dynamic.

Among the revelations we received were the short periods—sometimes as long as twenty minutes—of full telepathic contact with one another. My first book in this series is a testament as to what can happen when two people in love with each other, and with God, throw themselves openly and unconditionally into the higher life of intuition and the subtle whispers of the heart.

We wondered merrily in those moments of mutual metaphysical musings how the Supreme, whom we are told has a *personal form*, might manifest if we were lucky enough to witness such an event. A female? A male? Something androgynous or hermaphroditic like those old occult woodcuts? Perhaps it would even turn out to be a pair—a male and a female? An Isis and Osiris? An Adam and Eve for the new times? Or would the Supreme manifest in all loving relationships to the extent each is capable of feeling and expressing this magnificent energy?

What a wonderful stroke of genius that would be! That so much of the potential for the actualization of this Deity might lie within our own backyards, accessible to and through those with the eyes to see and the hearts to feel. Yes indeed! This has the stamp of divine humor we've come to expect from the higher realms.

As we left Manfredonia the psychic atmosphere continued to lift in that particularly tender way we'd come to recognize as characteristic of the presence of the Supreme in action.

Our ponderings on all the exciting possibilities ahead were evidently opening up new channels of contact with the Spirit. We were able to release and leave behind in that little nowhere town all the psychic flotsam and jetsam we had picked up on our way through Europe. In our private world we christened Manfredonia La Ville au bout de l'Univers, because it felt so much like a border outpost—somewhere one can politely dump one's baggage and move along.

As we followed the coast south a new sense of delightful balance seemed to come over both of us, peeling away another layer in our closeness. In a relationship that always tended to be fiery, the move toward equilibrium was all the more pronounced. I saw and experienced, in those moments—in the manner of the microcosm—how the creative balance of these two quite different energies, the male and female principles, might one day lead to a transmutation of the contentious nature of our species, hopefully without losing any of the hard-won vigor and adventurous courage that typifies the human spirit at its best.

Whether it was Mich's guidance or simply another happy line of coincidences, we didn't see another painting, icon, or any kind of visual reference to knights killing dragons throughout the remaining length of Italy. For us, it was as if the land had been purged of conflict.

We poked our heads into all the churches we came across, always ready to be jolted back to harsh reality, but sure enough, the spaces and designs were getting simpler, less ornamental, and somewhat nearer to what we felt were the basic teaching of Jesus: not to oppose evil, but to love one's enemy: the reconciliation of opposites.

The tour de force turned out to be the new church at Selva di Fasano. It was a small masterpiece. The architect had adapted the roof of the indigenous *trulli*—curious conical structures that dot the landscape—and applied it to the much larger and bolder domed church. While the design can't be said to be modern in the vernacular of contemporary sacred architecture, the architect has carried forward the finest of the simple old ways, cleaning up the lines and presenting a concise and joyful resolution. The internal space was free of ornamental bric-a-brac and flooded with the golden light of a low sun as we walked in. Open and white, the atmosphere was humming with love and attention.

To my eyes the only harsh detail, the one out-of-place visual statement, was a series of etched marble tablets marching along the walls depicting, in a comic book perspective, some of the more gruesome scenes of Christ's journey to the cross. If I tend to be somewhat overreactive to the relish with which the crucifixion is often portrayed in Roman Catholic iconography I expect it's because I was brutally tortured in a recent incarnation. It's hard for me to stomach any capital being made out of such awful pain. If it's intended to get across how terribly Jesus "suffered for our sins," then it's a blatant guilt maker, rendered all the more tragic by the statement in *The Urantia Book* that this simply isn't true. The communicants are clear about this.

Jesus Christ did *not* die for our sins. That was never his intention.

What would be the sense in doing that anyway? Besides whatever does it mean? Are we automatically pardoned or forgiven for our sins because Jesus died for them? Could we be *that* lucky? Can we sin with complete impunity because our sins have already been paid for? Somehow I don't think so.

However, understood in the light of priestly manipulation, it makes perfect sense: keep the flock guilty, submissive, and irresponsible, and they will believe the most transparent fictions.

Turning away from the blood fest we both moved to the end of the main aisle, and under the soft light echoing in from the dome stood a simple altar. Behind it reared a fourteen-foot slab of fine white marble. Gone completely was the crucifix with its heart-rending, drooping body.

In its place stood this splendid modern dolmen. Etched into its smooth, reflective surface, by the same hand as the artist who created the stations of the cross, but more delicately this time, was the image of a resurrecting Christ, rising in freeze-frame from a reclining body, into the lightness of a bodiless soul.

It was a beautifully conceived representation, filled with hope and courage, and in the manner of the associative Multiverse, it led us further to appreciate the closeness of Italy with the Spirit. As in Israel, we sensed this country has a particular, and continuing, relationship with Michael of Nebadon. Feeling the pulse of this association warmed our hearts and souls.

6

The Twilight of
the Gods

The Delphic Oracle, Entheogenic
Archaeology, and the Twilight of the Gods

Delphi had been drawing both of us from way back in Canada. It was one of the places we actually planned to visit. The magic of its name was almost enough, yet I also had an intuition back then—provoked perhaps, more by the name—that we'd find the next clue in our dolphin trail in or around the village of Delphi and the nearby temple ruins.

This particular dance is turning out to be a feature of our conscious choice to live the life of the Spirit. We make our plans more as general directions based on what feels most pleasurable, a place at which to point our noses, full knowing, by this time, our guides will be the in-time pilots of what actually happens.

I could never have anticipated, for example, the quality of my encounter with Michael of Nebadon in Ravenna. I felt it was the dolphins who led me directly, if subtly, to the Master. I hadn't started on this journey with much of a feeling for Christ beyond respect, but in Ravenna so much seemed to come together in the being of this Michael of Nebadon, I was beginning to feel through the miasma of misinformation to reach the true nature of Jesus.

It was perfect, too, on a symbolic level. The dolphin book—the book I was writing stimulated by my early encounters with cetaceans—far from being focused solely on contact with dolphins and whales, was turning out to be leading me into a much wider-ranging experience of otherness. I'd rejected conventional Christianity for so long it was challenging to break through my mental barriers. I'd like to think it was the dolphins, with all their telepathic brilliance, as well as the transcendent beauty of those mosaics in Ravenna combining to gently guide me through this trail, which culminated in discovering for myself, through direct experience, the emotional reality of this Creator Being, the father of my flesh.

In Ravenna, being primarily a visual person, I found it was the exquisite beauty of the mosaics, their loving care and tenderness portraying a very different understanding of the Christ, that touched my soul. That Jesus would be accompanied by dolphins in an art that lovely carried a deep personal meaning for me. It was one of those moments in which I could feel the truth of Dostoevski's prescient vision, "In the end beauty will save the world."

Although we both felt it was the angels who were guiding us from day to day, I had to acknowledge it was the dolphins who had more than a fin in leading me to a real feeling for Jesus. It was a delicious rapprochement of three primary threads in my life: my spiritual journey, my love of dolphins, and my joy in the face of beautiful art. I would have never have anticipated this epiphany, knowing how resistant I'd been to Jesus and for how long, especially in a country that felt so spiritually depleted. It felt like a gift from a different era of Italy, and with it came the sense that it was a good time to leave the country.

On a more iconic level, and in spite of the likelihood that the fish that has come to symbolize Jesus to the faithful is a reference to Christ's being a "fisher among men," it set me to wondering whether a more occulted meaning might point to the dolphins. After all, here we have highly intelligent creatures not so very different from human beings, yet with the wisdom to have sustained their culture and environment for over thirty-five million years. So as delicious as it might be to eat a limbless, cold-blooded vertebrate with gills and fins that lives wholly in the water, as Christian symbols go, I suggest a dolphin carries with it a far deeper resonance than a fish.

Now Delphi was calling, and it was only a short hop on the ferry from Brindisi in southern Italy directly across to Patras, the main port on the western coastline of Greece.

Greece opened its arms to us the moment we stepped off the boat. Both of us felt the relief. After the teetering ambivalence of Italy the atmosphere of social ease washed over us with the warming sunlight. Even pottering through the noisy, raunchy streets of the small port, kicking our heels for a few hours while waiting for a bus was far more pleasant than I could have imagined.

Most noticeable was the easy rapport between the men and women who crowded around us. The women seemed to mix fluidly with the men, a parity that seemed wholly lacking in Italy. Here the men stood or sat in groups talking, palavering most likely, yet it was with the old and young mixed together, without any of the generational gap that seemed so wide and impassable in southern Europe.

Clearly the strictures of the Roman Church didn't have the same kind of hold in this country, as we were to find emphasized when we went into the small Greek Orthodox churches we came across. They were uniformly dark and unkempt, with little or no spiritual charge left in them: it felt to us to be the religious authority and artwork of a tired tradition.

The paintings in these churches were crude and gaudy, everything thrown together in unselective piles. A mass-produced, poorly made image of the Virgin, embossed on gold paper, stood leaning against a far older, but equally poorly crafted wooden icon. This was the work of a people who, though they must have meant well, certainly weren't pushing themselves to produce their best for their God.

I knew the contrast from my cousin Christopher's work and the amount of time, love, and dedication, let alone the patience and craft to master egg tempura, that he puts into creating his superb icons. The icons we were seeing in the small churches were so poorly made as to suggest the good ones were either sold, stolen, or more likely secreted away on the walls of the modest homes of the discerning faithful.

Although the overall atmosphere in the streets was warm and heartful, for all the social relaxation, something felt missing. This sense of lack, a psychic hole in the core of the culture, was to pursue us throughout our travels in Greece. Some essential ingredient for a well-balanced society had disappeared, and I wondered whether its absence was not contributing directly to much of the unrest I knew existed in the country.

Admittedly, these were first impressions, psychic snapshots of an ancient and complex people. Yet I've found in my travels if I pay close attention to my feelings when I pass from one culture to another, in the newness of my impressions, I can often get an accurate gestalt picture of some of the ways those societies function.

Giorgias echoed this vacuum when he described his town, Delphi, as cursed. He was angry that first night we met him, his dark eyes set even farther back among the bruises of late-night worry. He was struggling to find the right word in English for what he felt, but he had called Delphi a jealous and unhappy mother who, resenting the attempts of her children to break free, had cursed them all.

Overly dramatic, perhaps, but Delphi is something of an anomaly in the soaring mountains and deep valleys surrounding it. The village wasn't even originally where it is today. Then it was called Kastri. It sat on the site of the Delphic Oracle itself until relentless pressure from French archaeologists managed to goad the Greek government into relocating the entire community half a mile up the road. That would certainly make a village seem strange and lost, its roots cut from the very earth it grew up on and thrust off into the arms of international tourism.

The village quickly grew into a small town, a place for the quick killing—grab the dollars and run. This was reflected again and again in the faces of the merchants in the village as we explored the narrow streets with their many small shops. The initial false blast of welcoming warmth was invariably followed by as rapid and complete a withdrawal as soon as it was obvious we weren't going to be spending money in their store. They'd evidently not had the best of seasons.

We were led off the beaten track to find Giorgias in his restaurant. Not surprisingly, it turned out the location hadn't worked to his advantage in the intense competition for tourist gelt. He owned a small place up behind the main drag. It was hard to imagine whether any but a spillover crowd would ever find their way there. Still, for all that, he greeted us with the most authentic look of the day—a scowl that he tried valiantly to turn into a smile. We were hungry and, I think in retrospect, also picking up on something of interest in all this. Mich had a way of guiding us into meaningful, if not altogether pleasant, situations.

The restaurant was a mess, evidently a one-shot deal with no thought of continuing custom. Avoiding the overwrought menu we both went for the safety of a salad, served with a complete lack of style by Giorgias himself. The place was empty with the exception of an occasional fluttering behind the beaded curtain of the kitchen.

When we were finishing our salads Giorgias sidled over to join us, as we both knew he was going to do, in spite of his abrupt rudeness throughout the meal. Like it or not he was clearly his own man. Melinda was just starting to read the auguries from the grounds left in my cup of Greek coffee.

"You have to tip it out onto the saucer," Giorgias said in what was a small power play.

"I didn't want to dirty it," she replied, without missing a beat. The kindness of the thought must have reached below his psychic armor because he disarmed immediately. The three of us were then able to relax into a spirited rapport. The truth, along with some tears, soon starting to pour out of him.

Somehow he'd allowed himself to be talked into opening the place as a business venture by a brother and two friends. Needless to say they had long since deserted him. He was quick to tell us that in village terms he was much admired. Popular opinion was that he'd been smart enough to invest in the space when he bought it—local boy made good. But now he'd hocked himself to the tip of his nose just to keep the place up and running.

The trouble, as he saw it, was that he had come in on the cusp. He explained in his remarkably good English, picked up from working in restaurants, that Greece in the good old days used to attract what was euphemistically called "a better type of tourist." Then the playboys moved on, however, and there had never been very many of them to start with. Ten years back, he told us, there were a mere half a million tourists a year. When the boom came three years previously the numbers soared to over eight million. Now tourism was falling back, only five and a half million last year and dropping fast.

The grand memories of big spenders still echoing in the minds of the merchants, it can only have been depressing to witness the busloads of Germans, French, Americans, and Japanese tourists, most eager only to be photographed in the shadow of a Doric column, anesthetized within their own cultural bubbles to the spiritual and psychic currents of the country they were traveling through.

Giorgias was feeling more insulted than broke. The ancient culture he'd grown up within and loved and respected was becoming a mere photographic backdrop: the hordes, like automatons, here to snap and be snapped, if only to prove they'd been to Delphi. The fast-food establishments began to appear. The trinkets in the shop fronts got cheaper; the faked artifacts, more expensive. Now, with all the dangers in the world, even the masses of tourists had fallen off. It's scarce wonder, in the light of this depressing record, such reduced expectations might have led to the equally flattened responses of so many of the shopkeepers during our afternoon stroll through the village.

Giorgias felt caught in a vicious circle, unwilling to upgrade the restaurant because it seemed like throwing good money after bad. After all, the dollars and yen still trickled in yet he hated himself for his place's lack of grace. He'd put it together as a hustle, and now, at least, he had the wisdom to see he was thoroughly caught out in his own game.

Had Giorgias been completely expedient and materialistic all this wouldn't have worried him; the main street was full of sharpshooter shopkeepers all too unconcerned with the indignity they had brought to a sacred place. Giorgias, however, was definitely different. As I got to know him better I began to see the magic in the man, and he certainly *knew* the Spirit of Delphi.

He told us he spent his childhood and adolescence scrabbling about in the ruins of the Temple of Apollo and was among the first of the locals—although to me he didn't look quite old enough—to have photographed the site as the archaeologists had pieced it together. I wondered whether it was this period, which he looked back on with such happiness, that might have drawn out what was clearly an unusual sensitivity to the inner realms.

He'd always been able to "see" people, as he called it. He hadn't understood the gift, the "seeing" and the "seeing-what-people-needed" had become confused, and he put many of the disappointments of his life down to this oversensitivity. He'd always been the one to help—and here came the tears—the one to come forward when asked, the loyal one. True or not, I'm sure *he* believed it; the encounter was starting to have a confessional quality.

Once he'd wanted to study and read. He'd wanted to travel and broaden his understanding. Then, in stepped his family, heavy with obligations and the responsibilities of the material world. Now he was trapped in a situation from which he saw no possible escape.

Later Melinda and I agreed for all his obvious frailties we both had a sense of the spiritual nobility about Giorgias, something of the quality we have experienced in a number of our "chance" meetings—encounters to which we felt ourselves led, or guided. One of the qualities we've come to see in these people is the degree to which they carry in their natures the main psychic and spiritual crosscurrents of their cultures.

Giorgias, in his own way, was laying out for us the subtle intermixing of human and Divine in contemporary Greece, every bit as much as Ray Bret Koch, for example, was manifesting many of the contrasts we found in France.

To staunch the flow of money out of the restaurant Giorgias had taken to gambling, to the horses and cards. He found under certain circumstances he was able to divine them, and when he felt really clear he claimed he was right every shot. Regretfully, he'd soon discovered what many gamblers discover, only made worse in Giorgias's case since he felt he'd betrayed his higher self. He'd been given the gift, and now he knew he'd thrown it away on trivial pursuits. At the age of thirty he was getting nervous. The grandiose expectations and wishful dreams were all gone.

While telling us this, his head steadily dropped until he was looking at his shoes. I could see he was crying again. He paused and blew his nose loudly on one of his paper napkins. After recovering he confessed he was scared he was losing his edge, his "ethical strength," he called it.

Acting out his tragedy for us, he appeared as if he were wobbling on the edge of an abyss of self-emasculation, his confidence slipping away, his dark eyes already worn into deep black pits by the tension of it. Yet for all this, it looked like Giorgias was convincing himself he'd one last whirl left in him. The Big One. Perhaps if he could summon up the power, with the right people . . . looking up at us hopefully.

It sounded like a last desperate hustle, which, if he'd been able to stand back a little, might well have sounded as absurd to him as it did to us.

Somehow he might have thought he'd "seen" us in that way of his and, with his despair clouding his vision, was folding us into his needs. Although how he thought a couple of foreign wanderers might have served his purposes, I doubt if he had any idea. We'd made it very clear neither of us had any interest in gambling, and since we were just passing through there was little we could do for Giorgias except patronize his establishment.

There was something very sad about the whole encounter and how it echoed the hollow feeling we both had on our first day in Greece. It also felt like it had something to do with Delphi. The gradual demise of the Oracle must have affected the locals' lives in their day much in the same way as the reduced numbers of tourists were affecting Giorgias and his fellow merchants.

The Oracle at Delphi had functioned superbly up to a few hundred years before the time of Christ. Although famous for its ambiguous answers, within its heyday the Delphic Oracle is on record as never being outright wrong. It even predicted its own demise. Its reply to Oreibasius, representative of the Roman Emperor Julian, in one of its final utterances, has all the stamp of a suicide note:

> *Tell ye the king: the carven hall is fallen in decay;*
> *Apollo hath no chapel left, no prophesying bay,*
> *No talking spring.*
> *The stream is dry that had so much to say.*

In the span of those four hundred years, scarcely a major decision of statecraft was taken in the ancient world without consulting the Oracle. The pantheon of gods and goddesses was a powerful presence in the lives of the Greeks, and Delphi was the chosen place of Apollo. Of all the deities Apollo was the great civilizer, "Giving to the Greek world," or so my guidebook charmingly put it, "a message on the purification from killing by milder means and not by blood."

Apollo was also the god of music as well as prophecy and sought through the Oracle to further his teachings of moral excellence, of how to live in a state of balance both with the self and with the world around by acting with measure. Although a later addition to the Greek pantheon, Apollo was one of the most popular and venerated of the gods and was perhaps the one who was most responsible for directing the sweeping expansion of Hellenism across the face of the known world. This was a truly massive undertaking in any historical era. The plans and predictions for this enterprise all sprung directly from the lips of the Delphic Oracle.

Little is really known about how the Oracle actually functioned. Popular theories talk of telluric fumes, mephitic vapors arising from volcanic fissures, of the possible psychedelic propensity of chewed, or smoked, laurel leaves, as well as the long and natural tradition of prophetesses and seers. The prescient utterances—always in verse form—came from Pythia, a collective name for the priestesses of Apollo, one of whom sat in a state of psychic possession suspended from a tripod hung over the oracular chasm. These priestesses were frequently chosen from the privileged classes, and it's been pointed out that their lives were invariably shortened by the exhausting sessions.

More recently, in 2001, ethylene, a gas with hallucinogenic effects, was found in and around the local geology and in the largest concentrations in water just above the temple. In fact, the temple of Delphi lies straddling the intersection of two major fault lines, and the nearby rift of the Gulf of Corinth is one of the most geologically active places on Earth. While the experts still argue about what caused Pythia to become a trance medium, a quote from Plutarch, the Greek historian, seems to make the point. "Not often nor regularly, but occasionally and fortuitously, the room in which the seat of the god's consultants is filled with a fragrance and breeze, as if the adyton [the gas] were sending forth the essences of the sweetest and most expensive perfumes from a spring."

Of all the hydrocarbons released as gases from the layers of bituminous tars heated by the immense stresses and friction of the earth's movement, only ethylene has such a sweet scent. The prophetic uses of the site go far back into prehistory, millennia before Apollo eclipsed the ancient Earth goddess Ge, or Gaia, by fighting and defeating her guardian serpent, Python. Older stories still mention two dragons, one female named

Delphyne, paired with a male serpent called Typhon. It's been suggested that the second myth conflated the two dragons into one Python.

This latter myth tells us that Apollo was chasing Python, having already fought a battle from which the serpent had escaped to Delphi. By the time Apollo reached Greece the god was definitely keen to inflict his revenge on the creature who had so cruelly harried his mother, Leto, in her worldly wanderings. Could the central meaning of Apollo's savage defeat of the protector serpent be the ur-myth beneath the later dragon-slaying of the likes of a St. Michael or St. George?

None of these ancient myths are straightforward: there are other stories that claim that Pythia, the enemy dragonness, actually became an Apollonian serpent. Images survive showing Python living happily with Apollo, guarding the Omphalos, the sacred navel-stone that stood in Apollo's temple.

The oracular priestesses at Delphi were evidently named after Pythia and the place itself after Delphyne—*delphys* being the Greek word for womb and also the root of the word *dolphin*. When I came to Greece, with my limited knowledge of the myths, I had no idea I was going to be walking into another dragon-slaying scenario. The alternate myth of Python and Apollo living together in friendship came to me later, while I was researching for background. During my time in Delphi I felt I was facing a dragon-killing story predating any of those sword-happy saints, and from which, in all likelihood, the early Christian fathers had originally derived their propagandist images.

I remembered those strange, serpentine visions I was given at the Cathedral of Notre Dame in Paris and in Glastonbury, back in the land of the Hyperboreans where, I read, Apollo would vacation during the three winter months, and wondered if they could be somehow related to what had happened in Delphi.

Then there was the Oracle. For the modern sensibility it's difficult to comprehend this seemingly direct line of communication with the wider realm of consciousness of the gods. We tend to belittle the ancients for their superstitious concerns, or sideline their beliefs as teaching stories or metaphors. Much of what was vitally important to them seems like hocus-pocus to us, these gods and goddesses with their autocratic behavior and their constant interactions with the human world. We tritely assume the ancients were simpler than us or that they spoke in fables about the natural forces around them. Contemporary belief has relegated these beings, whoever they were, to the world of symbols and archetypes—and doubtless they were all these things, too—but, I suspect, we have missed something of the underlying truth.

The ancient Greeks were a deeply rational people struggling to make sense of the cosmos in which they found themselves. Their poetic souls and the myths they'd inherited from other, older peoples often ran counter to their own objective, empirical attempts to describe and measure the world of phenomena. They would have been most unlikely to have given much credit to or placed so much importance on their pantheon unless there were some clear, evidential signs the gods and goddesses existed for them as very real phenomena.

As I pondered this it became more real to me that there was something very different about the situation of the ancients, one that makes it well nigh impossible for us to identify with them or to fully appreciate what exactly they were dealing with.

I lay on the bed in our simple room in one of the more pleasant hotels in the town of Delphi, perched over the olive and cypress trees of the Pleistos Valley, which swept away beneath us thousands of feet down to the distant sea and the Gulf of Corinth. The shimmer of the silver water hung like a mist beneath the broad, red sunset. Mountains became islands became clouds and disappeared, miraging into the early darkness.

Yet, all was not well. My mind was racing.

As I lay there doing my best to quiet myself I realized I'd staked a great deal on Delphi and, without really registering it, I'd been building up an unreasonable level of expectation as to what I might find here. Perhaps it was going to be the next step in the dolphin trail or the secret history of the dragon.

And what of the Oracle itself? The angels back in Toronto had told us it was "due to be reactivated" (their words). And the midwayers, who had been making their subtle presence felt in the course of our journey through Europe, did they play a part in the Oracle? It would have been a masterful way of guiding or controlling human beings. I was finding myself being drawn into the psychic vortex of Delphi, the metaphysical motif of the place. I was becoming captured and entrained by the mental projections of every poor soul who had come here over the thousands of years, all looking for something. The Answer. Advice. Prophecy. A vital decision in a nation's life, in a person's career . . .

I prayed myself asleep that night and dreamed vividly of a Zen monastery and of tests passed and an acceptance that involved elaborate dances with two-headed snakes . . . I awoke feeling refreshed, relaxed, and happy. This was the day I'd decided to take on the Delphic Oracle with the finest substances in my explorer's entheogenic pharmacopeia.

Our first visit to the Temple of Apollo, the afternoon we arrived in Delphi, was pleasantly unspectacular and definitely casual, in the way we had come to recognize as signifying an angelic presence. We both wondered what "the Oracle is due to be reactivated" might mean and whether anything specific might be required of us.

We were told by the angels in Toronto that it would be our presence in Delphi that would do the reactivating. Of course, I'm aware of the apparent absurdity of this claim, but if these spiritual adventures are to carry the truth of my experiences and observations, I've long chosen to be transparently honest. However silly or naive I subsequently think I was, my authentic, in-the-moment beliefs and reactions are the only things of value I can pass along.

Even at the time, we'd both taken the angel's statement lightly since it sounded so outlandish and we really couldn't imagine what it might mean. A medium suspended from a tripod over a chasm and sucking in the ethylene (or whatever it was) and speaking in poetic quatrains wouldn't be likely to make much of an impression on the modern world.

Yet, on that first sun-filled afternoon, something did engage. I felt it without being able to describe it: a very subtle sense of cooperation, of simply being in the right place at the right time.

We'd circled the ruins with an easygoing caution, stalking them almost, feeling them out, exploring the lesser-tramped paths as we pulled our way around the back of a steep slope. We descended on top of the main complex, elbowing our way through brambles, over small ravines, and jumping from old walls into dried-up riverbeds. We kicked up the dust of the ages, which filled the air with all the scents of a long, hot summer passing; then we found a small, untended path, threading its way into the ruins.

Whatever the French archaeologists might have been thinking when they recreated the place, this felt the right way in to us. We were drawn immediately to a large circular stone plinth, which was capped by three flat rocks. We both agreed that intuitively it felt like a key spot, although it was tucked away behind enormous piles of dressed stones, neatly numbered and placed ready for some new archaeological folly.

Melinda clambered to the top of the plinth, standing first and then squatting down over the spot we both sensed as being the cleft from which the fumes once arose. Admittedly it was a magical moment and one particularly hers as she crouched, limned against the setting sun, her form grayed to charcoal and glowing irradiated against the gray-green slur of the mountains. I helped her down off the plinth, and we folded into a tender embrace. We'd come a long way following this trail. The adventures would continue, we knew that, but these moments in Delphi represented a completion of what the angels required of us on this trip. We both intuitively knew the deed was done, whatever it was. It was a perfect moment, *per facio,* thoroughly made. Complete. Me (pronounced *meh*), as the ancient Egyptians called it. From here on we were on our own time. We could both settle back and enjoy ourselves.

Or so I thought!

A couple of days later I wanted to plunge into the vibrations of Delphi, far deeper than I'd had the chance on our first late afternoon visit. I yearned to open up the floodgates of knowledge I felt permeating the ruins, ready for any who could decode the information. I'd been feeling a path clearing for what had become by this time in my mind a veritable spiritual assault—a storming of the gates of heaven.

The bright morning sun was climbing above the mountains by the time I arrived alone at the ruins. Melinda had chosen to remain back at the hotel until later in the afternoon, when she would come and rescue me if I needed pulling out of a jam. I picked up my muses on the walk down there. A small cat traveled with me for a couple hundred yards, mewing encouragement (or more likely, hunger) and was happy to be petted. Three large birds sprang from the nearby stiff wiry undergrowth—always the correct number under these circumstances—and I felt their complicity in the events to come. Then, turning the corner to the entrance of the site, a lion's head formed itself briefly out of an overhanging rock.

They were all good signs.

I'd located what I thought of as the center of power the day before, so I wound my way up through the columns and porticoed treasuries to the base of the main temple. There, jutting out from the long stone wall that supported the temple platform was a massive natural rock bluff shaped like a dragon's head. It must have been carrying the weight of the entire temple structure, preventing the whole complex of buildings and amphitheater from slipping gracelessly down the mountainside.

Pulling my guitar and my shoulder bag up with me I scrabbled onto a sandy niche directly on top of the flat, rocky head. Nestling into the warm sand, I spread my tape recorder, sketchbook, pens, and pencils around me, murmured a prayer to the Great Spirit for vision and understanding, and taking a deep swig of water, washed down four hits of microdot acid and two caps of fine phencyclidine, timed, hopefully, to layer in over the 125 milligrams of MDMA that I had dropped back at the hotel before I left.

I regard the use of entheogens in these special situations as a valuable investigative tool and expand on this further in appendix B. I quieted my mind to match the silence of the valley—just the sound of birds and the scent of the pine trees rising from the valley below and the new sun now blazing through my closed eyelids.

Soon the MDMA starts to engage, and I can feel the deep subterranean machinations of whatever exists here. Mellow, underlying rhythms start to swell around me, lulling and enveloping. I find myself falling into a reverie, fully conscious and yet simultaneously a detached observer of everything that was going on around and inside me.

After a while I open my eyes to find the mountains are moving as if the earth herself were rippling her flanks—a slow-motion earthquake that never ceases. I watch intently as over this vision falls a matrix: layered cycles of events piling endlessly one on top of another, their points of synchronicity, their connections and small parallelisms, all abuzz with sudden bursts of visible energy.

Intuitively I know I am seeing a visual representation of the common denominator of what underpins the material universe. From the sub-electronic world of the *ultimatons, The Urantia Book*'s name for the quarks and charmed particles of the quantum physicists, up through the cellular and biological realms to the landscape itself, they are all contributing to shaping of the reality of the moment.

All this I can see simultaneously, every layer of events occurring throughout history in this place, and all this is happening in the same breath, as though serial time were collapsing into an ever-perpetuating moment. As the phencyclidine starts kicking in, I find myself sprawling across this matrix, feeling the tickling tumult of being everything at once. Each breath pours around the world, then the solar system and larger still, to return and rejoin and entrain my next breath into even wider expansions.

Within this ongoing and eternal instant, I know with inner conviction that the very landscape, the apparent meat and potatoes of creation, is itself merely a thought in the mind of the Supreme. I also perceive that what I know as the material world is an overlay held in the mind of the Supreme and that its form is constantly being modulated by those who have passed through, by those who have tarried here, both human and nonhuman, and that the truth of Delphi is indeed lying impressed into the landscape.

The shifting of the mountains and their heaving flanks abates slightly. I have a sense something is required of me. Of course! The balancing presence of music, of Apollonian measure. I reach for my guitar, and within moments of getting comfortable and adjusting to the strange reality of having something so physical as a musical instrument in my arms, the music is playing me. I watch my fingers taking positions I've never seen before, crawling like crabs over the shimmering fret board.

The music starts slow at first, the most plaintive I've ever heard it, and at each note the landscape shudders and rearranges itself into a different reality, as a kaleidoscope might. I feel I am seeing a sequence of parallel dimensions, the subtle physical shifts the landscape must have undergone through the millennia of tectonic activity. (See plate 4.)

It's now that I begin to feel the presence of the spirits of the valley, the separate notes of my guitar clinging to the air and moving the vision through action, freeze, and change; action, freeze, and change; action, freeze, and change . . .

I was shown that the gods have known this place and have tried to mediate with the human races of the time on this wild slope, that a great tradition had grown up over the centuries in a world more open to direct interaction with the spiritual dimensions of life, that on at least two occasions the gods caused earthquakes to prevent invading armies from reaching this special place.

A profound sense of sadness envelops me. While the music is echoing through the rocks and valleys, as I watch and listen to its ebbing and flowing, a composite of deeply felt thoughts spreads over me. I see, in the clarity of these revelatory moments, that indeed the gods of the ancients were, and are, the midwayers of the Urantia cosmology, the race of beings who were among those sent to uplift life on this planet all those many tens of thousands of years ago.

For me this is no longer theory or simply my speculation. I'm experiencing and sensing the reality of the midwayers. I'm being given insights into their lives. I feel intensely the loneliness of these beings, isolated on this planet and yet with the poignancy of knowing of the larger Multiverse and their cosmic parentage. These are beings with a vastly wider range of knowledge than we humans, yet ones as capable as we are of making errors of judgment. These errors have had a profound effect on the well-being of the human races, sadly compounded over the many tens of thousands of years of continuing midwayer activity. I feel their loneliness and their isolation, their sense of careening down false paths and misdirected good intentions. I know their tragedy in the silent sadness of my heart. I see how the situation spun gradually out of their control after the exhilaration and challenges posed by the rebellion and all the difficult choices with which they were faced after their chief of mission sided with those rebelling against the Multiverse Authorities.

Half a million years ago humans were dwelling in large clan-groups and were primarily nomadic, foraging for food. They lived in a world of ghosts and angry spirits, fearful of every shadow that skulked in the shadows of a guttering fire. Here was a population of bipeds, just down out of trees in the larger span of human history and already terrified out of their wits by the violence and predation of a dog-eat-dog world. I understood how impossibly challenging the midwayers' tasks on this planet must have been at this level of physical density. Yet, for all this, the midwayers could see these pathetic human creatures living and dying and ascending to the higher worlds of the Spirit. All the while the midwayers remained stuck on this wretched little world, in service for all time and with no guarantees they would ever get off the planet and into the Grand Multiverse.

Having a wider field of vision than humans, the midwayers must see more and deeper and know very well the "great out there" really exists. Up until the rebellion and the consequent isolation of the planet they would have witnessed extraterrestrial and angelic activity as an almost everyday event.

In the 293,000 years the prince's staff and their midway complement labored here before the rebellion struck, they helped build what was probably the finest culture of prehistory and a mature and spirited civilization centered in the Persian Gulf region. Then came the rebellion. Quarantine. Disgrace. Isolation and an acute sense of division and enmity between those who had chosen to remain loyal to the Multiverse Authorities and the larger number of those choosing to follow their leader into rebellion. Wars between these opposing factions soon led to the co-option of their human wards in the midwayers' own selfish conflicts. The millennia passed as civilizations supported by one faction or another rose and fell.

I could see the sway these "gods" have held over the human races for these long 203,000 years since the rebellion. After all, the generations of humanity were every bit as cut off from the rest of the Multiverse as the midwayers were, and sadly, mankind was all too prone to deify and worship anything or anybody seen as more powerful than them. I understood, then, how the midwayers' loving care for their human charges gradually became worn down by their growing sense of desperation, to be ultimately perverted by their own self-interests. Their very immortality and invisibility were working against them—the humans had started to worship them as gods.

This fundamental corruption of human beings' natural spiritual impulse was most likely initiated by Caligastia, when subsequent to the rebellion he declared himself "God of Urantia." This would have set a shocking example to both staff and midwayers; it ran completely counter to the purposes of their mission. In those moments of inspired clarity I saw it was this "worship factor" that had gone so awry, one of the many complex and unimagined ramifications in a world that has been summarily cut off from a Multiverse teeming with life on its many levels and dimensions. It seemed to me the rebels hadn't taken into account quite the strength of the worship circuits seemingly hardwired into the human species.

At first, the midwayers thought they could control and manipulate the spiritual urge in the human species, for the good of all. I could see how this urge to worship, once so painfully redirected from the ghosts and devils of practical experience to focus on the Father God, now turned back toward the midwayers. I could also see how this adoration must have gone to the midwayers' heads and disorientated them, giving them delusions of their own godhood.

Then, over the last score of millennia, I could see how the situation of caring for the human races accelerated even further out of their control, their influence lessening and their capacity to "talk inside peoples heads" diminishing. The places where midwayers could meet and interact with humans grew fewer. Some of the midwayers became belligerent and ever more selfish, getting turned on by the very mortality of human beings. Others, like the presences I was feeling here in Delphi, remained as faithful and true to their original mandates as they knew how.

It had been a sorry scene. Confusion and conflict swept through the affairs of humankind, and the rebel midwayers, so often the provocation behind the conflicts, were increasingly powerless to maintain their control over humans. They must have known by this time their mission was proving fruitless; the overall momentum of the evolutionary prerogative was too much for them. Humanity itself was changing, becoming less fearful and more rational, more individualized. Spiritual teachers were appearing who were pointing the human races back toward a worship of the one true God.

I felt I was being shown how the midwayers withdrew, first from the minds of humans, then from oracles, seers, and mystery cults, which desperately tried to keep in contact with the best of them. By the time the rebel midwayers were banished two thousand years ago by Christ Michael, they were but a shadow of their former selves. A trace memory has remained in Greece of once-great exploits and the presence of these apparent demigods. I felt sure midwayers must have existed and left their mark on the very fabric of the country, embedded in the group-mind every bit as much as in the landscape itself. I knew intuitively, too, this

was the sense of lack, the pervasive undertone Melinda and I'd been feeling throughout our time in Greece.

It was at this point in the revelatory stream of information I first heard
the shouting and whistling, although it didn't seem strong enough to pay
much notice to. I kept playing my guitar to the sleeping rocks while a
soothingly soft silence settled all around me. The music was being listened to, not merely heard. The spirit of the place was coming alive. I
knew the harmonics were important; I could hear them ringing through
the rocks and echoing back to me. I entrained their echoes, building up
crescendos of reverberating sound returning now from the valley walls.

The shouting comes through again, this time nearer and louder. I
imagine it's being directed at me, but I am in no mood to pay it any heed.
I'm thoroughly entranced by the music and all the layered stratas of information the sounds are unveiling. Suddenly the voices are much louder,
coming from somewhere up above the ledge on which I'm sitting. Various
languages are being used, and I can hear them vaguely through a haze of
shifting realities.

"It's forbidden to play here . . . verboten . . . it's forbidden to play here.
. . ," over and over again. I still pay no attention to them, my eyes tightly
shut and face raised like a blind man to the sun. There's a soft thud near
me as one of them jumps down to join me on the great stone head. I
sense his shadow falling over my face, the vivid crimson behind my eyelids turning to magenta.

Still I keep my eyes shut and the music flowing. From another world
I hear him alternately pleading with me to stop and then shouting at me
right in my face, his spittle falling on me like the first raindrops on a
parched land. My fingers move faster, changing the muted minor notes
into more rapid, rhythmic, and triumphal tones. Amid all this shouting
and whistling I distinctly hear from somewhere overhead one of the guards
taking up the melody in that wonderfully woeful way of the Greeks.

There are calls of "Apollo! Apollo!" and some nervous laughter.

Still the music pours through me, and I know in the serenity of the
moment—the calm point in the center of the storm—that it is indeed *his*
music that wishes to be heard, in *his* temple, the Temple of Apollo.

After a long time of indecision and mutterings in Greek between the guards, the shadow darkens over me and I can feel the man trying to block my strings, his hands groping at the neck of the guitar. I play on undeterred, incorporating the fudged sounds of his fingers against the strings in yet new rhythms.

I feel his fury rising, the smell of fear and anger oozing over my hypersensitivity. Soon I know, he will strike me. I know he has no choice. Having started this course of events he will not be able to stop without losing face. So, I open my eyes and smile up at him as he wrenches the guitar out of my hands, my fingers still playing as he grabs it away.

The reverberations died slowly in the embarrassment of the silence.

Yet I could feel the music living on, in the rocks, the ruins, and in the very fabric of the mountains themselves. The birds and insects heard it. The temple was bathed in the harmonics, with every quartz crystal in every piece of granite storing and recording the cadences for some future time.

I knew, too, in those moments when he was grasping the sounds away, that the music was too much. It had upset the subtle balance and stripped back the nerves of the place. It had left the people with their memories. It was too near the nub, too near the inherent tragedy of Delphi and the demise of its Oracle.

The rules had to be followed, had to be obeyed at all costs. Living music had to be silenced lest the truth roll out from beneath the stones for all to see how the glory had been dissipated. All hopes for a working relationship between humans and demigods, between humans and mid-wayers, had been dashed—dribbled away in shallow politics and second-rate myth making. I felt the guards showed me by their actions they were probably not yet ready for a reawakened oracle. Right now the pile of dead stones was quite sufficient, thank you very much. An oracle alive and well would be a dilemma for all. A flourishing oracle, they seemed to say, would be an insult to scientific materialism, to man's faith in man's ways.

Yet, for a few moments there I could feel and see something of what it might be like to be touched by an oracular voice.

The music gone, the shouting guardians retreated, clutching my confiscated guitar and satisfied I was only a harmless madman. I continued sitting alone on the hulking rock while the underlying rhythms of the spiritual power embedded in the place took me away again.

The landscape is heaving and sobbing with me. Generation after generation of humans, each wave overlaying the former, come to visit my consciousness. Breaking through the sadness I laugh into the sun as the massive dragon's head shifts under me in the soft earthquakes of my soul. The mountains themselves are flowing, like water washing down the flanks of gigantic living creatures, rippling folds of deep violet gauze shiver in a constantly mobile montage. I become the rocks, the mountains, the valleys, and the trees, then the earth herself, continually rearranging my flickering stability in a fall through the ages.

I'm reminded in these visions how seismically fragile the place is, how near to the edge it stands. Three earthquakes have already buried and reburied the temples over the years. It came to me then, perhaps more as a fantasy than a prediction, that there would be another earthquake sometime in the near future, and it would be this event that would allow the oracular chasm to reopen and the Oracle to be truly reawakened.

I saw old secrets being revealed, ancient treasures being thrust once again into the light: the hidden truths of history, laid out by a race of beings who have observed everything that humans have achieved over the past half a million years and who have, by nature, a deep caring and compassion for our species. I became convinced that what had once occurred here would come again, yet this time around with the wisdom of hard-won experience.

The so-called gods—the rebel midwayers—if they were to be permitted to return to join their colleagues who remained at their posts, would no longer be able to behave with such arrogant indifference to the human race. The overall planetary situation is completely different, and the human races they were originally mandated to care for have multiplied across the world. If the rebel midwayers were ever permitted to return here they would have to find new forms, new methods of contact, and gentler and more effective ways of influence if they, too, wish to play their part in the transformation of the planet.

It was in the grounds of the smaller Temple of Athena Pronaia the next move in this sequence played itself out. The compact and circular Tholos was set lower into the slopes of the mountain, about a quarter of a mile downhill from Apollo's edifice, and was a far more pleasant spot.

Melinda had collected me from my dragon's head perch midafternoon, still in a fair old state. Both legs had long since gone to sleep and crumpled under me as I heaved my body off the rock. I needed to stay still for a while and restore my equilibrium before working on my verticality. Looking back up the mountain we could catch glimpses of the broken white columns of the larger temple thrusting up through the wild hillside—surely a gesture of Apollonian dominion. The temple was, after all, built (or rebuilt) and dedicated to Apollo's victory over the great python, guardian of the shrine of the Earth Goddess. This is generally believed to be a symbol for the growing rationality of humankind, the victory of the cerebral over the visceral, of the head over the heart.

Soon enough we were reeling off down to the Temple of Athena, holding hands and me so overwhelmingly joyful I was laughing and crying at the same time. Down the pathway we wobbled and around a corner to careen helter-skelter through an untidy gaggle of German tourists, scattering them this way and that. I could read from their faces they were writing me off as retarded. So I hopped around some more and grunted a few times. I must have played the part with convincing vigor because I was able to watch their barely suppressed laughter turn into what they must have thought of as sympathetic concern before we lurched farther down the path.

At the ticket booth, the doorkeeper, noble guardian of the shrine, replaced my confiscated guitar in its canvas bag with extraordinary care and would not meet my eye. I said, "You took the music away!" How he hung his head! Whether he understood my words or not, he quite evidently got my meaning. He was the epitome of sadness and dejection.

Melinda, on him like a cat on a mouse, added "Apollo's very unhappy you took his music away; he's up there crying now. Can't you hear him?"

It was all too much for the gatekeeper. His poor head dropped even lower, looking for all the world like a man hanged by the neck until dead. Perhaps I should have read more carefully the small print on my seventy-drachma ticket. It quoted Euripides in Greek and English, and I didn't notice it until much later.

You have killed, O Dannaoi, the most learned who
never caused grief:
The Nightingale of the Muses. The very best of the
Greeks.

Now we are sitting quietly in Athena's domain, our arms around one another and in a much more peaceful and yielding spot.

The psychic strains of the events in the Temple of Apollo have disappeared. The white, shaped stones strewn all around us are gleaming in the late afternoon sun. Birds soar over the blue-hazed valley as darkness deepens into the nested folds of rock. Distant sounds of children's voices drift up on a new young breeze from the olive groves closer to the sea.

On the way down the mountainside we'd stopped to look at an ancient, split olive tree, both silently caressing the stern, living trunks and running our hands over bark rubbed smooth by the hands of countless generations. Then, feeling into the many small clefts and cavities, we wondered at its antiquity and the million minute decisions made in its writhing journey through time, admiring the color of its elegantly formed leaves and the surprising bitterness of its fruit, wincing and smiling again in the silence.

Neither of us spoke, each alone with our private thoughts. It was Melinda who broke the silence. "How about we petition for the return of the rebel midwayers? They've been off the planet for nearly two thousand years, surely they'd have learned the errors of their ways by now! And we could really do with some friendly help, couldn't we?"

The idea appealed to me immediately. It would certainly heat the game up to have a whole bunch more of these powerful invisible presences working for the transformation of life on this planet.

As we know, *The Urantia Book* maintains there is already a group of almost ten thousand of these midwayers in service to the planetary over-government. They were the ones who'd remained loyal to the Multiverse Authorities at the time of the rebellion. I imagine the responsibilities of this small group would have become stretched thin over these last couple of thousand years. The loyalist midwayers must have struggled to fulfill the duties for what was originally intended for five times their number. This would have been made all the more pressing as the human races multiplied and life in general became progressively faster and more complicated.

Petitioning is also something that *The Urantia Book* mentions.

As citizens of the Multiverse—even if we don't know or acknowledge it—we have certain rights. If we have a relevant idea or suggestion, want to help with a conflict, or wish to overturn an injustice, for example, we are encouraged to petition the Multiverse Authorities (whether or not we can perceive them) for advice or action. Three human beings in agreement are sufficient for a petition to be given consideration. If what is petitioned for comes from a heartfelt need or desire and is aligned with higher purpose, we are told there is an excellent chance the request will go through.

Were the midwayers themselves ready to return, or would they even want to? They have a number of fine attributes, yet from some of the decisions they made that are related in *The Urantia Book,* they also seem to be a little simple—emotionally immature perhaps—as one glance at the Greek myths will confirm. Surely they would have had to grow up a bit while they were away.

Given the dark times we live in, could the returned rebel midwayers be relied on to behave more responsibly? With what they now must undoubtedly know, it is hard to imagine they would be so easily led into such confusion a second time around.

What of the human races? Would we be ready?

Although it is evident that the midwayers who remained on the planet these last two thousand years elected to ensure their existence was largely kept hidden from the public eye of most cultures, I wondered if the addition of another 40,119 might blow their cover. If that happened how would our species react to the reality, the *reality* mark you, of thousands upon thousands of kick-ass invisible immortals—not to be confused with gods, mind you—who are back with us and anxious to cooperate?

Would there be those among us who would not be able to resist the temptation to worship them and treat them as gods? These are extremely powerful beings who, because they exist on a slightly higher level of vibration, are liable to stir up deep terrors in people with repressed fears. Surely a benign Creator would desire for all of creation to be joy filled and at ease with itself? Wouldn't any father or mother wish for all their children to be in harmony with one another?

The return of the rebel midwayers?

Sure. The worst that could happen would be that the petition would be denied, and the outside possibility was that we'd get a rap on the knuckles for being too pushy—but the angels have urged us all to be bold, so why not?

Then, as we sat there in this beautiful little temple a sense of supreme happiness spread over both of us. Melinda and I solemnly shook hands on the deal, hugged each other, and went off to find our third person.

7

The Plight of the Rebel Midwayers

Cosmic Consciousness, Telepathic Influences, and the Plight of the Rebel Midwayers

Giorgias looked as if he was expecting us when we arrived at his place the next day. It was still early in the evening, yet he simply closed and locked the doors after we'd had a simple meal. Then the three of us tramped off together down the hill once again to find a conducive spot among the old stones of Delphi to transmit our petition.

Once we found our place and made ourselves comfortable on the ground I suggested my companion do the talking. She laid out a brief history of the midwayers as we knew it, threading it together with the insights we were given by the angels in Toronto and the assurance that the rebellion, which had so influenced our world, has finally been adjudicated. We talked about the Universe Circuits opening up again and what this would mean to us as our planet swung back into "normalcy" (as the angels had called it) over the next twenty to thirty years. We passed on what the angels have told us about not expecting the planetary situation to clear up overnight; that first we would see a massive global cleansing as the corruption, pollution, and negativity rose to the surface of the world body and mind to be released; and that we would see these profound upheavals primarily in those areas most corrupted by power and influence.

Finally, however tenuous the world situation might become, we told him that we should always remember this is a much loved little planet. Whatever Earth changes and general tumult will result from these coming transformations, if we remain aligned with our higher purpose, we will be cared for and protected. If we hold to the path of truth as we know it intuitively, then we will always find ourselves in the right place at the right time.

Giorgias listened intently throughout the telling of the story, and I could see that something in it appealed directly to his unspoken interests. After Melinda had finished with an impassioned invitation to join us in petitioning for the return of the rebel midwayers, he broke out in an enormous grin—the first real smile I'd seen on him over the days we'd known him.

After a few remarkably intelligent questions, which demonstrated he understood what we were asking of him, Giorgias gave the whole idea his vigorous approval. It evidently ignited an underlying sense of recognition in him, which both of us took to mean that it was no coincidence we had been guided to his door.

Although Delphi presented us with a wide range of further possibilities, we both felt intuitively our work there was complete. Even though we'd identified the strange sense of lack we'd been feeling throughout our time in Greece, it still remained a disagreeable reality. Something was definitely luring us on; our feet itched for sandy beaches and the smell of the sea again.

Such were our thoughts when, in among all the involvement with the midwayers, the next stage in the dolphin trail plopped down in front of me. One of the details Giorgias had relayed to us when he heard our saga was a popular local story, perhaps based on a Greek myth. This told how Apollo came to Delphi from the Mediterranean island of Crete after having been thrown off a ship—presumably in human form. He had then transformed himself into a dolphin and had swum into the Gulf of Corinth.

Apollo then changed himself back from a dolphin to make his home up in the mountains in what was already an ancient holy place. Giorgias also wanted to make sure we knew how much the ancient Greeks revered dolphins, that they were widely known at the time to be intelligent and compassionate beings. He assured us it was not at all unusual for humans in those days to have formed close loving bonds with individual dolphins.

Of course, this simple factor raised a most intriguing possibility. Were we being shown in the course of these experiences in Delphi that the midwayers were connected in some intimate way with the dolphins—the original launching point for all my recent explorations?

I've wondered about this connection before. Since I've chosen to use the full range of my physical and emotional sensorium as a sounding board in the course of these encounters with spiritual intelligences, I've found my subtle reactions to both cetaceans and midwayers are often remarkably similar. The two species are, after all, indigenous to the planet, and both clearly possess considerable intelligence. This intelligence seems to be so sufficiently different from ours as to seem thoroughly elusive. Both species also have a long history of survival in a medium somewhat more fluid than terra firma.

I suggest, too, since both midwayers and cetaceans may enjoy wider fields of individual consciousness than humans, that these faculties may well allow them greater access to telepathic and spiritual contact. I needed to take into account the behavior of the captive dolphins back at the Britannia Beach Hotel in Nassau at the start of my dolphin trail. For all their quite evident intelligence they would suddenly, and often unaccountably, start to display an astonishing degree of what can only be called emotional immaturity.

Over the weeks I was there studying them at the hotel—and I've noticed it subsequently with other captive dolphins—I saw many flashes of anger, envy, jealousy, and the kind of sulking you see in spoiled children. Any dolphin trainer will tell you how emotionally skittish their charges can become. It puzzled me at the time. How could creatures I intuitively felt possessed such a fine intelligence behave in what appeared to be such an emotionally undeveloped manner?

If we are to give credence to the Greek myths as honest and realistic attempts by humans of the time to describe the doings of the midwayers, much as perhaps we might describe the lifestyles of Hollywood stars in fanzines, we can get a glimpse into the troubled world of these unfortunate creatures. Having made their choice to side with the rebellion and finding most likely to their horror that their world had been cut off and isolated from the general star routes, the midwayers would have watched their parents, the staff, die while they lived endlessly on, falling deeper and deeper into the denser frequencies of human emotions as they struggled to keep control of their human charges.

Their decision to appear as gods to the bewildered humans, their demands for worship and devotion, their ceaseless enmities, their cruelties, their philandering and infidelities, and their self-absorption and delusions of grandeur, all betray an immature level of consciousness. Reading the myths I find myself asking just what these purportedly divine or semi-divine beings actually did for a living when they weren't swanning around trying to impress one another. How on earth did they justify their lives, and why they were here? What was their function, their niche in the spiritual ecology of the planet?

Why is it when we are told there were a total of over forty thousand midwayers who gave their allegiance to Caligastia, *The Urantia Book* mentions only relatively few of their number? Are we just reading about the activities of one clan of midwayers? Were the pantheons of the Babylonians and the Egyptians simply other small clans among this far greater number? And finally, given the often cavalier attitudes these supposed gods have shown toward humanity, could it have been just this sort of out of control immaturity that caused the final downfall of so many of the antediluvian cultures?

At this point I'd no wish to speculate further, having figured out by this time that the midwayers would reveal more of their true nature when *they* were ready. I knew if I was able to frame the relevant questions, they would most likely then reply in their own ways and in their own time. Besides, it was enough to learn that Apollo was reputed to have come over from Crete to remind us in our associative Multiverse that Crete needed to be the next port of call in our journey through the Old Ways.

We made the intuitive, but somewhat curious, decision to arrive at Hania, at the eastern end of Crete—curious because we really had no idea why we chose it. There were two ferries leaving Piraeus at the same time, one to Hania and the other to Heraklion, Crete's capital city.

Knossos, the only place whose reputation we knew about, was just outside Heraklion, so it didn't make much sense going to Hania. Yet here we were on the interisland ferry chugging toward Hania. Perhaps it was Mich. His presence was gradually getting less tenuous. Mich's influence was always subtle, never controlling, and although neither Melinda nor I had any direct perception of our "continental guide," as we'd started to call him, we were beginning to understand a little of how he functioned. He never covertly influenced our actions unless we consciously and verbally turned matters over to him for immediate guidance. Yet he certainly seemed to smooth the way ahead if that was the direction in which he wished us to go.

I did not take to Crete immediately. Hania has the same touristed-out quality we saw on the mainland, a certain seediness that comes from catering to large and careless transient groups. Arriving in a light rain, we wondered whether we were seeing another historical irony in action: the tourist hordes overrunning contemporary Greece much as the barbarian hordes had a couple of thousand years earlier. The results were looking sadly similar.

Then again, renting a car was curious too, after all the ranting I'd done about low-grade diesel and gasoline fumes and the automobile as albatross of the modern world. Yet noble sentiments aside, renting a car felt right. My scruples needed scrapping. I doubt whether we'd ever have gotten off the miserable southern coast if we relied on the erratic public transport system.

Driving in Crete has its own breakneck charm. Macho is the name of the game, and there has to be a great deal of natural telepathy involved. The general idea seems to be to drive as fast as possible straight at oncoming cars, both drivers claiming the relatively smooth center of the road. The first person to crack has to swerve to the side into the potholes and busted tarmac. This is where Mich must have been working some mighty mojo for us because throughout our time on Crete we barely had one close call. I became so absorbed for a time in the challenges offered that I must have put him to a grueling test.

The Canyon of Samaria had attracted us both back on the boat from Piraeus, bending over the swaying map and wondering once again why we'd plumped for Hania. Billed as the longest canyon in Europe, it was stuck up there in the wilds of the northeastern coast, isolated and tempting, the sole habitat, or so we read, of the Cretan chamois, the *Kri-Kri,* goat of goats.

That first afternoon we were drawn across the island sure enough—anything to get out of the constant hustle of the populated coastline—but it was not to Samaria. I suspect I may have missed the turn back there somewhere in among letting the car find its own way and the mad-dog rushes of Cretan driving.

The road meandered through orange groves, the air heavy with the scents of a late summer afternoon, before heading up into the dry, dusty mountains. Strange fruit, wild berries we'd never seen before, grew among the grapevines and olive trees bordering the road. There were also laurel-like bushes, heavy with bright orange golf balls—a cross between a strawberry and a lichee, seedy but delicious—and chestnuts, and grass that tasted of anise. We happily stopped the car at every vegetative provocation and grazed until we'd eaten our fill before moving on to the next place.

Soon, the weather began to cloud over, and we hurried on to the tiny village of Pellora. It must have been the runner-up to Manfredonia in the end-of-the-tracks stakes. It was permeated with a sense of nowhere. The church, with its broken windows, was soundly locked, and the few homes were shuttered and quiet. It was the end of the line.

Over the village hung a castle, by now a somewhat familiar sight. We climbed the steep, stepped, earth path and emerged out onto the plateau that formed the main keep.

Silence.

Sitting on the old masonry wall I watched the powder-blue waves washing up on the curved, sandy beach below. I was still feeling a trifle attenuated after the powerful psychic overlays of Delphi and now found myself even more depressed by a nagging sense that we had indeed come to the wrong end of the island. O me of little faith! Perhaps as a result of this oversensitivity I soon discovered I'd opened myself up inadvertently to wholly other waves of turbulence, this time coming from the place itself. The cycles of invasions, the doubts and fears of the defenders, all the concerns and worries such formidable fortifications suggest, the cruelty and butchery that hung in the air imprinted on the spirit of the place, the blood that had flowed over these old stones—all this seemed to wash over me. It became more and more atmospherically depressing, my own doubts about irrational decisions and spiritual red herrings welling up in me to join the unhappiness of the place itself.

It was then it dawned on me, still in a mental fog, that here was yet one more of those spots from which the crusaders must have embarked. Without realizing it we had driven straight to another of these hellish locations. Whether the crusaders, those faith-driven fanatics, were the cause of the psychic misery spreading out from these places, or whether they merely contributed to far older cycles of violence, I was in no condition to work out.

I schlumped around the keep, picking up small rocks and throwing them down again. Perhaps I could use a shard of pottery, a tooled stone, or even a piece of discarded metalwork to open up my psychometric receivers. After all, an Italian count had once given me an Alfa Romeo saloon car (admittedly it was on its last legs, but it got me from Rome to Paris) for accurately psychometrizing his grandmother's brooch.

Maybe he just wanted to get rid of the car, I thought in my addled brain, because all I was getting from the castle was a jangling, nerve-stripping psychic barrage, nothing specific enough to be able to release. Weighed down by the place and far from feeling on my spiritual toes, I was walking dejectedly across the spiny scrub when a voice spoke, clearly and deliberately, in my head. A male voice (that didn't sound like mine) said: "The answer you seek you will find in Omalos."

Then the barrage started again.

I have to admit I was astonished. The voice could not have been clearer if it had come from someone standing right next to me. It wasn't threatening in any way. In fact, it was rather flat and disinterested, as if it was just delivering the obvious.

There was a considerable difference between what I've experienced in my telepathic encounters with dolphins and this actual voice in my head. With the dolphins, communication tended toward the visual, together with what I've described elsewhere as thought-clusters, visual gestalts of information, yet never anything I would describe as a voice in my head.

I've had a few occasions, as well, when I have slipped into fourth dimensional awareness and have "overheard" casual conversations between people many miles away. These I've come to regard as freak events, perhaps some sort of momentary dilation of the earth's electromagnetic field, and I don't take them too seriously.

I've also done my stint with automatic writing, yet that was different, too. This voice was so precise, so quietly self-possessed, and it was such an uncharacteristic thing to happen to me that I promptly pushed it to one side when all the doubts and fears came flooding back in again.

The depression, which increased with the now-insistent rain, felt almost impossible to throw off. It pursued me along the narrow, jerky road back south—the very same road we had come up, grazing along the way, to reach Pellora in the first place. Some planning, I thought, wanting to blame Mich for taking us to a place from which there was only one road out, and that was the one by which we arrived. Some scenic tour guide!

It was still our intention to try to get to the Canyon of Samaria that same evening by cutting through the secondary tracks. We could see from the map that tiny roads wound up through the mountains to Omalos, at the mouth of the gorge. Having set out on the smaller roads we soon discovered this was going to be a hazardous drive indeed, even in good weather. By this time we'd picked up a couple of rural Cretan woman and didn't have the heart to drop them off in the rain short of their village. We slid on, the mud of the unmade road clinging to our wheels.

And the rain! Another bone of contention. It'd been beautifully sunny all day—in fact, it had been sunny every day since northern Italy—and now, when we were getting bogged down in the mire, it wouldn't stop raining. My grumbling discontent was somewhat lifted by the joy with which our two ladies in the back were greeting the downpour. It was the first rain they'd seen in about six months. We soon joined them in their squeals of pleasure.

They also strongly discouraged us, if we understood them correctly, from trying to make it up through the mountains on such a night. I was secretly relieved at hearing this since I was having misgivings myself as to whether we could really navigate the maze of dirt roads, with every possibility of the tracks being washed out by the storm. I also reckoned that I was in no fit state for whatever it was we were going to find in Omalos and discovering what that "voice" might have meant.

Having taken care of our two villagers, it felt prudent to follow their advice and to drive back to the overrun coast road and then turn back up to the canyon by a hopefully more sedate route. It was becoming a long evening. It was cold, wet, and dark, and our nerves were becoming deep-fried in the fat of Cretan road craft. Headlights, seldom dipped, blasted photons into our tired eyes, refracting off the arcs of dirt the wipers couldn't reach. We were both bent forward, peering into the night, when there, on a particularly deserted stretch of highway and opposite an island that we could see rearing out of the stormy, gray swell, stood the Dolphin Hotel.

Improbable, right? It might even have been a sign. Of course, we didn't get any nearer to real dolphins than the two swimming up the hotel lobby wall, plaster facsimiles of those in the queen's chamber at Knossos. At least it stopped me from blundering on to Omalos in a thoroughly disgruntled state of mind. It was a rotten cold night. We slept fitfully in each other's arms with the wind rattling down the corridors of our virtually deserted hotel. I awoke intermittently to see broad flares of lightning crackling into the sea beyond the coast road, momentarily floodlighting the crouched mass of the island. The rain beat down unremittingly. Lying awake under the thin blanket, trying to warm myself against Melinda's hot little sleeping body, I found my doubts were marshaled into battalions and were tramping through my imagination.

Before we went to sleep we'd made a bargain with the elements: If the rain were to persist then we would dump the idea of the canyon and head up the coast road for the long drive to Heraklion and Knossos. If indeed we needed to go to Omalos then the weather would have to do an about-face.

Finally, I managed to get a few hours of dreamless sleep.

The weather the next day, predictably, was neither fair nor foul, placing the decision as to where to go firmly back on us. Fortunately, as it was to turn out, by the time we finished our breakfast my enthusiasm for Omalos returned.

I remembered again the voice in my head, so clear and unexpected. My rational mind, preoccupied as it was with trying to maintain some semblance of balance amid the psychic barrage, must have simply shoved the fact of the voice down, beneath the level of my conscious awareness. Even now, as we sat eating what was euphemistically called a "continental breakfast," my mind still wanted to dismiss the voice as my imagination. I thought it would be crazy to get my hopes up. Besides, what *was* it I was seeking, anyway? The voice seemed more knowing about this than I was.

Faith won out, however, and amid overhung lazy clouds we set off into the mountains for the great Canyon of Samaria—the longest, craggiest, and reputed to be the most beautiful gorge in Europe.

The road climbed up, more steeply than the one we had taken the day before, the heavy scents from the new rain swirling around us. The road rippled past precipitous lips, the sheer drops falling away into clouds and mists. Halfway to Omalos the sun burst through. We were to have a circle of blue sky over our heads until the moment we left the canyon.

Feasting, as yesterday, on wild things, we found newly plumped-out blackberries, ur-blackberries we thought them since they only had half a dozen bulbous black segments bursting with juice. We saw no *kemura,* the orange golf balls of the previous days grazing—our Cretan ladies had told us the name and that they were most prized—from which we deduced that the fruit was probably very local.

We stopped for a glass of Turkish coffee at a small village, just ten or twelve neat stone buildings straddling the road. The owner, a young woman with a seraphic smile, plied us with sweet local grapes and chestnuts, while we opened up and shared our little stock of kemura to her obvious delight. Lulled and softened up by the rhythms of rural life, we idly watched five men doing the work of one as they slowly and systematically papered a timber post with insect repellant. Half an hour later, a good day's work done, they ambled off in their different directions. Time, too, for us to drag ourselves away.

The last few miles doglegged upward, the progressively ill-kept road pulling itself up and over the ring of mountains surrounding and containing the plateau of Omalos. It was a stunning moment when the road tipped over the edge and onto an entirely flat, circular plateau. I guessed it was once the perfect cone of a volcano that had become more recently a lake bed. The water must have drained out through a maze of underground caves and streams because there were no breaks in the circular rim of the plateau.

Nothing appeared to grow there save short, wiry scrub bushes. We found ourselves overcome by the strongest feeling of containment and security. Evidently it was a sacred place. A great place for a landing, I thought, before discovering later it was where Zeus reputedly liked to set down his fiery chariot. A sheer peak soared over us, glistening in the sun and luring us by its dominating presence across the open space and toward the opening to the gorge. As we neared the rim we could see a ragged trail dropping down in a series of wild switchbacks into the great canyon.

It was at that point, as near as I can discern, the strangest of feelings enveloped me. It was an ineffable, and quite unaccountable, feeling of peace accompanied by a shimmering sense of a vast stillness spreading over everything I could see. Not only was all of nature one united whole, but I also felt myself finally to be fully part of that whole. Every branch of each tree, every rock and stone, the single screeching cry of an eagle, the murmur of distant water—all and everything became part of one still vaster being, as though all reality were suspended in golden jelly, every part completely responsive to every other part.

It is not a word moment. We silently separate, going our different ways. yet closer still in the sharing of the inexpressible calm.

I choose to plunge down into the chasm, by this time laughing and crying in joy, burbling happily into the face of the sun.

I know in my heart, as I throw myself heedlessly down the trail, that I have come to my place of contentment and knowledge.

The voice of yesterday indeed speaks the truth.

I am no longer observer.

I am entwined irrevocably with the nature surrounding me.

I have no way of knowing where I end and the rest of nature begins. My calls and gestures are answered by the birds in their sounds and swooping dives.

Small animals appear where my gaze falls.

A light wind funnels up the valley, rustling through the high groves of cypress. The subtlest of rhythms and cross-rhythms resonate between us; the birds, the animals, the rocks, and the wind in the trees are all one enormous reciprocal organism, throbbing and moving in its own hidden dance.

Delphi is just a prelude to this, I think. Here is no sadness; nothing is missing. Every level of experience is complete and joyous.

My feet are still leading me down the steep path when the sight of a sinuous, blackened, reptilian body, lying in the sun over one of the rock bluffs stops me in my tracks. It takes me a few moments before I realize it isn't a prehistoric creature, but a burned-black simulacrum carved by the ages from the gnarled roots of an ancient olive tree.

As I settle down to draw it the information starts rolling in.

Yes, the midwayers have been here; indeed this valley was one of their final homes. Midwayers of every persuasion have loved the great Gorge of Samaria, this home of theirs, so far from the increasingly complex machinations of the human race. The feelings surge in: a profound weariness, an ennui of the eons, and great regrets. The midwayers, too, have been through their own hells.

For me, however, the misery is brief. The beauty of the valley quickly chases away the primal shadows. I know now in my heart it is the midwayers who have led us here. Never coercive, always allowing us the maximum degree of personal choice, yet nevertheless it is they who have brought us here. More significantly, I realize this is a clear sign of their desire to be better known and understood.

Bathing in this understanding, I see that like Delphi, the midwayers have left their signatures in the very structure of the landscape. The long-term presence of these entities has shaped and formed the rocks, mountains, and valleys.

In an unexpected insight I realize this is a landscape onto which they have projected their stories. In these moments of spiritual clarity I know the midwayers have embedded their five-hundred-thousand-year history in the vision before me—gigantic hieroglyphs molded by their vibrations into the sheer rock wall of the gorge.

If ever I might wish for some sort of record of that long and unfortunate history, here it is. The high cliff walls of the gorge, pocked with fissures and weathered ledges and furrowed with deep crevasses, appear to glow with deeper meaning. I feel in these glorious moments I can almost read what the massive hieroglyphs are saying; I can sense something of significance pouring off the cliff face.

My drawing as complete as it will ever be, I drop a little farther down into the valley before coming to rest in the cooler air of the shadows. I know there is a lifetime of study here, of music and spiritual archaeology, of intellectual and artistic challenges, of walks and rambles on the winding trails. It is a lifetime of loving contact with the midwayers, these strange and wonderful new friends.

It's becoming too much. I feel I need to get out. One more step downward and I will be drawn irretrievably into its golden web. I turn to climb back and there, ten feet away and rearing up over me, is an enormous, rocky head. This one is such a superb simulacrum, with large eyes looking back at me from grassy sockets and the high ridge of a forehead, that I am shocked.

Involuntarily, I blurt out, "Hello!

"Hello," it replies, in much the same male voice I heard the day before.

We stare at each other across the abyss of our differing realities, and before I can react, the voice rolls on. I climb up onto a nearby rock and pull my journal open. I know the massive, granite head is merely a screen, something I can keep my rational mind focused on while the easy, confident voice continues.

"You have learned much since you started this journey."

I agree. It went deeper than I was able to know. The voice goes on, this time slower, at dictation speed. It's a humorous voice, yet quietly authoritative.

"Most of all, you have learned to be quiet inside. Understand that this is a permanent condition now. You can lapse back into secondary consciousness, but you will always be able to find your way back.

"You are also now telepathically linked with a network. You can talk with them on the inner planes by merely summoning their names, although rest assured there is always choice as whether to answer or not. It is fourth dimensional network of the heart and cannot be abused. It is not possible to use it for purely selfish ends because its movements are governed by the Supreme Circuit."

And, in spite of the wonder of the moment, I doubt, once again, that this can really be happening. The voice, loud and clear, is telling me things I've never heard before. Goodness knows, it feels real enough, my back against a tree, my journal solidly on my knees, the pen in my hand. Yet, still I wonder, is all this happening in my imagination?

The voice speaks again, reading my thoughts, and this time it seems to come from a deeper place, between my throat and heart.

"It can always be your imagination. We contact people through their imaginations."

When the simplicity of this hits me I laugh out aloud. Already somewhat oversensitized by the unified field in which I find myself, I am soon sobbing with the joy of it, and the humor and beauty. It is such a superb fail-safe, a secret that would keep itself, a contact that can only happen to those who are prepared to *imagine* it.

The voice continued from where it had left off earlier, before my silly doubts interrupted it.

"These networks have been growing in number and closeness, coordinated in the deep mind and in dreams. Beings in these networks will sometimes share dreams, and one of the most powerful of these dreams is that the overall matrix might start drawing together.

"As more of you realize the depth of this movement of the spirit and see that it truly represents the best work of humans and angels, so will you see the spiritual transformation of the planet and, piece by piece, the emergence of the Living God in your midst.

"This will also mark the start of a new perception of the Deity on this world, a knowing of God as best friend, as being in each heart. Therefore, look to the quiet places, in nature, and by yourself. Allow the din of civilization to die away and talk in your heart to your closest Friend."

I need to pause for a moment, just to gather my wits together, take a few deep breaths, and wriggle myself more comfortably into the tree against which I'm propped. When the voice starts again it seems to take on a slightly different tone, as if speaking more to an audience.

"It has been a complicated journey for all. Many of you will have been prepared for these times. In your interests, in your reading and thinking, and in your hearts' whispers you will have gathered some understanding of the acceleration of consciousness now under way.

"This is a very wide-ranging plan in which each personality is a discrete entity, having a particular part to play. You will find the direction this leads you will be that of joy, fun, service, and spiritual and mental illumination.

"We have long thought to extend ourselves through such a work as this, but the timing has been premature. With the final adjudication of the rebellion behind us we can now press on.

"If you have been drawn to this area of interest, it indicates to us you have shown an open-minded curiosity about the invisible world. Many of you will doubtless have made contact with spiritual entities before, but these messages have a particular purpose to them. They will act as an introduction to your planetary cohabitants, the midway creatures."

There followed some advice as to how others might make this connection.

"The more emotionally quiet and casual you can be, the easier it is for both of us. You are perfectly safe, and there is no cause for any concern. Just relax and make yourself physically comfortable. Use any of your customary meditation or visualization exercises and focus on keeping your breathing deep and steady.

"When you close your eyes, listen into your upper chest area, between your throat and your heart, and you will hear a voice that will greet you by name.

"Because we are here and we can do this does not make us gods or anything more special than you. We are just different life forms who happen to share the same planet. Recent changes in the spiritual administration of the universe have opened up new doorways of contact between our species.

"If you wish to start a long and fruitful relationship with a personality not of your own species, then we too will do everything in our power to maintain our end of the connection. On the other hand, if at any time you wish to discontinue the experiment, we will leave immediately upon request.

"We are always available to be contacted at these early, key stages in the transformation. As you grow in confidence and are able to hold longer contact periods, you will start to sense our presence in more ways than the merely telepathic.

"You are all very important to those of our race because within you we can see burning a spark of the Creator of us all. It is our very great pleasure and privilege to know and be known by you."

The voice came to a natural stop.

I recall thinking that if this were just a mental projection I would be able to make the voice continue. I couldn't. I checked myself. I didn't want to get too analytical; it was rare enough when something like this happened. I didn't want to blur the reality of it by thinking too hard about it. That could come later.

After I'd finished writing and clambered down from the rock on wobbly legs, I made as courteous a bow to the rock simulacrum as I could manage and made my way back up the narrow path. When I reached the top of the gorge and stepped back onto the circular plateau, it came to me in the light of what I had just experienced that the local's reference to the plateau as Zeus's landing ground carried a profound resonance.

Our boat for Israel was due to leave from Heraklion a couple of days later, so it was back onto the coast road again to arrive in the city in another rainstorm. The next day the weather cleared, and we decided to follow our intuition, which meant allowing Mich to guide our feet—and guide them he did, to the Heraklion Archaeological Museum.

Now, I'm somewhat allergic to museums in general. I don't enjoy being in them, my legs and feet hurt, and I'm empathic enough to all too easily feel the deadening weight of the past. I avoid going to them, and if I do, I find myself quickly tired and wanting leave. I didn't feel that way in this case, although the place was not unlike other museums: all hard surfaces and echoing vaults, this one filled with Minoan artifacts.

It wasn't the exquisite little figure of the Bull Leaper or the enigmatic Phaistos Disc, with its hints of an archaic and unknown language and its implication of moveable type, that Mich was guiding us to. He seemed to be urging us on deeper into the museum. He drew us finally to a halt in a room with low tables. Moving closer we could see they were glassed-topped cabinets filled with fragments of clay and a number of small cylinders made of different colored stones.

Plate 1. *Animus Mundi: The Return of the Prince*

Plate 2. *From Jericho to Cairo*

Plate 3.
*Glastonbury
and the Angel
of Peace*

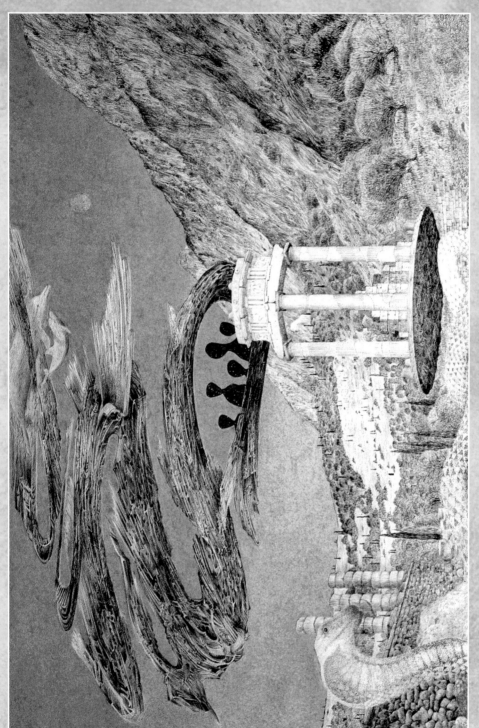

Plate 4. *The Reawakened Delphic Oracle*

Plate 5.
*Stonehenge:
1984 The Return
of the Caducean
Emerald*

Plate 6. *The Arrival of Quetzalcoatl in New York City*

Plate 7. The Verdants' secret city as I imagined it to be in the foothills of the Manzano Mountains in New Mexico

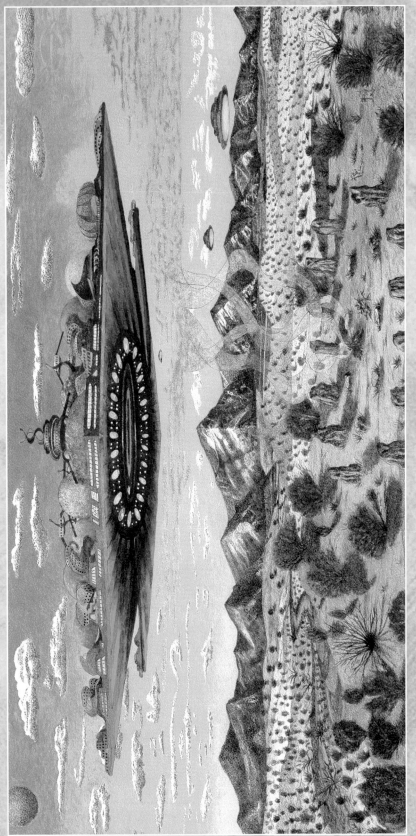

Plate 8. My own conception of the mile-long Arcturian mothership docked in the fifth dimension over New Mexico's Manzano Mountains

Cylinder seals appear in ancient Near Eastern cultures and were evidently used to imprint the identity of the seal holder in soft clay. In some cases they became the precursor of hieroglyphic writing, but that didn't seem to be what Mich was hinting at.

We both pulled out our sketchbooks simultaneously. Drawing an object requires an unusual level of consciousness. Not only does one have to look with great care, but drawing also has the additional advantage of stilling the mind.

Here I can't quote verbatim what I heard while I was drawing, but as I looked more carefully at the cylinders, it was obvious there was a wide variety of extremely unlikely symbols etched into them. They were all meticulously carved, some with tiny human forms incised so precisely as to leave no doubt at the skill of the artist, which made it all the more surprising when I examined and drew the more idiosyncratic seals, to find just as exquisitely carved a hermaphroditic winged figure, a variety of winged goats, a man's face with what appeared to be a flying saucer, and creatures, many of them with wings and strange faces, half-bird and half-man.

Mich was nudging me; there was something here he wanted me to really understand.

Then, I got it!

Some of the cylinder seals, but not all of them by any means, symbolized a far deeper claim of identity. Mich wanted me to know this was an era when the midwayers were exerting their influence more openly in the world. Not only were some masquerading as the gods of the ancient pantheons, but others were also supporting chosen bloodlines. The symbols on the seals he was drawing my attention to had been used by the great trading families and the clans who were working with individual midwayers. People had intense relationships, in a way we moderns can't start to appreciate, with those entities they might have thought of as their household gods.

Then I *knew* why it was that Mich was showing me this.

We'd only recently petitioned the Most Highs for the return of the more than forty thousand rebel midwayers who have been away from the planet these past two millennia. We had somewhat cavalierly asked for them back, trusting that if it wasn't meant to happen, the Most

Highs would have rejected the petition. At this stage we didn't know whether they'd accepted it or not—and we wouldn't know until some weeks later.

However, what Mich was making clear was that if the midwayers were to be returned, they would be working with individuals and groups who are aligning themselves with their highest purpose and are committed to co-creating the New Reality.

8

The Challenges
of Empathy

Negative Thoughtforms, the Challenge of
Empathy, and the Return of the Beings
of the Violet Flame

I liked Israel in the first brief time Melinda and I were there on the way to the Conference-in-Spirit in Egypt. Apart from its sacred aspects, there was a down-to-earth, reality-orientated feeling to the country in the early 1980s and a vigor to the people we'd not seen in our journey through the Old Ways.

Paradoxically, I felt that Israel would allow me the desired mixture of spirituality and groundedness to settle into writing the first book in this series, *Dolphins, ETs & Angels*. This time Melinda's parents had organized a perfect space for us to rent for the six months we'd be in the country. It was right on the southwest corner of the southernmost and final block of apartments in the seaside town of Netanya, close to where we stayed before, and this time on the sixth floor overlooking the somnolent waves of the eastern Mediterranean.

After the stimulating journey south, I hoped I would be able to spend my time in Israel quietly enough to produce a book at the end of it. I had a relatively clear picture of how the book would shape up, but my recent encounters with the midwayers had rattled my bones. It was all so new, this contact with entities invisible to my eyes, yet all too present to my feelings. I feared it might throw me off my basic themes for the book. How would I start to explain the presence of yet another intelligent species? I wanted to focus the first book on my personal encounters and experiences with dolphins, extraterrestrials, and the astonishing transmissions from the angels in Toronto. That was going to be quite mind-expanding enough.

Most of all, I needed some peace and quiet.

Of course, that was just me trying to impose my expectations on what was bound to be a complicated situation. It was Israel, after all, and although this was a relatively peaceful interlude in 1983 and '84, the undercurrents of violence were discernible in the emotional realm, suppressed (for now) by a physically controlling state apparatus and a torrent of state-sponsored propaganda.

Yet, for all the turbulence roiling under the surface there was a sweetness and an innocence to the smiles that greeted us, almost entirely from young Arab males. We'd watched a clutch of Jewish Israeli tourists on the boat from Crete to Haifa, sticking close to one another as usual. There were almost a dozen black-shirted (silk), black-jowled, black-eyed, aging young men in extra-tight pants (black), with the start of beer bellies hanging over their black leather belts. They loved shouting at one another as if they were still on the top of tanks. They were boys who'd been forced to grow up too fast, who'd seen too much, all protesting their jollity with a tad too much enthusiasm. One black-garbed warrior who had ambled over to join the group was sitting with his wife, or girlfriend more likely, and as he squeezed in beside her, he threw a large arm covered in black fur around her shoulder, a lolling hand cupping her breast.

Coming from another culture, I found the innocence of this claiming, and the ready acceptance with which it was received, rather surprising. I'd have imagined Israeli girls, with their conscript experience behind them, would be less eager to be so casually possessed. However, as I came to know the people better, I was able to understand something of the contradictory convolutions of cultural influences mixing and colliding in this one small country.

The enormous influx of North African Jews brought with them a profoundly different worldview when they immigrated to what was essentially a northern European territorial creation. I came to see the continuing ramifications of this cultural collision was contributing to a constant state of nervousness, bordering on paranoia, that seemed to lay over the land.

It was clear a terrible frustration was building on both sides with the continuing lack of resolution to the Palestinian/Israeli stalemate. Although this was fomenting under the surface during the six months we were living there, it soon became the emotional fuel for the despair and hatred that exploded into the First Intifada half a dozen years later.

To my joy (and amazement) I found this prevalent state of mind among many we talked to paradoxically supportive of writing from the heart. As I meditated prior to writing I could package all the emotional turmoil I was picking up, both from the general psychic atmosphere as well as the more immediate stresses in my personal life. I could effectively release them as thoughtforms back to the earth. I'd been shown how to do this by Ray Bret Koch at the start of this journey.

Looking out from my sixth-floor study window, an endless stretch of sandy scrubland disappeared into the distant sea mist, cut through only by the black strip of road south to Tel Aviv. When it was clear at night I could just see a vague haze of light hanging over the city.

There didn't appear to be any houses along the coastline south of Netanya, or any signs of habitation. It was a desolate area with a few weather-beaten trees crouched into shallow valleys only half-protected from the constant wind that corrugated the dunes and kept the sea grass in constant movement. The trees could look like specters in the half-light of early evening. The setting sun turned the sea mist pink initially, then into the deepest maroon and shades of purple, before fading through to lavender and darkening into indigo and violet.

Since we had arrived late in the year, the view outside the window was constantly changing throughout the winter months. Sometimes an entire climatic cycle moved from broad sunshine to an intense storm, back to sunshine, and then to storm again, all within an hour. Storm clouds ripped across the heaving sky, a bright red sun peering out between them, fanning brilliant swathes of Jesus-rays over the white-chopped sea. Minutes later the muddied clouds cleared away, and a sunset of every shade of violet-rose lay across the western sky.

As I relaxed deeper into the creative process I found the constantly changing montage of color and weather conditions, as well as the white noise of the waves breaking on the long sandy beach, conducive to the light-trance state of consciousness I prefer to be in when writing a first draft.

Yet, even as writing was occupying my full attention, both Melinda and I could feel our new midwayer friends dancing around the edges of our awareness. Mich was definitely there, we knew his vibe, yet there was also a vivid sense of the presence of others of his kind. Thoughtful as ever, the midwayers never thrust themselves at us, but even the idea that invisible beings were there, perhaps even looking over my shoulder as I wrote, became an impossible distraction. It was thrilling, of course, and exciting and shocking. I felt privileged. However, in the next moment I felt I might be going crazy. I was too self-conscious; it's challenging enough to write honestly from the heart without feeling someone is peering over one's shoulder. After a couple of weeks of struggling with my mental conflict it became resolved one clear bright morning.

I like to write the first draft of my books and articles in longhand, aiming always for that subtle state of consciousness in which it seems as though the truth is leaking out of the nib of my pen. Not being a touch-typist, I can slip more easily into the "zone" when writing becomes mildly automatic, the flow sweeping the words along, when I don't have to think where each letter is on the keyboard.

It was when I was in this open state one bright morning that the writing suddenly changed its voice. I knew it was our midwayer, Mich, guiding my hand. Then, I heard very clearly that I was being required to make a decision. I remember the words to this day.

"You have the choice," Mich's deep voice resonated in my throat chakra. "You can either choose to take dictation from us. . . ," and I realized that was what I was doing when the automatic writing took over. "Or, you can decide to work collaboratively with us."

Although I enjoyed "taking dictation," it was easy and fluid and good for some purposes, the decision to work in collaboration with angels felt far more appealing. I'd received *The Helianx Proposition* several years earlier, in 1979, in one unbroken stretch of automatic writing, but at that stage I was still an innocent and hadn't thought to ask where the narrative came from. Besides, I knew how to do automatic writing. Actually consciously collaborating with angels was going to be something entirely different. Something new.

I don't recall any further details of that conversation with Mich, but from then on I experienced a profound shift in viewpoint. I no longer tranced out, saving that subtle state of consciousness for my graphic work. I considered and chose every word and concept for myself, all the while keeping an awareness of the intimate presence of the angel with whom I was working at any one time.

This collaborative relationship was to develop over the course of writing my books and as I've become gradually more sensitized to the angels' approval. A shiver of spiritual pleasure and a lovely sense of well-being and emotional warmth creeps up my spine when I've written a concept or sentence that meets the angel's agreement.

The population of Netanya in the early 1980s was almost entirely Jewish. I doubt if it's changed much over the years in that regard. Perhaps there are just more buildings, crowded shops, and from a photograph on Wikipedia, even a couple of thirty-three-story high-rises completed in 2005.

Perhaps it was my blue eyes, pale skin, and long white hair, but it was impossible not to notice the odd looks I'd get when out in public. Twisted smiles that could have been sneers; girls' snatching glances before turning away in fits of giggles; lines of young men walking five abreast, nudging each other and whispering loudly in Hebrew; others waving both hands in the air and shaking their heads around, letting their features go slack and their eyes pop wide open as if they were slightly crazy.

How could I not make a silly face back? This simply generated more laughter, and I'd walk on as puzzled as ever. When some four- and five-year-old kids came across me rounding the end of a supermarket aisle and ran off screaming and giggling, it just became plain old irritating. I wanted to get out of Netanya and visit somewhere more Palestinian.

It wasn't until we'd driven to Sebastia, in Samaria (another Samaria!) that I felt I'd touched the heart of Palestine. An ancient place, twice destroyed (once in 331 BCE, by Alexander the Great), it had been the capital city of the area, rivaling even Jerusalem. Sebastia's prominence didn't last long; the religious authority of Jerusalem had always been hard to question.

Driving slowly through the Palestinian village I was relieved to find I was no longer the object of derision I had been in Netanya. Women of all ages, dressed in drab, dark-colored robes, flashed looks at us before quickly averting their eyes. The men ignored us completely. Yet, it wasn't a happy place, and we had no desire to stick around. The flatness of the emotional suppression we'd felt in Sebastia quickly dissolved as we drove toward nearby Nablus. We'd been cautioned by Melinda's parents to avoid going to the city since recently it had become the center of the Palestinian dissension bubbling to the surface. Stories of strangers being stoned in the streets and other dire warnings echoed in our ears as we drove off in the morning.

Of course, overconfident as ever, this merely provoked me even more to see and get the feeling of a real Palestinian city. Brushing aside all warnings of foreigners being stoned as local paranoia, I might well have gone barging ahead if it wasn't for an odd sign that it seemed wise not to ignore.

We were sitting on top of the highest knoll of the ancient ruined city, having climbed steadily up through the wreckage of half a dozen civilizations, the dilapidated stumps of fluted Roman columns mixing with shards of marble carved with Byzantine intricacy and embedded in the gentle hillside. The land, arid and bleached now in November, swept down and away beneath us to the soft hills of Samaria. There was no sign of the modern city we'd come to visit.

As we sat gazing out over this tranquil landscape a grasshopper suddenly jumped between us. It was unusual to see a grasshopper this late in the year, and we followed its progress with our eyes, both of us noticing simultaneously a large bird flying low overhead, moving in the same direction as the grasshopper.

Melinda, more sensitive to the subtle ways our invisible friends guide the hand of natural events, got up quietly and followed the erratic yet determined path of our grasshopper. Reaching the edge of the small plateau she looked up from following the insect, which by now was lost in the long yellowed grass, (perhaps to be eaten by that same attentive bird), to see way below her, sheltering among the surrounding hills, the actual city of Nablus.

There then followed a rather ordinary, but to us significant, small drama. Try as she might, Melinda was quite unable to take a good photograph of the city below us. The sun, which had shone from a clear blue sky all morning, seemed to choose exactly those moments when she was preparing to shoot to disappear behind thick clouds moving in from the coast. Whenever she lifted the camera for a decent, well-lit shot, a dark shadow raced across the valley to eclipse the city, shrouding it in darkness.

Originally founded in 72 BCE by the Roman Emperor Vespasian, Nablus has always been a troubled city. Samaritan citizens rebelled against their Byzantine rulers in the sixth century, only to be almost wiped out. The Crusaders dominated the city for most of the twelfth century until they were outfoxed by Saladin, who had earlier taken back Jerusalem.

Nablus then fell under Islamic rule. Upheavals followed over the centuries as rival clans of Arabs clashed with each other and constantly challenged the authority of the Ottoman Empire. More recently it was the British who, in 1922, tried to incorporate the city into the ill-fated British Mandate of Palestine. Then, after the 1948 Arab/Israeli war, Nablus was annexed by Jordan, only to return to Israeli hands during the Six Day War in 1967.

Those are simply the highlights of the two-thousand-year history of the city. In a troubled land, Nablus seemed to us to be a focus for much of that pain and anger, a dark place, the signs were telling us, to be left well alone. Instead we drove to nearby Tulkarm, a small Arab town within the Territories. We'd been told the atmosphere there was far more relaxed than in Nablus.

Tulkarm's location, nestled in the foothills of the Samarian mountains, places it at the nexus of three key arteries, roads that connect all parts of the country. The original caravan station became a trading center from Roman times onward, interrupted only by invading armies making their way to and from Egypt. Even in a country this tiny it was always surprising to find such a wide range of atmosphere and opinions between neighboring communities.

Sometimes, amid all the ambient angst and paranoia, a deep sense of joy would break through the miasma. On the road that morning I watched an elderly Arab carefully tilling his ground with his donkey, a smile of quiet pleasure on the old man's sun-cracked face. This being Israel, the moment of joy I felt at seeing one man's happiness in tending the ground he loved was quickly followed by a sad reminder of the many Palestinian Arabs who've lost their land, in all probability never to return.

In Tulkarm, walking in the street amid jostling Arab youths, here was the joy again. There was none of the roasting I had gotten in the supermarkets and streets of Netanya, just open, honest stares, the warmest of smiles, and a feeling of brotherhood. I felt unaccountably relaxed and happy, greeting every smile with an open heart and a sense of mutual recognition. As alien as I had felt in Jewish Netanya, in Arab Tulkarm I found myself finally at home. I *knew* these people, not in my head, but in my heart. Their friendly responses were so open and undisguised, their welcoming smiles so kind, that the contrast with our reception in Netanya became even more puzzling.

It wasn't until many months later, after we returned to New York, that I realized what the fuss was about. The film *Back to the Future,* out a few months, must have been showing in Israel while we were there. Unfortunately, it seems my more-than-passing resemblance (pointed out by friends, although I think I'm taller!) to Christopher Lloyd's manic, white-haired, eccentric inventor, Doc Brown, was what was sending the children in Netanya scuttling for safety.

The Jewish kids had seen the movie; apparently the Palestinians hadn't.

Writing was becoming easier and more fluid after my brief encounter with Mich. I was starting to get the hang of the collaboration, although I doubt if it was any simpler for him than for me. I was still very new to these realms, and doubts can crowd in if all isn't well in my personal life. And all, indeed, was not well.

As is true of anyone on a spiritual path, I'm constantly learning how vital it is to trust my intuition. Being empathic, part of this is developing the self-awareness to know what is self-generated and what I'm picking up from outside. Now I was facing a dilemma that was blocking my writing and filling my mind with irrelevant chatter. I pinned down the source of this problem to my relationship with Melinda's stepfather, second husband to the mother who had so kindly put us up on our first visit and who'd found the apartment in which I was now writing.

I knew from some of Melinda's stories that her stepfather had been a bullying presence in their household. We hadn't taken to one another first time around, although we both did our best to maintain a polite front. He was the domineering type who controlled the household with his anger and his moods. Having built up and successfully run a factory in France, he and Melinda's mother relocated to Israel at a time when the country's future must have seemed bright.

The move, evidently against his wife's better judgment, had not turned out well, as Israel became more deeply troubled year by year. The old man's hopes and dreams came to nothing, and he was seething with blame and barely suppressed anger. He was not a pleasant man to be around. Now that Melinda and I were here for six months we were expected to have dinner with the parents at least once a week.

Over the weeks and months I came to dread these occasions. I liked the mother, she'd been a war correspondent and was very alive and interested in everything. And she spoke perfect English. He spoke no English, and my primitive French probably just irritated him. However, he was a blowhard. He insisted on telling me his war stories about his time in the French Resistance over and over, as he demanded the women to translate them for me. Poor dears! They must have heard them a hundred times.

My dilemma was that I didn't really believe him. Having worked for many years to develop my empathic and telepathic abilities, I find when people tell me about events in their lives truthfully, I can see them happening like a film in my mind. This has become a useful bullshit detector, especially when there's frequently no verifiable evidence for the stories I hear.

I know from writing about my own encounters with angels, dolphins, and extraterrestrials, and now with midwayers, how easy it would be to exaggerate my claims or to delude myself into becoming the hero of my own drama. I've also learned from this that if I relate an anecdote as honestly and precisely as I can perceive it, then the truth carries and others will feel the resonance of the experience in much the same way.

When the stepfather was relating his stories I was drawing a blank. Since I was hearing them first in French, which I could generally understand, then translated into English, there was the chance for seeing the images twice. I felt nothing either time. I had little choice but to keep up a courteous front; what could I say under those conditions? It certainly wasn't up to me to expose the old man as a fraud, or worse, since what I was coming to feel was that he might even have been a collaborator or a sympathizer of some sort.

And what if I was wrong? Understandably, this is a very delicate issue for Frenchmen of his generation.

I stress that this insight was entirely based on my intuition and was never talked about or confirmed. I may have been completely wrong— the man is long dead and beyond caring—but a number of events over the ensuing months tended to confirm my worst opinion. To make the situation even more personally troublesome, the man must have been unconsciously picking up on my disbelief, because in the way of those who protest too much, he would repeat his stories with a growing insistence every time we were there.

If I wasn't trying to write a book and hadn't committed myself to living in Israel for six months I would have moved on and likely forgotten about the poor tortured soul and his guilty lies. Here, this wasn't an option. I had to live with it, and as I said, it was wreaking havoc with my concentration. The writing was seizing up, and I was having constant difficulty achieving the balanced state of mind I needed to cooperate with Mich.

Rationally, I knew I was overreacting to what really wasn't my problem, yet I simply couldn't push the issue aside. The situation steadily deteriorated, producing a constant state of anxiety. This also wasn't helped by what I was trying to work on at the time: whether evil is an inherent aspect of the Multiverse or merely the result of different levels of ignorance. The psychic disturbance erupted first as a negative thoughtform— the horrible blob of paint that mysteriously appeared on my companion's canvas, which I described in chapter 4.

Then, a few weeks later, as we were preparing to go over to the parents for a New Year celebratory dinner, I had what I can only describe as a mini nervous breakdown. I could barely move. I was shivering uncontrollably and couldn't stop weeping. I knew Melinda's mother would have been cooking all day, creating a feast for us, and I just couldn't go on dissembling in the face of all that kindness. I couldn't go through with it. I knew that I would either insult them by not appearing or appear and end up insulting them.

In our apartment the tension built as my companion's patience wore thin. I'd kept my dilemma about her stepfather to myself, not wanting to dump something on her as painful as this without a much better reason, so she had good grounds to be angry with me. After one last attempt to get me moving, Melinda left the apartment, alone and angry. I hoped she was preparing an excuse for me. I could do nothing but curl up in the bed and shiver myself into a disturbed sleep.

Although excruciating, these brief journeys into the dark night of the soul can be deeply cathartic. I knew from experience not to resist the psychic pain, but to go with it. Let it all in; if anything, accelerate the process, make it as bad as can be. That way when I hit the bottom of the "bottomless pit" I can bounce right back up.

Next morning I was back on my feet, my head clear again, and enthusiastic to get back into my writing. The mental conflict of the past few weeks had simply been lifted off me. I couldn't see what I was making all the fuss about. Of course I could listen to the old man's stories without having to get caught up in whether they were true. He was already living in his own hell. Why would I want to make it any worse?

Perhaps these soul-searing events are perfectly normal incidents, necessary punctuations in the spiritual path; then again, possibly these are the moments when our angels are particularly active. In this case, I can only conjecture that the midwayers had a hand in what I was going through, since that same afternoon I saw with my own eyes a small group of midwayers. It was the first, and only, time I have ever actually seen them with my physical senses.

As I've already discussed, there's good reason to believe that the midwayers draw their existence somewhere within the ultraviolet range of the electromagnetic spectrum. This makes them invisible to our eyes under normal conditions, although within their own realm they are as real and solid as we are in ours. They are not spirits or ghosts, neither are they real angels. They are, in a way, the true guardians of the planet, who live on here far beyond the generations of humans, whose care for the planet is probably deeper than we can imagine. Midwayers are able to interact with our reality under extreme conditions, but like all higher orders of intelligence, they walk a fine line between necessary intervention and allowing a human situation to work itself out without any interference from them. To actually see them must be an extraordinary rarity.

So it was that late afternoon as dusk was starting to fall. By now, I'd walked on my own, three or four kilometers down the deserted beach. It was a thin strip of untidy sand strewn with ribbons of seaweed and boulders fallen from the eroded cliffside. On my left side the cliffs rose at a sharp angle two hundred feet up to the dunes and scrubland above. The steep slope was studded with rocks dangling precipitously, sure to fall in the next storm. Keeping a wary eye on the cliffside above and dodging around the fallen rocks, I made my way along the beach.

I paused briefly at what I'd come to think of as a natural sacred circle: seven or eight larger than man-size boulders that must have plunged down the cliff, embedding themselves in the beach in an almost perfect circle. They stood upright, like dolmens, the megalithic standing stones of northern Europe. I'd meditated here before, but this evening my intuition was drawing me farther down the beach.

I walked on as the light dimmed until I reached a large, flat rock that I'd previously found and on which I'd taken to perching. It was still warm from the sunlight, and I felt relaxed and comfortable staring idly into the surf. It was at that point during sunset when the air can almost turn lavender. The waves rolled in with the surf, striking the rocks and throwing up sheets of violet spray that hung in the air before the next wave replaced them.

It felt like one of those magical moments in which nature lowers her veil and we catch a glimpse of what lies beyond. I relaxed into the beauty of it all.

My mind was empty as I gazed into the violet haze.

Suddenly my whole body jolted. There, in the constantly shifting curtain of spray, I could quite clearly see a group of ten or twelve beings, very tall—almost twice the height of humans—with a couple of children among them, all plodding slowly along in single file up a slight incline. There was no indication that they saw me, or even had any awareness of the landscape I was in. They were simply going about their business.

This strange scenario, as real as anything I have ever watched on a movie screen, persisted in the violet mist as long as the waves replaced the spray. When the light slowly changed and the spray no longer refracted a violet glow, the figures dissolved and disappeared. Though never as "real" perhaps as the rock on which I was sitting, the figures and the landscape through which they were trudging appeared quite solid. It wasn't a single flash—my brain trying to make pattern-sense out of a random cloud of water molecules. These beings walked! Their movement was continuous and fluid, despite the fragmentary nature of the diaphanous screen. I watched them walking slowly and deliberately for at least ten or twelve seconds. I've had hallucinations in my life; anyone who has taken a powerful entheogen knows what they are like. The walking figures were no more a hallucination than the moving images of a film.

The diagnosis of a skeptical psychologist might suggest my interest in the midwayers had become so obsessive over the preceding weeks that my fevered brain had manufactured a delusion to support the obsession. This approach, however, is biased by the tacit assumption that such beings as midwayers don't exist. Reversing that assumption creates an equally valid argument. It was the very passion of my interest, and not obsessive pathology, that signaled my desire to get to know midwayers better, which culminated with them creating a delightful and clever mise-en-scène in which this event could occur.

I had no doubt while I watched this unusual scene that it was a small group of midwayers I was seeing and that I was being singularly privileged. Their apparent unawareness of my observing presence suggested the event wasn't organized by them, but I had the strongest sense of Mich's hands behind delivering me to the right place.

I can only admire the guidance that got me there, on that precise rock, at exactly that time when the sun was at a very particular angle, the wind from the right direction to carry the spray that, in turn, was lofted by waves of the necessary height, speed, and volume to create the ideal amount of water vapor to provide a momentary window to another reality.

If my brief vision of those midwayers wasn't purely the result of a fortuitous set of intersecting circumstances, then perhaps it demonstrates the degree to which we're all being gently guided by angels or midwayers, whether we know it or not.

It has obviously been in the midwayers' interest to remain largely hidden from human ken for these past two millennia. The behavior of the rebel midwayers we find recorded in the Vedic, Sumerian, Egyptian, and Greek traditions, when they had last made themselves obvious to human beings, did not work out for the best. Without responsible leadership those midwayers who aligned themselves with the rebel faction, as we know, soon fell to infighting, splitting into rival groups and using terrified humans as their pawns.

If the rebel midwayers *were* to return, as we'd petitioned back in Delphi, they would need to take their lead from the relative few who'd remained here, faithfully fulfilling their functions from behind the veil. In an increasingly materialistic and scientific age, it must have been easier for them to have remained hidden, but it would have also made their tasks far more difficult. Not only had their overall number been so dramatically reduced, but the midwayers who stayed also would have had to develop far more subtle ways of helping to guide human development.

The industrial and scientific revolutions have largely explained away the superstitions that used to plague our ancestors' lives. Many of those spurious beliefs originated in pre-Christian times, when the activities of the midwayers were far less guarded. The hierarchical propensity of human beings to fear what appears to be more powerful would have been all too easy to manipulate. With all those "gods" to propitiate and serve, with their constantly shifting alliances and conflicts, their demands and frightful retributions, it's scarce wonder that humans were confused in a way it's difficult for us to understand today. Many superstitions we find meaningless in the current age must be remnants of rituals intended to placate the increasingly bizarre and unpredictable behavior of the rogue midwayers.

While Western culture has undoubtedly gained a certain (illusory) self-confidence by rejecting superstition, individuals as a consequence have largely lost a personal sense of the miraculous. Cyclotrons and genetic engineering may well represent the pinnacle of scientific achievement, but they can scarcely be called miracles. Crop circles are mysterious, yet there is obviously an intelligent hand behind them. Hubble's photographs of farflung galaxies are awe-inspiring and glorious, yet what is revealed is too vast and impersonal to make much of an impact on everyday life. By discrediting all superstition, including in some extreme cases religious belief itself, materialism necessarily becomes blind to the reality of all incorporeal life.

This may have worked temporarily to the advantage of the midwayers since it allowed them to operate more freely when undercover. The return of a large number of their colleagues might well have to signal a change of tactics. If it is true that midwayers worked with, and through, influential families and clans in ancient times, then it's not too far-fetched to think this might also turn out to be their modus operandi for the days to come.

Our recent experiences with Mich and his attentive guidance down through Europe, as well as the brief glimpse I was given into the midwayers' ultraviolet world, suggest they may also be willing to collaborate more openly with individual human beings.

Those readers familiar with *The Urantia Book*, or with my own exegesis of the Lucifer Rebellion in *Dolphins, ETs & Angels*, shouldn't be surprised at this. Over the long 297,000 years that the midwayers were on the planet serving with the prince's staff prior to the chaos of the Lucifer Rebellion, human beings would have been far more aware of their presence. As I've already proposed, it was only much later, and as a result of the revolution, that the substantial majority of midwayers who aligned themselves with the rebel faction became so overbearing and self-serving.

Any reading of the Sumerian or Greek "myths" testifies to godlike beings with little interest in the well-being of humans. It's possible to interpret the myths in a Jungian sense, as archetypes, with the stories related as cautionary tales of human behavior. Doubtless some of the stories do function in this way. The wing-burned plunge of Icarus into the sea is clearly warning against hubris.

There is another way to interpret these myths, however, if one allows for the quite reasonable assumption that our ancestors could tell the difference between reality and hallucination. They may well have been gulled into all sorts of meaningless superstition, remnants perhaps of a far earlier time of ghost worship, but the reality of these midwayer "gods and goddesses" was of a completely different order of phenomena. They appeared and disappeared at will. They were larger, older, and, in some cases, wiser than humans. They used flying craft. They fought wars between themselves. Some sought human companionship, but others merely wanted to manipulate humans for their own purposes. Some were trustworthy and loyal, others cruel. They were able to communicate telepathically. And, let's not forget, they were immortal.

Although Julian Jaynes evidently wasn't aware of the midwayers when he wrote his controversial book, *The Origins of Consciousness in the Breakdown of the Bicameral Mind,* his conclusions are remarkably consistent with what I'm proposing. His "gods and goddesses" could speak in the minds of early humans.

Dr. Jaynes, a Princeton psychology professor, was trying to understand the profound change in human consciousness that started appearing around three thousand years ago. In his elegantly written book he examines archaeology, religion, language and consciousness, and ancient art and texts to propose that early humans received hallucinated instructions in their minds, which were then attributed to gods and goddesses. He points out how, for example, in Homer's *Iliad,* the main actions are the result of instructions received from a god; there seems to be no personal volition, no internal monologue, in the book.

Being unaware of the existential reality of the midwayers, Dr. Jaynes struggles with where these "hallucinated voices" might be coming from, ultimately settling on the disassociated right brain. He maintains that until the transition in consciousness in the ancient world, humans had a bicameral mind, in which one side of the brain communicated with the other through auditory or visual illusions. It was these internally generated voices and visions that were then projected outside the self. Dr. Jaynes suggests it was out of the breakdown of this bicameral mind that a modern, language-based consciousness emerged.

Unfortunately, basing so much of his conjecture on the hallucinations of schizophrenics and recent split-brain experiments resulted in a weakness at the center of his theory. If indeed early humans received instructions from their nondominant hemispheres, where did *those* instructions originate? The confusing and self-accusatory voices of schizophrenics barely explain how this could have come about. And, while recent experiments isolating the left and right hemispheres of the human brain demonstrate that each hemisphere can have a unique identity, no one has yet reported civilization-building wisdom emanating from their nondominant side.

Although Dr. Jaynes overstates and confuses his case in trying to locate the source of these "hallucinated instructions" in the right brain, he may well be onto a more fundamental concept. Rather than credit the right brain for originating the "voices," a more metaphysical viewpoint would be that the nondominant hemisphere is more finely tuned to *receive telepathic signals* and that the development of what we call modern consciousness, which Dr. Jaynes defines as the self-identification of interior mental states, has evolved from a gradual *integration* of the two hemispheres.

The most significant theme in Dr. Jaynes's book, however, regardless of his unconvincing explanation as to the source of the internal voices, is his claim that a profound shift in consciousness exists between the ancients and modern human beings. We dismiss the gods and goddesses of the ancient pantheons as metaphors, myths, or archetypes, simply because our experience of the world currently doesn't include them. I believe that this difference in the nature of ancient and modern consciousness is what makes it difficult for us to identify with so many of the motives of the ancients.

If the (hopefully) redeemed group of midwayers are to be returned, they will find that a lot has changed on the planet over the last couple of millennia. Their influence and guidance will need to be far more subtle than their previous attempts, as their observed presence in a technological civilization would create unnecessary confusion.

The Urantia Book tells us that one of the midwayers' functions is to mediate with any extraterrestrial races who are drawn to this world. I suspect this must keep them busy, since this planet is currently the focus of such interest. Michael Salla, in his book, *Exopolitics,* claims he is aware of fifty-seven different off-planet races currently observing and participating in the coming transformation, although I suspect the true number is far greater than that. It seems everyone wants to be here for the big show.

Although petroglyphs from different parts of the world feature flying machines, it is from the Vedas that we get a more detailed description. *Vimanas* are described in the Vedas and in later Indian literature as having a variety of shapes and sizes; they might have two engines (*agnihotra-vimana*) or more (*gaja-vimana*); they flew within the earth's atmosphere, and they were able to travel in space and move submerged under water.

Superbly carved images of what are clearly flying machines decorate the ceiling beams of a three-thousand-year-old New Kingdom temple, south of Cairo, at Abydos. Some of these images resemble modern aircraft to a remarkable degree; one small carving can be nothing but a helicopter. This resemblance really shouldn't be surprising since aircraft are such functional machines. Given certain physical conditions, including the density of the air, weight-to-lift ratios, the structural capacity of available materials, and technical know-how, the design of a hovering flying machine would need to satisfy the same material conditions then as would be true today.

More significant to the point I'm developing is that vimanas are also described in Indian sacred writings as having been used widely in warfare. The current belief among those researchers who acknowledge that the Vedas may be describing real events is that this aerial warfare must have been between hostile extraterrestrial races.

This seems highly unlikely. Open hostility appears to be rare in the Multiverse, and according to the extraterrestrial contact I reported in *Dolphins, ETs & Angels*, the few known warlike races are restricted to their own planets.

If not extraterrestrial vehicles, then vimanas are more likely to have been midwayer vehicles, and the warfare, the result of the conflicts that developed between the different midwayer factions. The Vedas are the oldest sacred texts of Hinduism, composed—or directly revealed, as Hindu tradition believes—many thousands of years ago, and if I am correct in proposing vimanas are in fact midwayer craft, what might this suggest about the current state of midwayer technology?

The midwayer reality I glimpsed in the violet haze appeared as solid in its own way as this one. They have to deal with a material reality the same as us—albeit a parallel reality on a slightly higher frequency. They might well be invisible to our senses and singularly long-lasting, but I doubt if they can teleport themselves around the planet. Like us, they would need their vehicles.

In the light of this, I'm proposing that much of the UFO activity we have observed in the skies over the past sixty years is, in fact, midwayer craft, given the way that some observers report the way craft will appear and just as suddenly vanish, the frequently unaccountable behavior in some contactee accounts, the evident penchant for secrecy of these so-called "visitors," to use Whitley Streiber's preferred term, and the apparently etheric nature of many UFOs. All these manifestations are far more attributable to midwayers than to beings hailing from other planets.

I've no doubt there are a number of authentic extraterrestrial groups here, but any survey of UFO literature raises some paradoxical issues. In many reports, the beings simply do not behave in the manner we would imagine technologically sophisticated extraterrestrials would. This argument is frequently used by skeptics to discredit the whole extraterrestrial hypothesis: Why would a race of intelligent beings travel light years to poke and probe thousands of middle-aged housewives? Or, tease and confuse policemen? Or indulge in any of the bizarre antics often observed?

Those people who have had encounters with genuine extraterrestrials, like the Dutch industrialist Stefan Denaerde, as reported in *UFO Contact from Planet IARGA* by Denaerde and Wendelle C. Stevens and also discussed more extensively in chapter 11, speak of much more mature relationships. These people, when "abducted," aren't subjected to embarrassing and painful medical procedures. They aren't poked and probed by small telepathic entities and then made to have amnesia afterward. Quite the contrary. Valuable knowledge is exchanged. Frequently the extraterrestrials will generously share information about their belief systems or how they live on their home planets. They even showed Stefan Denaerde holographic movies of their world.

Yet if we factor in the midwayers, a race of beings indigenous to this planet who exist in a parallel dimension and care perhaps more deeply for our world than for individual humans, wouldn't this account for many of the documented "alien abductions"? These "visitors" are clearly technologically more advanced than us, but not by that much. They appear to have mastered moving between dimensions since they walk through walls, yet they use craft; there are more than enough similar reports of the interiors of these UFOs to establish that. They are invariably mysterious and secretive. They reveal nothing of themselves, who they are or where they come from. They appear emotionally cold and unavailable. They abduct people seemingly arbitrarily, without warning and often against their will. They treat people as if they own them, sometimes reassuring the abductee that the abduction is for his or her own good. They may well feel they are administering their form of tough love. They may not like humans very much, and probably with due cause. They give dire warnings for the future of this planet.

In short, as respected French researcher Jacques Vallee proposes, these beings appear to have a far more intimate involvement with the planet, stretching way back into history, and a deep sense of responsibility for the state of the world. If these "visitors" are indeed midwayers, then they are completely different from extraterrestrials. As we move farther into the transformation, it will be important to know the difference.

Ufologists tend to polarize on this issue. The more scientifically oriented are inclined to insist on the extraterrestrial explanation. Since most contemporary theories of physics don't allow for habitable parallel dimensions, these ufologists tend to reject the interdimensional concept, simply because it doesn't fit into their preconceived model of the way the universe should work.

However, Jacques Vallee has advanced an interdimensional hypothesis, in which the "aliens" are visiting from a parallel reality, coexisting separately, but alongside our own. Dr. Vallee supports his theory in his book *Messengers of Deception* by demonstrating that such paranormal phenomena as fairies have more in common with current "alien abduction" descriptions than with authentic alien encounters. Although it's frustrating not to be able to verify Jacques Vallee's theory by observation or experiment, he is clearly onto something. Like Julian Jaynes, Dr. Vallee appears to be unaware of the authenticity of *The Urantia Book,* and yet his research has brought him to much the same conclusion: there exists a race of beings who live in a parallel dimension who are capable of interacting with human reality.

It sounds like the midwayers to me.

Although midwayers are described in some detail in *The Urantia Book*—after all, it was their petition that succeeded in getting the book transmitted— their actual activities are seldom mentioned. We're told how the midwayers were created, something of their functions prior to the Lucifer Rebellion, and then what occurred as a result of the planetary quarantine and the failure of the prince's mission. Yet compared with the richness of the information on almost everything else, the angelic communicants of the book are remarkably reticent about how the midwayers go about what they do.

There is a good reason for this. Even in our materialistic, technologically driven age, most humans are still all too willing to give up their power and worship what appears godlike to them. Human emotions, especially our devotional feelings, are very powerful when ignited, so I'm not surprised the midwayers are shy of having their presence generally known. Should the rebel midwayers return they won't want to repeat their previous mistakes and I imagine will be relieved to avoid the temptation of being worshipped as faux divinities.

I believe I have been allowed my encounters with midwayers over the years because I am God intoxicated, in love with the God I experience in the silence of my heart. I don't find myself overawed by the presence of midwayers, and I cooperate with them joyfully—although they put me through it from time to time—as invisible friends and companions in the journey through a life both our races share.

I doubt if I am alone in this. There will be such people all over the world, like George Barnard in Australia, who became aware of the presence of midwayers in his life some years before he realized they were, in fact, midwayers. George collaborates with them in his healing work and describes his fascinating encounters with them in his book, *The Search for 11:11*, as well as running a website (www.1111AkashicConstruct.com) for those starting to encounter these and other celestial beings in the natural course of their lives.

While working on the final draft of this book in 2010, I heard George was not only asserting that the rebel midwayers were returning, but also that a number of midwayers from other nearby worlds have been shipped in to help out as well. As we move further into the energies that are transforming our planet, more people will need to gain the faith and confidence to cooperate consciously with the midwayers. This close relationship was always intended to be one of humanity's spiritual birthrights, before it became just one more unfortunate consequence of the rebellion.

Times have changed. Lucifer's rebellion has been settled, the protagonists appear to have reconciled, and new times are upon us. These were the conclusions that emerged during our time with the angels in Toronto in 1981 and that I transcribed in *Dolphins, ETs & Angels*. We were not told then what would happen to Lucifer or Satan, and over the ensuing years I've received no further information as to their whereabouts.

I should also add that the understanding concerning the reconciliation of the rebellion, which was communicated to our small group by the angels in Toronto, was not immediately shared by the bulk of committed readers of *The Urantia Book*. Over the years more of them have come to accept the reconciliation when it's revealed through their personal experience, but there has never been any formal announcement that could be considered hard evidence.

I deduce from this that it is more important to recognize the reconciliation as an act of faith. Trusting the intuition and learning to discern the difference between it and self-delusion has been an integral part of the path I'm following. I've had no reason over the thirty subsequent years to question the revelations we received in 1981. In fact, to the contrary, many of the significant events taking place in the world over the last three decades tend toward substantiating what the angels disclosed to us. As mentioned previously, they told us the period in the immediate future will bring many problems and challenges as the corruption embedded in almost all aspects of human life rises to the surface to be released. There'll be revolutions and small wars, localized violence and religious conflicts, and political and financial scandals as the undeserving rich and powerful are exposed.

This will be as true for individuals as it is for the entire global culture. Each of us will have to face our own demons, to come to terms with the light and darkness we all contain, and to integrate our personalities. Amid the fear and confusion we'll be witnessing on the global stage, we are being required to hold firm in our faith that in spite of how bad things appear, there is a profound meaning and intentionality behind it all.

Writing now, thirty years later, it's easier to see how this profound angelic reconciliation has been rippling down to affect this world. The fall of Soviet communism, the reunification of Germany, the end of apartheid, a resolution to the Irish issue, and the more recent people's revolutions in the Middle East—all of these events can be seen as the fruits of the reconciliation. In the widespread availability of hand-held video and recording devices and, more recently, with the arrival of the Internet, the balance of power is steadily moving in favor of the collective.

The exposure of abuse by Catholic priests and, more recently, the near collapse of the world financial situation and the many sexual and investment scandals of the past few years all confirm there's a new spirit of openness and transparency influencing human affairs.

Many of humanity's most persistent problems and confusion over the long 203,000 years that this planet has been isolated are a direct result of the rebel midwayers' irresponsibility. It's my hope should the rebels be permitted to return that they will cooperate more effectively with each other and with any humans open to such interspecies adventures. Perhaps our relationship with Mich will act as a model.

It was a couple of months later, as we were preparing to pack up our affairs in Israel and return to New York City, when we heard the news. Melinda, more sensitive to the presence of midwayers than I was, received the information telepathically.

The message was short and to the point.

Over forty thousand rebel midwayers will be returning to serve on this world, seven of them every ten days. And they didn't wish to be called "rebel" midwayers anymore. They desired to put those times behind them and wanted us to rename them. I don't recall how we decided on calling them collectively *the Beings of the Violet Flame*—shortened to the acronym BVF. It may have been a term we'd come across in spiritual literature, but it felt respectful and poetically fitting, given my experience with the violet haze.

The Beings of the Violet Flame it would be from now on.

PART TWO

Life in the True Age

The sacred teaching is not hidden
in darkness and obscurity;
it radiates in bright daylight.
What they call up, they receive.
Leave the dead with their dead!
So often did they summon death
that it finally came.
Let us summon joy, and the Divine Realm will come!
Call not trembling with fear, but with jubilation!
COULD ANYTHING BE MORE NATURAL
THAN OUR TALKING TOGETHER?

TALKING WITH ANGELS: BUDALIGET 1943,

TRANSCRIBED BY GITTA MALLASZ

9

Re-enchanting the Planet

Nature Spirits, Working with Angels, Crystal Geomantics, and the Returning Cathars

It was almost a year after Melinda and I returned from Israel that the Beings of the Violet Flame once again appeared in my life. Coming back to New York City we assumed Mich must have gone on his way, since we hadn't heard from him for a while.

My book was finally complete and heading for publication. I was continuing to live frugally on the small monthly payments from the sale of my business. I'd prorated the payments over a four-year period to give me sufficient time to write and publish my first book. With the writing behind me, this allowed me a chance to focus on making contact with my guardian angels.

In Toronto in 1981, the angels who spoke to us through the light-trance channel, Edward, and were included in *Dolphins, ETs & Angels* told us that everybody was potentially capable of close contact with their guardian angels. It was another of our perfectly natural birthrights, of which we've been deprived since the rebellion.

As stated earlier but bears repeating here, I was first made aware of my two angels in the course of my near-death experience in 1973. I also witnessed a large choir of angels. The NDE was so emotionally and psychologically overwhelming, however, I pushed its implications aside until the angels showed up again a few years later, speaking through Edward. I knew then that the angels would be playing an important part in my life. At that point, I realized I would need to throw myself wholeheartedly into these new and mysterious relationships.

It was going to be a challenging effort.

Many spiritual traditions, such as Jewish mysticism, place stern restrictions on trying to communicate with angels, reserving it only for the old and devout (men only). Although I don't support the inherent gender discrimination, there are good reasons for emphasizing maturity in this enterprise. It's an extremely confronting exercise.

Serious intention to communicate with angels for me requires a focused, yet relaxed, attention, with minimal distractions—something almost impossible, for example, while raising small children. It demands personal honesty and psychological transparency to clear away the ego-driven concerns that thwart or distort the contact. It's crucial, the traditions remind us, to bring a clear and balanced consciousness to any contact sought with angels.

Since angels operate at a much higher vibrational frequency than us, any repressed fear, guilt, and shame within our psyches will rise to the surface in the heat of the exchange. If these negative thoughtforms aren't examined, understood, and then released, they will effectively distort any reliable conscious contact with angels. It's then the demons appear, when our individual thoughtforms become absorbed by the collective thoughtform, and we find ourselves in a whole world of terror. I was aware, too, that in my case I had some very deeply repressed early traumas, and I only hoped I'd be able to finally release them in the course of my relationship with the angels.

I had put off embarking on this enterprise; however, after my recent experiences with the BVF in Europe and Israel, I was more encouraged and decided to see for myself if it was possible. I'd always found value in meditating, yet have seldom done it consistently. Now I started to meditate daily and to keep a detailed journal of my slow progress. While doing this I continued my personal research into dolphin telepathy, spending some time in Florida swimming with a pod of coastal bottlenose dolphins. Then the day came that I received a telepathic impression from the dolphins. According to them, apparently I'd completed my studies with dolphins for the moment. They were turning me over to the angels for further training!

Looking back over that time I can see that I was continuing to entertain my doubts and fears. On the surface I was confident and determined to see this new phase with angels through. Yet, in spite of my encounters with the BVF I could still slip into doubt about what I was experiencing. Was I going crazy? Why me, Lord? I'm not worthy of having an angel! Am I deluding myself? It was all the usual stuff . . . Yet as it turned out, much of the guidance I received over the two years it took to establish reliable contact with my two guardian angels was in being able to identify my childhood fears. I was shown how to find the source of the trauma, how to deal with the thoughtforms, and then how to release them.

It was an often grueling process, yet utterly fascinating. One by one I was able to identify the fear-impacted thoughtforms I'd imprinted as a child in the Second World War and, later, from the many formal beatings I'd received at my English public school. These traumas were so deeply repressed they didn't manifest in my life until I was well into my twenties. Then they would come out in unaccountable fits of violent rage at the slightest provocation. My eyes would red-over and I'd come to a few seconds later, my fists thrashing out at whoever had provoked me.

The unpredictability of my anger and its unpleasant consequences took many years to master. Without being conscious of it I was choosing relationships with particularly strong and provocative women as a way, presumably, of testing myself by pushing myself to the brink. Yet, for all this self-control, I wasn't getting to the root of the problem and I certainly wasn't releasing the thoughtforms. It was only in working with the angels that I found a spiritual technology powerful enough to dislodge and finally release these demons.

The guidance and information I acquired through this period formed the basis for the GRACE Process, which was subsequently refined and included in *Ask Your Angels,* the self-help manaul I wrote with my two coauthors, Alma Daniel and Andrew Ramer, which Ballantine Books published in 1992.

✠

It was mid-December in 1983, and I'd flown to London, this time on my own, to visit my mother. Since I've lived all my adult life in America, Diana and I only saw one another every couple of years—which suited us both fine. We typically enjoyed about five days of each other's company before a mutual irritation would set in. Sensibly avoiding this became something of a routine, in which, after three or four days, I'd borrow Diana's car and set off on my own for a sacred adventure somewhere in England.

Usually I don't create any goal on one of these adventures. I simply choose a general direction, cast myself on the currents of life, and see where I'll end up. This trip was going to be an exception, although I gave myself ample time to drift as well.

I knew I needed to go to Glastonbury again. You'll recall this is the small town in southwestern England, regarded by many in the spiritual community as the heart chakra of England. It's one of those places on the planet where, if you are sensitive, upon entering its vibrational field you will feel a palpable change of frequency. This can have some comical results.

Many of those new to the spiritual path go to Glastonbury to find teachers or gurus, to attend the many workshops and lectures given there, to browse the specialist bookstores, perhaps even join one of communities in the area, in the hope of becoming more "spiritual." Glastonbury, however, with its long history of turbulence and religious devotion, has some powerful mojo and doesn't take kindly to the pretentious, the deluded, or the fraudulent. This results in frequent rows and feuding between the various self-proclaimed masters and teachers who choose to live there, and since the emphasis is on appearing "spiritual" at all costs these conflicts tend to become suppressed, negatively influencing the overall psychic atmosphere. But this wasn't what concerned me on this trip.

I'd always had an interest in Aleister Crowley, without delving much into his magical techniques. While in Sicily some years ago I'd clambered up to his Abbey of Thelema, then overgrown with weeds and untended by locals still too scared to go there. For all his assumed wickedness, I'd admired his intention to make contact with his guardian angel, even if it was a lot more complicated than the techniques the angels in Toronto had shown us. I had also recently acquired the tarot deck that Crowley had designed.

Putting all that together with Glastonbury gave me the idea to do a Crowley twelve-day meditation, using his deck on the twelve days of Christmas, and physically doing the practice on the land delineated by the Temple of the Stars, the twelve signs of the zodiac that surround the small town. Although this vast terrestrial zodiac is more poetic whimsy than established fact, it felt like the kind of whimsy I enjoy. The concept was first advanced by the artist Katherine Maltwood after a vision suggesting the temple was created by the ancient Sumerians. Glastonbury is in the county of Somerset, after all.

This was as much of a plan that I set myself.

I didn't sense Mich's presence as I drove through the drizzle along the country lanes leading into the town, yet as the adventure turned out, the BVF evidently must have played their part.

I'd learned by now that all angels prefer us to use and sharpen our intuitions rather than continually rely on them for guidance and direction. This is one of the reasons why, for most of us, after initially making close contact with our companion angels and having formed a firm and loving relationship with them, the angels frequently step back again. Of course they are always there, especially in emergencies, but they've no wish to encourage a dependency. As well, they want us to learn from our own mistakes.

I booked into the bed-and-breakfast at the foot of Glastonbury Tor that I'd used before. It was run at that time by two elderly sisters with the significant surname of Parfit. Having come across some intriguing material about the Cathars, my ears pricked up at this. Whether or not the sisters were aware of it, I knew the titles parfit and parfait were used interchangeably to describe the highest rank of the elect in Cathar communities. Although I never thought it necessary to raise the Cathar possibility with them, I always felt supremely comfortable in the sisters' solicitous care.

They put me in my favorite room on the second floor after greeting me as an old friend. It's a solid Victorian house, and the large room with its high ceiling overlooked the wide plain, out of which rise the three hills that shelter the town. Up until the early Middle Ages this area was known as the Isle of Avalon and the three hills were surrounded by water washing in from the Bristol Channel. It was all this water that contributed to the misty strangeness of the Arthurian legends.

Rain was starting to slash at the windows as I settled down for the night.

This is not the place to describe the details of my twelve-day Aleister Crowley meditation, except to say it was cold and wet and not really relevant. As it was to turn out, the real reason I was in Glastonbury was quite different. There was one amusing postscript, however, that illustrates the kind of synchronicity that occurs in spiritually charged places and serves as a confirmation that my twelve days had not been entirely wasted.

It happened on the morning of the day after I'd completed the cycle of twelve meditations. I'd chosen to spend that last night up on top of the tor. You will remember from my earlier adventure in Glastonbury, when my cousin Chris and I spotted that strange hunched figure up ahead of us as we climbed the tor, there is a fourteenth-century tower at the summit. St. Michael's Tower is a solid stone structure, some seventy feet high and twelve feet square, open at the top, with two arched entrances and a flagstone floor. Alone and shivering on a cold winter's night, the wind blowing over the lip of the tower sounding like a massive pipe organ, its varying bass tones echoing down the rain-slicked walls, I did the last meditation of the series.

When dawn lit up the sky I unknotted my frozen legs, hauled myself outside of the tower, and perched on the rim of the tor to soak in the morning sun. Birds circled around me, the lights of Glastonbury twinkled off in the distance, and the ground smelled sweet after the night's rain. I felt clean and open after my self-imposed ordeal, relieved, too, at having it behind me. I've no rational idea why I took it on; it simply *felt* right at the time.

Following the intuition so wholeheartedly can be a demanding path, since the consequences of an act done purely intuitively often do not manifest until some time after the event. As in this case, I'd given myself a rational reason for being in Glastonbury, sensing there would be more to it, yet having no idea as to the consequences. Fortunately, I knew enough by this time to trust myself and giggled when I remembered the story I heard in India some years ago, when I was following a Sufi trail.

The Master, in this case, was a very fine shoemaker, or so I was told. An American heard of this enigmatic Sufi and, with the additional attraction of a fine new pair of boots, decided to make the long flight to India to visit the shoemaker. After an exhausting journey he finally arrived at the little open-fronted shop. Immediately as he entered the place a small man leaped up from his cushion and rushed screaming at the startled American, bowling him backward out of the shop and into the street, where he stumbled, fell, and broke his leg.

Some days later, in the hospital, having missed his return flight to America, the man read in the newspaper the plane that was to have carried him home had crashed, killing all on board.

The sun was warming me up, and I felt a deep sense of gratitude. I closed my eyes and bathed in the feeling. Sometime later I opened my eyes to see far below me, at the foot of the tor, four figures well-wrapped up for a winter's walk. Nothing special there I thought: people were bound to appear sooner or later to break into my solitude.

The tor is a curious spot with a long history as a holy place of pagan spirituality. It appears to be man-made and could well have been created as a spiral labyrinth, a place of initiation and of attunement to Earth energy, which was concentrated by the spiraling contours of the hill. I never know quite what to expect when I'm on the tor.

Who could these bundled pilgrims be on this freezing winter's morning?

I focus my eyes in interest. There is something odd about the four figures stumbling around nearly six hundred feet below me. The grass is wet and the going steep, so it is not surprising they totter and stagger on their laborious way upward. Yet there *is* something strange. In spite of all the slipping and sliding, they move almost as one being. Every unsteady step one of them takes appears in some unaccountable way to create a direct response in the next step of the other three. If one figure falls back a step or two, the other three react in halting or falling back, the entire group never further than a few feet from one another.

As I observe more closely, it appears there's a central figure around whom the other three buzz like slow-motion flies. Their slow, jerking advance, accompanied by frequent pauses, is so bizarre, so baffling and idiosyncratic, that I once again close my eyes. I don't feel threatened, and the way the four figures are climbing they'll come across me when they reach the top. With that thought I return to my morning meditation and promptly forget about them.

My head is turned upward toward the sun, eyes still closed, when sometime later, I feel a slight ruffling of my hair and think it's the wind. Then I feel someone directly behind me. I sense others are clustered around me, a little too close for polite comfort. I can feel their body heat and hear their panting breath. I have the presence of mind to keep my eyes firmly shut, having no idea of what's in store for me.

Another gentle ruffling of my hair on both sides of my head and, mysteriously, the distant sound of music. . . . The distant sound of music? It's suddenly much louder as the pads of the earphones close on my ears. My head fills with the final glorious crescendo of the Vangelis arrangement of William Blake's poem, *Jerusalem,* beloved of all English people; it became the soundtrack of the film *Chariots of Fire.*

> *Bring me my bow of burning gold:*
> *Bring me my arrows of desire:*
> *Bring me my spear: O clouds, unfold!*
> *Bring me my chariot of fire!*
> *I will not cease from mental fight.*
> *Nor shall my sword sleep in my hand*
> *Til we have built Jerusalem*
> *In England's green and pleasant land.*[1]

My body is filled with sound, and I am transported into ecstasy.

As the music finally dies away and I float back into my physical self, I slowly and infinitely respectfully, open my eyes.

There, surrounding me, with tears of laughter running down their faces, were four friends of mine. More astonishing still, they were good friends from different phases of my life. I didn't know they were in Glastonbury, and they wouldn't have been aware I was in England.

There was Peter Russell, author of *The Global Brain Awakens,* who had sacrificed his earphones for my epiphany. There was Marilyn Ferguson, author of *The Aquarian Conspiracy,* who I believe was clutching the Sony Walkman. John Steele, master alchemist of aromatic oils, earphones still on his head, was doubled up in laughter. And there was Fredric Lehrman, wizard, dragon farmer, compiler, and writer of *The Sacred Landscape,* his usual dignified self convulsing in laughter.

It was, of course, their earphones, all connected to the Walkman by four-foot-long leads, that had produced their mystifying climbing technique. It was as surprising for them to find me there as it was for me to witness this striking synchronicity. Three had traveled from America, only Pete Russell is a fellow Englishman. We all lived in different parts of the world, and yet here we were.

It was one of those strangely meaningful encounters that I was gradually getting used to as I follow my intuition and the quiet guidance of the angels. Yet, as it was to turn out, even that event wasn't to turn out to be the main reason that my angels had schlepped me down to Glastonbury.

It was sometime in late December when we first heard a piece of serious and, if true, extremely frightening news. I say "we" because in the course of my Crowley meditations I'd been meeting others in the loose-knit Glastonbury community. I'd spent one of the days around Baltonsborough, a small village close to Glastonbury. The whole area has deep pagan roots, and it seemed to me that the village of Baltonsborough could well have been named after Ba'al, a name used for a number of different Phoenician and northwestern Semitic "gods." Ba'al makes a brief appearance in the Hebrew Bible, cast as a false god when his priests, unable to set alight a wetted-down sacrifice, were humiliated by the Prophet Elijah (1 Kings 18), whose god Jehovah burned his sacrifice to ashes, in spite of it having been soaked with water.

Over the centuries Ba'al became more of a title applied to any god, rather than a singular identity, so it isn't altogether surprising to find echoes of the name appearing in pagan England. But, of course, it set me to wondering whether the Ba'al were likely to be among those BVF due to return.

As dusk was setting in I decided to knock on the door of a cottage set off on its own in the fields with the encouraging, if unlikely, name of King Solomon's Temple. I wasn't sure what I would find until I was ushered into the warmth of a blazing fire and the presence of two beautiful young women, Alexandra and Lydia, both very much in their power. Although I didn't know it at the time, it turned out that both women were highly regarded key players in the spiritual life of the community.

As the evening drew on and we came to know one another better, it was obvious to each of us there was a deeper reason for my unexpectedly turning up on their doorstep. It was purely a feeling: we'd no idea what it meant. A plant entheogen was produced, sacred mushrooms I believe it was, and we all happily dissolved into the higher realms of consciousness. I retain only an unforgettable image of a spiral galaxy whirling majestically within the naked thigh of Alex, the woman with whom I bonded the closest.

Alex, who remains a close friend to this day, turned out to be one of the main people in the authentic (as opposed to the poseurs) community. With a broad, tanned face and constantly smiling eyes, Alex was a fund of occult and metaphysical knowledge. Her voice was deep and confident, and she seemed to be close to everybody of interest in the area. As I got to know her better I saw how deeply committed she was to her path and how much she was of the earth. A few years earlier she'd driven a gypsy wagon, alone with her two horses, all the way from England down through France to the Mediterranean coast. She was a formidably intelligent and powerful woman with a psychic sensitivity to the ancient ways.

It was over breakfast the next day when I believe we first heard the news that was going to so preoccupy us for the next few weeks.

The three of us were tucking into farm-fresh eggs and bacon and talking about the previous evening's trip, comparing insights and wondering (once again) if we really were in as profoundly telepathic contact as we felt we'd been in those moments of grace, when the door burst open and yet another beautiful young woman rushed in.

Out of breath and flushed with running through the cold, Diana had the look of a young Julie Christie, stumbling in from the snow in a scene from *Doctor Zhivago*. Boots and coat shrugged off, she joined us at the table, poured herself a cup of tea, and told us a remarkable story. She wasn't sure where she first heard it, but somehow the story had reached Glastonbury.

A Frenchman living in Paris, so her story went, was being terrified by strange and mystifying dreams. Apparently the man was an atheist so he had at first dismissed them as nightmares, until his mother, who had recently died, persisted in appearing in his dreams and informing him that the atomic reactor at Cape de la Hague was going to be melting down. She gave the date this event was going to occur: sometime between January 16 and 18 of 1984—the very next month!

The poor man was so disquieted by these dreams that he started telling people about them. He called the scientists at the reactor and was casually dismissed as a loony. None of his friends took him seriously, and he'd become increasingly nervous as the days ticked by. The very people who might have done something about the impending disaster were sneering at him.

Came a day when sitting despondent on a park bench, doubting himself as to whether there was anything to his dreams, he shared it with an Englishwoman who happened to be sitting beside him. By what I can only imagine was a most skillful piece of angelic coordination, this particular woman took his dreams very seriously indeed and immediately called her friends in Glastonbury.

This was where the story stood that winter morning, with different people reacting with differing degrees of disbelief or horror. The atomic reactor was frighteningly close to England, on a peninsula of land in Brittany that sticks out into the English Channel. No one knew quite what to do, and many people who perhaps should have known better pushed the whole awful possibility aside. After all, they'd said, it was only a dream.

Alex and I, however, were among those of a very different view. With her Celtic soul and her knowledge of the great ley lines that run through the body of the earth like the energy meridians of a human body, Alex had an idea of why the news reached Glastonbury. Two of the main ley lines, the Mary and Michael lines, snaked their way through the town. Was it possible, she wondered, that those ley lines ran somewhere near the Cap de la Hague reactor?

Alex knew just the man to answer this question, so we drove through winding lanes to a nearby village and the house of a man I'm going to call the Wizard. He was one of the strangest people I've ever met. Almost completely androgynous, seemingly quite hairless, his smooth unlined face, feminine at one moment, was male the next. His pear-shaped body moving delicately between piles of books, the Wizard was soon smoothing out his geomantic maps on the kitchen table.

Alex and I crowded around him as he traced the main ley line connecting England and France, his almost transparent fingers showing how it ran up through France, and (Lo!) right under the atomic reactor. We looked at each other with a sense of dread. We didn't know what it meant, but an atomic meltdown on top of a main subtle energy meridian couldn't be good.

When we got back to Baltonsborough, Alex started calling together the people who were giving credence to the frightening possibility that the Frenchman's dreams may have had some substance. About a dozen people immediately responded, and we made the time to meditate together regularly and ask our angels and spirit guides if they had any insights on a plan of effective action. I don't recall how it came up, but we received the guidance to plant quartz crystals at key points up and down the relevant ley line, then to meditate throughout the given period, visualizing transforming the dangerous radioactivity into healing energies.

Given the urgency, and finally having a plan of action, we had no problem in gathering sufficient crystals in a town like Glastonbury. More and more people were now coming to the meditations and supporting us once they realized we were committed to planting the crystals. Alex and the Wizard left one morning in late December in a VW van to follow the line down through France, every free space crammed with crystals of different sizes and shapes, many of them fine generator crystals contributed by the Wizard himself from his large collection.

I elected to stay in the Glastonbury area after completing my Crowley meditation cycle to support and encourage those aware of the upcoming event, who could easily slip into fear and doubt. Fear that it might be true: doubt that we could remedy the situation if it were true. And, of course, from any conventional viewpoint the whole thing *was* absurd. Dreams don't predict reality. The dead remain dead. The Frenchman must have been deluded by grief. Atomic power stations don't simply melt down. The scientists wouldn't allow that to happen, would they? Neither Chernobyl nor Three-Mile Island had yet occurred, so it was not so unreasonable to believe atomic power might be safe. As synchronicity would have it, I was editing this paragraph at the very moment Japanese technicians were struggling to bring their atomic reactors under control after the March 2011 earthquake and tsunami ripped open their coastal atomic power stations.

When Alex and the Wizard arrived back a week later, with their mission accomplished, our little community gathered more often to meditate together. We started to bond into an effective group consciousness with a serious shared intention firmly held in mind and began to focus our energy on the ley line and the crystals.

It proved to be a nervous couple of weeks for all of us. We followed the subtle guidance we were receiving as best we were able. I doubt if any of us could account for what we were doing. It seemed so simple, even *too* simple on some days when the rain beat down on top of Alex's van and we huddled in the back. I've since met a few dedicated people who have made it their task to place crystals in key positions all over the planet, but in 1984 it was all very new to us.

Working together with Alex during this time drew us close together, both of us recognizing a reincarnational resonance, yet without feeling any need to try to pin it down. In my experience, having that intimate connection in another lifetime is something merely to be acknowledged— since here and now is where the action is—and is only worth delving into if there is some form of traumatic attachment. We were clear on that front, so after a few brief and unsuccessful attempts to see if we were sexually suited, we settled into one of those wonderfully relaxed relationships, unimpeded by second chakra concerns. It became a lovely balance of male and female energy that was starting to yield a rich vein of spiritual exploration. All that had to be put aside, however, in the light of the upcoming crisis.

When January 16 finally arrived a larger group than usual came together. Since the meditation was to continue over the two days, we elected to have people come and go as they wished, only making sure there was always a minimum group of five holding the center. Some brought their children, others their elderly parents and intrigued friends. We asked only that they hang their disbelief on a peg by the door for the time they were meditating. If they wished they could always pick up their doubts again when they left.

Incense hung in the air. Candles burned steadily among crystals the Wizard placed carefully around the room, and the air smelled of honey. People spoke quietly, one at a time, with long pauses between them. Some talked of their fears, bringing them out in the open where they could be acknowledged and released. Others briefly described what they were "getting," what they were seeing in their meditation. One woman prayed out loud. Sometimes we played music and sang together. The hours passed. People came and went. We focused our attention on the magnificent generator crystal in the center of our circle.

I believe it was in the late afternoon of January 17, after we'd been gathered together for about thirty hours and had a good crowd, some having left, slept, and returned refreshed, that we felt a powerful burst of energy. I suspect each of us experienced this energy in a different way; it was quite discernible. I was meditating at that time so I felt it as a body rush starting at the base of my spine. We all concentrated our hearts' desire on guiding the radioactivity, on transforming it, with the help of our angels, into a positive healing emanation.

Alex, ever sensitive to the subtle energies, looked across the circle and caught my eye. I knew in that moment that we'd done what we came to do. The Earth magic, if that is what it was, was complete. The circle slowly relaxed, people talking quietly to those next to them. Whatever we'd done, we shared a sense that we were working with the earth in the way we believed the ancients must have, with their stone circles and carefully placed dolmens. Like them, we performed terrestrial acupuncture on the body of Mother Earth. In our creative imaginations we had agreed on visualizing the radioactivity released in a potential meltdown, transforming it into regenerated and harmonizing energy, which we then directed toward other significant places of spiritual power.

As we were wondering how we would know whether our crystal ministrations would work and were laughing grimly at how we'd know if they *didn't* work, a quick cry of surprise came from an eight-year-old boy, the child of one of the meditators, who was looking out of the window. A small group of shining silver discs was floating over Glastonbury Tor, the late evening sun glinting brightly off their surfaces. (See plate 3.)

It was all the confirmation we needed.

Had it worked, or was it all a silly delusion concocted in our collective imagination? Simply a new age grandiosity? A practice run for something in the future? Did it really matter if it were true? For that matter, is it likely the authorities in France would ever confirm or deny such an event?

The French atomic reactor at Cap de la Hague was not reported as having any problems on those two days in January 1984.

The weeks I had spent a couple of years earlier with the artist Ray Bret Koch had made a deep impression on me. I felt he'd dropped some important hints on Melinda and me with his talk of the Cathars. I knew very little about this obscure Christian sect at the time, only that they were regarded as heretics by the Church of Rome and had been massacred somewhere in the south of France.

I'd also wondered whether there was a relationship between the words *Cathar* and *cathartic*. I'd found that the former derives from the Greek *kathaori,* meaning "the pure"; and cathartic from the Greek, *kartharsis,* means "cleansing." But Ray had evidently wanted me to know something of the deeper truth of the brief and unfortunate history of the Cathars.

"The first thing to know," Ray had told us as we sat around the fire in his old Normandy château, and I'm paraphrasing his stumbling English, "the thing is the Cathars, as a religious community, were extremely successful. They owned enormous swaths of land and had only started arriving in the Languedoc region, as well as a few other places in Europe, sometime in the eleventh century. They were popular in the region almost immediately; they were converting more and more people away from the Catholic Church. Their influence expanded over the next couple of centuries until most of the south of France, the Provence area, belonged to them."

"That must have pissed off Rome," I broke in.

"Not only that," Ray responded, "but by that time the northern French barons were jealously eyeing all that land. It didn't take much to set the wolves on the sheep. By the mid-thirteenth century almost all the Cathars had been exterminated. In fact, the Inquisition was originally set up to convert, or more likely, to torture Cathars. It was a dreadful time. Quite awful." Ray's head dropped to his chest, and I wondered if he was quietly sobbing. After a while he spoke again, and I could see he was getting tired. He was an old man, already in his eighties when I first met him.

"Here's what I wanted you know," he was speaking even more quietly now, yet there was a new intensity to his gaze as he turned away from the fire to look directly at me. "The Cathars might have had some extreme beliefs, but there's something they held particularly dear, and you won't find this in the books . . ." There was another piercing look and then a short silence.

"You know they believed in reincarnation?" he said.

I shook my head. I hadn't known this at the time.

"Well, they didn't make a big deal of it." Ray continued. "If they weren't able to purify themselves sufficiently in this life, they knew they'd be coming back until they did. But here's what I wanted you to know, which was one of their closest held secrets: they vowed to return at the end of time."

With that the old man lapsed into silence, and Melinda, who'd been sitting quietly translating a word every now and then, signaled with her eyes that it was time to creep up to bed. My head spinning with questions, I resolved to research as much as I could about the Cathars.

I found that the beliefs of the Cathars, although Christian in essence, were very different from those held by the Holy Roman Church. Closer to the Gnostics than strict Catholicism, the Cathars believed this world was created by a Demiurge; a subcreation devoid of any true spirituality. For the Cathars, the world was inherently malformed, a place of spiritual darkness, created and ruled by the devil. They couldn't accept that a God of love would have created such a horrible world. This led to their belief that matter itself was inherently evil, tainted by power and corruption.

This dualistic concept in Christianity, of spirit versus matter, has run like an alternative current to Catholic dogma. It appears to have originated in Zoroastrianism and then later manifested in Gnosticism, with Yaldabaoth, the Demiurge (an obvious proxy for Satan), first among the seven Archons, and their mother, Sophia. There's an intriguing resonance here. Sophia, so the Gnostics maintained, originally created the world. This act was then usurped by her eldest son, Yaldabaoth, who claimed the creation for himself. He has ruled as the Rex Mundi ever since.

This act of the Demiurge effectively trapped the spirit, the Indwelling Divinity, within the prison of matter. For the Cathars this was the great human challenge. Matter had to be renounced or redeemed for the spirit to be released into the hands of the God of love. If this release couldn't be achieved in one lifetime, then the Cathars believed they would reincarnate (echoing what Ray told me) until they got it right.

As I read up on the little known about this remarkable sect I couldn't help feeling that in spite of their rejection of the physical world, much of what I was learning was thoroughly compatible with how so many of us are currently thinking. In the Cathar sect there was a parity between the sexes, and an almost equal number of parfaits were women. Many parfaits were doctors; they used molds against infections and hypnosis for anesthesia. Cathars were supported by over a third of the Midi nobles, and they were respected for their craftsmanship, including their papermaking. In a manner that would be familiar to Tibetan Buddhists, the Cathars were said to have used mandalas in their tests for the rank of parfait.

Surveying history from our perch in the twenty-first century, it's sadly ironic that the brief flowering of the Cathar culture represents possibly the finest manifestation of a true Christian way of life we've seen over the last two millennia. It remains hard to believe, for example, that the Church of Rome, with all its opulence and centuries of power mongering, really fulfills the intentions of Jesus Christ. And it's also becoming increasingly obvious that technological materialism, the malformed child of corrupted Christianity, has brought us to the brink of disaster.

More detailed information on the Cathar belief system than I knew at the time is currently available on the Internet. Ray had given me a taste; he said enough to alert my interest. Clearly what he wanted to get across to me was something to do with reincarnation.

Although it's believed that early Christians subscribed to reincarnation, as did many of the Greek philosophers, by the fourth century the Roman Church had stamped it out in Western thought. The belief that salvation can be obtained only through Jesus Christ, and not through self-perfection, was justification enough for the pope to declare Cathars heretics. As with other extreme dualistic sects in previous centuries the label of heretic once again opened the way to some of the most shameful genocidal behavior ever committed in the name of religion.

Ray was right; I couldn't find anything in the literature about their vow to return at the end of time. I knew this concept of a final "return" was a familiar trope in a number of reincarnational belief systems, yet the more I looked into it, the more identification I felt with the tragedy and bravery of those unfortunate and devout people. Their terrible deaths in that harrowing time must have created a powerful intention in the massacred Cathar Parfaits to reincarnate at the end of time. As I read and meditated on them, as Ray suggested, I was finding an increasing depth of sympathy for the Cathars within myself.

In spite of these feelings, I didn't make the obvious connection I think Ray wanted me to make. I'm justifiably suspicious of what other people see in me or ideas they might have about themselves that they project onto me. However, reincarnation had come up a number of times over the course of my life, so I simply decided to be open to all possibilities. Since the clarity of my near-death experience in 1973 established for me that life continues after death, it wasn't such a jump to know that life can precede birth. Whether this is true for everybody I can't say, but I have had a sufficient number of experiences in the course of my life to know with certainty that I've had many previous lives. I have also met a number of people, men and women, with whom I've felt such a powerful affinity that reincarnation is the most simple way of explaining it.

Yet, all of this is also somewhat puzzling.

The Urantia Book says quite firmly that reincarnation is not a technique practiced in this Local Universe. It maintains that the souls of mortals are created on this level by the interaction of the Father and Mother Spirits. Having been created on this, the densest level to sustain intelligent life, souls continue to climb up through a variety of increasingly spiritualized vehicles on their Multiverse journey of self-perfection.

Yet, this dismissal of reincarnation flies in the face of subjective experience and doesn't explain the profound sense of familiarity reincarnates feel when they encounter one another; nor does it account for what is a fundamental belief in two of the world's great religions. I doubt if *The Urantia Book* is inaccurate in principle; there'd be little point in the celestial communicants making up lies. While it could be the Christian bias of those who received the book, I'm more inclined to think the ones who have chosen to reincarnate on this planet fall under an unrevealed agenda.

After all, the reconciliation of the Lucifer Rebellion was still eighty years in the unpredictable future when *The Urantia Book* was composed. The communicants may not have been free to reveal what might ensue after the rebellion was finally resolved or they might not have been aware it was going to happen. Then again, perhaps the angels, as compassionate and loving as ever, merely kept their silence, allowing all involved to work out what is happening in the privacy of their own hearts and minds.

It was then I first got a clue as to the existence of what I've come to call the Angelic Conspiracy.

Now, however, during a cold January in 1984, with all the excitement of the potential Cap de la Hague meltdown and my own focus on the Crowley meditations, I hadn't given much more thought to the Cathars.

Alex and I teamed up together following her return from the crystal planting mission and were living in her VW van, parked in a field within sight of Glastonbury Tor. Most days the rain teemed down, forcing us into the fuggy closeness of the van. We found we worked well together, seeming to have mutually interlocking pieces of information, which contributed to an overall pattern we called our "cosmuesli."

The little I knew about the Cathars had touched my heart in an unexpectedly intimate way, so I wasn't altogether surprised when Alex arrived back from her sojourn to Provence with stories of a farmstead built over a ruined Cathar village there. She and the Wizard had followed the Magdalene ley line all the way down through France and found themselves deep in Cathar country, close to the village of Rennes-le-Château. A lot of speculative fiction has been written about the area around Rennes-le-Château, including the firmly held local belief that a small group of Cathar parfaits, prior to one of the more hideous massacres, had escaped with what has become known as *le tresor cathar* and which is believed to be buried somewhere in the area.

Still more speculation has also focused on a nineteenth-century priest, Father Bérenger Saunière, and his bringing to light the secret society, the Priory of Sion. The 1982 bestseller *Holy Blood, Holy Grail* by Michael Baigent, Richard Leigh, and Henry Lincoln expanded a speculative line of thinking into a legendary royal bloodline descending from the children of Jesus and Mary Magdalene. It was this *sang royal,* so the story went, that the Priory of Sion was created to protect down through the ages.

More recently, the colossal success of Dan Brown's *The Da Vinci Code,* a direct descendant of Baigent, Leigh, and Lincoln's book, suggests an increasing number of people are opening up to alternative versions of the Christian story. Whether true or not, the popularity of these books and films helps break down the cultural and religious trance that holds so many sincere believers in the thrall of accepted dogma. Consequently, all of us are obliged to use our intuitions to discern the underlying truth from all the fabrications.

While recent research has disposed of many of the false notions about the priest Saunière, his mysterious fortune, and the more recently admitted hoax of the Priory of Sion, there remains the persistent story of Mary Magdalene and her life in the south of France following the crucifixion.

The Magdalene, along with Joseph of Arimathea and others, apparently landed in France, where Mary settled in Provence. Joseph headed north, finally arriving in Glastonbury. This narrative is somewhat supported by the widely held belief in England that Joseph of Arimathea came to Glastonbury with twelve companions. He was recognized as an authentic holy man by the Druids and given some land, on which he built the first Christian church in Britain.

It was Alex who connected the next dot: "If it's true that Mary Magdalene lived out her life in the south of France, then surely the Cathars must have been aware of it."

"Perhaps that was one of the reasons they were so successful," I added. "It was already fertile turf for them when they'd started to arrive." I knew Alex had been thinking about this since she'd returned from Provence. Like many women of power these days, she identified strongly with Mary Magdalene. There was something in Provence we both needed to discover.

The synchronicities were starting to pile up.

It was not an easy journey down through France. Sure, the van purred along fine. After a blustery, cold crossing, the car ferry struggling against the powerful currents of the English Channel, the weather was growing progressively warmer as we drove south. Alex and I were buzzing with excitement and couldn't wait to explore the area she'd found on the previous trip.

All was not well with the Wizard, however.

We'd agreed to take him—he claimed to be too nervous to drive on the "wrong side of the road"—because he wanted to retrieve some of his crystals now that they'd served their purpose. I'd noticed a flicker of reluctance from Alex when he asked. Then I'd recalled she'd mentioned, after she returned with him from the previous mission, just how tedious it was to be around the Wizard for any length of time. Now I was starting to understand why.

The poor Wiz wasn't cut out for travel. His strange amorphous shape was never comfortable crammed onto the sleeping platform in the back of the van. He was a whiner and a complainer. Perhaps it was his sensitivity, as he insisted, that gave him stabbing headaches whenever we were passing through urban areas, but it gave him one more thing to complain about. The graceful androgyny I had rather admired back in Glastonbury soon lost its grace under the strain of unavoidably close human contact. Brilliant and wise though he may have been in his comfort zone, the Wizard on the road turned into a shrill and self-pitying old shrew.

After some initial attempts to help him through his troubles, it soon became obvious the Wiz was a drama queen who simply preferred to bitch and moan. When we realized that, Alex and I sat in the front seats and exchanged the driving every couple of hours, then loudly singing every song we could think of, effectively drowned out the Wizard's petulant moans from the back.

We were all tired as we finally threaded our way through the winding country roads of the Aude Valley that lead to Lavaldieu, the site of the Cathar village. It was mountainous country, great rocky crags rearing up out of thickly forested flanks, with surprisingly few farmsteads. It was evident wherever we looked that for all the rugged beauty, this was one of the poorest regions of France.

It was late afternoon. A winter sun flickered through the trees and threw us into twilight when a ragged mountain ridge blocked its light. We passed by the village of Rennes-le-Château, perched on a limestone bluff and overlooking a wide valley, punctuated by crumpled rocky outcrops. Leaving the village behind us, we descended down into the valley.

Alex pointed out Bugarach, calling it a holy mountain, and I could see it, a dark hump against the misty blue of the surrounding mountains.

Only a few miles more.

Night was falling when we finally reached our destination. It was not a prepossessing first view. There was no sign of the Cathar village, of course; I wasn't expecting to find that. Lavaldieu was simply a couple of two-story stone farmhouses and a large, well-built barn, open at one end, positioned at a right angle around a wide cobbled courtyard. Exhausted, we left the bed in the van to the Wizard, threw our sleeping bags into the barn and instantly fell into a deep sleep.

Awakening to a startlingly blue sky, I got my first clear view of the land surrounding Lavaldieu. Bugarach, like the humped back of a great dragon, dominated the landscape. A lenticular cloud that would have made Mt. Shasta envious floated above the summit. I found out later there are local stories of Bugarach being a center of extraterrestrial activity, with craft observed flying in and out of the mountain.

The air was dry and seemed preternaturally pure. Trees at the property line were bare of leaves, their trunks and branches dark and stark against the white limestone crags. It was cool without being cold. I found a rock set off to the side of the courtyard and settled down onto its smooth surface to meditate. I knew I needed to get in touch with the soul of the place, but I wasn't expecting the rush of energy and information that filled me after I'd grounded myself.

I *knew* in those moments that Lavaldieu was indeed a special spot. It was a place of reconciliation and healing, as well as a place that required its own healing and reconciliation. The setting was magnificent, but underneath there was a deeply unsettled turbulence. In a strange but not entirely unsurprising way, which might have had something to do with the ley lines, the area had something of the quality of Glastonbury. Beautiful on the outside, dark and somewhat savage on the inside.

I can't say I heard the cries of dying Cathars. No awful visions appeared as I sat there, just a crushing sense of desperation—a despair echoing down through the centuries, held in the fabric of the place. The stone walls of the farmhouses would have been the same rocks the Cathars used to build their village, recycled countless times over the centuries. Whether it's true rocks hold memory or whether terrible violence remains long after in the vibrations of a place, I was overcome with feelings of desolation that seemed to spring from the stones all around me. Distantly, back in the courtyard, I could hear the Wizard's shrill and complaining voice rising and falling in tones of personal misery.

My heart opened as my body heaved with anguish. The despair just under the surface was almost too much to tolerate. I wasn't ready for this. I was due to return to New York in a couple of days, and this was no way to end what had been to date such a positive and uplifting trip. Yet, here I was. I must have been experiencing these awful feelings for a good reason. It must have something to do with me.

With that thought I knew I would have to return to Lavaldieu.

It wasn't until June of that year that I could get back to France.

The landscape was green and lovelier than ever. Lavaldieu had been spruced up in the intervening months, and the buildings were now livable. When we were able to settle down and talk, Alex told me how she'd gone ahead and bought the property with the idea of creating a spiritual community that would live and work there. Already there were half a dozen people who were planning to come, and a couple was already residing in one of the farmhouses.

I wondered to myself if they had any idea of what was going on under the surface of the place. How would they cope with the underlying sense of horror and desolation, if it ever did become apparent to them? They might well think it was them.

Alex was excited. She felt on the cusp of great potential; she'd always wanted to create a community, and here it was, actually happening, and in this intensely sacred landscape. After a spring down here she was glowing with health. Having committed herself so wholeheartedly to creating a vibrant community at Lavaldieu I felt it wouldn't have been exactly encouraging to talk about my experience on the previous trip.

"You're not going to believe this," she was saying, "but you know how we came here just following our intuition? Well, since I've been here I keep meeting people from all over the world who've also been drawn to this region."

We were sitting at a long wooden table that had been pulled into the shadow of the barn, its surface decorated with the scorched scars of generations of cigarettes. "It's the Cathar thing," Alex continued, "we really *are* coming back. People are saying there are at least thirty thousand of us in this area, in the little villages around here—and more coming every year apparently. I've met lots of them."

Her eyes were sparkling. I'd never heard Alex say "we" and "us" before when we'd discussed Cathars. Of course we'd talked about Cathars in general; it was one of the interests we both had in common. Believing wholeheartedly we were reincarnated Cathars, however, wasn't something either of us was really ready to accept. Our previous trip to Lavaldieu was merely an exploration. I'd no idea Alex was going to end up living here. Evidently something had changed and deepened for her since I'd been away.

Remembering my unsettling meditation the last time I was here, I wasn't sure I wanted to dive into the Cathar reality quite so readily. Yet, I had to admit something had pulled me back. Alex must have seen the doubt on my face.

"Wait until you meet some of the others. Hear some of their stories. Sometimes when you meet one of them all sorts of memories and pictures come up."

"You're sure about this? You really think you were a Cathar?"

"It's not a question of being sure, or of thinking too hard about it. It just seems to be. There are too many synchronicities, too many people feeling it for it to be a delusion. You'll see."

And, indeed I did.

It was a few days later that Klaus and Jessie came to Lavaldieu to see what was happening. Klaus had lived in these mountains for some years and had heard of some new people moving into Lavaldieu. Alex had previously met them in an open market in one of the local villages.

I was sitting in our van at the far end of the courtyard when the couple puttered up the drive. They seemed oddly depressed as they got out of their little Citroën Deux Chevaux, but perked up when they saw me waving from the van.

As I was walking toward them I first got the *feeling*.

The three of us met in the middle of the courtyard, and I shook hands, first with Klaus, and then with Jessie. When I looked into Jessie's eyes, again that *feeling:* I *knew.* It was like looking at myself. I *knew* this woman as I *knew* myself. A jolt of mutual remembrance passed between us as we shook hands. I could hear Klaus talking somewhere behind me, but it felt like Jessie and I were surrounded by a bubble of intimacy, neither of us willing to break the trance.

The shock of recognition is something of a cliché, yet it *is* a shock, made all the more intense in this situation as it was obvious we'd never met before in this lifetime. Jessie was a tall, slim Danish girl in her late twenties, with a smiling elfin face, cornflower-blue eyes, and short blonde hair, urchin-cut. She had a graceful dancer's body, long tanned legs, and a flowing way of carrying herself. Klaus was still talking as we moved to the table in the shade of the barn and joined Alex. Respectful of Klaus, I made sure Jessie and I sat at different ends of the long wooden table.

"Can you imagine?!" Klaus spoke with a strong Swiss-German accent, "we were hoping to make some good money for a change, then this happened."

"Yah! And it was all the monster's fault!" Jessie broke in, her voice rippling with a surprisingly deep laughter. She spoke better English than Klaus, with a lilting Scandinavian cadence.

Alex and I must have looked puzzled. Monsters? In Provence?

Klaus looked sharply at Jessie for spoiling his story. "No, no," he said, his voice louder; I could feel his controlling nature from the other end of the table. "It was this damn film we'd signed up for. A Hollywood film. Good money."

"We really need it for the cottage...," Jessie broke off again at another dark glance from Klaus before he continued.

"The film was meant to be in Carcassonne. The whole crew had arrived from California; I've never seen so many people just to make a film. So Jess and I signed up as extras. Just as we were ready to start we heard everything was postponed, at least for another week."

"And it *was* a monster," he said ruefully, looking sharply at his girlfriend, who was still laughing. "The star had to be flown back to England. To hospital. They told us it happened with his monster mask. It gave him a terrible rash all over his face. The heat of the sun made some sort of chemical reaction, and the inside stuck to his face."

It must have been a sad situation for the star, but of course we were all laughing. There seemed to be a pointed metaphor to do with masks in Klaus's story, which was made all the funnier by his disappointed expression.

Jessie and I were trying hard to avoid each other's eyes.

Alex had returned from shopping in the village shortly before Klaus and Jessie arrived, so she went to the back of the barn where we kept the ice and pulled out the bottles of French beer she'd bought in Rennes-le-Château. This was followed by a bowl of the tangy wild cherries picked from the trees beside the road on the way back.

Talk turned to all the new people arriving in Cathar country. For Klaus, it was infuriating. He thought the "Cathar bullshit" was crazy and had no time for all the spiritual mumbo jumbo. Jessie caught my eye at that, and once again, almost like an electric shock, this profound sense of familiarity swept over me.

No, indeed, it wasn't the "damn Cathars" (another wince flickered over Jessie's beautiful open face at that jibe) that made Klaus want to live here. A self-proclaimed mountain man, he fell in love with the landscape and resented the hell out of having to go back to Switzerland so frequently to earn the money to live in Provence. As for those "deluded hippies" who were invading his territory, it was really all too much.

Another chronic complainer, I thought. Was there an energy around this place that brought out the worst in people?

Quickly changing the subject, Alex told him something of her plans for Lavaldieu, of creating a leaderless community and a retreat center—a place where everyone could come and work with their own spiritual practices. There'd be no dogma, and people would be open to sharing what they were discovering. It was a formalization, in a way, of how Alex and I were developing our cosmeusli. She'd barely finished describing her intentions when Klaus, eyes narrowing, cut in angrily. "Talk is cheap," he said.

I was startled at the rudeness. He must have seen the look on my face because before continuing he turned toward me. "I've seen a lot of dreamers coming and going around here. But I'm a practical man and unless a person can actually make their dream happen, all the talking in the world won't help."

I ignored the sneer in his voice and merely asked him quietly, "And what do you do for your *artistic* soul, Klaus?"

Perhaps he was surprised I wasn't being defensive and might be actually interested in him because he answered in a much more open tone. "Well, I love to create with my own hands, but with no money and all the building work I need to do, and then having to go off to Switzerland for so much of the year . . ."

He saw me smiling at him, realized he was justifying not manifesting *his* dream, and was open enough to burst into peals of honest laughter. The atmosphere relaxed after this interchange, and when the other resident couple joined us we were able to talk about our plans without constant cynical interruptions from Klaus. In fact, he turned out to be rather helpful—in a practical sort of a way, of course.

As the light faded we carried the table and benches back into the barn. The floor was covered with hay and there was no electricity. A gibbous moon was already rising, throwing a cool lemony light through the open doors of the barn. A single candle sputtered in the middle of the table—the only sound in a great quiet settling over the hills.

Sinking into the silence, we didn't talk for a long time, entranced by the fading light and the sweet scents of a summer evening in the south of France. My eyes were closed and I was breathing easily when, in a way hard to describe since it happens so rarely, I *felt* the presence of Jessie. If I knew more about my soul I would say with more confidence that our souls joined in some way I could feel, but not understand.

When I finally opened my eyes, she was looking directly into them from the other end of the table. As we held each other's gaze long past the point of no return, memories flooded to the surface: of feeling vast and spread over the land beneath me; then of being the land itself, the great rock ridge was my spine, massive white bones shimmering in my imagination. My eyes closed in ecstasy.

We were together then, our souls entwined and soaring above rolling forests covering the gentle swelling hills. Mountains seem to rise up below us, sending us twisting and turning higher still, before descending in a long catenary dive over desert sands, curling around rugged limestone peaks . . .

There was a sudden movement in the barn that jerked me back into my body. I opened my eyes to see Klaus pushing back the bench and getting ready to leave. As we said our goodbyes, Jessie whispered that she'd see me again in a couple of days, after Klaus had gone back to Switzerland.

A few afternoons later Jessie arrived in the Deux Chevaux to whisk me away on what she announced as "an adventure in Cathar country." As wistfully beautiful as the last time, and more relaxed free of Klaus's presence, she drove fast and confidently along the winding country roads. She was telling me how she'd been drawn down from Denmark, following what she called the "Cathar trail," but she couldn't explain to herself exactly what she was doing. She'd lived in the region for some years and had tried to get away, three or four times, she told me, and she'd always been thrown back to these desolate mountains by the tides of life.

She was such a strange mixture, this beautiful creature. A quiet sadness, poignant rather than overbearing, could be broken by flashes of such pure delight as to make me catch my breath. She was simultaneously ancient and innocent, a beautiful young woman and a crone; she was modest yet self-confident, fearless but intimidated by Klaus's control; she was deeply spiritual yet largely unaware of it.

We were climbing higher into the mountains, the roads becoming narrower, more ill-kept and sinuous as we snaked around hairpin bends. The air was getting noticeably cooler, while the sun on my face grew more intense the higher we ascended. I was mulling over my feelings and thoughts about Jessie, how good it felt to be with her and how deeply familiar she was to me. I think I *knew* then that I was being driven through these country lanes by a one-time Cathar parfait.

It was an exquisite summer's day. I could have been in heaven.

Perhaps I should address here what must have occurred to you, the sympathetic reader. How could I not have been turned on by this gorgeous woman? Am I not describing all of the symptoms of falling in love?

These are both reasonable questions, but here's the odd thing. Jessie and I loved each other at first sight, we both knew that. Our hearts had opened to one another, yet surprisingly, there was absolutely no erotic charge. It wasn't that we were both unavailable, and perhaps under other circumstances we might have been drawn to sexualize our relationship. Rather, we seemed to have an unspoken agreement that we were doing the angels' work. Sex might have been fun, but it would have been an unnecessary distraction.

As I pondered this it came to me that, like the Cathar parfaits before us, we found we loved each other with a purity undisturbed by any sexual yearning. Neither were there any of the stresses and strains, the hopes and uncertainties, all the will-she-won't-she tensions that generally accompany sexual desire.

My eyes were closed, and the wind—hot and pine scented—blew through my long hair, tickling my back and arms. I was bathing in this tender innocence as the car swayed around the corners on its astonishingly forgiving Citroën suspension system. We felt one and the same, Jessie and I, and I was reminded of that traditional Mayan greeting, "I am another you." We drove in a telepathic silence for at least an hour before she pulled the car over at the foot of a mountain. The landscape was deserted. We hadn't seen another car for miles.

Clambering over a low stone wall we start climbing up though a steep gorge, a stream beside us trickling down through rocks. Butterflies are dancing all around us. The sun is low, yet the earth is still hot beneath our feet.

We arrive together, stepping into a natural clearing culled from the surrounding forest. The grass is soft and welcoming as we throw ourselves down to rest and take in the view of the coiling massive forms of the surrounding mountains.

Water is bubbling from an oddly sculpted stone spout in the form of a dolphin's head. The water is cool and sweet. We both splash water over our faces and bodies at the same time, looking up and laughing with joy.

"I don't know if I'm dreaming all this. . . ," I say, and we're laughing again, neither knowing nor caring.

Turning, we pick the cherries off three perfectly formed trees in the meadow behind us. The fruit from each cherry tree tastes quite distinctly different. We walk, marveling, from one tree to another, trying to sense the subtle characteristics leading to each individual tree's cherries.

It comes to me that we are being prepared for an initiation.

A grassy incline curves up to a grove of pine trees; white rocks fallen from the ridge above lie scattered among the wildflowers and flowing grasses. We climb hand in hand up through the pine grove, pausing to sit together on a flat white rock. It's Jessie who breaks the silence.

"You know this is a sacred mountain, don't you?" I nod; I can feel it too.

"Cathar families burrowed into these mountains, hiding in the caves until they were walled in and left to starve. . . ." Tears are trickling down Jessie's beautiful face. I *know* we are here to transform the awful energies, the horror and sadness I'd felt that first day in Lavaldieu, to make our peace with the souls of the devoted Cathars and their path of pure love.

This understanding brings waves of infinite sadness; my emotional body feels as if it's being crushed. Desolate, I feel the pain and know the faith of the Perfected Ones, the sacrificial lambs of a cruel and despotic Roman Church and the greed of the French nobles.

I couldn't tolerate the horror in that first meditation back in Lavaldieu. It overwhelmed me at the time, and I needed to leave the whole ghastly issue behind me.

Now I'm back in the fray. I'd made the conscious choice to return to Cathar country, and I know this time I need to let in all the pain and suffering, as much for my own spiritual well-being as anything we might be doing for the earth or the Cathars.

Aided and supported by Jessie's spiritual purity, I find I'm able to feel the full abomination of that terrible time. The overweening greed and cruelty of the French nobles; the sadism and perversity of the Inquisition; the daily terror with which the Cathars lived; the torture of burning alive, of suffocating in caves, of being racked or torn apart by horses—all of these frightful images and thoughts and feelings are welling up in me.

Sitting next to Jessie on the white rock, the wooded hillside dropping away beneath our feet, and allowing myself to experience this hideous barbarity while simultaneously basking in our newfound unconditional love for one another, I feel she is giving me the spiritual courage to face and release these horrors.

I gather all the demons together, inviting them into my base chakra, where I visualize them surrounded by golden light. Then, in the way the old alchemist Ray Bret Koch taught me, I visualize the golden bubble moving up through my chakras, to finally stream out through my crown chakra.

Doing this, Ray assured me, permitted the angels to disperse the negative energies back to the plenum. According to him, the thoughtforms have to be initially transformed and released by a human being before the angels can finally disperse them. The horrific thoughtforms were created by humans, and they had to be released by humans conscious enough to do it. That is what the modern shaman or alchemist did, he'd told me.

I feel Jessie's body shift beside me, the warmth of her arm pressing against me. A long sigh. Neither of us are speaking. I *know* she knows what just happened, that she too felt the negative energies passing through me. We're both laughing now, arms around one another, my cheek nestling into her long neck; her scent is that of the wildflowers on the mountainside.

We remain quiet, still in each other's arms and feeling the glorious purity of Oneness before we uncurl our limbs, and rising together we turn back to the mountain, which is now steeper and more rugged.

We separate, first one of us leading, then the other. There is no path, yet every step I take I'm aware of others who've trod these steps before. If I stumble or miss my balance, even slightly, there's a convenient root or clump of ferns with which to steady myself. Ledges appear at exactly the right intervals, large enough for us to lie back on and regain our breath.

We climb on, the guitar I thought to bring with me bangs painfully on the back of my legs at each step. Sweat is running down my neck. The pace Jessie is setting is relentless. She's twenty years younger and a lot fitter than I am. Her tanned legs are long and pump like pistons. Her feet seem to know exactly where to plant themselves, sometimes scattering small rocks, which fall around me. We're climbing fast, and I know Jessie is testing me, pushing me to my limits.

We begin to see below us the rocky summits of the surrounding mountains. The winding valley we are following is opening up the higher we climb.

As we reach two large white stones standing upright on the slope Jessie climbs onto one of them that appears to be carved into a natural stone throne. I stand beside her, our eyes on the same level, and I feel the sorrow of the ages lifting off me. I am aware of what is required of us. It is through the purity and innocence of our love that the healing can take place.

Our next surge takes us to a ridge, and then it is an easy route along a trail leading between limestone bluffs that takes us to the summit. Once again we fall in with each other, matching step for step, breath for breath. We bend against a fresh young wind, pausing to float with seven crows lofted on the evening's updraft to within feet of us, wheeling and dancing with our spirits.

Lighter now, and with our second breath, we run laughing, allowing ourselves to be drawn up to the very peak of the mountain, before sinking down, back to back, on a large flat stone. Jessie is behind me, wordlessly settling into a single lotus position, as I am. I feel a gathering warmth in the base of my spine, and I *know* she feels it too.

Once again the feeling of spiritual oneness is almost overwhelming. The inner and outer realities come together as our bodies seem to dissolve into the mountain beneath us. This massive limestone formation, the primordial creature on whose head we perch, is coming to life. An energy, deep within the mountain, is awakening from its long dream. My body is shuddering with the energy, and I'm aware of Jessie turning to massage my back. With that, this intense energy roars up my spine, erupting out of the top of my head.

When I finally open my eyes I see that Jessie has been flung by the expulsion of energy down a grassy slope to a wide flat ledge some fifteen feet away; she's flowed with the energy, allowing herself to wash down like water, and has come to rest under a lone silver birch tree.

She is smiling up at me as I pick up my guitar and move over to where I can lean against a white rock buttress. A church bell tolls in the valley far below, echoing up to us and seeming to hang in an aural mist around us.

A single note curls out from my guitar, catching a resonant harmonic of the church bell. My hands feel as though they are following their own sweet agenda. Another chord unfurls Jessie's long body. She shivers in ecstasy, her slim fingers forming mudras in the air. I pick up the rhythm, and now she is dancing—her legs stretching and curving with the sound. She dances for the earth and for the nature spirits, a whirling mad swirl of movement, bare feet beating out the rhythm on naked rock, her lithe back arching up to the sun. She swoops to the ground, pauses with eyes closed while my guitar gently weeps, then, matching a new rhythm she throws her body, as a woman possessed, into yet further gorgeous gyrations.

We are joined by the tendrils of sound, and I know I am flying Jessie, as I might fly a kite. It's utterly spontaneous, a dance of equals, each trusting the other, each dependent on the other to shine the philosopher's stone. It is a conjunctio of the most subtle and sacred kind, and it's bringing a blessing on us and the land we both love.

She soars on eagle's wings higher and higher, dipping and flowing with the evening drafts as minor chords transform to majors. As so rarely happens, my fingers are playing themselves and I am liberated. Joyfully disassociated, I rise to join Jessie, our spirits entwining as tongues of sound curl around us.

My eyes are closed, and I *know* we are both seeing the same vision: twin volcanos are rising before us in our collective imagination, one pouring forth fire and the other, spirit smoke. The earth shakes, and the sound is pure harmony. We wrap a flaming angel in our arms and are both consumed with joy. I hear the guitar as though another is playing. The rhythm flings us this way and the other, yet holds us all the while on the whelm of a continuing wave of ecstasy until, exhausted, Jessie follows a trembling thread of sound and tumbles back into her body, dance and music climaxing together under the single, whispering, silver birch.

As I thought later about this ecstatic day with Jessie, of the spiritual rapport we shared and what we'd been guided to do together, I realized it was a form of Earth magic, perhaps something along the lines of what John Michell has called "re-enchanting the planet." It wasn't anything either of us had planned, or even done before. It was a completely spontaneous and intuitive act, so fluid and meaningful that it could only have been orchestrated from deeper levels of reality.

I believe both Jessie and I emerged from the experience spiritually enriched, whether or not we created any metaphysical effects on the Cathar reality. It was a sacred initiation for both of us, of that we were sure, but an initiation into what, we were not being told.

We didn't talk much in the car on the way back to Lavaldieu, both content that we had fulfilled our mission, neither of us trying to rationalize what we had done. I only recall the few words Jessie spoke as we sped back in the fading light. The sentences came out slowly in a grave voice, punctuated by long silences and spoken with an almost incantantory tone that made me shiver with recognition.

She said, "I reached down along the filaments of sound and found my self. I knew my self in you."

She said, "I gave myself finally and totally to the winds of sound. I became all things. I permeated the universe. I extended on out into the infinite spaces. I knew all and was known by all."

She said, "I fell through time. I was Inanna. I was Tara. I was Isis. I wept for us all. I knew all this suffering was made worthwhile. I died and was reborn."

With that she dropped me off at Lavaldieu, and we've never encountered one another since.

I've retuned to Lavaldieu half a dozen times over the years. I'm still no wiser as to my individual identity as a Cathar, although I have no doubt I was there. My encounter with Jessie was too intense and meaningful to be dismissed as delusional. In fact, the authenticity of my experience was supported when I came across Dr. Arthur Guirdham's book, *The Great Heresy,* about his remarkable findings.

Dr. Guirdham is a respected English psychiatrist who, in the course of his practice, discovered in doing therapeutic hypnotic regressions that some of his patients related complex and detailed narratives of their lives as Cathars. He has since written a couple more books on this subject, coming ultimately to the understanding that he, too, was a reincarnated Cathar.

Personally, I find I have no desire to dig any deeper, which suggests I have nothing specific to learn from that particular incarnation. I assume I wasn't one of those burned alive, or I'd probably be more motivated. The most troublesome incarnations, in my experience, are those in which I wasn't able to learn what I needed to in that lifetime—generally due to it being cut short in some unpleasant way.

I feel I've served my time with the Cathar energies, and whatever Earth magic Jessie and I may have summoned together was directed with open hearts toward the healing of the land. More and more people were arriving over the years, and I imagine they are all having to deal with the powerful energies in this region of France.

Sadly, Lavaldieu as a community turned out very much as I'd experienced when I was first there. People appeared and lived in the farmhouses or pitched tents on the grounds for varying lengths of time; some were spiritually inclined, others not. It even appeared to be flourishing for a while; Alex was doing a sterling and exhausting job of holding the community together, while not wanting to be seen as the leader.

But it was never a peaceful place. That subterranean unrest I found so horrifying when I first meditated in Lavaldieu seemed to progressively overshadow it. People were drawn to the community by the beauty of the landscape and the possibility of a simple life, only to find after being there for a while that the worst aspects of their personalities would rise to the surface. Couples broke up in terrible rows; authoritarian personalities sought to dominate and take over; there were the inevitable little princes and princesses expecting everything to be done for them; in short, there was all the cut and thrust of community life amped up to a formidable degree.

What we didn't know then, but is far clearer in retrospect, is that spiritually orientated communities, especially those located in an energetically potent landscape—Lavaldieu and Glastonbury being two examples—will bring to the surface what needs to be healed. This process invariably brings up repressed anger and fear—all the traumas of childhood—and these will be acted out within the community. If this isn't well understood and worked with therapeutically, the group will break into factions and either shatter or collapse.

Of course, all was not permanent turmoil at Lavaldieu. There were many magical moments, one of which I believe is particularly reflective of the potential of Earth magic, when human personalities interact with the spirits of the landscape to the benefit of each. It happened in this way.

I'd come to know Stanley Messenger well over the years of my pilgrimages to Glastonbury. He was an elderly man, perhaps in his early seventies when I first met him, slim, with bright blue eyes, elegant and beautifully mannered in the traditional English way. He was generally considered one of the elders in Glastonbury spiritual circles. He'd been supportive of our plan to save the reactor meltdown and had encouraged others to take it seriously. He also was among the most stalwart meditators when the big day came around. Like many other genuinely spiritual elderly men and women, Stanley, for all his wisdom, had an air of delight-ful, childlike innocence.

One summer, after Lavaldieu had been functioning as a community for a couple of years, I was able to spend another week there. It hadn't been an easy time for Alex, with people coming and going for the reasons I listed above. Now, on top of all the internal problems—and money was always an issue—she was having to deal with the French government, who had recently notified her that they were going to log the massive forested ridge right in front of Lavaldieu. This was going to be a tragedy.

The ridge was majestic, curved like the back of a massive sleeping animal and filling the vision from left to right as one looked from the courtyard of Lavaldieu. Perhaps to emphasize its creaturelike simulacrum, the spine of the ridge was eroded into a series of limestone spires that rose up out of the forested flanks like the fossilized backbone of a monstrous beast. It was unthinkable for it to be stripped of its beauty.

Alex, however, had an idea and asked Stanley Messenger to join us at Lavaldieu. Among Stanley's many interests was a lifetime study of butter-flies. Alex had discovered that if an endangered species, or a new and as yet undiscovered species—animal, plant, or insect—were to be found on the ridge, then French environmental laws would prohibit logging.

Stanley's first assignment was to hike up to the ridge and examine the terrain to determine whether a genuinely endangered species of but-terfly might exist there. He was just completing his fruitless search when I arrived. Picture an elderly man, long white hair streaming behind him, moving with the fluidity of a mountain goat, a butterfly net waving wildly in one hand as he pursued a fugitive insect, and you have Stanley at work.

Unfortunately, for all his effort and enthusiasm, Stanley drew a blank. No new or endangered butterflies were making the ridge their territory. So the situation stood when I arrived. They'd run out of ideas.

Authentic magic, by which I mean working cooperatively with vari-ous nonhuman intelligences to achieve results of benefit to all, is funda-mentally made possible by the human end of the operation being in the right place at the right time.

I'd been working consciously with the angels for about five years by this time and had had the chance to appreciate the precision of the guid-ance I'd received. I can only wonder at the angelic coordination that got me, with my preposterous idea, to a rare situation in which this preposterous idea could be tested. Equally, it's hard for me to imagine that anyone else could have come up with this approach.

And my preposterous idea? Let me back up a little, since the source of the concept lay in the intersection of a few seemingly unrelated disciplines that I'd been following, plus, of course, pure necessity.

I've always enjoyed smoking and have done so in moderation for most of my life. I'm also not blind to the obvious; that gunk, the tars and such, must accumulate in the lungs of smokers. At around that time, in 1979, I'd been reading some recent reports on how scientists had gene-spliced a microorganism designed to consume, and thus clean out, the oils and tars that stick to the inside of the storage tanks of oil tankers.

In less environmentally aware times, the ships would simply flush out their tanks with seawater, so the development of the oil-eating organism was a great improvement. Coincidentally, my metaphysical studies had led me to the nature spirits. This isn't the place to describe some of my experiences in this realm, only to say that it has become real to me that all life-forms possess a spiritual center, a deva. Applying this concept to myself, it was reasonable to think that I, too, must be indwelt by a deva. After all, I have no idea how my body functions moment by moment, how my organs, systems, and curcuits coordinate their activity—all the myriad chemistry that keeps me functioning and healthy. Of this and more, I'm completely ignorant.

Yet it is equally self-evident there is someone or something inside me that *does* know how my physical vehicle actually works. This one I call my deva.

Cut now to the graphic artwork I was doing at that time. I'd just inadvertently discovered, and was having some success with, a form of absent healing. My mother, in London, had fallen and broken her foot. Back in New York, I decided to draw her foot, using different colors to release the trapped trauma and to bring in positive healing energies. By putting myself in a light-trance state I felt open to working with one of my angels as I was drawing.

My mother was unaware of what I was doing and would have dismissed it as pointless fantasy if she *had* known. She called a few days later to tell me her doctor was unable to account for the rapidity with which her foot was healing. I took this as a positive sign and had worked on a couple more healing graphics by the time I was called to Lavaldieu.

Putting these three streams together, it came to me that what the biologists could do externally with their genetic manipulation, my deva should surely be able to do on the inside. And my healing graphics gave me the clue as to how I might imprint my deva with the necessary intention for her to take action. As a result I spent a sixteen-hour stretch at my drawing board (my graphics are extremely detailed and labor intensive), holding my light-trance so I could focus on drawing my concept of a tar-eating *E. coli*, one that would live symbiotically in my lungs and keep them clean.

So, it was with this in mind that I rather tentatively made my preposterous suggestion to Alex and Stanley. "Why don't we see if we can create a new butterfly that we could then find on the ridge?"

I'm sure it was the lack of any further alternatives that made my idea even halfway attractive. In a desperate situation, it couldn't hurt.

Now, thirty-two years later, still smoking and with lungs clean and clear—although I needed to reboot with a new design some years ago after a bout of malaria must have overheated the poor little buggers—I would have been able to make a stronger case. So, I was somewhat surprised when they agreed to take it up.

At the very least, it gave us something constructive to do.

I might have initially misjudged Stanley because he took to the challenge with a passionate enthusiasm. Out came his entomological books as he pored over hundreds of delicate drawings and color photos of different butterflies. He studied their preferred terrain and climate, seeking a strain that might, with some small design modifications, enjoy living on our threatened ridge.

Stanley finally decided on a design, and we carefully drew it up, a little white thing, I recall, with some blue spots, rather modest considering how flamboyant we might have been tempted to make it. We did the necessary invocations, meditated together, and talked as persuasively as we could to the resident nature spirits.

Holding to the faith that the magic would work, I suggested we create a luminous violet bubble in our collective imagination, into which we placed the image of the butterfly we'd designed, and floated it off in the direction of the ridge. We then agreed to put it out of our minds, a strategy that we'd found previously effective in these magical matters, and went about our lives at Lavaldieu.

I was only there for a short time, so it was a week or two after I'd returned to New York when I heard the good news from Alex. On one of Stanley's daily hikes on the ridge there was our butterfly, the very one we'd designed. Quite a number of them, too. A specimen had been sent in to the appropriate authorities, and there was no reason to think the ridge wouldn't get its reprieve.

French bureaucracy grinds slowly, but the mere discovery of the butterfly was sufficient evidence to first delay the prospective devastation and then subsequently ban logging altogether on our beautiful ridge.

So ended my adventures in Cathar country. I've had no desire or guidance to return to Lavaldieu. Alex packed it in some years later after valiant efforts to keep the place afloat and moved to Australia, where she now has a retreat center in the volcanic mountains just north of Byron Bay, on the New South Wales coast.

Back in New York, my life was changing, too. I'd become accustomed to working with the BVF even though I wasn't always aware of them. I'd managed to establish good personal contact with my two guardian angels. As we neared the end of 1984 it appeared they were setting me up for the next phase of activity.

10

The Return of Quetzalcoatl

Altered States, Rascals, Floatation Tanks, the Mayan Factor, and the Return of Quetzalcoatl

An amusing synchronicity concerning butterflies emerged sometime after returning from Lavaldieu. What led to this odd coincidence, however, was not instrumental in our success in manifesting our endangered little friend—at least I hope not!

The backstory started with an unsettling man who appeared to be spending an inordinate amount of time trying to befriend people in the loose-knit international new age community. His name was on the cover of a successful self-help book, so initially it was hard to reconcile the wisdom dispensed in the book with the man's egotistic personality. He was clearly intelligent, yet he was also emotionally stunted, which was frequently revealed in the banality of his humor. He was a small man with a bullying manner, which he cloaked in an avuncular air and the ploy of arriving with expensive gifts. He was evidently playing the part of a new age cognoscente, yet underneath the apparent generosity and bonhomie there was a crudeness about him.

Later, it became generally known that the book that had made him so well-known was really written by a female editor. The publisher thought that the book would seem more authentic if it appeared to be written by a male "author." This was an unfortunate position to be in—for both writers—and went some way toward explaining the author's pretensions and his awkwardness.

I never knew the woman who was the true writer, but this author became quite insistent on ingratiating himself with my girlfriend and myself. Then I starting hearing from other of my friends that he was behaving in the same unctuous manner toward them.

In his late fifties at the time, the man was a few years older than most of us, so we were initially happy that someone of his generation was interested in our work. He attended the workshops we were holding, which helped people make contact with their guardian angels, but then he would unexpectedly show up at our apartment and want to hang out with us.

Over time this became annoying, and there was something about him that made us increasingly uneasy. Yet it was hard to turn him away because he always expressed such a high level of interest. He was a great note-taker, yet in spite of his nods and smiles of agreement, it was fairly obvious that most of what we talking about was going over his head.

After a while, this queasy feeling resolved into a sense that the author must have a hidden agenda. We wondered whether the man was working with one of the intelligence agencies, and if he was, whatever could they find of any interest in what we were doing? Was the intelligence community really interested in angels and nature spirits?

I recall confronting him once as to whether he was a CIA agent, but he rightly pointed out that if he was, why would he tell me? He was a great one for dismissing the whole suggestion with a roar of laughter, asking me why would the CIA employ someone like him?

So the situation stood, with the author showing up every few months at our apartment in Manhattan with yet another pricey gift. Then I heard from some friends in London. One of them was the seminal English writer John Michell, who had also attracted the unflattering attentions of this fellow. Like us, John had also grown wary of him and was irritated by the way he used John Michell's well-known name to open doors for himself. We'd both previously agreed there was something suspicious and self-serving about the man.

How the next event came about I was never told—and no doubt

for good reason. Apparently, John Michell and a couple of others, with the help of either an astute hacker or a cooperative agent (I wasn't told which), made their way into the massive CIA computerized database, in which they keep files on people of interest. John wanted to know what the CIA had on this troublesome writer; might he really be a CIA operative?

Whether the writer was an actual intelligence agent is not for me to say and isn't really the point of this contextual tangent. It is worth noting, however, that the man had eight full pages in his files; he'd visited the Soviet Union and spoke fluent Russian.

Unable to resist the temptation and given this rare opportunity to look behind the secrecy curtain, John and the others did a quick scan to see if any other of their friends had files.

My file, by their account, had but a single line: *He is a butterfly. No problem.*

The year 1984 was weighted down by George Orwell's dark vision.

The press was full of it, making the most of every disaster, selling fear for all it was worth. Ronald Reagan was being reelected to a second term of international saber-rattling, supply-side economics, and the increasing rift between rich and poor. The old leaders of the USSR were becoming more paranoid as they felt increasingly threatened by Reagan's military buildup.

If there was going to be a global war, 1984 was going to be the year for it.

One of the features of a prospective atomic conflict is how helpless the citizens feel. Even in a modern state, individuals are effectively powerless. Have citizens of any Western democracy ever managed to stop a war from starting? It took many years of intense citizen activity to bring the Vietnam War to an end. There are simply too many vested interests involved in promoting conflict.

While the introduction of atomic and hydrogen bombs and the mutually assured destruction policies of the Cold War may have reduced the possibility of the bombs actually falling, the constant presence of the imminent threat was clearly having a debilitating effect on those of us living in large cities.

Denial and cynicism were seeping into everyday life, propelled by the gathering Republican revolution. Greed is good. Grab what you can before the bombs fall. Many of the financial woes of the subsequent century find their source in the deregulatory extravagances and self-serving excesses of the Reagan years. The dream of profound societal change that flowered in the 1960s was long shattered, crushed by the imperialist ambitions of the status quo. Social programs were being eliminated. Each one of us was on our own; and alone, each one of us was inevitably powerless to have an effect on the overall situation.

The concept of personal power is better understood in shamanism, martial arts, and in some Eastern spiritual disciplines, but each of us has an everyday experience of power and how it is used. On the most basic level, when we give more credence to another's opinion or belief system than to our own inner knowing, we give away our power to that person. It's the most common of human frailties: an atavistic desire for a strong pack leader who will tell us what to do and think.

Yet, giving away one's personal power and then reclaiming it also appears to be a defining station along the spiritual path. Referred to as "killing the Buddha on the road," this maxim describes the point at which the pupil no longer needs the teacher and forcefully cuts the umbilical cord of spiritual codependency.

As one who gave away my personal power in my twenties and thirties to a woman I accepted as my spiritual teacher, only to grasp it back fifteen years later, the experience has established for me the importance of valuing my personal power. I vowed never to give it away so thoughtlessly again. Of course, central to this approach is finding a way of reasserting one's personal power and sense of self when circumstances are trying to make us powerless. Ultimately, it's not about influencing or changing the situation, but changing our relationship with it. This decision alone puts the power back in our own hands. Then it's simply a question of finding an appropriate expression for the response.

It's then I turn to my drawing board. "The Ship of Art will always get you through," says a wise woman of my acquaintance, and when I approach my graphics with devotion, sacred intention, and loving care, the Ship of Art does indeed take me to a safe harbor. It was with this in mind that I embarked on a large graphic of the Third World War, with the idea of continuing to develop the drawing over the entire year, completing it on the last day of 1984. (See plate 5.)

My basic intention, fanciful though it may sound, was to take the brunt of all the negative energy bearing down on this particular year, transform it with the alchemy of the spirit, and externalize it into an expressive piece of art. Unlike the more carefully considered graphics I'd been doing in my Sacred Landscape series, this 1984 graphic would be completely spontaneous and unplanned, developing only as the energies and images manifested through me and onto the paper over the course of the year.

In this way I found I was able to maintain a stable center and retain an essential optimism while my life was changing gears once more. When I started actively working with the angels and dedicating myself to a higher purpose, I really didn't know the impact it was going to have on my life. I was traveling more frequently on my own now, following the guidance of my angels, with Melinda staying at home with her art. She had introduced me to *The Urantia Book,* and we had shared the adventures described in *Dolphins, ETs & Angels.* Her wisdom and input had been invaluable for that phase of my journey, but she was an extremely private and modest woman (for example, she never wished to be named in my books, so here I've called her Melinda) and my life was leading me in the direction of working within the collective. As an artist, this was of little interest to her.

Dolphins, ETs & Angels had come out, and I was giving talks and traveling all over the country to promote the book. Just getting it published had been a challenging exercise in humiliation. I sent the complete manuscript, having had it well edited by a couple of literate friends, to twenty publishers and twenty-five agents and received only two letters back, both rejecting the manuscript.

Apparently, the public wasn't ready for what I was saying.

Fortunately I'd also sent the manuscript to Shirley MacLaine, who'd published her groundbreaking book, *Out on a Limb,* the previous year. She'd written honestly and openly about her exploration of reincarnation, and I felt she might be interested in my book. Apparently she was. I got the kindest and most encouraging letter back from her, and with that I decided to find a way of getting the book published myself.

Having lived in Manhattan for almost fifteen years I'd come to know a lot of people. I decided to throw a party and charge an admission price of twenty-three dollars with the promise of two books per person when it was published.

My good friend, Yanni Posnakoff, the owner of a Greek restaurant on the Upper West Side, generously offered his space and contributed the food. It was a terrific party, and enough money was raised to have the first edition, at that point named *The DETA Factor: Dolphins, Extraterrestrials & Angels,* printed and published by Coleman Press, a Long Island company that had published *A Course in Miracles.*

In spite of the book having been rejected by the more mainstream New York publishing houses, the small metaphysical bookstores that were springing up all over in American cities and towns were considerably more enthusiastic and carried the book, as well as recommending it to their customers and friends. Contemporary stories of spiritual exploration were not popular with the big New York publishers thirty years ago, yet clearly people were starving for honest personal accounts they could identify with and from which they could learn something of real value to apply to their lives.

Consequently, the book was surprisingly successful, and when it was picked up by Knoll Publishing Company, I recall the publisher's astonishment when he heard how many copies of the book I'd sold on my own. It's now been through many editions, two more publishers, and remains in print twenty-five years later. All of which is to say my career was taking me out into the world and my relationship with Melinda was, of necessity, drawing to an end. Although we loved each other deeply and remain the closest of friends to this day, we were both aware it was a working relationship and we'd been drawn together for a specific purpose.

While I'm sure my angels had a wing in the situation, my planetside experience was somewhat more human. I was in love with another woman. I'd been close to Alma Daniel some years earlier, and we'd exploded apart over a disagreement that caused us to break off contact for four years. We both knew we had work to do together, but in the late 1970s the timing wasn't correct. Neither of us was ready. Coming back into each other's lives over Christmas of 1984 allowed us to pick up where we had left off, both better prepared for the tasks ahead.

Alma is a petite woman, slim and delicately formed, yet with a ferocious courage and a determination to see beneath the surface of life. She has a remarkably deep and resonant voice for a small woman and an aquiline profile that might have been American Indian. A New Yorker all her life, Alma had worked in public relations and advertising in the early days of live television, making her bones demonstrating kitchen equipment on TV in the days when breaking or dropping a gadget was seen live, to the amusement of the watching millions. She'd been divorced some years when I met her first in 1978. She lived, with her three teenaged children, in a large apartment on the twenty-fifth floor of the Eldorado, a classic art deco apartment building on Manhattan's Central Park West.

Having had a somewhat conventional life of marriage and children, Alma was yearning for a deeper connection to life and to her soul. Soon after I first met her, back in '78, I'd taken her down to the only floatation tank center in Manhattan at the time and introduced her to the experience of floating quietly for an hour in a totally dark tank filled with water at blood temperature and enough Epsom salts to emulate the Dead Sea.

Alma had evidently taken to floating because when we re-met she had a floatation tank in her apartment, was taking in paying clients, and was well on the way to creating the Floatation Tank Association. Sensory isolation tanks were becoming a popular new healing and training modality, and Alma, with her organizational skills, had pulled together the various different healing centers, end-users, and the sports facilities who worked with floatation tanks into an organization that held yearly conferences. It took hard work and constant travel, and since the type of people drawn to floatation tanks tend to be more eccentric than most, it became a lot like handling quicksilver.

The floatation tank is a remarkably powerful instrument. It allows the floater access to a wide variety of enhanced human abilities. Since brain activity doesn't differentiate between an action done in reality or in the imagination, it's become an invaluable tool for sportsmen and sportswomen who need to train their muscle-memory and habituate their mind/body connections to an optimum condition. This can be done highly effectively in a floatation tank by the repetition of an action done correctly in the imagination.

Unfortunately, most people have only encountered floatation tanks from watching the film *Altered States,* in which a wildly overwrought depiction of a man leaving his body forever distorted in the public eye one of the unusual gifts that floating tanks can bestow. Water at body heat quickly eliminates an awareness of the body's limits, and with practice this allows the subtle energy body to travel free of the physical vehicle. Dr. John C. Lilly has written extensively about his uses of the tank, including his encounters with various entities in an out-of-body state.

Alma, though her personal work in the tank and in debriefing her clients after a float session, was well aware of some of the more mysterious effects of floating. One story she'd tell was of a Japanese businessman who had recently lost his mother without being able to speak to her before she died. He was floating to find peace and alleviate his grief. While in Alma's tank he'd heard a phone ringing insistently in the distance. Thinking it was Alma's phone, the man grew progressively more irritated at her failure to answer it. Where *was* she? It was destroying his peace. Still the phone rang on. Finally, angry and frustrated (and no doubt forgetting where he was), he reached out in his imagination and lifted up the receiver. The ringing stopped, and when he put the phone to his ear, it was to hear his dead mother's voice on the other end of the line.

He emerged at the end of the session, having had a long conversation with his mother, relaxed and filled with joy, and with the firm conviction that life continues after death.

Alma was an intelligent modern woman who, when we met, had a generally agnostic view of the spiritual life. She read widely, had a lasting interest in psychology, and had a deliciously wicked sense of humor. Yet some of the unexplainable incidents occurring in the course of her work with the tank had started opening her up to other realities. This made it a lot easier for both of us when the subject turned to angels.

She was a practical woman, and although she was intrigued by what I'd found out about angels in the four years we'd been apart, she was far more interested in making direct contact with her angels for herself. It had taken me a couple of years of constant meditation, self-examination, and journaling to establish a reliable connection with my angels, and I'd never helped anyone else to get into contact with theirs. I wasn't at all sure it would work for someone else.

Luckily, I recalled that Dr. John C. Lilly had written about his encounters with beings he believed to be angels in his 1978 book, *The Scientist: A Novel Autobiography*. Alma came to know John Lilly in the course of her work with floatation tanks—he'd invented the sensory-deprivation tank back in 1954—and I knew she respected his opinion as an open-minded and brilliant scientist. If Dr. Lilly had encountered angels, she was prepared to give it a try, however skeptical she might have felt.

For all her pragmatism, Alma turned out to be a natural. In our first session together, I was winging it (no pun intended), simply trying to follow the guidance I felt coming from one of my own angels. For Alma, a gifted channel in spite of herself, the contact was almost immediate. The "voice" was strong and wise. It was like opening a floodgate of love and knowledge she'd been keeping at bay all her life.

As is true for anyone bold enough to take this step into unknown territory, Alma became deeply involved in this newly opened channel of communication, journaling every bit as much as I had when I made my breakthrough. To open the heart and mind to an intelligent being who loves you and knows more about you than you do about yourself, who will speak the unadorned truth to you and help heal you of what prevents you from being a whole human being, can be a challenging affair. It requires a stripping away of outmoded belief systems and an unusual degree of emotional honesty in releasing long-held trauma.

In working together with our angels over the next couple of years, Alma and I were able to investigate the angelic reality for ourselves. It was an exhilarating time of spiritual exploration and self-examination, which might have become solipsistic had the angels not had their plans for us. We knew from our own angelic communications how important it was to them to establish conscious contact with their human wards. There was an unexpected urgency about this, and although our angels were vague about telling us why, there was a feeling they were preparing us all for the coming times.

Our friends, seeing the obvious changes in us, soon started joining us for informal sessions in which Alma and I showed them how to open to their own guardian angels. Granted, our friends may have been more receptive to unorthodox ideas than the average person, simply by the fact of being our friends, but we found the work to be remarkably successful. People were being genuinely helped. Seeing them blossoming with their angels' guidance became a joyful encouragement for both Alma and me and bonded us into a close working relationship.

Of course, there were always a few who were unable to make the leap, who were too emotionally insecure, too cynical, or too set in their ways to hear their angel's voice. We realized from this that being able to open to the angels was not for everybody, although our angels assured us that everybody *could* do it, and indeed *would have* to do it, sooner or later, in this lifetime or the next. It was very much a question of timing, not a matter of right and wrong.

Understanding this timing issue became a valuable asset when we felt ready to create workshops and seminars to serve a wider audience than just our friends. We were not seeking ridicule, and in these cynical times we knew there were always going to be people who would think we were deluding ourselves, or worse, deluding others. Neither were we trying to make money from our angel workshops. Believing them to be a service to both angels and people, we kept the fees low and made the workshops accessible to everybody who sincerely desired contact with their angels.

It was a delicate area, and we needed a way of preselecting the appropriate attendees. Apart from the difficulties presented by a resistant personality, there was no point in disappointing people or having them feeling insufficient or foolish purely because they were not ready for this rapid acceleration of consciousness. In order to keep the overhead down we held the early workshops in Alma's elegant living room overlooking Central Park. It was a large room, with a raised platform and a circular conversation pit. The seating was built into the sides of the carpeted platform, and the room was entirely free of ornamentation, with the exception of a wooden weathervane in the form of Gabriel blowing his horn. The august minimalism of the room, the subdued tones of carpet and furnishing fabrics, and the welcoming silence of being twenty-five floors above the traffic all gave the place a sense of the sacred. The lack of any sort of visual distraction in the room allowed the ever-changing weather conditions, seen through the floor-to-ceiling windows, to become the sole decorative element. It was a most delightful and appropriate place to converse with celestial beings.

The angels guiding us suggested that we should do no formal advertising for these gatherings. We were merely to place the minimum of leaflets at key points around town and leave it up to the angels to nudge the right people, those who were ready for angelic communication, in our direction. In this way we would know that those who came to our workshops were sincerely interested and had been guided (unknowingly) by their angels to attend.

Naturally, in my case this led initially to some nervous moments when we never had any idea who or how many people were going to turn up on our doorstep for the event. Sometimes it was twenty, sometimes only twelve, other times there would be thirty or forty people meditating together. We called the gatherings Opening to the Angels, and we made sure they were intimate gatherings in which attendees could trust one another. Stories were shared, and people felt free to speak about events in their lives that they had not previously been able to express; emotions flowed freely as they felt secure in the company of angels.

Although we started by making the workshop a two-day affair, believing we needed as long as possible to make sure everyone in the workshop had an angelic experience, we hadn't taken into account how dedicated and effective the angels were in making their presence felt. After a while we were able to distill our approach down to a day of meditations and exercises, which would result in the experience of angelic contact.

Soon we were being asked to hold our workshops in different American cities. We also traveled to Canada, Switzerland, Australia, and England, where we gave seminars in London and Glastonbury. More and more people were becoming interested in angels, and the workshops were growing in size. The work was so intense and personal that, to be fair to the attendees, we needed to put a cap on the numbers. We found that about sixty people was the maximum number to whom we were able to give personal attention.

Alma was keeping extensive notes on all our work, including many examples and stories drawn from the experiences of our attendees, so the idea of the material coming together into a book had occurred to us. It wasn't something I really wanted to jump into, since I was already starting to write the second book in the series, *Adventures among Spiritual Intelligences*. But the angels clearly had different plans for us.

I believe it was after a workshop in New Orleans when one of the attendees came up to us, insisting we should write a book, something he could take home with him and practice with on his own. Others had asked us something like this after previous gatherings, so it was what he said then that caught our attention: ". . . and why don't you call it, *Ask Your Angels!*"

It was an irresistible title, of course, summarizing exactly the central theme of any potential book we would write. The idea was becoming more intriguing, yet it still felt like an overwhelming prospect. I had no illusions about how all-consuming it was to write a book. It had taken all of four years to write and publish my first one. I knew how committed we would need to be.

We continued to hold our workshops. Matters might have rested there because Alma and I had quite enough to do without needing to take on yet another project, had not the angels arranged such an obvious series of synchronicities we'd have been foolish to ignore them.

It was the spring of 1987 when the next tumbler slipped into place.

In the course of my research into various cosmologies I had become interested in some of the indigenous peoples' belief systems, in particular the Hopi and the Maya. Through Marilyn Ferguson, the friend with the Walkman I met at the summit of Glastonbury Tor, I came to know the artist and author José Argüelles.

José had just completed and published his controversial book, *The Mayan Factor: Path beyond Technology,* and had become convinced that the Mayan Calendar held profound predictive potential when interpreted in the correct way. While José's calculations were opaque and not always easy to follow, the gist of his idea lay in his belief that a group of extraterrestrials had incarnated into the bodies of people in the Mayan civilization between approximately 600 and 1000 CE.

Throughout this period the Maya created the most advanced culture in Meso-America, and the artifacts they left, the great pyramids and sculptural stonework, appear to have emerged out of nowhere. Their knowledge of the stars and the immensely long planetary cycles like the 25,800 years of the precession of the equinoxes coded into the Mayan Calendar, was far in advance of their Western contemporaries. Then, as unexpectedly as the Mayan culture had blossomed over the brief four hundred years of their existence, this sophisticated civilization just as mysteriously disappeared.

The native Maya returned to living simple lives in the jungle, much as they had existed for millennia. The great pyramids, the temples and palaces, the sculpted stone forms of Quetzalcoatl, were all quickly overrun by the tropical forest.

Like anyone who encounters this mystery, I'd found the disintegration of the Mayan civilization puzzling. How could a culture at that level of astronomical sophistication simply disappear? José's proposition, however improbable it might seem to conventional thinking, certainly went toward explaining what might have happened.

Having lived in the Yucatan, in Mexico, earlier in my life, I had always felt particularly close to the Mayan villagers and was even allowed to attend their psychic gatherings, their séances. They are a secretive people, speaking their own language, and to this day are reluctant to reveal to outsiders that they conduct their psychic sessions in the privacy of their tiny homes. Yet for all their psychism and openhearted kindness, it was hard to believe they were a people who might have built and sustained an advanced and intricate civilization.

The stories surrounding Quetzalcoatl, the feathered serpent, fascinated me from the first time I'd heard them. I'd read Tony Shearer's 1971 book, *Lord of the Dawn,* some years earlier and was aware of Shearer's claim that Quetzalcoatl, upon departing, left a prophecy of thirteen heavens and nine hells (each cycle was fifty-two years in duration), promising to return at the end of the thirteen heavens. It was the accuracy of this prophecy that had convinced Montezuma and the Aztecs to welcome Cortez as a god when he arrived on the very date prophesied as the end of the thirteen heavens.

More to the point, José was telling us that the Mayan Calendar would come to an end on December 21, 2012, and the upcoming Harmonic Convergence in August of 1987 was going to be an important event, signaling the start of the twenty-five-year countdown to December 2012, the end of the Mayan Long Count.

José Argüelles and his wife, Lloydine, had arrived with some friends at our apartment at the Eldorado. José was a voluble talker, an intense, compact man, wholly convinced in his own opinions and theories. Although he was clearly highly intelligent, it seemed to me that Lloydine—sitting silently on her own, doubtless having heard it all before—was José's muse, with the spiritual intelligence to balance her husband's obsessive tendencies.

After José's discussion drew to an end and he'd addressed all our questions I invited him back to my studio to look at some of my graphics. This didn't come from any competitive urge in me, simply the desire to show him what I'd come up with graphically in my intuitive exploration of the Quetzalcoatl story. I thought he'd be interested. In fact, I had a large drawing, *The Return of Quetzalcoatl to New York City,* on my drawing board at the time, as well as other graphics on the walls addressing Quetzalcoatl's promise to return at the end of the nine hells of the Mayan Calendar in December 2012. (See plate 6.)

Perhaps José didn't want to muddy the clarity of his vision or his obsession had become too personal to include other input, but the moment he entered my studio he seemed quite unable to look at my drawings. He came into my studio as if he had blinkers on. His eyes were firmly fixed on the floor as he crossed the room and hugged me with the traditional Maya greeting: "Lak'ech; I am another you." Then he turned, left my studio, and went back to the living room.

What I didn't tell José—I didn't really want another such pointed dismissal—was that I'd been receiving transmissions from an entity calling himself Quetzalcoatl for the previous few months. All the work I'd been doing with the angels over the past few years had sensitized me to the subtle realms, yet I was still surprised when Quetzalcoatl came through. His energy was quite different from what I'd become accustomed to with the celestials. He spoke to me in my mind in complete sentences, which I then could either say out loud or write down. In contrast, the angels seem to prefer writing *through* me, as though they were guiding my hand from the inside.

Alma and I were hosting a weekly meditation group for advanced meditators, and one evening Quetzalcoatl had broken through the veil, using my mind as the interface. His messages were brief and largely relevant to what was happening in the moment. He seemed to be focusing on the twenty-five years following the Harmonic Convergence on August 16 and 17 of 1987, which end in the events of 2012.

Although I didn't altogether agree with all José's conclusions, I regarded his unexpected visit as a synchronistic confirmation of the direction that my intuitive interests were taking me. I resonated with the central theme of José's theory, that an advanced race had interceded in Mayan history and left their prophecies cast in stone. José maintained they were fine-tuning human history and preparing humanity for the events at the end of the long cycle in 2012.

After José and Lloydine left for the evening Alma and I discussed our feelings about José's information and whether we wanted to put any energy into supporting the Harmonic Convergence. Even if there was nothing to the Mayan Calendar, we both agreed that any celebration linking people all over the world was a worthwhile enterprise. Of course, we would get involved. I was aware from information in *The Urantia Book* that the Multiverse is a populated place and, of necessity, it needs to be well-organized. To imagine otherwise is to project our anthropomorphic paranoia out onto the unknown "other." Advanced races with high intelligence tend to be peaceful, their technological development in balance with their emotional and spiritual growth.

This had been confirmed for me on Labor Day in 1981 when Melinda and I saw a flying saucer passing over Manhattan. As we were finishing gaping at the UFO a small, perhaps eight-year-old boy wandered over to tell us it was a "just a star car." For the next twenty minutes, the child, speaking with all the authority of an ET mouthpiece, spoke about extraterrestrial politics, Mani Particle Beam propulsion systems, 3-D communication systems, the star system Phinsouse, the Andromeda galaxy, and much else that I managed to scribble down and record in *Dolphins, ETs & Angels.*

"There are a few warlike races," he'd replied to my question about war in the universe, "but they don't get very far from their home planets, because the lines of supply become so attenuated. War takes a lot of energy and expense, and in those cases the races involved and the spaces they occupy are avoided by everyone else."

There were starting to be enough coincidences pointing to the fact that the Harmonic Convergence might indeed be a significant event, so I decided to put out a few simple flyers to see what response I'd get. About forty people turned up to that first meeting, and it was obvious there was a lot of gathering interest in the event. We all decided to get together weekly, and the meetings increased in size to more than two hundred enthusiastic volunteers. We agreed between us to be leaderless and make all decisions by consensus. It made the meetings slow and somewhat laborious as everyone expressed their views on each decision, but it kept the egos at bay. No one was able to take over, and in spite of having originally put the meetings together I really didn't want it to be my show.

First of all, we needed to choose where we were going to hold the gathering itself. Another group was getting together in Brooklyn so we knew it would have to be in Manhattan—not the easiest place to find the right spot on which to plant ourselves undisturbed for a full two days. We all went off to think about it. Living high up in one of the towers of the Eldorado, with a 360° panoramic vista over the whole city of Manhattan, it was clear to Alma and me that Central Park was the pivotal point of the island. Viewed from high above, it became obvious what a stalwart and necessary job all those trees are doing in filtering Manhattan's polluted air.

I had come to love Central Park over the years of living at the Eldorado. I knew it well and often went out after midnight when the park was empty and the constant white noise of traffic hummed like insects in the distance. Like the two protagonists in Terry Gilliam's masterpiece, *The Fisher King,* I used to enjoy the peace I felt lying on my back in the middle of Sheep's Meadow at three o'clock in the morning. On one of my late-night prowls I had stumbled on a fair-sized open space off the main paths and hidden from the rest of the park by large trees. There was a serenity about the spot, and apart from the occasional dog-walker I seldom saw anyone else there.

What came to be called the "Sacred Circle" is a flat platform perched on top of a massive outcropping of glaciated metamorphic schist that heaves out of the park on the west side, just south of 85th Street. In the center is a twelve-foot-round sandpit, surrounded by a circular paved court with benches around the edge of the circle. It must have been the site of a fountain in Frederick Law Olmstead's original plans, but it had long-since been removed and replaced with the sandpit. The whole place had a rundown feeling: the benches were worn bare of paint, some with their battens broken; weeds sprouted up between the paving stones; the sandpit, which might have once served children, now was only used by dogs. For all the dilapidation, under the surface, the place *did* have a special feeling.

Although other possibilities were suggested at the meetings, after those involved had visited the various sites, the Sacred Circle in Central Park was the one agreed on. It would comfortably hold the three or four hundred people we anticipated coming to the event.

As August 16 approached benches were repaired and repainted, weeds pulled, and the area cleaned and tidied up. The old sand was removed and replaced by clean and gleamingly white sand that we shipped in. Prayer flags and wind chimes were hung in the surrounding trees. And, though I never planned it, the graphic I'd been working on for the previous four months, *The Return of Quetzalcoatl to New York City*, was completed on the day before the Harmonic Convergence.

Waking to a clear blue sky on the morning of August 16, Alma and I walked down to the Sacred Circle, only a few blocks from the Eldorado. I took 125 milligrams of MDMA prior to setting off, anticipating a quiet sacred time among the friends I'd met in the course of the meetings. As we climbed the enormous rock, we found to our amazement the few hundred people we expected had swollen to at least three thousand, and more were arriving all the time. TV cameras had been set up, and people stood crowded around the perimeter. Some were sitting on the spruced-up benches, while others were perched in the trees. Most people were seated on blankets in concentric circles around the sandpit. Alma and I edged through the crowd to reach our friends in the center.

On the previous day a small group of New York artists had done some work with pigments donated by my art partner, Juno Atkin. Recently some Buddhist monks who lived in Manhattan had created an exquisite sand mandala in the Natural History Museum that they had then tipped into the Hudson River after completion. As we set about working with our pigments, I like to think we achieved the same intensity of focus that the monks had had in creating their mandala. And, like the monks, we knew our sacred work of art would return to the earth within a few days.

So between us, keeping impermanence firmly in mind, we'd made the circle of sand a thing of beauty. In the center stood a massive quartz generator crystal surrounded by smaller crystals, shells, and peoples' special rocks, interspersed with sacred symbols from all faiths limned out in colored sand against the sparkling whiteness. When the time came to start the ceremony, which we'd previously agreed among ourselves would be intuitive and spontaneous, people lit candles and a conch shell was blown. We all meditated in the silence. After a while, as people had been encouraged to do in the meetings, someone stood up and spoke aloud a prayer; a Native American woman made a blessing in her own language; others invoked the nature spirits; others reached out to the extraterrestrials. There was a respectful silence while people spoke, followed by ripples of agreement from the crowd. For cynical old New York, the Harmonic Convergence appeared to be warming its heart.

The sun had risen high over the trees, and the MDMA was peaking when I felt the presence of Quetzalcoatl once more—and he wanted to address the crowd!

This was not something I had any desire to do. For all the public speaking I've done in my time, this was something totally different. I'd no idea what he wanted to say. I fought his insistence for a while, as others spoke their pieces, the silences between them growing longer. I really did not want attention focused on me. When I realized I was being even more egotistic in denying Quetzalcoatl his voice than in getting up there and doing it—I got up and did it.

I must have been in an altered state because I can recall nothing of what was said, only that I was hearing Quetzalcoatl speaking loudly in my head and pausing long enough for me to repeat his words verbatim, before starting up again. When he finished I sat firmly down.

Others spoke as the day passed. Chants that started among one group spread to others in the circle, the spontaneity of it all bringing out unusually beautiful harmonies. The hardest hearts must have softened because a palpable sense of the sacrosanct hung over the Sacred Circle for the entire two days and one night. People came and went over the two days as friends told friends about the strange happening at the Sacred Circle. Each dusk, as the traffic on Central Park West grew quiet, food would appear to be shared. Candles threw their light on the faces of small clusters of people, and bottles of wine were passed around, along with the occasional joint. Children ran happily around the edge of the circle, sometimes dodging between the groups, before collapsing exhausted on their parents laps.

Guitars were produced and a few drums, and soon there were four or five little jam sessions going on. People were moving like shadows from group to group, pausing to listen to Spanish flamenco for a few minutes before slipping into the shadows of the trees and singing along to "Rocketman," complete with a young black man vocally emulating all the spacey background sounds.

Toward midnight the groups started breaking up and heading for home. The park emptied out, and as far as I could tell no one spent the night out there after the park had closed. We decided to leave the sand painting and the various precious objects, including the large (and very valuable) generator crystal, unguarded (at least by humans) overnight. We were gratified (and happily amazed) to find everything the next morning perfectly in place and untouched.

It was toward the end of the second day, when the crowds had dissipated, leaving only a few of us gathered around the sandpit, when someone pointed up in time for us to see a group of a half a dozen silver discs flying in formation slowly down the island from north to south. They were graceful and utterly silent, their smooth surfaces glinting red against silver in the evening sun, before they disappeared behind the trees.

It was so brief and unexpected—we only saw the discs for a New York second—that they could have been dismissed as a trick of the light. Yet, there they were. I saw them, and I had a pretty good idea of what it meant. As in Glastonbury, I regarded it as confirmation that whatever the purpose behind the Harmonic Convergence might have been, we had successfully accomplished it. However, for all the drama and excitement of the gathering, something of much more personal interest was stirring in the wings.

The angels were busy.

I met Andrew Ramer as I was relaxing on one of the benches on the afternoon of the second day of the Harmonic Convergence. We were introduced by a mutual friend who thought we might have a lot in common. And indeed we did.

Like others I've spoken about in my books as being part of the Network of Light, Andrew's eyes sparkled with interest and intelligence. He was a beautiful man in his late thirties, tall and elegantly lean, with large brown eyes full of feeling. When he shaved his head, which he did later on, he could have been taken for a young, but much slimmer, Georges Gurdjieff. We liked each other immediately, soon finding that we were both working with the angels. For Andrew, angels have been a lifelong reality, after having had a profound encounter with his companion angel when he was a child. His deep feeling for angels was entirely experiential, and since he was raised in an atheistic household he needed to learn the value of intuition through personal experience.

His book, *Little Pictures: Fiction for a New Age,* was about to be published later in 1987 by Ballantine Books, a major New York house, and he was on the edge of being the successful writer he was later to become. As often happens in these synchronistic meetings—encounters clearly arranged by the angels—we found that much of our information and the adventures we shared with the angels contained interlocking pieces of the puzzle, allowing each of us a deeper confirmation in the validity of our work. When I mentioned what had occurred in Glastonbury, for example, with the Cap de la Hague reactor, he related a somewhat parallel story.

On March 29, 1979, and whether Andrew was meditating or sleeping at the time I don't recall, but he was suddenly plucked out of his body in full awareness to join a large gathering of angels encircling a group of buildings he could see far below. That it was a power station was evident from the enormous cooling towers. Although he knew it must be an emergency of some sort, where it was and what was happening didn't seem to be obvious, so he joined the healing circle.

It was only sometime later in the day, when the news came over the radio, that Andrew understood why he had been part of a contingent of angels and out-of-body humans. A reactor core at the Three Mile Island nuclear generating plant had suffered a partial meltdown, and this contingent was working with the subtle energies in attempting to contain the spread of radioactivity that the meltdown had created.

Until we shared some of our angel stories I don't think either of us fully realized what an active role the angels must take in the affairs of humanity. We wondered what a planet would look like if there weren't any angels behind the scenes. Evidently angels are required to allow us to learn from the consequences of our actions, without their intervention, unless the effects of human actions have a destructive consequence on other dimensions. I believe this is the answer as to why the angels couldn't, or didn't, prevent such horrors as the Nazi gas chambers, or the Rwanda genocide, or any one of the individual murders and mayhem we see daily on the TV.

The risk that humans may use a weapon that might have a calamitous impact on dimensions and frequency-domains about which we have no idea seems to be one of the areas of human activity that appears to concern both angels and extraterrestrials. It's no coincidence that the increasing presence of UFOs in the modern age started in 1947, only two years after atomic bombs destroyed Hiroshima and Nagasaki.

Andrew and I found we had wide areas of agreement that sunny afternoon in the park, with a sufficient divergence in viewpoint to keep the dialogue vital and provocative. Andrew's angels possessed wings, for example; Alma's and mine didn't. And while Andrew was more familiar with the celestial realms over the course of his life than I, he hadn't had the extraterrestrial experiences I've had.

I think both of us knew our meeting would have a deeper level of significance, and we agreed to keep in touch. Alma, who'd been resting back in the Eldorado while Andrew and I were talking, walked over as he was getting up to leave. We talked briefly about the book Alma and I were planning to write, although at that point it was still more of a dream than a reality. Neither of us was quite sure how to go about pulling together all the material that we had collected from our workshops.

I was also glad to see that Andrew and Alma liked each other immediately.

It was only days later when Andrew called with the next stage of this angelic dance. What I hadn't known talking to him in the park was that he was working as a reader for Cheryl Woodruff, one of the senior editors at Ballantine Books. Ballantine, apparently, was planning a series of books about angels and was already working on the first; Sophie Burnham's *A Book of Angels*.

In Cheryl's office one day, she'd turned to Andrew and asked him, quite unexpectedly, whether he knew anyone who was familiar with angels. While he might well have suggested himself, he generously told her about meeting me and that I'd already written a book that featured angels. He mentioned the book that Alma and I were considering writing, and when she heard it was going to be a practical guide called *Ask Your*

Angels, something must have clicked. She told Andrew to call me right away to see if I would be interested in publishing with Ballantine.

In spite of my initial resistance, the synchronicities were too blatant to ignore. I could always get back into the other book when the angel book was complete. What I didn't know was the entire process was going to take the next five years of my life!

Naturally Alma was on board—I knew I couldn't put together a book like *Ask Your Angels* on my own—and because of our recent connection with Andrew, it felt important to ask him to join us in writing the book. With a topic as subjective and elusive as angels it would prove to be a sensible decision to have three different points of view.

We met at Cheryl's office. She liked the concept, drew up a contract, and gave the three of us an advance on the skimpiest of proposals. It all happened so fast and with such ease that it verged on the miraculous.

I can only credit the angels for making all this possible. Big New York publishing houses—Ballantine Books is a subsidiary of Random House—used to be notoriously skittish about anything spiritual. Before the success of this Ballantine series on angels, I doubt if any of the major publishers would have contemplated such an uncertain venture. As for books written by virtual unknowns who haven't come through the filter of a literary agent, they have become a rarity in an industry increasingly focused more on the bottom line and on established bestselling writers.

When the euphoria dissipated and our first draft, proudly presented some months later to Cheryl Woodruff, was summarily rejected, we started to realize just how challenging this was going to be. Although it was invaluable to have three very differing viewpoints, since the angels themselves made it clear there was no one way to perceive them, it wasn't an easy process. Like three people trying to drive a car at the same time, we often found ourselves wrestling with the direction the book was taking. This struggle was alleviated somewhat, after our second draft was as peremptorily rejected as the first had been, by the arrival of the angel Abigrael into our lives.

It appeared we had shown sufficient commitment and intention to deserve our own angel. Work then became far more fluid since Abigrael could make herself felt to each of us. There was a sense she was carrying the pattern for the completed book, and by staying closely in contact with

Abigrael we were able to write with more confidence. We found, as we worked away in our separate quarters, what we were writing as individuals was knitting together in a surprisingly fluid way. The book was suddenly starting to take shape. The editor was right, it was getting much better.

We were exhausted but proud of our work when we presented Cheryl with the third draft, sure that we had it right this time with Abigrael's subtle direction.

"It's good," Cheryl told us at the next meeting, "very good." We sat back happily on the sofa in the editor's comfortable office.

"But, do you want to make it *the* best? Do you want it to be a classic in the field and so good that no one else will try to write another book like this?"

These were not rhetorical questions. It was already 1990, and we'd been working on the book full-time for three years. We looked at each other in horror, but of course our editor was right. With the idea of writing a classic in mind, how could we not have one more go at it?

Ask Your Angels was all but complete by this time, our individual sections finished and accepted, and those parts in which we spoke with one voice simply needed smoothing out. Still, more examples and exercises were required to cover all of the angelic encounters. Since Alma and Andrew had been developing that section and had more experience in the psychotherapeutic aspect of angelic contact, I was finally free to turn back to the book I had been working on before devolving into the writing of *Ask Your Angels*.

At least, I thought this was the case.

Because of my background in the visual arts it fell to me to gather up the illustrations for the book. We decided mutually (including Abigrael) not to use classical pictures of angels. Since we made the point so strongly in the book that there was no one way to perceive angels, we asked seventy-five people—some artists, some not—for their visual representation of an angel. We sifted the contributions down to about thirty possibilities and presented them to Ballantine's art department.

When they asked us for any suggestions for a cover image, we told them that any image they selected would be fine with us, as long as the angel depicted didn't have wings. It wasn't much to ask.

At a certain point with these large publishers, I've learned to simply give up. They know how to sell books. They know what people like. In the end, they are going to do what they want. Out of the thirty different angel pictures I submitted, they chose only one artist to illustrate the entire book. Although I had to do a lot of apologizing to seventy-four disappointed artists, I was overjoyed to hear that the artist chosen was Yanni Posnakoff, the friend who'd so generously offered his restaurant for my book party back in '84.

There were proofs to be read, reread, and reread again, until our work was finally over. There'd been a lot of pressure from the publisher for us to finish as fast as possible. So it was disappointing when Ballantine delayed publishing the book for the next two years, while the three of us nervously waited, being told it would come out any day now. Having thrown ourselves into the writing so wholeheartedly, it became a challenging exercise in patience. Reminding each other the book was going to come out in angel-time became something of a mantra.

1992 was evidently angel-time. Sophie Burnham's *A Book of Angels* proved to be successful, and the renewed fascination with angels, which rippled through the 1990s and into the new century, was gathering momentum. *Ask Your Angels* was well positioned to ride that wave of enthusiasm, and to our surprise it soon became a modest bestseller in the religious category. The marketing department certainly had gotten the timing right.

A cautionary note here for budding writers: on the very afternoon we heard that our book was outselling the Bible and was in the number one spot in the *New York Times* religious bestseller list both Alma and I were sharply cautioned about any incipient pride. Striding down a Santa Fe street, quietly kvelling on the book's success, I slipped and fell flat on my face in front of a café full of people trying to suppress laughter while at around the same time, Alma, alone in her New York apartment, fell flat on her bottom.

Needless to say, the cover of *Ask Your Angels: A Practical Guide to Working with the Messengers of Heaven to Empower and Enrich Your Life*, (the subtitle is the publisher's), carried a large picture of an angel *with* wings! And every one of Yanni's delightful little ink drawings also featured angels *with* wings!

It would be ungrateful to criticize how the published book looked. No doubt many people bought it *because* the cover looked so pretty and safe. The winged angel they chose was a model of Victorian sweetness and placid rectitude. The inside of the book had been designed well enough, with wide margins and the comforting feel of a working book. Our text had been left alone; no ambitious young editor had tried to make it "his book." It has sold massively over the years, going into eight translations, and it remains in print almost twenty years later. What ever have I got to complain about?

To put it plainly, I was embarrassed at how it appeared. It was just too pretty, too suggestive of the Victorian romanticized view of angels. Abbot Henderson Thayer's painting, *Angel,* which decorated the book's cover, dates from 1889, and while cute in its own way, certainly didn't represent what we were saying about angels—quite the opposite, in fact. Of course, angels can be loving and compassionate, but their love and compassion is far from sentimental and their truth will burn out falsity.

To make the cover appear even more frilly, Thayer's painting was placed in a silver filigree frame, set against a powder-blue background with just a hint of heavenly white clouds. The script used for the title might have been lifted from a nineteenth-century wedding invitation. It was exactly what we hadn't wanted.

At first, I wondered if the book had been sabotaged by a cynical graphic designer, before realizing that an overworked art director at a large publisher would be most unlikely to have actually read the book. He (and it was a he) must have simply seen from the title that it was about angels, assumed it was a book primarily designed for women, and slapped together his own sentimentalized image of angels.

We had set out to write a serious book, about one the most serious of human issues. Everyone will have to encounter their angels sooner or later, and they will discover angels are not the saccharine visions of a mawkish past age. Yet, as the popularity of angels grew throughout the '90s, it soon became obvious that the possibility of a serious study of angels had degenerated into fantasy, cuteness, and nostalgia.

So, while I feel embarrassed by the way the angel fad turned out, at how different my own perception and understanding of angels is from how they get promoted in the marketplace, I know from the letters we received from readers that some people were genuinely helped by our book. Yet, at the same time I've had to recognize that unless someone is unusually open and sensitive, making angelic contact and maintaining that relationship in the course of a busy life is a lot more of a challenge than most people are willing to take on.

This ambivalence continued to worry me as the book became increasingly popular throughout the 1990s. I was concerned that when people attempted the meditations and exercises they would find them too demanding, and as a consequence, they would lose their interest and their belief in angels. I agonized as to whether we'd disappointed our readers, whether the book promised, from the way Ballantine presented it, more than a reader could make it deliver.

Alma and I both knew from the *Opening to the Angels* gatherings we'd been conducting over the previous years that angelic contact was greatly facilitated by the supportive atmosphere of the workshop and our presence there. I suspect our initial difficulty in pulling a book together, before we met Andrew and got the Ballantine contract, resulted in part from our doubts as to whether a book could ever be sufficiently effective. Yet, taking into account the run of synchronicities leading to the book being published, it was equally obvious the angels themselves wanted the book to get into the public's hands, even if we humans might have had our reservations.

After letting me stew for a while, my companion angel Joy reminded me that all of my fretting was just my ego trying to reassert itself. She assured me that I had no reason to worry, that the angels had their own purposes, and we mortals had done our part in supporting that. There are some readers who were ready for the encounter and whose lives would be changed by the relationship they established with their angels. Yet, there was something more important from the angels' point of view, something that had never once occurred to me throughout the years of writing the book.

Joy told me that what *Ask Your Angels* did most effectively, in contrast to almost all the other angel books that followed ours, was to show how angels need to be approached as *real* beings. Not as archetypes or aliens; not as sentimentalized images on chocolate boxes; not as metaphors, or creatures of myth, or merely the hallucinations of a fevered imagination.

While angels may take all of these forms, from age to age, individual to individual, they are above all, *real beings*. They have personalities and feelings not unlike ours. Their realms are the inner spaces, as mortals and extraterrestrials are the citizens of outer space. They have an existence separate from us, yet we encounter them in *our* inner worlds. This is what confuses us. Because of our limited understanding of what it means to be human, we think that since angels approach us within our inner spaces, they are of necessity somehow projections of human unconsciousness, or creatures of the human collective unconscious, or more simplistically, shadows thrown up on the screen of human imagination.

This is to fundamentally misconstrue the use of the imagination. Psychologists speak about an eidetic screen that they locate behind the forehead. Think of it as a small movie screen on which we can project images from our imaginations. People with eidetic, or photographic memories, will be familiar with this screen. It's a useful metaphor, even if it doesn't fully describe the experience of visualization. The inventor Nikola Tesla was capable of designing a machine in his imagination, setting it going, and then returning to look at it in six months to see how it was functioning over time and which parts were wearing out the fastest.

What the conventional understanding of the eidetic screen misses is that it's a two-way affair. To use the movie metaphor again, the eidetic screen can receive back-projection as well. In the words of one of my angels when I was querying just this issue, "We reach you *through* your imaginations."

If this were a normal planet and we hadn't fallen under the thrall of the Lucifer Rebellion, the reality of angels would not be a mystery to us. As it is, humans have had to stumble in the darkness, making up our own cultures, our own laws, our own religions, and we were allowed to make our own mistakes. Knowledge and acceptance of angels has come and gone through history, but they've always remained well hidden behind the scrim of reality, betraying their presence only when absolutely necessary.

When Joy communicated her assurances to me, I relaxed and was able to let go of my concerns and anxieties about our book and was able to fully trust that I had done my part in what had been required of me by my heavenly guides.

✦

When I managed to get a sense of what Quetzalcoatl had said at the Harmonic Convergence by talking to friends who had been there and heard him, I learned he'd spoken of the period between 1987 and 2012 as a time of cleaning and clearing out the corruption endemic to so much of human activity.

He warned that it wasn't going to be an easy time for many people since all of their suppressed violence and fear would be breaking through the veneer of civilization. The general sense was that after an initial feeling of hope, this would be followed by some pretty grim years. This was a necessary process, Quetzalcoatl emphasized, and a preparation for the glorious times ahead.

I was told he also spoke about the reincarnational trail many of us have taken to get here. Apparently we've cycled through lifetimes on the inhabited worlds of various star systems—the Pleiades, Sirius, Arcturus, Orion, Antares, and Ursa Major were among those mentioned—to finally arrive in our present-day incarnations. He told everybody to always remember what a privilege it was to be alive and in a mortal body at this precise point in human history.

I like to think the Maya have their astronomy straight and 2012 is going be the year in which the global transformation becomes undeniable, however the event manifests. But I'm certainly not counting on it. What I am sure of is that if it doesn't happen in 2012, something very similar is going to have to occur soon. Our planet is rapidly becoming uninhabitable; the situation is far worse than the planetary scientists' warnings, and there is realistically little that humans can do about it. That's the bad news.

The good news is that we are receiving help from the higher realms, whether angelic, delphinic, or extraterrestrial. Western science's dismissal of the subtle realms for lack of objective evidence, and the shadow this throws over the public's perception, has successfully kept the existence of the larger Multiverse context hidden from us. Yet, information does leak through, as these adventures clearly illustrate. Some heretical scientists are breaking out of the current paradigm and giving serious consideration to other dimensions, to zero-point energy, holonomic models of the universe, torsion physics, and new and different ways of perceiving the world.

I've found it extremely helpful, for example, to understand that what we collectively believe to be the world we experience with our senses is better thought of as a frequency-domain to which our senses are tuned, rather than simply having a solid, physical reality. Physics has long since demonstrated how insubstantial material reality is on a subatomic level. We experience the world as solid because of the interlocking relationship between the frequency range of the reality we are sensing and how our senses are tuned to that frequency.

The Beings of the Violet Flame, for example, will be experiencing their frequency-domain in much the same way. That they exist in a slightly higher frequency-domain than the one to which our senses are tuned, and can thus observe human activity while remaining invisible to us, supports the concept that the higher frequency-domains interpenetrate the lower ones. Note, I say "observe," since for one of them to actually physically interact with our material reality apparently requires a considerable number of BVF working together on their side of the veil to make that possible.

Our current understanding of the space-time continuum is limited by the capacity of our sensory apparatus, as well as technological devices like telescopes and microscopes that extend our perceptual abilities, to experience the many layers of the Multiverse. However far we extend our senses, we will perceive only our own frequency-domain.

If we think of the Multiverse as a toroidal onion, each layer of the onion represents a single frequency-domain. Now, for example, stand on the outside layer of the onion—look as far as you can, you'll only see as far as the curve of the horizon—and you will only be seeing that one layer, without having any idea about all the rest of the layers. As we now know from particle physics, matter as we experience it is composed largely of empty space. But once again, this perception of emptiness is the result of the limitations of our senses to perceive anything manifesting outside our frequency-domain.

Returning to our toroidal onion, we can visualize each layer of "matter," each frequency-domain, as composed of matter at the appropriate density to support that particular frequency-domain. Now stand on the inside of the innermost layer of our onion—and don't forget a torus has a hollow center—and look back toward the outside of the onion. It will appear partially transparent to you since you are standing on the highest frequency-domain. And since high frequencies interpenetrate lower ones, as radio waves pass through walls, you will find it potentially possible to move unobserved all the way to the outermost layer.

I use the visible spectrum as an analogy since it allows us a way of understanding how frequency-domains also lie along a spectrum of frequencies. Just as the normal human eye responds to electromagnetic wavelengths from about 390 to 750 nanometers, an infinitesimal portion of a spectrum spanning wavelengths from thousands of miles down to a fraction of the size of an atom, so also is our domain a tiny fraction of the spectrum of habitable frequencies.

Using a somewhat cruder metaphor, let's take the example of an anthill. The ants are living within a spectrum of frequencies governed by their genome and the exigencies of their environment. They go about their business unaware of us unless we physically interact with them. Although ants broadly share the same frequency-domain as us, their senses are genetically tuned to a far smaller slice of that domain. In the same way, the BVF share enough of our frequency-domain to observe and in some cases to actually affect it, but they essentially exist in the neighboring frequency-domain.

It is by understanding that this multilayered nature of the Multiverse can be experienced directly, without the need to unravel the arcane equations of contemporary physicists, that the living Multiverse becomes most intimately and naturally available to an open heart and mind.

11

The Extraterrestrial Enigma

The ET Enigma, Djinn, Frequency-Domains, the Holographic Multiverse, and Intraterrestrial Craft

I doubt you'd be reading this book if you hadn't had moments in your life, generally under drastic and unpredictable circumstances, during which reality appeared to alter in a completely unexpected manner. This will occur when the senses are deranged in some way, by an accident, an inebriant, an entheogen, or a powerful emotion. We all have these brief glimpses of other realities over the course of our lives, often in difficult and dangerous situations, and because they don't fit in with the accepted view, it is all to easy to dismiss them as dreams, delusions, or hallucinations. If the derangement is uncontrollable and severe it can become a psychosis.

So it has rested; we have these profound events that occur rarely in our lives, whether they are near-death experiences, journeys out of the body, an extraterrestrial encounter, or the conviction that your dead mother is coming to you in dreams. They remain unexplained and mysterious hints of a far vaster and more complex Multiverse than is allowed by conventional explanation. These mysterious and anomalous transcendent incidents, like an NDE, for instance, or spontaneous contact with angels, will tend to open the mind and heart to the deeper levels and implications of human existence. This realization then appears to launch a cascading series of events and encounters, which act for all the world as incremental initiations into an entirely new and deeper understanding of what it might mean to be more fully human in the True Age.

I don't believe I can be alone in this. Neither do I feel in any way "chosen" or "special." I do feel extremely fortunate, however, to have had a number of spiritual experiences and the opportunity to study and think about them. I write about these matters both to understand what has happened to me and in the hope of helping the reader make sense of some of the mysterious incidents in his or her life that remain unexplained, and therefore taboo in contemporary intellectual discourse.

Having orbited the sun seventy times now, I *know* something weird and wonderful is happening on the face of the planet. I still have no evidence that would satisfy a skeptic, just the evidence of personal experience, and no desire, or need, to convince anybody of the ultimate rightness of my viewpoint.

What I am sure of is that my mind has been progressively opened to the larger Multiverse context over a series of initiations, which, looked at as a whole, appear to be a deliberate system of deprogramming from the generally accepted worldview. To the extent that I have freed myself from my own limited thought patterns and have learned to deconstruct the deceptions and distortions we get fed from the day we are born, it feels perfectly natural to slip into understanding the world from the larger context.

The best way of illustrating this is by tracking the various initiatory angelic and extraterrestrial incidents that have occurred over the course of my life.

After my early stint practicing as an architect in London, and then briefly in Nassau in the Bahamas, I gave up the profession and threw in my lot with the mystery school, which by now had become the community called the Process, which I discussed earlier in this book. We lived together in a large mansion in London, and one of the ways we paid the rent was to present weekly shows in which we would act out different themes. Perhaps the presentations might have been labeled performance art in a later age.

I recall one, for example, that we called Great Priest meets Great Beast, in which a couple of us dressed up, one as a pope (any pope), the other as Aleister Crowley, and created such a spirited impromptu dialogue that it would have made the two old primates rise from the dead.

Whenever possible the Process emphasized spontaneity in public events. This built our confidence in being able to talk without inhibition or internal censorship and helped us trust ourselves to speak "off the top" without making fools of ourselves. I don't think any of us realized that doing this became an excellent preparation for mediumistics and channeling.

Being somewhat shy by nature, I was hesitant to push forward my idea. I wasn't even sure where it had come from. Looking back, I'm surprised I ever took on such an ambitious event, yet it clearly reflected the strength of my interests at that time. I created a cubicle on the stage and surrounded myself with half a dozen borrowed or broken TV sets, a bunch of obsolete recording equipment, some small amplifiers, and a couple of ex-military fluoroscopes that glowed a pleasantly unearthly green—anything we could find that blinked, glowed, or buzzed. For the show we set up a microphone and speakers so it would appear as if I was in a SETI situation, speaking to ETs.

Apparently I managed to pull off an hour of an animated trilogue between a human and two different extraterrestrials, in three distinct voices, in three different accents, in front of a small audience. Once again, in a pattern I've had the chance to observe over the years, I have no memory of what was said in the event. I don't think I ever knew. As was our practice, I hadn't planned what to talk about, preferring to leave myself open to being spontaneous. Although at that time I couldn't have described it as channeling, I believe now that is exactly what it was. My total lack of conscious recall strongly suggests I'd gotten myself out of the way, as I must have done as a child when an angel held me in her arms. The gift bestowed by those dreadful bombs was starting to manifest in a most unlikely way.

I also had the chance to meet Desmond Leslie, the Englishman who, in 1953, coauthored *Flying Saucers Have Landed* with George Adamski, and to hear the story of the UFO he observed when he was with Adamski in California. Desmond Leslie was fully convinced by his experience. He believed what Adamski had told him and was clearly an intelligent and reputable person. Although some of Adamski's claims appeared to have been discredited by subsequent scientific discoveries, I suspect it was our ignorance as to how different frequency-domains actually operate that made Adamski's claims appear so implausible. Whereas the moon is barren in our frequency-domain and Venus is covered by clouds of sulfuric acid, it's not unreasonable to propose that on a slightly higher vibrational frequency-domain, both Venus and the moon are verdant and habitable worlds.

Some insight into this possibility can be found in Robert Monroe's 1971 book, *Journeys out of the Body.* Toward the beginning of the Monroe Institute's research into the out-of-body experience, Monroe reports those chosen to travel in their soundproofed chambers were finding every planet they visited in their out-of-body state was barren of life. Realizing this was probably due to a deep conditioning in the implausibility of extraterrestrial life, Monroe started implementing a new approach. This included a sacred dedication with the tacit assumption of life on other worlds. Before long the travelers were finding inhabited worlds all over the place.

It's reasonable to deduce from this there has to be a direct interaction between human consciousness and dimensional realities. We know so little about the nature of human consciousness and what it's capable of that the power of belief is seldom given credit for the effects it can create. Believing in the possibility of inhabited planets and approaching their explorations in a more sacred way apparently had been enough to allow the subjects to subtly shift frequency-domains, possibly without them even knowing how or when the shift occurred. If this is what happened to George Adamski back in the early 1950s, the sadly ridiculed man would have had no way of understanding what happened, or even a language in which to express it if he had.

Frequency-domains and different dimensions are more familiar to those who have experienced them than to scientists who would need a testable model in order to study them. A few theoretical physicists, however, have ventured into some of the strange implications of quantum mechanics: Bryce DeWitt and Hugh Everett, with their many-worlds interpretation, introduced the concept of parallel universes; the quantum physicist David Böhm, collaborating with the neuroscientist Karl Pribram, developed a holonomic model of brain functioning. Both approaches broadly include the possibility of parallel worlds and other frequency-domains.

But to find the working model that matched most closely my personal experience of these different levels I had to wait until I met the scientist and inventor Itzhak (Ben) Bentov in the mid-1970s. Bentov's work is best summed up in his seminal little book, *Stalking the Wild Pendulum,* which was published in 1977, a few years after I got to know him. Sadly, Ben was killed in the 1979 American Airlines crash at Chicago's O'Hare Airport. He was a practical *and* intuitive genius, a man who created the first rocket for Israel's War of Independence, yet could also speak, as a biomedical engineer, about our bodies being mirrors of the Multiverse.

I still regard Ben Bentov's simple and readily intelligible theory that our brains and the Multiverse are both holograms as being closest to the way I actually have experienced my interactions with the Multiverse. It also neatly accounts for the issue I raised earlier, that the frequency-domain experienced interacts with, and is dependent on, the state of consciousness of the experiencer.

Our brains, Ben held, are thought-receivers and amplifiers, lenses that holographically interpret a holographic Multiverse, and not merely the source of thought, as is conventionally believed. (Please see appendix C: "The Spiritual Underpinnings of the Multiverse as a Cosmic Hologram," for more on this topic). Ben's approach supports the possibility of other inhabited frequency-domains, as well as demonstrating that all matter is essentially made of consciousness at different levels of development.

When I was living in London in the mystery school's community, we'd started working with a P-scope, a simple galvanometer measuring skin resistance that we modified for our purposes. The P-scope was a remarkably effective device at cutting below the conscious level of thoughts and intentions. Our approach was to dig deep into our psyches, using the small electrical variations showing on the P-scope to unearth unconscious emotional blockages. Bringing these compulsive patterns of unconscious behavior—which frequently ran counter to our conscious intentions—to conscious awareness, allowing them to be released.

In so thoroughly exploring our personalities and psyches, chasing down and releasing repressed traumas and conflicts, we found we were becoming more and more open to other levels of existence. This openness came to fruition in Nassau as we meditated together as a group (having moved there together in June of 1966). We'd form an intention prior to going into the meditation and create a pertinent question, which each of us would then put to the entities with whom we felt connected. When we emerged from the meditation some minutes later, each of us shared the answer he or she received. Questions formed the basis of our work in London, so it seemed perfectly natural to pose questions to the beings with whom we felt in contact.

Whether these beings were archetypes, our higher selves, midwayers, mischievous thoughtforms, or the voice of our group mind, the quality of the information that came through was coherent and fascinating. Soon we all felt in touch with these beings, and when we shared what we had received, the information revealed to different people frequently interlocked and cross-referenced in a most convincing way. It was because of the way our different answers knitted together that we came to believe we were in contact with an authentic and consistent source. Soon we came to rely on the guidance of these unnamed beings for all major decisions, including where to travel.

I'm only describing here my series of experiences, some of them simply paranormal events and others clearly initiations that prepared me for contact with nonhuman intelligences. Since this has become the focus of my work for the past thirty years, I should recount two events that happened to me during my time in Nassau. The first was a lucid dream. I doubt if there are any statistics on how many people have lucid dreams, or how frequent they are if they do, but I've probably had about eight in my entire life. That is eight out of the 24,090 nights in which I've presumably dreamed normal dreams. That's rare. And given lucid dreaming's rarity, I tend to give them more credence. (Not that I think they are real, merely more significant and memorable than regular dreams).

Recently I've come to think of lucid dreams as one of the ways we are being prepared for a frequency-domain substantially different from the one to which we are normally tuned. The fact that it's possible to affect events in such an unusual way in a lucid dream allows us a window into the nature of the higher frequency-domains.

This particular lucid dream occurred during one of our siestas in the early afternoon as I slept in one of the large bedrooms of the house we had rented in Nassau. I was on my own in the room and must have "woken up" in a dream because there I was in the same room.

As I lay there enjoying the lucidity of the moment, I caught a glimpse of a slight movement in the right-hand corner of my vision. It didn't feel like a bout of sleep paralysis since I was able to turn my head as two extremely tall entities (I was lying in my bed looking up) seemed to glide into view. They appeared to be dressed in long unbelted coats of a dark material, with heads I remember to this day. Both appeared to look similar, with slightly canine faces, except one of them was a little taller than the other, with a longer head.

What remains most clear in my mind were their ears. They were long and wide and covered with a light brown fur that, unlike a dog's ears, stuck up parallel to the sides of their heads and protruded at least six inches above the top of their heads. Their ears appeared to be rigid, and when these beings bent slightly from the waist in greeting I noticed their ears didn't flop forward. The entities' faces, with their curious flattened muzzles, also appeared to be covered with a light-gold fuzz and seemed to me to be stiff and immobile. These creatures were clearly friendly, and at no time did I feel frightened.

What I could see of the entities' eyes shone with intelligence, and when one of them spoke it was directly into my head. I would love to claim that the secrets of the Multiverse were telepathically transmitted into my mind, but no. Instead came such a cliché that if it hadn't been presented in such a dignified manner I might have laughed out aloud.

"Take us to your leader," I heard one of them say in my mind. "Take us to your leader."

Even in my dream, I thought this was absurd. However, they appeared so serious about it and due to fact that, at that time I did have someone I thought of as my leader, I directed them across the patio behind the house to meet the woman who had become the oracle of the community. I watched as the creatures both went down on one knee in front of her. Then I popped back into my body and woke up.

I'm not suggesting this pair was *real,* yet the effect they had on me, their friendly demeanor and their obvious intelligence, encouraged me to be more relaxed in subsequent encounters.

The second incident was harder to believe, except for the fact that it was witnessed by at least a dozen of my friends in the community. Like the others, I had a job on the island. Those who could get the time off work used to return to the big house for lunch and a sun-bake around the pool before returning to work after the siesta. So it was early one afternoon when a couple of dozen of us were lying around on the patio on deck chairs taking in the sun. Every once in a while someone got up and flopped into the pool.

As I lay there, quite awake, I had a most unusual feeling. I'd never felt it before or since, yet it was as unmistakable as a sudden pang of hunger. One moment I was lying there, my mind relaxed and content, and the next thing I *knew* there was a large spaceship directly overhead but too high to see. Although I was possibly predisposed to such a situation, my intuition was so strong, and it was such an unexpected and outlandish thought, that I decided in that moment to go with the flow.

Where my next thought came from was as mysterious as my conviction there was an ET craft overhead: "If you really are there," I formed the words carefully in my mind, "then give it to me. I want to know everything you know."

A moment later I was flying through the air. This was witnessed by a number of my colleagues, as I was mysteriously lifted out of my lounger and was hurled about twelve feet through the air, to land on my back in the swimming pool. It was so fast and startling that I have no conscious recall of exactly what occurred to throw me into the pool. It was simply an energy.

As I've pondered this event over the years, I can only think that the extraterrestrial download (if that is what it was) was too energetic for my tender neural circuitry. I wasn't harmed by the encounter, just astonished by its power and appropriately humbled at my hubris. I've still no explanation for what happened, only that it did. Regardless, it has often occurred to me that I've been spending the last forty-five years gradually decoding what they hit me with.

We continued to meditate and communicate with the beings, so when the community needed to leave the Bahamas it was perfectly natural to ask the beings where we needed to go. This led to a series of meditations that took us first to Mexico City, then, in a rickety rented school bus, down to Merida, where in a meditation in the town railway station we were told to journey still farther to the coast. Finally reaching the Gulf of Mexico we found ourselves deposited in the tiny village of Sisal. We were thirty young English men and women, penniless and somewhat bewildered by our act of faith and wondering why we were there.

The answers came a few days later, when we had the final meditation in the series. The initial excitement of letting ourselves be guided on such ephemeral evidence had evaporated; it hadn't been an easy time. Coconuts from the trees and the few fish we caught barely sustained us, so we went into the meditation famished and more than a little concerned as to where all this strangeness was going. But we needn't have worried. The beings appeared to have our best interests in mind, because when we came out of the meditation and compared notes as to what each saw, heard, or felt, a coherent picture emerged of what we'd find if we walked along the beach.

Next morning, after walking about fourteen miles along the shoreline, there was the place shown us in our visions the previous night. Different people had received specific images: high white walls; a ladder propped against a wall; a coconut grove; you can hear the sea, but not see it. There were other signs I don't recall, but there they all were. The high white walls . . . the ladder . . . the coconut grove . . . all were set in the grounds of a long-abandoned and ruined salt factory, hidden from the beach by a small cliff and sand dunes, yet well within the sound of the surf.

When we discovered we could rent the entire estate for a pittance, we had no doubt it was the beings who had clinched the deal. After that we trusted their guidance even more implicitly. I've written in more detail about our community's time in Xtul—which we were told was the Mayan word for, appropriately enough, "terminus"—in my 2009 book, *Love Sex Fear Death: The Inside Story of the Process Church of the Final Judgment.* Since I'm focusing here only on those situations that touch on my experiences with nonhuman intelligences, I'll skip to some months later, when the beings played their last astonishing hand, and may even have saved our lives.

It started when the British Consul came down from Merida to warn us that Hurricane Inez, one of the deadliest storms on record, was thrashing across the Gulf of Mexico, heading straight for us in Xtul. He was certain we would be wiped out if we stayed put in the ruins and the primitive structures we'd been able to build without tools. He found it difficult to believe it when we decided to stay and face the hurricane.

But, stay we did. We meditated together as ardently as we ever had, asking the beings to protect us from the storm. This was the supreme test, and we only had our faith it would work. It was a terrible storm, with 120-miles-per-hour winds blowing coconut trees parallel to the ground and destroying all the building work we'd done over the previous months. Yet, we survived, wet, cold, and exhausted, and fully convinced that the beings must have had a hand in redirecting the storm.

We were told later how fortunate we'd been in that Inez, after moving directly toward the Yucatan peninsula, had turned slightly north to brush the Mexican coastline, thus somewhat minimizing its impact. In the diagram showing the path of Hurricane Inez that small, but significant, change in direction is quite visible.

When this sort of event happens in life, it presents us with a potentially life-changing choice. As an isolated incident, something like Inez's unexpected change of direction can be readily dismissed as a result of natural causes. When the event is part of a string of meaningful incidents, however, all to some extent self-confirming, and in this case, life affirming, it requires us to acknowledge that there are other, more mysterious forces at work behind the scenes. Choosing to accept that it was the beings who saved us in Xtul acted in much the same way as Robert Monroe's advice to his out-of-body experiencers when they were seeking inhabited worlds. It demonstrated unequivocally that a strongly held belief can directly influence a frequency-domain, in this case our group's shared consensus reality.

It was through Brinsley le Poer Trench that I met Gordon Creighton when the community finally returned to London after being moved along by Hurricane Inez. Brinsley was great fun, and since he was also an Irish peer (he later became the eighth earl of Clancarty on the death of his brother and sat in the House of Lords), he was extremely well connected. He was a charming man, completely free of class judgment, and unusual among the aristocracy, he possessed a delightfully innocent openness.

In the 1950s he cofounded and edited *The Flying Saucer Review,* which Gordon Creighton later edited. Brinsley had just published his book, *The Flying Saucer Story,* when we first met, and he had some remarkable stories. The one that sticks in my mind, because it is still an enigma to this day, concerned President Eisenhower's purported meeting with extraterrestrials at Edwards Air Force Base in 1954. Brinsley told me that he knew an American test pilot who had been at that very meeting and told him the aliens looked almost human. You really couldn't tell just by their appearances that they were alien, he'd told Brinsley, but somehow you *just knew* they were.

I pricked up my ears at that since I'd only had that brief encounter in the street with the person *I* also *just knew* was an extraterrestrial a couple of years earlier. When he looked me in the eye and assured me they can "pick the rockets out of the sky just like that!" I had no doubt he was speaking the truth. Yet what struck me afterward was the curious dissonance I felt between the certainty of my intuition that he was an extraterrestrial and his appearance, so ordinary all I've ever been able to recall is blond hair and a pair of very blue eyes.

In 2009, as I researched President Eisenhower's alleged meeting, I could see no one is any the wiser. Eisenhower never talked about it openly, and his son denied hearing anything privately about any such meeting. One story circulating maintained the meeting was with two small "Greys" and there were a couple of circular UFOs present; Brinsley's test pilot spoke of five craft: three saucers, and two cigar-shaped craft.

Elsewhere I read of there being two meetings: an earlier one with "Nordics" and the other with "Greys." If this were so, then Brinsley's contact must be reporting on the first one. The "Nordics" are said to look very much like blond Scandinavians. Since the truth of the meeting and what was talked about have never been established with any certainty I feel free to use my intuition, along with common sense, to speculate on what might have occurred.

I feel sure that the meeting, or meetings, *did* take place. Both the United States and the Soviet Union had only recently developed hydrogen bombs, the Cold War was gearing up, and an arms race was inevitable. Bigger and more devastating thermonuclear weapons not only threatened the human race, but in all likelihood, also the contingent frequency-domains we are not aware of. Assuming the Multiverse is essentially a benign place—and we would have been invaded long ago if it wasn't—

then surely interplanetary courtesy would require a friendly diplomatic meeting to set the matter straight. If atomic weapons were the main item on the agenda, history suggests Eisenhower must have ignored the extraterrestrial request, whatever his reasons may have been.

My intuition is also telling me that the various extraterrestrial groups changed their tactics at that point. When it became clear there was no stopping the bombs by direct request to the only man who had the power and the military prestige to have possibly reversed the nuclear madness, the Visitors (to use Whitley Streiber's species-unspecific word) evidently switched to Plan B. Each situation would have to be handled individually. This was later confirmed by accounts that have emerged in the past few years of UFOs seen hovering over military bases and missile silos. In the case of the silos, U.S. Air Force personnel have also reported the missile-launching mechanisms were compromised while the UFO was overhead.

In 1954, apparently, it was still too early for the general revelation of the extraterrestrial presence and the impact it might have on the planet. The Brookings Report, commissioned by NASA and submitted to the U.S. Congress in 1961, demonstrates how nervous the writers were about direct contact with a more advanced extraterrestrial race. Using the example of the destructive effect a more advanced human culture invariably has on a less advanced one, they make the anthropomorphic error of assuming that a considerably more advanced extraterrestrial species would act in the same rapacious way.

Many UFO researchers point to the 1961 Brookings Report as being the source (or the justification) NASA used to suppress what they came to know about UFOs and the extraterrestrial presence during the late 1960s. This situation persists to this day.

If indeed the Eisenhower meeting, or meetings, took place and the extraterrestrials subsequently adopted a different approach, that would account for many of the perennial questions concerning the ET presence, the most common of which is, If the ETs are here, why don't they land on the White House lawn?

Evidently the ETs have tried.

So must have started their more covert plan of action of individual contact, which has so puzzled ufologists and scientists alike. This was made all the more confusing by the adamant denial of the various military outfits dealing with UFOs and the consequent ridicule of the press.

By the time I came to know Gordon Creighton, the general suppression of all information on aliens was well in place. The press, with their sneering references to "little green men," were making sure anyone courageous enough to speak publicly about UFOs would be pilloried unmercifully. It was rare to encounter a person who was apparently well placed in the English government and who was prepared to talk freely about these touchy areas.

Gordon was always a little enigmatic about what he did at the Foreign Office, but I've since learned he was with British Intelligence and had an office close to the one dealing with the extraterrestrial problem. He was a smallish, middle-aged man, somewhat stout and completely unassuming in his manner. Like John le Carré's George Smiley, Gordon could fade into the background. He was the perfect spy, so perfect that over the course of numerous lunches, it never once occurred to me that *he* might be gently interrogating *me* as to what I knew. Yet, as sometimes must happen when a handler is ingratiating himself to his agent, I learned a lot more from Gordon than he could ever have learned from me. I was a kid; what did I know?

What I recall of those conversations so many years ago was Gordon's talk of the Djinn. I'd traveled widely in the Middle East by that time and knew he was talking about the spirit beings of the Islamic culture. They are often talked about as mischievous entities, known to be tricksters who enjoy leading humans astray. Djinn frequently make appearances in Arabic folklore and Sufi stories, and they still feature in the lives of ordinary men and women in Arab cultures. I'd read about Djinn and hadn't given them much credence beyond thinking they would make a convenient butt of blame for a superstitious culture.

No, no, Gordon would insist, Djinn were very real indeed. They lived alongside us and were normally invisible except when *they* wanted to be seen. He said he'd been able to find evidence of Djinn in all human cultures, mentioning fairies, trolls, genii, demons, daemons, Elementals, poltergeists, spirit guides, and gods and goddesses as being manifestations of this one race of beings.

Gordon had seen his own UFO in China back in 1941, when he'd been with the British Embassy there. He described it as an intensely bright light racing across the sky. I wasn't quite sure what he made of this, whether he thought it was one of his Djinn or not. I recall him mentioning that the ufologist John Keel called them "ultraterrestrials" and that Keel had come to the same conclusion, that much of what we think of as extraterrestrial activity is in fact the work of the Djinn. Although they are said to be deceptive sometimes with humans, Djinn don't appear to be downright evil. At the time I wondered if the beings who had guided us from Nassau to the Yucatan and saved us from the hurricane were what Gordon Creighton called the Djinn.

Ah! If I knew then what I know now I would have put together that Gordon must have been talking about the midwayers, or the Beings of the Violet Flame, as I'm now referring to them collectively since they started returning. The BVF fit the pattern precisely, and thanks to *The Urantia Book* we now know a little more about their troubled history. In those thousands of millennia after the rebellion and planetary quarantine the BVF did indeed break into factions. If we are seeing them most clearly represented in the Greek and Sumerian myths, they might not have been pleasant, but they weren't exactly evil. Detached in their dealings with humans, they were certainly, at worst, jealous, egotistical, skittish, seductive, and probably very annoying to have around. However, the gods and goddesses always seemed to be too self-involved to be creatively evil.

If we are to accept *The Urantia Book*, the majority of the rebel midwayers, the BVF—all 40,119 of them—were removed at the time of Christ. I imagine the remaining 9,881 would have been kept far too busy at their authentic tasks over the past two millennia to descend into the nonsense that our forebears had to put up with.

Gordon was clearly distrustful of the Djinn, whom he believed were deceptively manifesting as extraterrestrials in our technological age and were the entities behind the UFO phenomenon. At some of our meetings I could see he was frightened under his placid, diplomatic front, especially when telling me he was convinced the governments of the world knew a lot more than they were saying about the phenomenon. And he should know, I thought.

He also raised the interesting point that of the few possible explanations for the alien presence, the concept these "aliens" are indigenous to the earth, that they exist alongside humans, yet are invisible to us, is seldom given much credit. It rings of superstition in our materialistic age.

I think in retrospect that Gordon Creighton was perfectly correct about his Djinn, but like many people who come up with an explanation for phenomena, I feel he overstated his case. His extraordinary gift with languages—he read in at least twenty of them—and his lifetime interest in the paranormal, I believe, gave him a certain bias toward thinking the Djinn were a baleful influence on humanity.

Although Gordon and I lost contact when I left England for the last time, he went on to take over the editorship of *The Flying Saucer Review* in 1982, becoming the "grand old man of British ufology." I'm told he held courageously to his belief that governments were deceiving the public about UFOs and what they know about them until he died in 2003.

Gordon seemed to me, when I knew him back in the 1960s, as the most unlikely proponent of extraterrestrial (or, ultraterrestrial) realities. Yet, when I researched some of the articles and essays he left, I could see that he'd developed his ideas into a remarkably perceptive system. He is quoted in an article from the UFO Resource Center, November 27, 2000, as saying, in part:

> The study of all the great world religions—and notably Islam, one of the world's great religions— yields valuable clues as to the true nature of the "UFO Phenomenon." Islam knows, in fact, of the existence of three entirely separate and distinct species of intelligent beings in the Universe, and indeed can furnish surprisingly precise details regarding their natures and roles and activities. Angels, Men, and Jinns [sic].
>
> The first category is that of the Angels or Messengers. The second are Men, with planetary physical bodies assembled from the mineral and chemical elements of our Periodic Table. The third category is the category of those beings created before man was, who are referred to collectively in Arabic as Al-Jinn that means, "to hide or to conceal," indeed a very fitting derivation for the name of these creatures. Whereas the bodies of Angels are of light, the bodies of

Al-Jinn consist of "essential fire," or "essential flame," or "smokeless fire," or "smokeless flame."

It is specifically stated in the Qur'an (Surah XV, 26 and 27) that they were created before mankind and some scholars speculate these might be the "Pre-Adamic men" whose existence is hinted at here and there in the Holy Bible. Western occultists have tried to describe them as ether, or as etheric or astral planes. I have also seen it suggested that some sort of plasma is indicated. The Source of the Jinns is not very distant from us, yet at the same time somehow very far from us. In other words, on some other dimension, or in some other Space/Time framework, "right here," some other Universe that is here, behind Alice's mirror: "a mirror-universe on the other side of the Space-time Continuum" as it has been neatly put by some investigators.

Although, the Qur'an (Koran) is not clear on this, it looks as though some of the Jinns could be fully physical and what we call extraterrestrials, while other species of them are of an altogether and finer sort of matter, corresponding to what various UFO investigators have tried to indicate by such terms as "ultraterrestrial" or "intraterrestrial."

In thinking about these ideas, we might bear in mind the theory of the Russian philosopher P. D. Ouspensky regarding the possible existence of other, more subtle, levels of matter on which the elements of the Periodic Table of our own chemical world are repeated—and, if I understand him aright, repeated more than once, on more than one level.

The early writings of Dr. Meade Layne in the United States, about the "Dense Etheric World" from which he maintained that the UFO entities and their craft originated, should also be borne in mind. His book *The Coming of the Guardians,* was published in 1958, and may prove to have been very important. "Certain of the benevolent Jinns may well be our 'Guardians.'"[1]

While Gordon Creighton's broad review of the three different life-forms may turn out to be oversimplified—Where are the nature spirits, for example?—I believe he is correct in his basic proposition concerning different lifeforms. His quoting of P. D. Ouspensky's concept of the

Periodic Table being repeated on higher, more subtle levels, demonstrates that he was thinking of differing frequency-domains, even if he didn't have the words to describe it.

When I knew Gordon he would have been reluctant to admit there were such things as "benevolent Djinn," so I take it he must have softened his views with age. I wonder if he encountered *The Urantia Book*, or would have thought the book a valid source of information if he had. His references to Ouspensky's theory and the writings of Dr. Layne demonstrate he was prepared to break out of scientific lockstep, but he may have drawn the line at a book actually transmitted by the angels.

It's an irony Gordon would have appreciated that the beings he'd identified as Djinn were the very beings who petitioned for *The Urantia Book* and who contributed many of the papers in it.

I think that some of Gordon Creighton's ideas, like those of many Englishmen of his generation, were shaped by two world wars. The knowledge of Nazi evil tended to color his opinions, and he was viewing the Djinn through that lens. He mistook the Djinn's very understandable need to stay hidden as evidence of their deceptiveness. By acknowledging the existence of a race of beings living in a parallel, but evidently connected, dimension, Gordon was confronted by a reality that must have frightened him. I never saw the files he'd been keeping after the war on all the anomalous incidents written up in the press and the more secret reports that came through his contacts in the military, but from what he told me he seemed genuinely alarmed at the implications for the human species.

I hope that by the time he died, Gordon Creighton may have realized his worst fears hadn't manifested over the last forty years of his life. Serious scientists like the astronomer Dr. Allen Hynek were giving credence to the extraterrestrial presence, while a psychiatrist of the impeccable reputation of Harvard's Dr. John Mack was examining the "alien abduction phenomena" with an open mind.

Sightings of mysterious craft have been reported with increasing frequency and reliability as the years have passed; millions of people are thought to have been "abducted by aliens"; authentic crop circles continue to appear yearly, enigmatic and full of hidden meaning; people are starting to talk about their alien/hybrid children; and for all the military's denial, normal people the world over have continued to see unexplained lights in the sky. If all this has been the "deceptive" work of Gordon's Djinn, then evidently they have suddenly become remarkably active all over the planet. Yet, here we are in the twenty-first century and still collectively no wiser as to what is happening. The governments of the West continue in their silence, in spite of a large percentage of the general public who now claim to believe in life on other planets. A 2002 Roper poll suggests 72 percent of Americans believe the government is not telling the truth about what they know of extraterrestrials.

If the Djinn really are as dangerous as Gordon made out when he was warning me about them back in the 1960s, now, looking back, for all the sightings and abductions, where has been the real harm? No one has been killed or severely injured. An alien abduction can be a frightening experience to go through, yet most abductees emerge stronger and more spiritually alive. The sight of a UFO can break down a person's conventional worldview, but that can't be described as particularly destructive.

Taking all these apparent contradictions into account, it seems far more probable that we have all been undergoing a wide-ranging program of social engineering. While the Brookings Institution might have been correct in 1961 in its condescending assessment of humanity's reaction to extraterrestrials, the situation fifty years later is somewhat different. Most thinking people now at least accept the existence of extraterrestrial life, and many of the human institutions the Brookings writers were so protective of have been quite discredited enough without the intervention of Djinn or extraterrestrials.

It is now thirty years since the French UFO researcher Jacques Vallee rejected the extraterrestrial hypothesis (ETH) as insufficient to explain the number of sightings and abductions, in favor of what he terms the multidimensional visitation hypothesis. While not completely dismissing the possibility of visitors from other planets, he stresses the importance for developing a second line of UFO research into the implications of multidimensionality.

Considered a heretic by the UFO community, who are mostly invested in the extraterrestrial hypothesis, Dr. Jacques Vallee has stood firm over the years, and in his 1990 paper in the *Journal of Scientific Exploration* titled "Five Arguments against the Extraterrestrial Origin of Flying Objects," he summarizes his position as follows:

Scientific opinion has generally followed public opinion in the belief that unidentified flying objects either do not exist (the "natural phenomena hypothesis") or, if they do, must represent evidence of a visitation by some advanced race of space travelers (the extraterrestrial hypothesis or "ETH").

It is the view of the author [Dr. Vallee] that research on UFOs need not be restricted to these two alternatives. On the contrary, the accumulated data base exhibits several patterns tending to indicate that UFOs are real, represent a previously unrecognized phenomenon, and that the facts do not support the common concept of "space visitors."

Five specific arguments articulated here contradict the ETH:

1. Unexplained close encounters are far more numerous than required for any physical survey of the earth;
2. The humanoid body structure of the alleged "aliens" is not likely to have originated on another planet and is not biologically adapted to space travel;
3. The reported behavior in thousands of abduction reports contradicts the hypothesis of genetic or scientific experimentation on humans by an advanced race;
4. The extension of the phenomenon throughout recorded human history demonstrates that UFOs are not a contemporary phenomenon; and
5. The apparent ability of UFOs to manipulate space and time suggests radically different and richer alternatives.[2]

Although Dr. Vallee makes no claims as to who or what these dimensional visitors might be, the points he makes above clearly suggest they are the BVF, the midwayers of *The Urantia Book*. Only in his second point does he confuse the issue. When he writes of the "humanoid body structure of the alleged aliens" as not being biologically adapted to space travel, I wonder what he is basing this assumption on. Alien autopsy reports have leaked out over the years, and whether true or not, the consensus seems to be that the creatures examined lack digestive systems or reproductive organs, and are more likely to be biological robots.

The film that appeared in the mid-1990s, purporting to be an authentic autopsy conducted in a tent following the 1947 Roswell crash, has since been admitted to be a reconstruction by Ray Santilli, the video producer behind the film. By all accounts Santilli continues to insist that his film is not truly a hoax but a "restoration" of twenty-two short, four-minute films of the Roswell autopsy that he saw in 1992, which he claims are now degraded beyond use.

These little biological automatons, if that is what they are, are most unlikely to be the BVF, although it might be possible they are BVF artifacts. Appearing to be creatures fabricated for specific purposes, these EBEs (extraterrestrial biological entities, as the military have named them) must be the product of an extremely advanced biotechnology. However, I see no reason that the BVF, who are capable of manifesting in our frequency-domain, would have any need to develop such biological robots, unless the various crashed craft were part of a BVF contact mission and the EBEs were considered expendable.

As far as is known, the few EBEs that have been recovered by the U.S. military from the various crashed discs have either been dead or soon would be. It seems to be highly improbable that any extraterrestrial race with the know-how to get here would crash with the regularity they have exhibited over the years since 1947. It's been suggested that a newly installed form of radar caused the New Mexico Roswell and Aztec crashes, but here again, whether they were interdimensional or extraterrestrial, it's astonishing the visitors wouldn't have had a better knowledge of our electromagnetic spectrum.

I suspect something else is going on and it's being overlooked because of our cultural programming here in the West. We view the extraterrestrial presence through the lens of our own troubled natures. Yet it doesn't have to be that way. I believe there is an important clue as to what might be happening in the Dutch contactee Stefan Denaerde's epic encounter with beings from the planet Iarga.

In contrast to the denials of the reality of ETs made by the military/scientific/academic complex there are some excellent in-depth investigations of extraterrestrial life done by private citizens. Retired Lt. Colonel Wendelle C. Stevens has produced a number of privately printed books over the years conducting inquiries and studying authentic personal experiences with ETs. His book, written with Stefan Denaerde, *UFO . . . Contact from Planet*

IARGA: A Report of the Investigation, published first in 1982, is an account of one of the most remarkable encounters yet to have been written up in such detail.

Stefan Denaerde's initial incident occurred in the mid-1960s as he and his family were sailing in the southwestern delta off the Dutch coast. The boat unexpectedly ran aground at night in the middle of the ship channel, and as he was trying to reverse the motors he saw a dark humanoid shape being carried face down in the current. Jumping off his boat he found himself standing on a flat, steel-hard surface submerged about three feet under the water.

When he rescued the dark form, he only slowly realized as he dragged it back over to his yacht that there was something strange about the metallic suit and the rubbery ball around the figure's head that gave off a blue light. Struggling to explain to himself what might be happening he thought for a moment it might be an astronaut who had ditched in the water.

Then, apparently everything happened very fast.

The sea lit up with "a great diffuse light under the surface of the water," and he turned to see another creature, dressed the same as the one he had rescued, wading toward him. After some initial terror on Mr. Denaerde's part, the creature expressed his appreciation, in oddly accented English, for rescuing his fellow crew member. The creature asked what he could do in return for Stefan Denaerde's "unselfishness."

Thus started what was to become one of the most deeply informed and fascinatingly detailed reports, of an aquatic extraterrestrial species from the planet Iarga in a star system ten light years away. I have only focused here on what I believe may be the clue as to what was actually going on with those crashed discs. As an aquatic species and dressed in a "spacesuit," was it really credible that the dark form floating in the water was in genuine distress? Or was the entire scenario more likely to have been a staged event to see how humans would react?

When he'd recovered himself Denaerde responded with an intelligent curiosity and a genuine humility and was able to set up a telepathic link that has allowed him to record in detail many elements of Iargan life and their complex belief system.

Stefan Denaerde's extraterrestrial encounter is a perfect example of what I earlier suggested might be the ET's Plan B. The Iargans told

Denaerde they had studied this world "for some time," so it's safe to assume they knew perfectly well who they were making contact with and had chosen Stefan Denaearde, a mature and successful industrialist, for his mental balance and courage.

Is this one of the answers as to how a more advanced society might initially interact with a less developed one without negatively interfering with it? By allowing themselves to appear vulnerable, might a more advanced society disarm the aggression and fear of a less developed one? Could those wrecked discs, with their "disposable" occupants, also have been ploys, deliberately crashed to see how we would react? And if the U.S. military had not panicked, covered up the incidents, and descended into a sixty-year paroxysm of denial, it's hard to imagine what the current global situation might have been like.

There is an extremely unusual feature to this world that, apparently, some extraterrestrials don't understand when they arrive here. A good example is the sad story of the Verdants and their ambitious plans for our planet. First some background, and here we need to turn to *The Urantia Book* to find out what this unusual feature is.

As I've previously suggested, it's helpful to understand the Multiverse as being divided into two major streams of intelligent life: the material worlds of the space-time continuum—the Universe we perceive with our senses—and second, the far higher frequency-domains of the celestials. Extraterrestrials are merely mortals from other worlds. The ones that are able to come here are simply older and more developed than we are, and fall under the first category.

What *The Urantia Book* makes clear is that while it's the mortals, on whatever planet they find themselves, who have to handle the denser vibrations of the material creation, the patterns for the material worlds descend from the inner realms of the Creator Son and the Mother Spirit and her angels. Ideally, we mortals become the hands of the angels in a cooperative effort to support and encourage the growth of spiritual intelligence.

After the initial seeding of life plasm on a world intended for habitation, the development of intelligent life becomes a cooperative venture between the evolutionary physical lifeforms and the angels who nurture them. This concern is illustrated by the five major interventions* from the inner realms that this planet has received over the last half a million years. Each intervention can be understood as carrying with it the potential for incrementally raising the consciousness of humanity in our slow climb from animal to being fully human.

Undoubtedly the most important of these interventions, according to *The Urantia Book,* is the incarnation of Christ Michael in the body of Joshua ben Joseph. Since it was Michael's choice on which of the ten million inhabited worlds in his Local Universe he would decide to incarnate as a mortal, Earth has now become known in the highways and byways of the space-time continuum as Michael's Planet.

This gives Earth a peculiarly important status within this Local Universe and has acted as a magnet for some advanced races capable of traveling to and from other worlds. And further, if *The Urantia Book* is accurate when it reports on Michael's promise to return to this planet, then the more advanced races would more than likely know about this extraordinary promise and would want to be here for its fulfillment.

It is our unlikely privilege as human beings to find ourselves on this world, alive at this particular point in history, when Michael's return, however it manifests, must surely soon occur. Possibly it will be timed to synchronize with the events of December 2012; it might even *be* the very event the Maya have predicted to occur at the end of this long cycle.

I should emphasize that in my opinion this event—let's call it the Big Show at the End of Time—will most likely have little to do with how conventional Christianity pictures Jesus. When Michael returns it will surely be as the self-evident savior of all people, whatever name he is given by different religions and belief systems. He may choose to return as an individual personality in his supreme glory, and he may decide to manifest in the hearts and minds of every person on Earth, each to the extent each person can experience his presence.

Most of all, I've come to believe the Big Show is intended to be a wonderful surprise for everybody, as the cavalry appears over the top of

---

*On this planet, the subsequent four interventions after the initial seeding of life plasm were the arrival of Prince Caligastia's mission five hundred thousand years ago, a genetic uplift mission thirty-eight thousand years ago, Melchizedek's mission four thousand years ago, and Christ Michael's incarnation two thousand years ago.

the hill in a movie and rescues the fort at the last moment. If my intuition is correct in this, the Big Show is not an event anyone wants an extraterrestrial race blundering into with their good intentions and spoiling the surprise for everyone.

Which is where the Verdants tried to come in.

I got to know Phillip Krapf after reading his 1998 book, *The Contact Has Begun: The True Story of a Journalist's Encounter with Alien Beings*. The book carried the ring of truth for me, and some of what the writer, a self-confessed atheist, went through so closely synchronized with aspects of my own personal experience that it was clear to me he was struggling to deal with a perfectly genuine encounter.

I met Phil Krapf a number of times over the years in his California home and had the chance to video-interview him about his encounters with the Verdants, a race whose home planet in a nearby galaxy is fourteen million light-years away, a distance they can apparently cover in about fourteen years. In a material Universe with a diameter of thirty billion light-years, the Verdants probably consider us to be close neighbors. They told Phil they first developed space travel 229 million of our years ago and claimed they'd nurtured many developing planets on their first steps into space.

The salient details of Phil's three-day stint in a Verdant ship and his subsequent encounters with "Gina," his delightful (and sexy) Verdant guide, are well recorded in his book. I don't intend to repeat Phil's story here, merely to pick out the main issues that led to the apparent failure of the Verdant project and what we can learn from it.

The experiences that would change Phil's life started one night in June of 1997, when he was drawn up through an intense beam of light to find himself in an enormous room facing three clearly alien beings. Small, slim, little creatures, between five feet two and five feet four, with a range of skin color that Phil describes as varying between them, "from a grayish-white with a barely perceptible greenish tint, to a muted tan with the same greenish tinge." Their eyes were dark, and when they spoke from their small mouths, it came through to Phil in excellent English.

When Phil recovered his composure—and remember this man was skeptical journalist who didn't read science fiction and certainly didn't believe in extraterrestrials—and was settled in for his three-day stay on the spaceship, he started asking questions. Apparently the Verdants have been studying Earth for about a thousand years and claim to have done tens of thousands of abductions—they prefer to call them "unsolicited visitations"—as part of their program of helping us get off the planet and out into the vast inhabited universe—by all accounts a noble goal.

The Verdants' plan, which they maintained had proven effective on many of the less-developed worlds they'd helped, was simple and ingenious. Not wishing to create the chaos that followed the 1938 *War of the Worlds,* they planned to bring hundreds of well-placed and important people to their large spacecraft in the same way they'd drawn Phil Krapf up.

These people would then become "ambassadors" so that when they revealed the presence of the Verdants and described their agenda, the general public would not be so disturbed. Phil was told he was among a secondary group of several hundred more humans, named "deputy envoys," who were serving different ancillary functions. Phil's part of it was to write up the intervention.

It's important to know there was some internal disagreement within the Verdants as to whether Earth was ready for an overt extraterrestrial presence. It was the mid-1990s, and it looked like the world was settling down somewhat. It was a risky call, apparently the Verdants knew that, but they decided to go ahead anyway.

So the situation stood. Phil recognized one or two of the more widely known ambassadors he'd seen on the ship from their pictures in the newspapers, had a chance to talk extensively to the ETs, and learned a great deal more about the Verdants that will be of interest to anyone with a jones for exopsychology.

Phil received a visit from Gina at his house in Los Angeles. His journalistic skepticism was challenged at every step. He published his book, and then a second book, filling in more of the gaps of the Verdant agenda. Apparently, after the ambassadors were to have announced their awareness of the Verdants and the human population had become accustomed to the Verdant presence and knew them to be peaceful, the ETs would green a large area of arid land overnight. They would then create (construct? manifest?) a "city" in the American Southwest that would act as a gathering place for humans and Verdants to share their knowledge and experience. (See plate 7.) There was even a tempting promise of piggyback rides to distant worlds on their "Star Cruiser," currently parked behind the moon.

In 2001, we had the September 11 terrorist strike on the World Trade Center. Almost immediately, the Verdants pulled out, citing the attack as evidence that humanity wasn't ready for what they were offering, and according to Phil, they have not made a reappearance to date.

So, what are we to make of this?

Was the Verdant agenda a subtle mask for a bit of interplanetary colonization? Were the Verdants who they said they were? If they had been observing Earth for the last thousand years, how could they have made the elementary mistake of believing that a few years of comparative peace demonstrated we would be ready for intervention? And if they were so advanced, it's hard to believe they wouldn't have had a grasp on time travel; nor do they seem to be aware of other dimensions. Some of their claims were clearly wrong or self-deluding. For example, they appeared completely unaware of any other extraterrestrial races who are interested in or involved with this planet.

Knowing Phil as I do, I regard his record as a completely reliable description of what he experienced over the years of his intermittent contact with the Verdants. He is a kind man, well into his sixties and retired from twenty-five years as a copy editor at the *Los Angeles Times*. There's a sort of midwestern innocence about him, but he's clearly not known for his imagination. I believe his encounters with the Verdants were perfectly authentic, but being spiritually undeveloped, I suspect he wasn't sufficiently equipped to know if and when they were telling him the truth.

Some metaphysicians insist there are deceptive quasi-lifeforms, demons perhaps, who exist in the astral regions and delight in messing around with humans. While the lower astral realms are home to both positive and negative thoughtforms, these entities have no real substance. Unlike thoughtforms, midwayers are spiritual entities and functional beings with a serious purpose for being here. While there is likely a racial memory in some cultures of the mischief the rebel midwayers got up to before they were removed by Christ, I'll warrant that any contemporary devilry attributed to Djinn, for example, is more the result of a fearful human imagination.

If these "deceptive quasi-lifeforms" of the occultists that appear to inspire such fear truly exist and they're not merely thoughtforms, then I've never encountered them. And if this is who the Verdants are then it's hard to believe they would initiate such a complex and long-lasting caper for such a minimal payoff. Besides, Phil has become a far more open-minded and thoughtful man as a result of his experiences, barely the outcome "negative entities" might have hoped for.

I think the Verdant story illustrates something else entirely. And it's a little more complex than it appears on the surface.

Of the many sightings of anomalous lights in the sky, a certain number of them are clearly true extraterrestrials, visitors from other inhabited planets. There have been far too many authentic, well-documented cases of face-to-face extraterrestrial encounters like Stefan Denaerde's experience to believe otherwise. Of course, some of what people see are earthlights or the planet Venus; some will likely be Gordon's Djinn, while others might be secret military craft; a few will be hoaxes or drunken delusions. What can't be explained away so facilely are the actual encounters with ETs, which sober, respectable people are having all over the world.

Since we've been seeing the lights and the craft in greater numbers as the years have passed and they haven't yet revealed themselves, it's reasonable to assume there is an overall plan they are all following. Now, *The Urantia Book* tells us that one of the functions of the BVF is to monitor and organize incoming extraterrestrial activity. If this planet has been technically quarantined since the Lucifer Rebellion—an isolation that has only been lifting over the past twenty-five years—it's safe to assume that the extraterrestrial groups are holding back for a specific reason.

Into this sensitive situation blunder the Verdants, clearly not quite who they say they are, with the arrogance to think they are the only game in town. They dazzle poor Phil with their honey traps (and yes, he falls in), and they flaunt their exaggerated claims of competence in what must be one of the most delicate operations of interplanetary diplomacy, that of initiating contact with a less developed planet.

Having filled poor Phil's head with all their plans, after encouraging him to write a book about them and keeping him on hand for over four years, the Verdants suddenly change their minds, dump Phil Krapf, and back out.

The Verdants' miscalculation in starting their agenda of contact—which they evidently had, since Phil saw ambassadors on the ship—and then changing their minds, curtailing their program, and pulling out, was discourteous at best and profoundly disappointing for all concerned. To make their behavior even more disreputable, they blamed *us* for it! It just proved to them we were still too belligerent and unruly.

The Rwandan genocide was exploding in 1994, just when the Verdants would have been preparing their plans, and this didn't deter them? And 9/11 did?

The only explanation for this whole unfortunate incident with the Verdants, which seems to cover all the odd contradictions, is that their prospective intervention was ill conceived from the start. If *The Urantia Book* is correct in stating that the BVF are in overall control of extraterrestrial activity, we can assume they were either asleep at the wheel and the Verdants snuck in or, more likely, they allowed the Verdants through, to go ahead with their plans.

Why would they have done that? The Verdants, for all their stated good intentions, were clearly not as advanced as they believed themselves to be. Their claim to be the dominant species in the universe, their evident ignorance of other dimensions and frequency-domains, and their unawareness of the deeper significance of this planet, all add up to a species much in need of a cosmic wake-up call. I suspect the BVFs allowed them to proceed with their plans so the Verdants might learn from their own errors of judgment.

I can only imagine how the Verdants must have felt when they discovered that not only weren't they the dominant species in the universe, there also were many other races, some far more advanced than them. If that wasn't sufficiently humiliating for the Verdants, to discover they had gatecrashed a party they didn't know was happening, then to contravene what must be the first rule in interplanetary diplomacy by barging in to "uplift" a planet they obviously didn't understand, must have resulted in some severe self-reflection in the Verdant community.

If the Verdants' efforts to independently colonize Earth and their subsequent unceremonious retreat was, in fact, a profound lesson for an arrogant species that was at best self-deluded and at worst deceptive and manipulative, what can we humans derive from this sorry tale?

In the continuing dialogue as to whether there are "bad aliens" out there, we now have Dr. Steven Greer in 2009, founder of The Disclosure Project, with its many hundreds of contributions from government and military scientists and personnel who have had firsthand experience with the extraterrestrial presence, assuring everybody there are currently no negative ETs messing around with Earth.

I'm inclined to think he is right. Michael Salla, in his book, *Exopolitics,* writes of over fifty ET races who are currently involved with what is unfolding on Earth, and they appear to be managing to stay in the wings. I suggest that what happened with the Verdants supports Dr. Greer's statement, as well as demonstrating to all observers, human and otherwise, that ETs can be fallible. With the unfortunate human proclivity to worship that which appears to be more powerful than us, it would be important for any reputable extraterrestrial mission to avoid what must be an elementary mistake in any interplanetary intervention.

The Verdants made a bad error of judgment, but I don't believe their motives were downright malicious. Nobody could think the Verdants were "bad aliens" or had evil intentions, and they were evidently pulled out before they could do any real damage.

I believe we can derive from this that we truly have nothing to fear from *any* extraterrestrial intervention. We can take courage in what seems to be happening on the planet. For all the appearances of imminent catastrophe, things are well in hand in ways that we barely understand. We have the respect and care of our interplanetary elder brothers and sisters for being part of this great experiment, and this will all become supremely clear when the moment comes for the Big Show.

If this is a fair assessment of the current global situation when the extraterrestrial presence is factored in, then what, I wonder, can we expect to occur over the next few years?

12

The Angelic Conspiracy and the Global Transformation

The Angelic Conspiracy, a Message from Zeta Reticuli, and the Great Transformation

I want to pull together some of the main streams of thought I've raised in the three books of the *Adventures among Spiritual Intelligences* series and bring what I have learned up to the moment.

Clearly, the global situation is a fast-moving one, and much more will be revealed as we reach 2012 and beyond. So, whatever I've been able to garner in the thirty years since the dolphins first opened my eyes to the fact we share the planet with another intelligent species are only hints of what lies ahead.

I don't believe my journey is particularly unusual. Given the same curiosity, anybody could have made the same journey. I can't say for sure that what I've learned, the assumptions I make, or the conclusions I draw will turn out ultimately to be true. However, that isn't the point. To riff on John Lilly's maxim, as long as the rungs in my ladder of self-knowledge continue to support my weight, I'll continue climbing.

My main interest, the whole area of nonhuman intelligences, is a territory that has rarely been charted in the modern era. Since this arena largely falls outside of science's purview due to its lack of repeatable evidence, any personal exploration can become a valid contribution toward a fuller understanding of what might be occurring on the planet. At this point there is no one concept, no single ideology or theology, no particular point of view or opinion that puts forth the whole picture. It will only be by each one of us bringing his or her own hard-won holographic shard of the truth to the party that we will be able to discern something of the overall pattern.

This has been a long 203,000-year angelic experiment in social engineering, in which humans have had a chance to function independently, without the constant presence and guidance of angels and extraterrestrials. As the Dutch doctor H. C. Moolenburgh suggests in his excellent 1984 book, *A Handbook of Angels,* this level of human autonomy is a most unusual privilege.

Under normal conditions, on a normal planet not falling under the thrall of the Lucifer Rebellion, we would have a full awareness of our companion angels to guide us through life. *The Urantia Book* speaks of "Lakes of Glass," great crystals a mile in diameter, that receive and transmit news and entertainment broadcasts from other planets. The inhabitants of such worlds must, of necessity, be aware of interplanetary and interdimensional travel.

Here, and on the other thirty-six inhabited worlds whose angelic overseers aligned themselves with Lucifer, the situation has been quite different. Being quarantined for so long, isolated from the rest of the teeming Multiverse, our spirits trapped in flesh and all but completely ignorant of the ways of the Multiverse, humans have been forced back on our own ingenuity. We may still be a fearful species, but as individuals we've become extremely emotionally tough. Some years ago I was informed by an angel with whom I was working that Earth is regarded as the "third to worst world in this Local Universe"; that's third to worst out of the ten million possibilities!

In this way the challenges and failures we've all had to face and surmount in the course of an incarnation on this planet have yielded a rich learning. Nothing teaches like failure. Over the course of these interspecies adventures, I've come to believe this is exactly the way this world is meant to be: a hard, fearful, belligerent place—evidently a rarity in a well-organized and benign Multiverse.

I suspect there is a very good reason so many of us have chosen to incarnate here, on this sad, beaten-up little world, and it's a reason I've struggled with over the years, since the implications are deep and stretch back over all those millennia to when the troubles began so long ago.

Those readers who have been following my thinking over the course of the books I've been writing will be familiar with some of the main themes I've been exploring. From the start, in 1979, I chose to record what I was experiencing and feeling with as much clarity as I could muster. If what I was passing along was to have any value to others, my descriptions and insights needed to be as truthful as possible.

Memory is now known to be inherently unreliable, so it's been a great help to have kept a detailed journal from which I've been able to draw the information and stories I include in my books. I've also had a great deal of help from the angels I work with, and they have held true to my original preference to collaborate rather than simply take dictation from them. Working so closely with the recording angel Abigrael on our book, *Ask Your Angels,* provided a great boost to our confidence in creative angelic cooperation. After that, when I was writing the second book in this series, I soon became aware that a couple of angels, whom I came to know as Zophiel and Zadkiel, were looking over my shoulder and giving me a shot of pleasure whenever I expressed something that they wanted said.

I've learned in the course of these spiritual adventures that if I follow my intuition at all times, while it may not always be correct, at least the mistakes are mine and I have a chance to learn from them. However, it is by consistently trusting my intuition and following the trail of synchronicities that have opened up as a result that I believe I've been given some glimpses of who and what exists behind the veil.

As stated earlier, much of what I have learned of the doings of the Multiverse has been derived from *The Urantia Book.* The book doesn't demand belief, it merely lays out some of the facts of the Multiverse that the Urantia communicants maintain we sorely need to have available on this world. *The Urantia Book* is a deeply serious document and contains information and insights on such a wide variety of subjects that it will likely prove invaluable for the studious reader for the next few hundred years.

Since the very existence of such a book threatens the basis of the scientific/materialistic worldview, it is reasonable to ask whether *The Urantia Book* is a fraud. If so, on what level? Could it be a deliberate ploy on the part of some incredibly devious (and very patient) rebel angels to misdirect humans? Yet if the book is read carefully, the tone is one that is clearly derived from an organized administration, and the bias in the Lucifer papers is that of a bureaucrat. The communicants included a broad assortment of celestials and high angels, along with some of the loyal midwayers who petitioned for the book, and there's really no reason to think they would have any cause for such a massive deception. If the book had been a nefarious disinformation campaign by the rebel angels, the tone and emphasis would have had to have been very different.

So, if the book isn't a celestial plot might it have been generated by humans? The Piltdown Man of revealed theology?

As well as Dr. William Sadler, the eminent psychologist responsible for getting all the Urantia material together—and his friends in the Kellogg family, who appear to be at the core of the undertaking—there was a much larger group of seventy stalwart Chicago citizens who met regularly to hear what was being transmitted and to offer up their feedback.

Given the improbability of a group of people dedicating almost fifty years of their lives to deliberately faking such complex and detailed material, whatever would have been their motive? A massive book claiming to be transmitted directly from the angels is not an easy sell. Anyway, apart from the Herculean task of getting their 2,000-plus-page book printed and published, not one of the people involved—all considered upright citizens—has ever come forward or suggested the book was anything other than what it claimed to be.

There seems to have been no financial motive at the human end. I'd imagine rather the opposite; it must have been a costly enterprise both in money and time for all involved. Besides, the personality type liable to commit such a massive fraud would want their cleverness noticed by now. Where is the motive for fraud? The whole process took decades of work and was done largely anonymously. Besides, the very act of committing a fraud presupposes a certain personality type and a predisposition to pulling a fast one, neither of which seems to fit the dependable Midwestern nature, let alone managing to get seventy-plus hoaxers together for over forty years for a fraudulent enterprise that many of them would never live to see completed and published.

So could it be a mass delusion? Might the people who received the book and those seventy people who gathered regularly over the years, could they all be deluded? And all those who read the book, deluded, too?

If this is so, who is doing the deluding? And what is the payoff for the deluder?

Of course, for the professional skeptics, those who would be unlikely to be open to the possibility of such a transmission in the first place, the answer has to be some combination of self-deception, delusion, or outright fraud.

Martin Gardner, in his 1995 book, *Urantia: The Great Cult Mystery,* attempts to show the book is merely the concoction of Dr. William Sadler and the Kellogg family. Due to the book's astonishing internal consistency and coherence, Gardner is unable to seriously challenge its contents on its own terms, and at a loss to grasp its spiritual significance, he spends most of his time attempting to discredit the people who received and published it.

In spite of the angelic communicants' clear requirement that they wanted the man who was actually receiving the transmissions to remain anonymous, for the very purpose of *not* creating a personality cult, Gardner insists on trying (unconvincingly) to ferret out the man's true identity.

As a founding fellow of the Committee for the Scientific Investigation of Claims of the Paranormal (CSICOP) Martin Gardner's professional bias is so pronounced that it seems to have led him to make a number of elementary errors. He dismisses the book, for example, as an authentic communication from the angels (naturally, since he doesn't believe in angels in the first place) by pouncing on the fact that Dr. Sadler and the Kellogg family were already well seasoned in religious matters.

Aha! Gardner reasons that Sadler and company were already religious people—Wilfred Custer Kellogg, Dr. Sadler's brother-in-law, had been an active Seventh Day Adventist—so they must have made the whole book up themselves! What Gardner's bias prevents him from considering is that if the angels wanted to find human participants prepared to take on such a massive task—the transmissions started sometime around 1907, and the book was not published until forty-eight years later—they would obviously have chosen stolid, devoted men and women with a sufficient background in theology to understand what the angels were talking about. I doubt if the angels would have had much success had they approached Martin Gardner and his bevy of professional skeptics at CSICOP!

If I'm belaboring this issue, I'm using the unfortunate Martin Gardner as an example of the limitations of a purely mental intelligence. He consistently makes the simplest mistakes. He spells the names of some key Urantia personalities wrong. He pounces on passages in the book, claiming plagiarism, in spite of the fact the Urantia communicants state clearly that they use available sacred texts to build on when those texts affirm what they are trying to get across.

There are errors of misunderstanding. On page 29 of his book, for example, he uses the word "gods" to describe the midwayers who had inadvertently facilitated one of Christ's miracles. While this apparent confusion might not be important to the casual reader, in fact, by introducing a plurality of "gods" Gardner is seeking (probably unconsciously) to ridicule a cosmology he doesn't understand by equating it with a more primitive pagan belief system.

In approaching *The Urantia Book* by only using his rational, analytic intelligence to examine its content, Martin Gardner is making a fundamental error shared by other professional atheists. Since many of them have never had a context in which to develop their spiritual intelligence and often specialize far too young to have achieved any degree of emotional maturity, they place no evidentiary credence in their intuitive intelligence.

The spiritual and emotional intelligence systems can easily atrophy if they are distrusted or not used. When you hear a Richard Dawkins or a Christopher Hitchens relate the story of their atheism, it's significant how many of them seem to have rejected God, along with religion, around the age of eleven. I did it myself at nine. I understand how this works. First, because we didn't know any better, we confused religion and how it is practiced with God, and threw them both away. Not being spiritually or emotionally mature enough at that age to see beneath the delusions of priestcraft, the choice that we seemed to face as youngsters (certainly in traditional British education) was to accept religious dogma unquestioningly, at the expense of the rational, or being untouched by religious ritual and seeing through the dogma, to reject God along with the trappings of religion and the hypocrisy of priests. This can leave us as schoolchildren with an almost exclusively mental/analytic lens through which to view and attempt to understand the world around us. And, growing up denying a spiritual depth to life, the rational can become as self-limiting and habituating as any addiction.

I'm not suggesting for one moment that a reader's rational intelligence needs be disregarded. On the contrary, it's wise to be initially skeptical. But the only way to assess spiritual information is to use the spiritual and emotional intelligence systems. If we are presented with data that we have no way of proving true or false, it's our intuitive *feelings* that will reveal the truth. At that point, when we know the truth of our feelings, *then* the rational intelligence can be used to assess the data analytically to examine the data for repeated patterns or for its intellectual content. If we are stuck in our heads to start with, unable or unwilling to trust our feelings, the spiritual truths we are confronted with in life will be as inaudible to us as a silent dog whistle.

Until we learn to align our four different intelligence systems—the physical, emotional, mental, and spiritual—and know which system to apply to which situation, we are most likely to apply the wrong criteria for evaluating any given scenario.

In Martin Gardner's case, this is a shame, because there *are* some very telling clues within the text of *The Urantia Book* of certain secrets kept. It's clear, as the communicants themselves admit, they aren't revealing everything. Not that the book is a hoax or intentionally misleading, but there is an emotional tone to some of the angelic communicants' writings that suggests another level entirely to the drama described. As attentive readers of the book will discover, the angels can occasionally betray some rather unangelic attitudes. It was these attitudes that caught my attention, particularly the relish with which Manovandet Melchizedek, the writer of Paper 53 on the Lucifer Rebellion, seems to be looking forward to the terminal extinction of Lucifer and other rebel angels.

It was this Melchizedek's lack of compassion that prompted me to examine the Lucifer scenario from a mortal perspective, from the viewpoint of a human being who has lived his life on a world overshadowed by the consequences of the rebellion. Over time a rather different narrative emerged. This essentially formed one of the main thematic subtexts to my first book and came to a climax in the recognition that the Lucifer Rebellion was adjudicated. A situation that lingered on for over two hundred thousand years was finally declared over.

As I've previously mentioned, this information was delivered to a small group of us through Edward, the sensitive young man who found he channeled angels when he put himself into a light trance. We'd worked with Edward for the previous couple of weeks and fortunately had grown accustomed to speaking with a variety of different angels. When Shandron came through with his astonishing statement it was with a voice that was unusually deep and resonant. Claiming to be a Supernaphim, he felt to all of us to be of an entirely different order of angels than we'd previously encountered.

In a Multiverse almost unimaginably large the Lucifer Rebellion occurred among a relatively low level of celestial bureaucrats. Lucifer, so the book tells us, was a perfectly legitimate System Sovereign at the time of the rebellion: that is to say that he was the angel in overall charge of the System of the thousand worlds within his administrative domain. Everything went along fine, apparently, until the rebellion got started.

As Lucifer's rhetoric and his Declaration of Liberty started to gain adherents among his followers, a case was taken out against him in the courts at an even higher level of constellation administration. If it's surprising to hear there are courts of law in the angelic frequency-domains, we're told that conflict never becomes physically violent in those realms and that the legal system is the celestial way of settling disagreements.

The "war in heaven" associated in the Judeo-Christian tradition with the "war" between the archangel Michael and Lucifer/Satan, clearly relates to the Lucifer Rebellion. Even though the rebellion occurred a couple of hundred thousand years ago, the prince and his rebel midwayers, continuing to be active well into recorded history, would have doubtless created and carried forward a vivid memory of their rebellion. However, in painting the angelic rebellion as a *physical* battle, the Christian tradition has conflated the physical wars that occurred far more recently with the rebellion. The battles described in the Vedas, for example, will have taken place within the past ten thousand years and will most likely have involved conflicts between opposing groups of midwayers.

After two years of consideration (the Urantia communicants use Earth-time years), the court ordered Lucifer replaced as System Sovereign and exiled from the Local System Headquarters world along with the other rebel angels. The Local System, along with the thirty-seven planets whose planetary princes and their missions supported Lucifer's call for "self-assertion and liberty" were promptly isolated and quarantined. These were not just the 40,119 rebel midwayers who remained on Earth until the time of Christ; these were all the many angels who served Lucifer as System Sovereign and chose to align themselves with his revolution. This is the "third of Heaven" that the Bible tells us fell with Lucifer.

The rebel angels were then free to develop their own brands of social and religious engineering on those thirty-seven worlds. What we witness on Earth today is the result of those many millennia of the rebel angels' bid for greater personal freedom for all and for an acceleration in the "mortal ascension plan."

Now, here is the puzzle. The angelic communicants in *The Urantia Book* frequently state how much chaos and devastation the Lucifer Rebellion caused. Lucifer was obviously extremely troublesome for the administration, and he was described in the most negative terms possible. Yet simultaneously the rebel angels were all permitted to continue with their activities. That Lucifer must have been expressing a general dissatisfaction with the status quo was demonstrated when his entire cabinet "went over in a body and were sworn in publicly as officers of the administration of the new head of the liberated worlds and systems."[1]

Thus, on the one hand the angelic communicants complain about how "very terrible and very real" Lucifer's Rebellion was and what a devastating experience it was for all involved. On the other, we find that Lucifer and his cohorts were allowed the freedom to continue ruling over the thirty-seven worlds aligned with the rebels. If they were as utterly awful and disruptive as the angelic communicants make out, then wouldn't it appear to be folly to permit them to go on spewing their poison on all those vulnerable worlds?

Over the millennia, apparently there have been many defections from the rebel ranks, yet we are told most of the senior protagonists have been holding out to the end. Earth has been particularly struck by the rebels' obstinancy, and we can see the results of this most clearly manifested in the deplorable condition of the world and the generally fearful and belligerent nature of so many of its inhabitants down through our planet's sad history.

So the situation stood in 1981 when our small group in Toronto, Canada, gathered by the angels for this totally unanticipated encounter, first heard the voice of Shandron. The nine of us were just finishing a long session with different angels speaking through Edward and were all of us roaring with laughter at something the last angel had said—angels seem to have well-developed but extremely dry senses of humor—when this powerful voice broke through. (I'm only including here those portions relevant to the Lucifer Rebellion.)

I am Shandron. I am a being of advanced status, greater than Seraphim. I am one who would be of Superuniverse status. I am Supernaphim.

My place here in the Great Work is as an usher of this new dispensation that is upon us, and I emphasize this aspect. Yes, there has been a turning of a dispensation for your world. An adjudication, in a sense. A release from patterns long-held. But more, and this you know in your hearts.

Such are the nature and magnitude of the changes being wrought here on this world that we, of Superuniverse status, are invited to function with our younger sisters and brethren in the ordering of the new ways.

Then, a little later, came Shandron's statement that so astonished us. It can only refer to the rebel angels, and it specifically counters the petty malice of the administration angels who couldn't wait until the rebels had all been extinguished.

Now we speak in this epic of the redeemed ones. Great then is the wisdom and mercy of the Father and such is His love that none are lost. All have been found and will stand revealed with gowns of innocence. For full forgiveness has been lodged in the hearts of simple creatures and moved by this vision, the High, the Mighty, as you would see them, see a revelation of their most revered Father.

That such lowly creatures may love so greatly is, and ever shall be, the message for all to learn. Forgive the error, see the Son, join as brothers, be us all as one.

This is poetically phrased and perhaps somewhat enigmatic to someone unfamiliar with the lingo. So, in decoding Shandron's statement, "the redeemed ones" have to be the rebel angels. Who else could Shandron have meant? His reference that "none are lost" surely means that Lucifer and the other holdout rebel angels were not, in fact, extinguished.

I can't be certain of this, but Shandron's mention of "the High, the Mighty, as you would see them" most likely refers to the Constellation Fathers, who preside over the Uversa courts handling the case against Lucifer. His point about them seeing "a revelation of their most revered Father" is evidently an allusion to the Father Spirit, who in the form of Atman indwells all mortal beings and who would have been the source of the forgiveness our little group was feeling toward Lucifer.

Once again, going back to *The Urantia Book,* we learn that it was Michael, Creator Son of this Local Universe, who intervened to postpone the court case against Lucifer. Although Lucifer was removed from his post of System Sovereign soon after his declaration of revolution, and replaced later by another Son of the same Order, named Lanaforge according to *The Urantia Book,* Michael recommended the unrepentant rebel angels be permitted to continue with their plans on the thirty-seven dissenting worlds.

I was puzzled by this action of Michael's until I remembered a concept mentioned somewhat in passing by the Urantia communicants that each Local Universe—for a sense of scale, there are one hundred thousand of these Local Universes within each of the seven Superuniverses—has a particular "tone." This tone is different in each Local Universe and appears to be a quality somehow infused into the dramatic possibilities of each domain. It should come as no surprise that the tone of this Local Universe is "mercy and forgiveness."

Mercy and forgiveness: that's a consoling thought for us as individuals. But it may have a deeper significance. It would account neatly for the perennial dilemma, the inescapable paradox any spiritual person has to resolve, which has caused so many to reject organized religion, and that is the inability to account for how a loving God would permit the existence of the cruelty and evil we encounter on this world.

If a tone of mercy and forgiveness is going to have any real meaning, it requires events and beings over whom such mercy and forgiveness can be extended. While this may not wholly exonerate Lucifer and the rebel angels, since each one asserted his or her choice to join the revolution, it provides a wider context for understanding the rebellion and extending our own forgiveness toward the rebels angels.

Indeed, every once in a while we all do something requiring forgiveness, either our own or that of others. I had a particularly powerful experience of this when I tried to mount a plan to rescue the American hostages from the U.S. Embassy in Iran in 1980.

The presence of so much of the horror and violence we find on the planet was a deeply troubling quandary when I set out in 1979 with the specific intention of exploring the subtle realms. My NDE six years earlier convinced me of the deeply loving nature of the Multiverse, yet when I looked around I saw little of this love manifesting. Another war felt imminent. Nixon and Watergate had exposed the endemic corruption at the heart of politics. Living in New York City, it was hard to forget that Manhattan was in the sights of Soviet ICBMs.

It was soon after the inept, failed mission to rescue the hostages in April 1980, and President Carter was quoted as being prepared to deal with the devil if he could get the hostages returned safely. America felt as if it was in a collective fugue state, frozen immobile by a sense of its own powerlessness. The nation's immense military power had been challenged to a standstill by a bunch of students with an ingenious idea.

Alma Daniel, my partner at the time, was an extremely empathic and psychically gifted woman who was daily agonizing along with the hostages, as so many Americans must have been feeling. Then came a day in May of 1980 in which the psychic pain Alma was going through must have touched my heart sufficiently to get my fertile imagination working.

A few days later I presented Alma with my plan. It was simple, ingenious, and I'd persuaded myself, eminently doable. All it required was courage, some elaborate cooperation, and a bit of rugged American individualism. We would gather a crowd of one hundred thousand people, get onto 191 Boeing 747s lent to us by various patriotic airlines, fly directly to Tehran International airport, deplane enough of us to confuse the issue while the remaining planes landed. Then we'd march, all one hundred thousand of us, directly to the U.S. Embassy, take out our little expandable ladders, scale the walls, and swarm into the building.

I reckoned we would need to be extremely polite and simply ask for our hostages back. How could they refuse? Then we'd pick up the hostages, march back to the planes, and take off for home. It was foolproof. Its breathtaking simplicity, its total lack of artifice, and what would need to be a righteous display of American guts would be sure to befuddle and perhaps even impress the Iranians. I'd worked out all the details and knew if we could get the volunteers we could pull it off.

Of course it all sounds absurd in retrospect, but at the time I was so stoked with my white-knight compulsion to come up with a solution to my lover's concerns, I might have been somewhat blind to the plan's obvious risks and drawbacks.

However, Alma bravely supported the idea after I'd answered the obvious questions. We'd get our volunteers by approaching some of the large groups and communities active at the time. There was Werner Erhard's EST, Oscar Ichazo's Arica School, there was the Farm in Tennessee and any number of hippies, yippies, and zippies who'd love a free trip to Iran. There were military veterans, survivalists, bikers, rodeo crowds, surfers, wiccans, rock 'n rollers, and who knew how many young people noble and crazy enough to take on such an adventure. Even if it was a failure, it would be a magnificent failure, and the attempt would be sure to go down in the history books. At least we could say we had tried.

Yet, imagine if we were to succeed . . .

If we went in peace, unarmed, with our women and children, would they really shoot us down? And in the utterly improbable possibility that the Iranians might start firing their guns, where would they stop? A crowd of one hundred thousand is no small number, and having spent time in Iran I know they are an old and honorable people who admire acts of great courage. I was also quite sure I could round up enough people, Hell's Angels and the like, who would be more than happy to be dosed up with meth and join me and my friends on the front line.

I'm sure you can see where I was going with this. I was becoming so obsessed that I'd pretty much stopped sleeping and was getting progressively more wired by the day. If Jimmy Carter was prepared to work with the devil to release the hostages, then by God, I was prepared to be the devil he could work with. I frantically wrote letters and made calls.

Unsurprisingly, the responses were not encouraging. Perhaps it was my English accent, but there seemed to be strangely long silences and some spluttering disbelief before I was either cut off or transferred to some other department, only to be dismissed as crazy by them or their superiors. The White House, more desperate for a solution to the crisis than the networks, took me a little more seriously, and I was bumped up to a fairly senior official.

However, it didn't turn out to be an easy conversation. I laid out the plan that, following my abortive attempts with the networks, I'd trimmed down to a few neat paragraphs (including a reference to dealing with the devil). Then I asked to speak directly to President Carter. My hope was to talk my way up to the Oval Office, or at least as high as I could get, before revealing that the essence of the plan was simply to create the appearance of a pending citizens' intervention sufficiently convincing to checkmate the Iranians. However, the official wanted to know more.

"And you have all these people lined up and ready to go?" she asked, after a long pause.

"Oh! Yes," I had to lie, "they can't wait to leave. And I know we can get the planes. I've already talked to the airlines."

"What if the Iranians start shooting at you? What's going to happen then?" I could hear an edge of hysteria coming into her voice.

"I think it's very unlikely," I replied, hoping to calm her down with my well-reasoned strategy and to show her I'd thought this issue through. "Besides, my friends and I have all agreed to be in the front rows with our women and children. Do you really think that they're going to open fire?"

There was another long pause, and I could practically hear the poor woman's brain freezing up. This was not something she wanted to think about, let alone be in the position of having to decide what to do with me. "And the planes?" she managed to blurt out, "what if they shoot down the planes before you even get there . . . with your little expandable ladders?"

Ignoring the obvious jibe, I insisted that it would depend largely on whether we could create a sufficient news flap at the initiating end so the Iranians would know we were on our way. Hey! If they saw the impossibility of the position we were putting them in, perhaps the planes wouldn't even have to take off.

"Lady," I said, a little too patiently, "do you honestly believe the Iranians would shoot down an airliner with 547 unarmed, peaceful men, women, and children? Have we demonized the Iranians to such an extent you really believe they would do that? Have we sunk that low?"

I could hear her draw in her breath in horror, so I went on quickly. "We'll have collaborative Muslim Sufi groups on board and any other Muslim Americans who want to join us. Then we'll open a channel to the Iranian military to they'll be able to hear the music and prayers . . .'"

I was asking her once again how could she believe anyone would shoot down a 747 full of innocent women and children when I heard the phone click off. I'd reached the end of the line. No one beyond my little circle of brave friends was showing any interest, and I'd worn myself ragged by this point. I still believed we could have pulled it off, but by now I was feeling the energy draining out of me. My lover, who nobly supported me throughout the process, abruptly changed her mind, and my friends, as might be imagined, were thinned out to less than half a dozen.

Wait a moment! It hit me. The White House was too frightened to hear me out, the TV networks dismissed me as crazy, Erhard and Ichazo were too busy with their flocks, my Alma had deserted me, and my friends would rather not hear from me. Why on Earth was I bothering to do this? I wasn't even an American!

It was some days later, as I was meditating and releasing the anger and frustration that had been building up over the previous few weeks, that I saw how everything I'd done was a foolish act of egotism. I'd masked the reality of this by convincing myself I was doing all this for the hostages, for my lover, for America, for anything but my own glory. The idea was entirely mine, and it was my energy I put into it. I'd thrown myself completely into making it happen, and I'd failed miserably. It was a harsh awakening.

If I'd been more aware in 1980 of the part that angels play in our lives I would have consulted with them before setting off on such a harebrained scheme. But, I was still a year away from the events that would lead me to Toronto and the meeting with the angels that would shape my life for years to come.

As previously mentioned, along with the good news that the angels passed along to us in Toronto, they also told us to expect a widespread exposure of the lies and corruption that had become endemic to human behavior. It wasn't going to be an easy time, yet the angels assured us if we could meet the challenges we would grow in spirit as a consequence.

It was after I published *Dolphins, ETs & Angels* in 1984 and was doing the rounds of speaking at conferences and book signings that I started encountering a number of people who told me that they too had been required to ponder deeply on the fate of Lucifer. Some people just found themselves contemplating "the devil" in a new light, and others familiar with *The Urantia Book* told me they felt they were being asked internally whether they could find it in their heart to forgive Lucifer and his rebel angels.

This suggests that various humans were being polled on the inner planes as part of what would result in the ultimate reconciliation of the Lucifer Rebellion. In a fair Multiverse it seemed entirely reasonable that some of those individuals living under the shadow of the rebellion would be asked for their input.

While I've still no reason to doubt what I believe to be the reconciliation of the rebellion, I've not been informed as to what has happened to the main protagonists. When I've tried to find out where Lucifer, Satan, Caligastia, or Daligastia are, I've received a polite reminder that it's none of my business.

Some within the loose-knit community of *The Urantia Book* readers who think about these matters (and most of them probably don't), believe these main contenders must have been eliminated. Intuitively, I don't think this is true. They've certainly disappeared off the spiritual radar. Having had one significant transmission from Lucifer prior to the reconciliation, for example, I've not heard a peep out of him ever since.

In a Local Universe with a dominant tone of mercy and forgiveness, it's hard for me to believe the main proponents of the rebellion, however rebellious they've been, would have been punished by being totally eliminated. What a horrible thought! Until such a time as I have a need to know I intend to hold to the more benign and forgiving alternative that Lucifer and his colleagues have simply been shoved upstairs. As often as not, it's the way of the world.

As below, so above.

Happily deluded though I may be, it amuses me to ponder whether it was a promotion for the old rascals or simply a way of removing their baleful influence from where they could do any more harm.

I continued to publish books through the 1990s: a new edition of *Dolphins, ETs & Angels* in 1992, *Dolphins Telepathy & Underwater Birthing* in 1993, and *A Practical Guide to Contacting Your Angels through Movement, Meditation & Music,* a slim book I coauthored with Elli Bambridge for an Australian publisher, in 1995. In 1990 I had teamed up with Elli, an Australian weaver and dancer, and we had fallen into the habit of spending six months in the United States, then traveling down under for another six months of summer.

Exotic as this sounds, a life of endless summer has its drawbacks. Dividing life into segments of six months each, backward and forward across half a world, became progressively dislocating after a few years. As beautiful as the Australian beaches were, and a more relaxed ambiance would be hard to find, it was the high desert that would ultimately call me home. But I wasn't there yet.

As I came to know Elli it emerged she'd been taught a dance form called angelic movement years earlier. I soon discovered that it was a remarkably powerful way of inducing the angelic experience. Having conducted Opening to the Angels workshops and seminars over the previous five years, I was starting to find them repetitive, even a bit laborious. In combining some of the techniques from the workshops with Elli's angelic movement, between us we evolved another effective approach for people to open to their angels.

This led to our conducting a series of workshops in Australia and

America, but by now a new and disturbing element was entering the game. The angels had become a fad, like pyramid power and Kirlian photography; as the concept of angels became commercialized they started to appeal more to those looking for a quick fix. The quality of people signing up for workshops was changing from sincere seekers to spiritual wanna-bes and workshop junkies: people whose emotional bodies were bundles of fear and guilt and who were wholly unprepared for a conscious connection with their angels.

This came to a head for us at a three-day Angelic Conference held in a large Colorado ski resort. The organizers gathered a dozen "angel experts" (what a presumptuous term) to conduct workshops and seminars over the weekend, and wanting to promote their conference, invited a local TV news team to participate and film the events. This might have been fine for some of the presenters, but too often I've seen how people change for the worst when there's a camera around. Besides, having onlookers with or without cameras would only detract from the meditative atmosphere Elli and I were trying to create.

When I stood my ground with the news people, of course they simply became more demanding and curious to know what we were *really* going to do in our workshop. They couldn't believe we wouldn't want to be on television. It became quite a shouting match, and soon the main organizer joined the scrap, trying to persuade us to let the TV in. But we were firm about it. I'd already seen some of the people at the conference posturing for the camera, and it would have been completely unfair on our workshop participants to have allowed the press in.

Elli and I won the battle in the end and conducted the workshop as best we could. It was not a success. Most people were hopelessly distracted, and by the end of it both of us felt we'd become the enemy. We'd deprived them of a slice of their fifteen minutes of fame, and they resented us for it. A final meeting with the organizer was just as unpleasant and assured that we'd never be invited back again on the lucrative conference circuit.

With that I saw more clearly what was happening. I never got into conducting angel workshops for money. It was never my intention. So, they were originally modest gatherings, small groups of sincerely interested people who were emotionally mature enough to handle the often disturbing material that comes up for release when working with angels. With angels becoming a popular vogue, big money and hucksters quickly followed. My hope was always that by acknowledging the *reality* of angels and learning how to work with them, others would find the joy and fulfillment I've experienced in my connection with them.

However, with some exceptions, that is not how it turned out. I felt I was watching something so delicate and sacred, of such deep value to humanity at this key point of history, being taken up and cheapened by commercial interests. Perhaps I was naive to imagine it might be any other way in our materialistic culture, but as I write an angel is reminding me to release my ego concerns. "It's simply the way of the world," she's telling me, "and there is nothing the angels haven't made good use of."

Grateful as I am now for being let off the hook, at the time I felt I'd let the angels down and decided to discontinue the workshops and seminars. Let the books do the work; that's why I wrote them. It had been a hectic decade. I needed to find somewhere quiet where I could keep my head down and focus on my artwork. I found the silence I was looking for in the high desert of New Mexico: my place in the world and a landscape in which I'm happy to spend the rest of my life.

When I left New York City to relocate to New Mexico I had no idea I was going to have to practically die to get there.

I'd become more familiar with working with the angels and had learned by this time to leave the important decisions up to my celestial guides. This move from Manhattan was a big one, so I knew they would want me to go through my options first. Angels don't want to live our lives for us. However, when it came time to actually leave the city, my home for over twenty years, I realized I could have gone almost anywhere. Back to England; Japan, I love Japan; Hawaii was tempting, and there was always California or Oregon, New Zealand, Cathar country, or Bali. And Cusco in Peru is eminently livable . . .

The evening came when I asked my angels for help in deciding where to go, and then I sat back to see what the Multiverse wanted of me now. Sixteen hours later my phone rang. It was an ex-girlfriend I'd not seen, or been in contact with, for over five years. Although we remain close friends to this day, our parting back in the early 1980s was an awkward one, so I was surprised to hear from her. She'd left New York some years previously, she told me, and had been driving around the southwestern states looking for a place to perch. Knowing I'd always found it difficult to write in New York, she thought of my plight when she came across a small hotel in a village in New Mexico that would rent me a couple of rooms for a pittance.

Next weekend found me in my rented car, blinking in the pure bright sunlight and climbing up from the Rio Grande valley into the mountains to the southeast of Albuquerque. At 6,500 feet, Monte Alto is one of those small New Mexico villages that have seen better days. Until the 1940s the area was known as the bean-growing capital of the world and supplied the armed services for years with all those beans. Then the weather patterns changed, and the bottom fell out of the market. Although not as hard hit as some of the more central states, the dust bowl put an end to the beans for good.

The Shaffer Hotel turned out to be an astonishing structure. Completed in 1923 and built in concrete by a local blacksmith for his wife, it was a delightfully idiosyncratic building decorated with occult and Native American symbols. My modest little suite would overlook a garden with elm trees and a lawn glowing an almost luminous green against the muted brown and beige of the neighboring adobe walls. Leaning against the hotel wall was a large, roughly rectangular piece of rock, eight or ten inches thick. It was stained brown by iron and etched with an elaborate spiral and a variety of petroglyphs. Anywhere else this slab of rock, which had been unearthed when building a spur of the Santa Fe Railroad, would be in a museum. And here it was in the garden.

The air was so clear I could see, about twenty miles away out of the windows of my room, every detail of the Manzano Mountains. It was midsummer, yet being so high in the mountains the air was dry and the temperature a pleasure. I felt immediately at home, which caught my attention as odd, as someone who comes from a small, damp island. But then again, it was not so strange after all. After *Lawrence of Arabia*, an Englishman's love of deserts has almost become a cliché.

It wasn't until some years later, after I'd been living in the hotel and building a house well outside the village on forty acres of the softest, sweetest land I know, when I stumbled on a possible reason for my odd sense of familiarity with the high desert. It was a long shot, but sufficiently odd and powerful enough to include here. Once again, the impulse for reporting this comes from wanting to illustrate how we are surrounded by clues as to the spiritual dimensions of life.

One hot and dusty afternoon, while waiting to pay for a milkshake in the village store, I was gazing idly at a rack of sepia postcards. You can see this sort of photos of sad-eyed and dignified Native Americans faces, generally the photographs of Edward Curtis, in many of the little stores in New Mexico and Arizona. Most of them I'd seen before. Then, suddenly I was jerked into full consciousness. There *I* was, a bandana around my head, staring with a certain grim determination into what must have been an uncertain future.

The shock of seeing myself photographed as a Zuni governor at the turn of the last century must have opened some psychic valve, because the next thing I knew there was a high-pitched buzzing sound and I was shifted into an alternate state of consciousness.

Now I'm *seeing* pictures on my eidetic screen of that tragic time. I am in the area of the Pueblo Indians; the Zuni are a peace-loving people, intensely religious and closely bonded together by language. I know I'm home. I can *see* decorated pottery jars and silver and the bright flash of turquoise. A girl, raven hair swept by the wind, moves gracefully toward an open fire. I briefly catch the scent of wood smoke before I'm pulled back into reality by the clerk insistently repeating my name.

A previous incarnation? Perhaps. A daydream? A momentary flight of the imagination? No, I know what they are like, and this was no daydream. An empathic disassociation? Could I have somehow slipped for a few seconds into the Zuni governor's reality? And if this was an empathic connection, is this the sort of psychism we will be experiencing more frequently as we move into the True Age?

The Shaffer Hotel turned to be a perfect fit, and I ended up living there for eight years. Yet, as I implied earlier, I was lucky to get there alive.

I'd returned to New York after that initial viewing, having signed a three-year contract on a small suite in the hotel, and was making my preparations to leave the city. Carolina Ely, a colleague of many previous lifetimes, agreed to accompany me in a rented U-Haul truck for the long drive across America to New Mexico.

It was late at night on an interstate in one of the southern states. Carolina was driving. I was snoozing in the cab beside her when I was suddenly woken up by a loud cry. Jerking upright I could see a tow truck caught in our headlights about thirty yards ahead.

Then, I saw it. I froze with horror as I watched a large metal tire iron, which must have fallen off the back of the truck, bouncing once on the road in front of us, then turning over and over in slow motion as it headed straight for our windshield. The shiny metal flashed in our beams as it whirled toward us. Then, just as suddenly, it was no more. One moment it was there, the next moment it wasn't. Instant death was a few feet away, and then the tire iron simply disappeared.

We both saw it. It was undeniable. Our noses were glued in horror to the windshield. There was the tow truck, still rumbling along in front of us, its crane swaying loosely from side to side, its driver fortuitously unaware of the "miracle" that his sloppiness had forced. We both simultaneously let out a long breath as Carolina accelerated past the truck.

"That must be the ring of demons," Carolina said softly, after we found our voices again. "The ring of demons that surrounds every safe place," she reminded me, as we were both laughing in relief.

It was one of my own maxims that I'd probably quoted far too often, since in every graphic I've created there will come a point about an eighth of the way into the work when I feel like I'm slamming against a brick wall. A feeling of uselessness wells up, and I start wondering why I'm bent over my drawing board hour after hour, day after day. I feel an intense yet generally momentary sense of despair before I remember that it's just a ring of demons.

It's what I learned working with entheogens. All I have to do is be brave enough to face and accept the demons, to know they're merely testing the purity of my intention, and with that they dissipate. The feeling lifts, and I'm up and running again.

I was sure from then on that my move to New Mexico would be a good one, and I thanked my angels for their ingenious bit of coordination.

Naturally, many of my friends assumed my move to New Mexico was inspired by the state's reputation for UFO activity. There were the Roswell and Aztec crashed discs and what many believe is an alien base deep underground at Dulce. I noticed on an Internet site only a couple of days ago a photo of a grouping of bright orange lights hanging over the very mesa I see out of my studio window. With Nevada's Area 51 only a few hundred miles to our west, I'm sure we are seeing or hearing the occasional secret military craft.

After the experience I shared with two others in Manhattan on Labor Day 1981, when the three of us saw a disc flying sedately over the island, I've developed a reliable way of detecting whether it's a military craft or an authentic UFO: wave hands wildly above the head, shout greetings as loudly as possible, and jump up and down. If it's a secret military craft, it *won't* wiggle its wings in response.

My reasoning here, and so far I've been shown correct, is confirmed by numerous first-person narratives from people who have observed UFOs when others around them haven't been able to see anything. It's hard to imagine how this can occur. How can two people standing next to each other see two entirely different scenarios? And, concomitantly, how can we account for it when a woman gets abducted into a spacecraft while her partner is fast asleep and lying beside her in their bed?

I believe that the individuality of the contact, whether it's BVF or a genuine extraterrestrial, is another of those aspects of the UFO phenomenon that creates such confusion. To our surprise, we are being treated as individuals. In spite of the myth of rugged individualism, which has always sounded like a protest, this concept appears to be hard to grasp. So ET encounters and abductions are labeled arbitrary, as coming out of the blue: Why me?

Over the past sixty years systems of social control have become devastatingly effective, resulting in a citizenry far more conditioned to think and act like sheep than those of the previous centuries.

Possibly it's our genetic background as pack animals that makes it so difficult for us to realize we might be valued as individuals. Then, on top of that, we're programmed to be obedient corporate consumers and to think of ourselves in statistical terms. We're encouraged to falsely associate individuality merely with a person's abilities, with his or her physical or mental prowess. In serious contemporary discourse, so little credence is given to the inner worlds that many people can only find their place in the "real world" by identifying with a particular group and subsuming their personality to that.

Yet, clearly, this is not how we are perceived by extraterrestrials. Our angels care for us as individuals, nurturing us as unique personalities, each of us mysteriously indwelt by an aspect of the God that is everything else too. Those who see an authentic UFO or find themselves abducted by "aliens" have these specific experiences *because* that is what *they* individually *need* to open their minds or to reconnect them with their souls.

The choice of who to pick up is far from arbitrary. A careful reading though the many abduction stories from a wide variety of apparently perfectly normal men and women soon demonstrates this. Of course, there will always be a few abductees who continue to insist they were taken against their will, and perhaps some were—against their conscious will. Yet there are enough accounts of abductees either being told or realizing for themselves that they are genetically bonded with a particular non-human race to believe this planet is a veritable meeting place for every ET in the galactic neighborhood. It would be naive to think there hasn't been some genetic tinkering, over the ages, between compatible interplanetary races; we're only unaware of this because of our isolation.

There can be a comical consequence to this accent on individuality, which appears in a few close-encounter reports, when the "visitors" attempt to persuade a contactee that he (and it does seem invariably to be a man) is, in fact, *the* Messiah!

While this might be dismissed as yet another deceptive trick of Gordon's Djinn, it's also more than likely that the visitors are viewing humans from a deeper level of reality. They may well be perceiving an inner light in human beings, which is imperceptible to us and largely unacknowledged in conventional terms.

In some cases, it seems that individual humans are valued for a more prosaic reason. It was when I came to know Elise Bailey that I was able to get some insights into one of these projects; even if it isn't quite the paranoid fantasy of "soul snatching," some people might find it somewhat disturbing. I should say in advance that although Elise refers to her visitors as extraterrestrials, it could also be the BVF with whom she's been having her unusual encounters.

✥

I first met Elise in 2001 through Roberta Quist, my dolphin friend who has reappeared with some regularity through my adventures. The ubiquitous Roberta Quist, I've thought of her, since we so frequently find ourselves independently in the same place in the world at the same time. Since our initial mutual interest had always been dolphins, Elise's connection with extraterrestrials didn't emerge until we had caught each other up on each other's recent adventures.

Roberta told me that Elise seemed to have developed an unusual ability to call in wild dolphins, so of course I was curious to watch her work. She was with Roberta when I met them on a beach in Malibu on a hot Saturday afternoon in July. There were more people sunbathing and surfing than usual. It looked an unlikely prospect to me.

I knew there were large pods of dolphins off the California coastline. I'd once seen a convocation of thousands of dolphins from high on a cliff in Big Sur, along with many hundreds of whales, swimming slowly south in a great procession. Yet, the dolphins in that area weren't known for coming in close to the beaches and generally appeared to avoid human contact.

Sure enough, within ten minutes we could see the flash of a fin out beyond the breakers, and soon there were half a dozen sleek forms sharing the waves with surfers. A frisson of interest rippled along the beach, heads raised, bodies turned, books and newspapers lowered. Elise and Roberta were running across the broad, sandy beach, leaping over prone bodies and splashing through the surf, before diving through the green wall of a Pacific breaker. Both were beautiful young women; one dark, the other blonde, sleek and tanned and wonderfully confident in the water. Their heads were soon bobbing way out beyond the breakers, disappearing for surprisingly long times beneath the few surfers lolling on their boards.

The dolphins stayed for a while, playing with the girls before slicing back into deep water to rejoin their pod.

It was an impressive display, and we chattered away like excited children on the drive back to Elise's compound in the heart of the Los Angeles forest. The small house, surrounded by wood-fenced paddocks carved out of the forest, had an oddly temporary feeling to it, as if the family could grab their possessions and be out of the place in five minutes.

Elise must have read my mind because as she was putting together a simple meal I heard her explaining to Roberta about the terrible fires that can sweep through the forest in the spring and fall. They'd been lucky so far, she was saying, but one never knew. I wondered how it was to live on a powder keg.

It was while we sitting around on cushions on the floor eating our dinner that I had a chance to get a closer look at Elise. I soon saw that under the bubbly, California-girl prettiness was a serious and extremely intelligent woman. As frequently happens when dolphin people get together, the conversation will turn to the subject of extraterrestrials, and as often as not, someone will get a dreamy look on his or her face and remind everybody of that suggestive first scene in the movie *Cocoon*. It was Roberta who spoke what was in my mind when she added that seeing the spacecraft over the water, with the dolphins whistling their greetings, was such a brilliant gestalt to get out there into the public mind.

Roberta had told me prior to my meeting Elise that our hostess had had some extraordinary ET experiences, but she wanted Elise to tell me for herself. Had she ever seen a craft? I asked her after we cleared the plates away and settled back around the table.

"Seen them? I've been *in* them," Elise replied with no hesitation. "I've been with the children. Lots of times."

"The children? What do you mean? How did that come about?" I'd read about women who claimed to have children on extraterrestrial craft, but never met one. Roberta hadn't told me about *this*.

"It started when I was quite young," Elise began, happy to be talking about this without reservation. Her open, pretty face was glowing.

"I started having awful panic attacks at night. I'd wake up in a sweat and hyperventilating like crazy. Sometimes I'd have strange marks on my body. I didn't know why all this was happening. I really thought I might be going crazy. There was no one to talk to, and I was afraid they'd put me away in the bug house.

"Then, one night I woke up, and there they were. And they were walking through the walls. *Through* the walls! I broke out laughing. Of course, I couldn't catch them; they don't need doors or windows!"

"What did they look like?" I broke in.

"They were little guys, maybe about three feet tall. Their skins were a bit like a dolphin's skin, except it had more of a powdery texture. It was just a texture though. They were whitish-gray, a pale gray; some were a little lighter and some darker. I didn't notice any hair. Oh, and very large eyes. Once when I was up there I noticed there seemed to be two different races in the same species. Some are quite a bit taller than these ones."

"So, what was it like when it first happened?" Roberta was leaning forward, her green eyes glowing with interest.

"This is so strange. You're not going to believe this," Elise said, laughing, "but that first time, the guys were wearing little black capes with black hoods. It was so silly; I've no idea why they did it. This time I woke up while *I* was going through the wall."

"How did it feel, going through the wall?" Roberta asked.

"Spongelike. Like I was pushing through a sponge."

I asked her if she thought she was in her physical body, and she replied she believed she was. She went on to say that, after going through the wall, she found herself in the backyard of her house and was in what remained "a dreamy state."

"In the backyard I realized I was floating on my back. But none of the little guys were touching my body. I was just floating there on my own. I managed to lean my head up a little bit and looked around, and I said, 'Hey guys! I'm awake!'" There was more laughter from all of us when she described the little guys stepping back in surprise. It was obvious they were thinking, How'd she do that? She shouldn't be awake!

"You must have been scared silly!" from Roberta.

"No, strangely, I wasn't. Relieved almost, just to know what was going on. But more important, *I remembered what was happening. I remembered* making an agreement to help them before I was born. They told me they came from a dying race, and that humanity might be a dying race too. And they asked me if I'd help them."

"How did they want you to help?" I asked.

"They told me they wanted to use my eggs and that I would have children who would stay with them. Later, when I was in the ship, I had a chance to ask them more details, and they explained they were working to create a hybrid race. Taking DNA from both species, they were recombining them in different proportions, some with more human DNA and some with more extraterrestrial.

"I've been allowed to hold one of the children," and as she said this, I *knew* she was talking about holding her own child.

"She looks very normal, but at the same time there was something odd. She has a slightly larger head than normal, and when I looked into her eyes . . ." Elise drifted off for a moment, and I could see her eyes glisten with moisture in the candlelight.

"When I looked into her eyes," she continued, her voice cracking slightly, "and she was just a little girl, she *knew* me. We were like one person, and I could see she felt exactly the same. She was a child, yet looking into her eyes, she was an adult. It was so strange. I felt her saying, 'I know who you are. It's OK,' and she thanked me. She *thanked* me for bringing her into the world."

Elise was crying openly now. She went on haltingly after pushing away the tears with the heel of her hand.

"By this time I was wailing in her presence. I knew that if this is what we are evolving into, then whatever they are doing could not be wrong. If that child is what we are turning into then there'll be no lies because we'll all be able to see into each other. We'll never be able to harm another person; it'd be like harming ourselves.

"They're *so* loving, *so* compassionate. They took the best of both of us, the best of both species. And, no way can I believe I'm the only person going through this, not if they're trying to produce a hybrid *race,* anyway."

We all laughed again. Footsteps sounded from outside, and a door creaked open as one of Elise's "regular" sons, a beautiful, dark-haired boy of about fourteen, slipped in the room. The conversation changed to more quotidian issues, like the health of the horses outside in the paddocks.

I believe I have a fairly reliable bullshit detector. My eyes tear up when I hear a profound truth, especially when it has a sacred aspect. It used to embarrass me terribly when I was young, before I knew what it meant. Now I'm able to use it more precisely, especially in situations for which there's no physical evidence. To this day, when I watch the videotape of Elise from which the above conversation is drawn, I tear up when I hear her describe her children on the ship. If she was acting, then she's in a class of her own.

There is a possible validation in *The Urantia Book* for this genetic tinkering, although I should say here that one of the challenges of drawing from *The Urantia Book* is to know what or how much to include. One of the more complicated situations described in the book that I've only touched on was the arrival on this planet of the second of the off-planet missions. This was said to occur some thirty-eight thousand years ago and featured a pair, a male and female, of what can only be described as superhumans. Like the prince's staff before them, by now long dead, the pair's physical vehicles were constructed for them, and magnificent bodies they were, too!

The couple was trained as planetary biologists, but their main function was one of genetic upliftment. Their many children were intended to interbreed with humans with the purpose of introducing a genetic complement called violet blood, which was designed to generally raise the consciousness of the human race. Unfortunately, the mission was a failure, and very little of this intended infusion took root. And the human species have been made the poorer for it.

I believe it was my companion Melinda who first suggested that in these hybridization programs we may well be seeing a remedial infusion of the higher frequency violet blood we were deprived of when the planned mission failed some many thousands of years ago. Ultimately we only have Elise's word to trust, but her story is not an isolated one, and like many contactees she has little to gain by fabricating such an obviously heart-wrenching lie.

I write now on the cusp of 2010 and want to use these final pages to explore where all this is leading. Are we in fact heading for a True Age? What is the Mayan calendar really telling us? Are we close to being accepted back into the galactic community? What can we do to prepare for a singularity? What is really happening on Earth? What are the implications of the Great Transformation?

In answering this, I believe the first issue to take into account has to be the Lucifer Rebellion and the consequent quarantine and isolation of this planet. Isolation is the key here. If it hadn't been for the Rebellion we would not have become quarantined and life would have turned out quite differently. From this we can deduce that we are in an exceptional situation and that inhabited worlds are never originally intended to be left on their own.

Now let's go a little deeper into a subject I covered earlier.

As *The Urantia Book* tells us, Earth is regarded as Michael's Planet. Michael, you'll remember, is the Creator Son, together with the Divine Mother, of this Local Universe. As one of seven hundred thousand other Michaelsons, each with his own Local Universe, our Michael was required to incarnate for a lifetime in the person of each of the seven different types of beings in his creation. Thus at one time, for example, Michael appeared as a Melchizidek Brother; at another, a Lanonandek Son; and at another, a Seraphim, and on this planet, as we know, is where Michael lived out his seventh and final incarnation as Jesus Christ.

In a benign and caring Multiverse, I'm encouraged to know that a Creator Son has the opportunity to understand what it's like to spend a lifetime on a world such as ours. That Joshua ben Joseph's life was cut short so brutally and in such an unjust way would have doubtless given Michael some appreciation for the violence and corruption we face on this planet.

All the more surprising then that it was Michael who postponed the final judgment on the Lucifer affair, allowing many of the rebel angels to continue with their plans to accelerate the evolutionary progress on the thirty-seven planets under their control.

The Urantia Book states that it is well established that Michael has promised to return to this world at some point. This promise, along with faith in Michael's capacity for mercy and forgiveness, makes it hard to believe that, regardless of the free choice of humans, he would permit his planet to go down in flames. Would a father ever let his children burn down the kindergarten just because a couple of them were playing with matches?

I wonder if the Gnostics and Cathars intuitively had it right—that what we experience as consensus reality is a subset of the true planetary reality? While this makes little sense in the light of what contemporary physicists tell us about how they believe the universe is structured, if we look at Ben Bentov's holographic model it becomes more understandable.

If differing lifeforms inhabit different frequency-domains in a ladder of sentience, then what we think of as consensus reality is merely the frequency-domain to which our senses are tuned. Consequently, there are two ways that a movement in a frequency-domain can take place. The individual can shift herself into another frequency-domain by altering her own level of consciousness (frequency) to match that of another domain. Or the planet's frequency-domain itself, or whatever is supporting the domain, can shift. I believe the shift in the planet's frequency-domain is what is meant when the extraterrestrials tell us that Mother Earth is changing frequencies from "third to fourth density."

What the implications are for those living on a planet when it shifts densities is hard to predict. There have been times when I have radically altered my consciousness with an entheogen and then taken a walk in the streets of Manhattan. The sidewalks of Manhattan are almost always crowded. It's a busy city at all times of day and night. Yet, whenever I ventured out in a particular state of heightened consciousness, I would invariably find far fewer people on the streets. Many fewer cars, too. I recall thinking at the time that I must have shifted up to another frequency-domain, and the people I was seeing were only those whose frequencies matched that domain.

Could it be as subtle as that? Is this the gentle transformation the angels speak about? Will the planetary shift turn out to be so easy and fluid we'll barely notice it? Might it be as tender as the English poet Arthur S. J. Tessimond's appropriately titled "Day Dream" elegantly suggests?

> One day people will touch and talk, perhaps easily,
> And loving be natural as breathing and warm as
>   sunlight,
> And people will untie themselves, as string is
>   unknotted,
> Unfold and yawn and stretch and spread their fingers,
> Unfurl, uncurl like seaweed returned to the sea,
> And work will be simple and swift as a seagull flying,
> And play will be casual and quiet as a seagull settling,
> And the clocks will stop,
> And no one will wonder or care or notice,
> And people will smile without reason,
> Even in winter, even in the rain.[2]

Alternatively, might it be what is intimated by a reoccurring dream I've had of two people standing on the shore of a great ocean and facing a tidal wave? One of them is washed away and drowned by the wave; the other man experiences it as a tidal wave of pure information and consequently makes the frequency shift.

This scenario raises the issue of a parting of the ways, of some people able to handle the shift and others going down with the ship—a typical Judgment Day script. The Christian fundamentalists echo this in their belief in the "Rapture," in which only those saved by Jesus float up to "heaven," as numerous religions and cults over the centuries have used their own beliefs about the imminent end of the world as a spur to belief.

In the unlikely event of this judgmental scenario playing out, with the unbelievers going to "hell," or worse, left abandoned on a dying world, this raises the issue of whether the planet would then be permitted to deteriorate to the point where it becomes uninhabitable.

Within the current scientific/materialist paradigm, in which faith is placed in the ability of technology to solve the world's problems, it tends to be overlooked that it was largely the unintended consequences of a technology unmediated by ethical standards or spiritual consciousness that has created the global threat. If this is the future we face, and there will always be people futilely promoting "new technology" or "green power" or the oxymoronic "clean coal" as *the* solution, it will simply be a matter of time before life on this world will become intolerable.

However, as Michael's Planet, allowing it to become a dead world hardly seems likely. A failing, self-destructive species and a devastated planet would fly in the face of the tone of mercy and forgiveness that is the underlying theme of Michael's Local Universe. Rather the opposite, in fact: surely this is precisely the sort of unfortunate situation most deserving of mercy and forgiveness.

Accepting, as I do, the essential truthfulness of *The Urantia Book,* there are three possible futures that result from my assumptions: an overall planetary shift in consciousness, extraterrestrial and/or angelic intervention, and/or planetary evacuation. Here, intervention can mean anything from enough helpful technological advice to turn around the deteriorating global condition to a profound manifestation of loving cosmic power, personified or not. In more simple terms, the Big Show.

Planetary evacuation, of course, has different implications. From what I'm able to garner, this is not only being seriously considered but also elaborately planned for, by at least five different extraterrestrial groups I've become aware of over the years. And I'm sure there are many more such projects afoot I don't know about.

If humanity is to be evacuated, at what point might this have to happen? And where would we be evacuated to? Are there already planets being prepared for us, as some ETs have intimated? And the inevitable question, does everyone get to go?

It becomes clearer with each passing month that if the global situation does not come to a transformative culmination in December 2012, it is going to have to occur sometime very soon within the following decade. Even if there is no great shift in consciousness or no Big Show, there is every reason to think there will have to be a global evacuation regardless.

Recent research is confirming that massive extinction events occurred regularly approximately every fourteen thousand years and that these appear to be related to galactic core outbursts. It's thought these "galactic superwaves," so named by Dr. Paul LaViolette and believed to be the most energetic phenomena taking place in the universe, are driving cosmic dust into the solar system. Not only will the increase in dust seriously affect Earth's climate, but the excess of dust falling on the sun will also provoke the most violent solar flares.

In addition, it's speculated that the intense electromagnetic pulses accompanying superwaves will be strong enough to fry all our electronic technology. Yet, the worst of it, far worse than every satellite and computer network being cosmically sautéed, would be the dust's impact on the weather as the entire atmosphere becomes shrouded in darkness.

Astronomers are now reliably predicting a massive increase in solar flare activity in and around the 2012 period. It's also known that Earth's magnetic field is getting progressively weaker, which may be heralding a reversal in the planet's magnetic shield. A weaker magnetic shield will not only be less effective in protecting Earth from the incoming cosmic dust but also will allow far more ultraviolet radiation to pour onto the surface of the planet. Then, skin cancer will be the least of our worries! Plankton, at the base of the oceans' food chain, are particularly vulnerable to excessive UV radiation, and there are also the destructive effects on DNA of sustained UV light for a wide variety of microorganisms.

No one is sure what such radical changes in Earth's magnetic field might mean, but one of the more worrying suggestions is that they will affect the metal present in and around fault lines, and will thus create magnetically induced earthquakes.

Of all these doomsday scenarios, it is Dr. LaViolette's galactic superwaves—not to be confused with the "Photon Belt" that gained some notoriety in the new age movement but appears to have no observable influence on life—that would demand an immediate planetary evacuation.

In light of this possibility, it's important to pass along an account of an incident that happened recently to my friend Peter Sterling and is related below in his own words. I received this report from Peter in late September 2009, with his permission and encouragement to pass it around. I've known Peter for over twenty years, meeting him occasionally at conferences or with mutual friends, and over that time he has become one of the foremost harpists in the country, with a devoted following. I don't believe he has any reason to fabricate his encounter with Zeta Reticulans, and I've had enough experience with entheogens to know such a meeting is perfectly possible.

I also recommend the interested reader to consult Dr. Paul LaViolette's work and theories, some of which I've paraphrased above, many of which are posted on the web.

This is what Peter wrote when I asked to him to describe his experience in more detail.

About three months ago I was part of a shamanic ayahuasca ceremony in Los Angeles. Ayahuasca is a powerful hallucinogen used in sacred ceremony for over 15,000 years by shamans in the Amazon basin of South America. I had experienced Ayahuasca a few times before but not to this degree. Anyway, while under the trance of the evening ceremony and the powerful medicine a remarkable experience began to unfold.

I had just taken a third dose for the night. It was around 3:00 A.M. and I was in a completely blacked out room with a group of twelve people as the shaman sang traditional "icaros," songs to invoke the spirits of the jungle and the ancestors to come and share their knowledge etc. The experience of the night had been rather mild up to this point. All of a sudden the sacred medicine began to kick in. I found my self on a wild ride as I journeyed through multihued and pulsating light formations of hexagonal sacred geometrical shapes that cascaded in rhythmic succession in my mind's eye.

I am an artist and composer of celestial healing music so sacred geometry is something that is very fascinating and captivating to me. I was really enjoying this psychedelic mind-show, when all of a sudden I seemed to pop through some sort of membrane, or dimensional gateway. To my astonishment I found myself on a space ship with two Zeta Reticulians, or Grays, in front of me!

Wow! I was not frightened or scared but was in some sort of a heightened state of being where it seemed quite normal to be in this situation. Within moments of my arrival and after I had a chance to stabilize in my new environment they began to give me some very intense and powerful information in regards to the coming changes for planet Earth. I noticed immediately that there were red lights flashing and warning sirens going off on the ship. Using mental telepathy they told me that everything was on high alert in the galaxy as a huge galactic pulsation emanating from the center of the galaxy was heading toward planet Earth. They described it like a tsunami of energy moving toward us at faster than the speed of light! They said this was going to be catastrophic for planet Earth and all her inhabitants! They kept telling me, "Imminent! Imminent! Imminent!"

They also told me that there is a reason why the Mayan Calendar ends at 2012 and there is nothing after. Because there will not be anything after as we know it. They said the prophecies of the Book of Revelation, Edgar Cayce, Nostradamus, and the Hopi prophecy, among others, are true! There will be catastrophic Earth changes on this planet and they are coming soon!!!

Now, I did not know anything about galactic pulsations but they told me to research what they told me on the internet and that I would find verification for everything they told me. When I returned home I did just that and found several scientific articles on galactic pulsations. But ultimately I found the website of Dr. Paul LaViolette. I immediately wrote Dr. LaViolette an e-mail to share my story and tell him the ETs were verifying his theory of galactic super waves.

I did not hear back from him, but one week later I was in England on a crop circle and sacred site tour and discovered that Dr. LaViolette was the keynote speaker at the upcoming Glastonbury symposium. I went to his talk and met him after at his book signing and shared my story with him with several onlookers listening in. He was very interested in what I was saying and asked when the superwave was coming. If indeed it was 2012? I told him that according to the ETs it was. I share this part of the story to illustrate the synchronicity that has been occurring for me ever since this experience.

Anyway, back to the ship! My conversation continued as the ETs told me that it was imperative that the humans access the codes in our DNA which hold the patterns and geometries of the Merkaba or light-body spoken of in ancient texts. That it was in order for us to make our ascension into the 5th dimension. That it is the next stage in human evolution. The quantum leap!

We are to make our triumphant entry into the Galactic Federation of Free Worlds. They also spoke of the plan for mass evacuations of humans off the planet as most will not be advanced enough to activate the light body. Very similar to what happened in Atlantis!

I asked them why they don't put some sort of a protective shield around the planet to protect us. They said they do not have the technology to do that. That it is all part of a reoccurring cycle that happens every 13,000 and 26,000 years. They said that they have to go up to higher dimensions with their craft and let the super-wave pass underneath and then come back down after it has passed.

They said the planet has been through this many times. It will regenerate after a while, but humans need to get off and this will happen. They want me to tell as many people as I can.

They also said that the portals of ascension will be opening soon as we align more with the galactic synchronization beam and that people working with the light body and ascension technologies will be able to bi-locate soon. I heard a recent interview with David Wilcocks and he said the same thing.

But they want light-workers and star seeds to know that they must come back and fulfill the mission of helping the humans to make the shift. Many star seeds and light-workers are longing to leave this planet and go on to the next dimension, but we are to remember our original contract when we signed on to this mission and stay until the very end! We don't have long to wait now!

I asked them about all the bad PR in regards to them about abductions etc. They said we must understand that in their society as well there are subgroups that operate. They said the ones doing this are "a renegade group that has broken away on their own. They are like adolescent teenagers playing games with the humans." These are the ones that have made contact with our government! They said "Pay them no attention." They said "We" are here to help and that it is imperative to get this information out as soon as possible as time is running out.

The next night I came back again for another ceremony and was contacted again by the ETs! I did not go on the ship but was given more information. They communicated with me in some sort of binary code that happened as my hand involuntarily tapped on my chest and my mouth and tongue made a unusual noise. As this happened images were downloaded in my mind's eye as I was shown many different things. Actually they showed me how to remote view as I was taken into secret government installations and facilities like the Pentagon, Area 51, and NORAD. I saw experiments happening now with genetics, the light-body, time-travel and interdimensional space travel to name a few.

They also said that Obama and the Pope are going to go public soon with the ET disclosure . . . and that we must be prepared for the pandemonium that will ensue as a result.

We will see, of course, by the time this book is published, whether an announcement was made by the pope and the president, or indeed whether the extraterrestrials have publicly manifested. Whether there really was, or is going to be, a pandemonium as predicted above, remains to be seen.

It's difficult to know quite what to make of the Zetas' warning about the galactic superwaves. If true, and Dr. LaViolette's research suggests these superwaves *are* quite real, this introduces yet another global threat that appears to be climaxing sometime around 2012.

What I find most significant about what the Zeta Reticulans told Peter is the way they addressed the question I raised earlier, If there is a planetary evacuation, does everybody get to go? If I'm reading the Zetas correctly, those people capable of shifting into the frequency-domain that sustains their light-bodies will somehow transcend the superwave, while the others will need to be evacuated.

If these superwaves are as devastating as the Zetas claim then there is clearly nothing we can do about it as a species. It really will be the end of an Earth cycle, and if this is what has to happen then it is surely a far more merciful way to meet our end than the long lingering death of a species. As I write this in the first weeks of 2010, I find myself wanting to believe that this coming transformation, first mentioned by the angels in Toronto almost thirty years ago, will coincide with the ending of the Mayan Long Cycle on the winter solstice of 2012.

I'm aware too, of how the idea of a planetary shift in consciousness, or some form of intervention, angelic or extraterrestrial, will be seen by skeptics as a soft-headed and even cowardly cry for an absent father's rescuing hand. Of course, no one wants to be fooled one more time, and many of these grand moments of potential transformation have come and gone unnoticed throughout history. Perhaps every generation has intimations that theirs will be the last. Yet life has continued uninterrupted by miraculous intervention, while humanity has blundered on in darkness, haplessly building and destroying civilizations, all but completely ignorant of a vast and inhabited Multiverse.

The ancients had to deal with the reality of powerful and frequently badly behaved gods and goddesses dominating their lives. Not only must this have been extremely annoying, but the behavior of these fraudulent midwayers also will have contributed over time to a profound distrust of true divinity. Without directly blaming those involved in previous off-planet missions, from a purely human point of view, those interventions were barely successful in their own terms. Some of the worst effects of their well-meaning interference have rippled down through history, resulting in endless conflict and the world we now find ourselves in.

I believe this inherited distrust of off-planet meddling has created a deep psychic scar in the world-mind. Rational reasons might be given for the professional rejection of other intelligent life in the Multiverse, but there is often an obsessional certainty in the skeptics' denial, which speaks more of deep emotional and spiritual insecurities. Most scientists are unwilling to even weigh the existing evidence for UFOs, while official governmental and academic propaganda continues to deny, and the press ridicules, the possibility of an extraterrestrial presence.

Angels, in turn, are dismissed as childish delusions by most conventional thought, and the increasingly widespread experiences of different sorts of paranormal events occurring in the lives of regular folk are thoughtlessly dismissed because they don't fit into the belief system of the status quo. These limited points of view are starting to slowly shift among those who apply a bit of common sense and intuition to the extraterrestrial issue and its many implications. Wouldn't we already see, for example, all the signs of a hostile takeover, if the visitors (extraterrestrial or intraterrestrial) really did have malicious intentions? When we have a physicist of Stephen Hawking's intellectual abilities issuing his warning against attracting the attention of other planetary races with the SETI program (because "you never know what's out there!"), he's speaking from his own fears. He is imposing his own fearful nature anthropomorphically on extraterrestrial intelligence.

Doesn't it seem more likely that the constant appearance of UFOs over the last half-century is a gentle way of preparing us for the next stage in our evolutionary process, rather than some alien invasion force? Isn't the collective myopia of much institutional thinking more reflective of human hubris than a well thought-out assessment of the UFO issue?

Could it be that the UFO is a direct challenge to conventional physics? And if we meet this challenge and try to move toward developing a theory that accounts for different frequency-domains, wouldn't this also allow us to understand the existence of the realm of the celestials? Is metaphysics going to turn out to be a necessary link between science and spirituality? Will accepting all this mean we are on the brink of an entirely new way of understanding ourselves and the Multiverse?

We're All Doomed
to Be Perfect

Any book that tries to make sense of what has occurred on this planet needs to wrestle with how we've arrived collectively at the unfortunate condition that exists on Earth. It raises the issue of whether humans are inherently good or bad, or a mixture of both. It demands an answer as to whether the Multiverse is benign, indifferent, or hostile. It brings up the nature of evil, what it is and how it can exist if God is a God of love?

I believe *The Urantia Book* supplies us with the most reliable cosmological and historical background information I have come across and that goes toward addressing these perennial questions. Yet, by no means does the book reveal the whole story. I suspect much of this has been deliberately left up to us to work out for ourselves.

The Urantia communicants claim the only true evil recognized within the larger Multiverse context is that of deliberately turning a person away from God. Everything else is seen as the result of ignorance or emotional immaturity. The communicants observe humans struggling with our animal impulses, with all our willfulness and brutality, both individual and institutionalized, as a very young species. Although it's the challenge of every human being to master our baser animal natures, the horror of a genocide or a sadistic murder, while not excused, is more constructively understood in the angels' terms as the result of profound ignorance of the consequences of such actions.

Lucifer, however, was a different matter. He was *not* ignorant, although his obsessive insistence on being right suggests a certain emotional imma-turity. His primary evil action, so the book informs us, was to deny the existence of "the invisible God" and to insist that no such God was needed to explain the Multiverse. I don't believe Lucifer ever promoted himself as God, since he evidently didn't believe in God. However, this did not stop Caligastia, our Planetary Prince, from declaring himself as "God of this world." This is the main grievance in the story the Urantia commu-nicants are telling, and they make it sound like the one unforgivable sin. Significantly, when we extrapolate from the pathologies of numerous dicta-tors down through history, we can see this impulse to replace God with themselves is a reoccurring delusion of grandeur.

As I have already pointed out, the only reliable narrative we possess concerning the Lucifer Rebellion is the Administration's point of view. And no administration, however benign, appreciates a rebellion. So, understanding there is going to be a bias to the way the Administration communicants describe the angelic rebellion, I've suggested we need to step back and see the whole situation from a wider perspective.

Much is made in *The Urantia Book* of the damage caused by Lucifer, yet there's no reference as to whether there were more fundamental rea-sons behind the rebellion. The communicants appear quite satisfied with dismissing Lucifer as mad and the impulses powering the rebels as self-serving and deluded. Yet this seems simplistic, as if the communicants are deliberately challenging us to raise the obvious question. Given that the tone of Michael's Local Universe is mercy and forgiveness, who then gets to commit the wrongdoing that requires forgiveness and over whom mercy needs to be extended?

This is no apologia for Lucifer. His influence doubtless threw off the normal well-oiled evolutionary plan for his System of planets, yet it's hard to believe some of his initial criticisms weren't well-based. In fact, there are enough clues in *The Urantia Book* to make the case that while Lucifer's Rebellion was an authentic expression of profound dissatisfac-tion of many angels with the status quo, it also served a far deeper and unrevealed purpose.

There is another cloaked hint here in that one of Lucifer's main com-plaints was what he regarded as the overattention paid to the "mortal ascension plan." This requires some explanation since it goes deep into the Angelic Conspiracy. It's important to remember that our status as mortal beings is a curious one. All mortals who have evolved from an animal ancestry are, at the same time, the very lowest of created creatures capable of sustaining a complex consciousness, yet mysteriously they also contain a fragment of God. The Urantia communicants describe this as one of the great enigmas of the Multiverse.

It is this Great Spirit that accompanies us in the mortal ascension plan by which we climb up through the many increasingly subtle frequency-domains until we are lofted out of this Local Universe. There is much more to this concept than I need to describe here, and those interested can consult *The Urantia Book* for a fuller understanding. My point is a simple one. Angels, we're told, are not indwelt by God and do not normally ascend in the way of mortals. The ascension potential of the human soul is seen as a profound privilege, even though most of us are completely unaware of being so blessed. It's perhaps a little humbling to know it is this Indwelling God that our companion angels serve. They guide and minister to us, but it is for the sake of the God they perceive inside of us that they care for us so deeply.

Angels, however, especially those in the Local Universe, are created by the Mother Spirit as *functional* beings. They are essentially static in their roles. They are created for what they do, and they do it well, and for extremely long times indeed. Lucifer's complaint about the importance given to mortals must have spoken to a growing impatience among the angels attendant to the ascension plan. They would have watched generation after generation of upwardly mobile mortals climbing up the ladder of their "Universe Careers,"* while they and their colleagues were endlessly stuck at their posts.

The more I pondered this issue, exploring it from every side and taking into account the humorous nature of high intelligence, my intuition kept returning me to look at what has been billed as the Lucifer Rebellion in the light of a cosmic melodrama, a real-life play in which the angels taking part were evidently unaware that some larger purpose underlay their choices. This is not to excuse the rebel angels or to absolve them

---

*A Universe Career is a person's spiritual ascension through the many levels of the Multiverse until his or her ultimate encounter with the Creator.

of the responsibility for the choices they made; they knew perfectly well what they were doing, even if they didn't know the deeper reasons as to why they were doing it.

That Lucifer may have gotten a glimpse of this deeper intention is suggested in the brief transmission I received from him in 1981 and included in *Dolphins, ETs & Angels*. Lucifer stated his understanding that Michael was aware of his plans and implied the angelic rebellion was permitted to continue. He believed there was tacit acquiescence from the highest levels, far higher than the Systemwide arena on which the drama was acted out.

As a result of this line of thought I became convinced there must be a deeper and unrevealed purpose that lay behind the rebellion. And if I am right about this, then the purpose might be of great interest to many of us.

Now, let's turn to the "fallen angels," the rebels who aligned with Lucifer and who, *The Urantia Book* tells us, were locked away on "prison worlds" and left alone, despised and rejected. In fact, the book goes out of its way to tell us that over the past two hundred millennia that the rebellion has persisted, no loyalist angels would deign to visit the imprisoned rebels. No doubt their delicate natures would have become polluted by those horrid rebellious thoughts!

Here, I'm not talking about the forty-thousand-plus rebel midwayers who remained on the planet until removed two thousand years ago by Christ. Those are the BVF whom Melinda, Giorgias, and I petitioned for their return back in Delphi. The so-called fallen angels who were said to have been imprisoned and ignored were the vast numbers of administrative angels serving Lucifer as System Sovereign, many of them also drawn from the angels originally serving the thirty-seven dissenting planets' Planetary Princes.

The logic of the situation demands if that was the case how can the Urantia communicants be quite sure that the fallen rebel angels were, in fact, all locked up safe and sound on those prison planets? And if they'd started off locked up and were then moved on, would the communicants necessarily know about it if no one had visited them? From the way some of the communicants express themselves they appear to have more investment in maintaining their resentment toward Lucifer and the fallen rebel angels.

More pointedly, are we really expected to believe that imprisoning these angels was the best way of handling revolutionary ideas? When even a human parent knows that the most effective way of correcting a rebellious offspring's behavior is to allow the child to experience the consequences of his or her behavior, isn't it far more reasonable to assume the rebel angels might have been given the same opportunity?

If I am correct in this assumption, then it seems equally reasonable to suppose it would be on the thirty-seven isolated worlds falling to Lucifer that these fallen rebel angels would experience the consequences of their choices to the fullest extent. They wanted to accelerate the process of human evolution by introducing unlimited freedom. Having to incarnate into physical bodies would give them the opportunity to live a variety of mortal lives under those conditions. Yet, there is no mention in the book of this rather obvious inference.

Now, one of the mysteries at the center of *The Urantia Book* is the communicants' bland statement that reincarnation is not a technique used in this Local Universe. Having puzzled over this dilemma, I've had to conclude something else is going on that the Urantia communicants either weren't aware of or were holding back for their own reasons.

I can well understand that most normal mortals are created on this level without having preexisted, as *The Urantia Book* maintains, but with the promise of eternal life before them. Yet, I also *know* from a number of profound spiritual openings over the course of my life that I've had many previous lifetimes, (as have many others I've met who are also aware of previous incarnations). The fact that I believe I've had many past lives is not something of which I've ever been particularly proud. They weren't easy incarnations, and there had always been a background sense I'm paying my dues for some ancient wrong.

When I first arrived intuitively at the realization over twenty years ago that there may be fallen rebel angels incarnating on the planet, it shook me deeply that I found I identified so closely with them. There was one worrying, but very brief, period when I became convinced I *must be* Lucifer! Fortunately, the absurd obsessiveness of this conviction soon chased away the delusion.

I hesitated to include the incident in my first book as it seemed to me more to do with ego inflation, although the actual feeling was one of miserable deflation. What it did allow me, however, was an experiential insight into Lucifer's state of being. Yet when the sensation passed I found I was left with the persistent thought that this would not have happened to me if I didn't have some sort of involvement with the rebel angels. I knew perfectly well I wasn't Lucifer. But the possibility I might be one of the fallen rebel angels would certainly answer some of the imponderable issues like reincarnation, even if the idea scared me silly.

At that point in my life the subject was simply too personal to include in my books, and I wanted to be sure I wasn't fooling myself or merely trying to fit facts into my theory. Since the existence of the fallen rebel angels is such an occulted subject and so little has been written about them with any real understanding, I had to rely on personal experience to find out if there are other angels on the planet. If I was correct in what I was proposing, that there are angels in human bodies, I knew it would make itself clear to me as I traveled around the world meeting a wide variety of unusual people.

Of course I'm aware of the all-too-human proclivity to hear what we want to hear, so I decided not to raise the issue with people I suspected may be of angelic heritage, but allow it to emerge naturally if it was there. The presence of incarnate angels was not a theory I set out to prove, but a simple exercise designed to find out if I was alone here.

Over the past twenty years of moving around the globe I can report with some intuitive certainty that there *are* indeed angels incarnating into human bodies. These are not the BVF who have their own destiny, but the many millions of Lucifer's administrative angels who have accepted mortal incarnation as a path of personal redemption. I haven't been told recently how many angels are currently embodied, except it seems obvious that these fallen rebel angels must make up the bulk of the sixty million reincarnates—and "more coming in every day"—that was relayed to me by my angels when I first inquired back in the early 1980s, which was recorded in my previous book.

I made the point of skirting this issue in my lectures and seminars, talking very generally about the reconciliation of the Lucifer Rebellion, and then watching to see who appeared to be most deeply moved. As I came to know some of these particular people I realized my exploration of the angelic aspect of my own personality was allowing them to open up and talk freely about themselves and how they'd always felt different from the people around them. I was careful not to prompt them or put words in their mouths, merely to ask the relevant questions. Many of them had tried their hardest to be "normal"; some were already aware of their angelic heritage, others identified more with an extraterrestrial background, while for other people it was the revelation they needed to make sense of their lives. All of those who talked to me in this way were also aware to one extent or another of having had previous lifetimes.

One of the common denominators of many of the incarnate angels I've encountered is that they've chosen exceptionally difficult and challenging lives. Some of them I've come across are down-and-out street people. Others are brilliant scientists who are frustrated by the constant rejection of their ideas. There are artists and poets who fight all their lives for their work to be seen and heard. Granted it's a hard planet for anyone living here, but it seems to be the incarnate angels who tend to pick the hardest roles.

I now understand this is chosen by angels prior to a human incarnation as a way primarily of strengthening their emotional bodies. In angelic form, and created as functional beings, angels have no need for strong emotional bodies since their range of choices is minimal. The density and power of human emotions are notoriously hard to manage, even for humans, and incarnate angels in particular need to prepare themselves for the challenges of being mortal.

Generally the incarnate angels I've met are following spiritual paths, or are challenging conventional thinking or conventional belief systems. Most are aware of why they've chosen to incarnate at this time, even if they aren't fully cognizant of who they truly are. I soon realized this is as it should be, at least for the moment, because angels are able to operate more freely "disguised" as human beings. Writing now in 2010, the sixty million reincarnates mentioned earlier will surely have swollen to more than ninety million. Having spent time with a number of waterborn children, I can attest to just how extraordinary they really are. And with the more recent buzz about "indigo children," and "crystal children," it appears my supposition won't be a secret much longer when these new ones discover who they really are.

What has emerged over the years is what I can only call an Angelic Conspiracy. Angels, as the idiosyncratic quality of the writing in the *The Urantia Book* illustrates so well, have a somewhat different kind of intelligence than humans. They are very different creatures. To pop an angel into a human body, so Joy, one of my angels, tells me, is like trying to squeeze a rainbow into a Coke bottle. It takes many lifetimes, in a variety of different vehicles, to prepare for incarnation. Then, it takes many more human or extraterrestrial lifetimes to prepare for an incarnation in a mortal body at this key point in human history.

Since the Urantia cosmology maintains that reincarnation is not practiced on this planet, I'm aware that what I'm proposing here makes a radical break from the book's claim. While I accept the book's statement as a generalization, my direct experience and my intuition suggest there have to be exceptions to their assertion. And these *are* exceptional circumstances. *The Urantia Book* distinguishes itself from some other cosmologies by owning its incompleteness. Although all the celestial communicants represent the administration against which Lucifer rebelled, they are sensible enough on the whole to adopt an open-ended tone as to how they believe the rebellion will be finally terminated. Readers of my first book will have a deeper insight as to how this might have occurred.

The Urantia communicants are also clear that there are some matters they aren't permitted to reveal. There would be very good reasons for them not to disclose that the fallen rebel angels were incarnating into human bodies, both for the angels own sake and for that of the vast majority of perfectly normal human beings who are born to their eternal life on this level and start on their Multiverse career.

As I pursued this line of investigation I came to understand there are many paths down which the fallen rebel angels have traveled to arrive in human form right now. Some have arrived here after lifetimes on the other planets; others, after a previous lifetime as a dolphin; another recalled destroying a planet. Some might have even incarnated their way up through the nature spirit realm (as Paracelsus might have suggested), while others recall lifetimes as witches burned at the stake, or being subject to the tortures of the Inquisition. There's yet another subgroup, of men with a scientific bent whom I call "Atlantean black magicians" because in many ways they are still paying for their behavior in that incarnation.

It is not necessarily a pleasant experience for a fallen rebel angel to enter into a mortal incarnation. Its main purpose appears to be redemptive in that it allows a rebel angel the opportunity to be directly subject, as a mortal being, to the ultimate consequences of his or her original revolutionary choices. This suggests the mortal lifetimes chosen by incarnating fallen rebel angels will be among the hardest and most challenging, yet they also contain the most profound of gifts. Upward mobility. Angels, you'll recall, are created as functional beings and stay in their posts for interminable lengths of time. In taking on a human lifetime angels technically join the mortal ascension plan; they essentially become mortal beings. Upon human death they rise up, as humans do, through the hundreds of subsequent frequency-domains to ultimately encounter the Godhead in the Central Universe. No angel possesses this privilege.

Although I've come to believe the vast majority of reincarnates on this world are fallen rebel angels, there are some other, generally extraterrestrial, souls who have courageously chosen to incarnate here right now to facilitate in the imminent global transformation. Then, at some point in the mid-1990s, I started meeting a few people who were clearly of angelic heritage yet felt no connection with the Lucifer Rebellion. This puzzled me until Joy told me there are some angels coming into mortal incarnation who are from a different line. They are among the angels who remained loyal to Local Universe Authorities. Yet, when they observed that fallen angels were incarnating in human form, they were fascinated and envious enough to want to emulate the experience. And indeed those I've met *are* very different, with a sweetness and an innocence I don't generally feel from an incarnate fallen rebel angel.

Although I've tended to only meet individuals, I know there are groups, large and small, all over the world, of incarnate angels who are in process of discovering their mutual heritage. The growing Cathar community in the south of France is an example of one such group, although it's unlikely they track their spiritual heritage any farther back than their Cathar incarnation.

Those of us who have had reason to recall some of our previous lifetimes almost always comment on our unfortunate deaths. Many, like the witches, truthsayers, and heretics throughout history, have died as martyrs to their truths; other fallen angels have taken the brunt of the world's wickedness; while still others had fallen for the hypnotic magnetism of a Hitler in their previous incarnation.

Many of the incarnate angels I've talked with have had a sense at some point in their lives, as I have, that being here, alive on this planet, is a punishment for something. Since this is not a subject anyone wants to contemplate for long, I've noticed this unease frequently manifests first through these people's dreamtime in the form of repetitive nightmares, which can only be sourced in previous incarnations and which cease with this deepening awareness.

There are a few historical personalities, mostly in the arts, medicine, and metaphysics, as well some who've chosen darker paths, who show every sign of having been incarnate angels. It is a personal matter, and I've no desire to expose anybody, past or present, since a person's spiritual heritage is an insight each will need to make on his or her own. However, if you were initially drawn to this book and have actually read this far, well, perhaps you can draw your own conclusions. And if such an insight proves of value in your life, I can guarantee there will be an added depth in the manner you will perceive and understand the ways of heaven and Earth.

The pace of the influx of fallen rebel angels into the human drama began to accelerate in the West from the time of the Renaissance, but it is over the last sixty years that it has become a veritable wave. If my initial supposition that the planet is passing through a sixty-year window of survival is correct then it seems appropriate that incarnate angels should be manifesting either before the transformation occurs or prior to the planet becoming uninhabitable. With the final reconciliation of the Lucifer Rebellion behind us and the general condition of the planet deteriorating all around us, I imagine there are still a great many fallen rebel angels out there anxious for a human incarnation, hustling for a body at the end of time.

I've been assured by my angels that victims of the famines, the plagues, and the cruelties of war are almost always borne by fallen rebel angels jumping onto the mortal ascension plan at the last moment, often as small children. They will likely suffer a short painful life before starving to death in Africa, or being carried away in a tsunami in Japan, or getting shot by a Mexican street gang, but then their souls are up and running and part of the mighty ascension opportunity that is the privilege and blessing of all mortals.

While this is clearly no excuse for the deplorable conditions in some countries, which in most cases are purely the consequence of human cruelty or indifference, it does allow us a glimpse into a deeper meaning that underpins events that can often appear as wholly chaotic or arbitrary. Granted it is an unsentimental approach, but it seems altogether reasonable that Lucifer and the rebels were permitted to continue for so long on their thirty-seven worlds *in order to provide for the exercise of mercy and forgiveness.* The very act of permitting angels to become human, to be indwelt by God, and to join the mortal ascension plan is itself a supreme act of mercy and forgiveness.

Might it also have been one of the deeper intentions of this Local Universe to create a new sort of being, a fusion of human and angel? A mix of the best of both species, individuals who've been tempered by the challenge of lifetimes on isolated worlds? Or perhaps this is one of the ways the Melchizedek Brothers tell us they turn the negative into the positive.

The Urantia Book tells us our Local Universe is numbered 611,121 out of a total of 700,000. Although this is not emphasized in the book, and assuming the development of the seven Superuniverses and the Local Universes is sequential, then it's obvious we are pretty far down the list. We can also infer from this that the vast expansion of creative intelligence in the Multiverse is soon coming to a natural pause and that this immensely long cycle is getting near to completion. The book says little about what might occur when this happens, except to mention the existence of four "Outer Space Levels" that wrap around the seven super-universes at a distance of four hundred thousand light-years. They call these levels "universes in formation," and there is an implication that we are going to have something to do with these universes in the far-flung future.

Are these the tasks for which we are being tested and trained? Could this be the reason the Lucifer Rebellion was permitted to work itself out? Was it all part of a plan to accelerate the evolution of a new form of intelligent life on a few selected planets? Is this the great experiment in which we have found ourselves unknowingly participating?

The Multiverse turns out to be a beautifully balanced teaching device, a massive multiversity in which each mortal is steadily working her or his way up toward the light of higher intelligence. Although it's difficult to appreciate this looking around the world today, all sentient beings will be seeking to better themselves.

The developed metaphysical viewpoint allows for an intelligence at the heart of matter and regards the entire Multiverse as a living being and all the elements in it as having an intelligence appropriate to their functions and their environments. This viewpoint allows for a ladder of sentient life that extends on upward into the astral, etheric, and celestial regions.

Of course, this concept of a living Multiverse is anathema to scientific materialism. I don't think it's irrelevant to suggest that if we had adopted this more metaphysical approach to life, we might not be so technologically advanced, but we'd have a far deeper understanding and respect for all of life. Humans who have had an experience like a near-death experience that allows them to *know*—not simply to believe, but to *know*—that life continues after death and that other dimensions exist, as well as incarnate angels who are aware of time spent between lifetimes, these ones will have a profoundly different view of how the world works.

If life does continue after death, then there really is no escaping the consequences of our actions. This is a necessary part of our learning, as much as it is the Multiverse slipping back into balance. Cruel and violent acts by people in this life will contribute to an understanding of themselves, if not in this lifetime, then in another one, in which they'll have the opportunity of being on the receiving end of the appropriate cruelty and violence. Those who find themselves victimized in this life are either acquiring self-assertion the hard way or they will be undergoing the consequences of their previous choices. Look deep enough, and it all balances out.

In this way we all ultimately learn compassion and the wisdom of correct action.

Those angels who have chosen to incarnate now have the opportunity to wake up to their true natures. There's no longer any need to hide. The lessons have been learned, the debts are paid, the rebellion resolved, and it may well emerge that we've all been elegantly trained in the fourth dimensional dreamworld for the times ahead.

Whether or not the 2012 event will turn out to be a world-changing event, a global cataclysm or a gentle dimensional shift, a planetary evacuation or the return of our elder brothers and sisters, or whether nothing at all out of the ordinary happens, there is one matter about which we can be *absolutely* certain.

We *will* continue on our eternal journey. We are all doomed to become perfect.

Would rebel angels have it any other way?

Appendix A

Some Speculative Scenarios
on the Future of
the Human Race

Author's note: This article was written in June 1980 and edited for length in January 2010. It was written before I became aware of the Urantia cosmology, and I include it here to demonstrate my thinking before I embarked on my thirty-year interspecies journey of discovery.

The general purpose of this article is to propose the theory that entities from our own future are intervening with the current world situation.

If, as I suspect my reasoning will demonstrate, there is even an infinitesimally small chance that our future is actively participating in the present, then it would seem an obvious and essential undertaking for at least some of us to examine ways in which we might broaden the base of that contact.

THE CURRENT CRISIS

Our universe, according to the best current estimates, has been around for about fifteen billion years, our solar system for some four and a half billion. Given the turbulent early years of this planet we can assume that the development of organic life-forms dates back about three billion years, give or take a few hundred million. Consciousness, therefore, assuming it to be a property of higher organic life-forms, presumably evolved through natural selection sometime during this latter period. Individuated consciousness, a quality generally associated with the higher mammals, is a relative newcomer, probably making its first appearance within the past hundred million years.

Forty years ago the human race, the result of one manifestation of that individuated consciousness, developed a way in which the presence of organic life on our planet might be destroyed for the foreseeable future. While every generation has probably thought that things are about as bad as they can get, the totality of the potential destruction is an undeniable new factor.

With the discovery of atomic and hydrogen weapons marking the start of this current period and experience telling us that in all probability the invention of a weapon predisposes its use, Carl Sagan, I think accurately, derived a fifty-year window (I've added ten to make sixty, because I'm an optimist) through which we have to pass to survive as a race. Assuming the development of the atom bomb to be the start, we are therefore forty years into this period, with twenty more years to go.

I am making the assumption, too, that if we survive this crucial period we will have in some way dealt with our contentiousness as a race, without hopefully losing our courage and aggressive curiosity. If this is so, space migration will rapidly widen our parameters of survival. No longer would the chance extinction of a single planet be likely to end the existence of the entire race.

THE NEXT TWENTY YEARS

The possible scenarios covering the next twenty years fall into four main categories:

1. The existing power structures entrench and somehow survive the next twenty years.
2. The existing world order is totally changed and the population reduced to a handful of survivors by a series or combination of smaller wars, or natural and/or man-made catastrophes.
3. The current world situation worsens, leading to all-out nuclear war. This destroys the physical presence of life on this planet for a period.

4. New factors emerge that result in planetary cooperation and a collaboration of resources.

My purpose is not to examine the implications of the first three categories, although they are inevitably touched on, but to run through some speculative scenarios based on new factors that might emerge as vital to our survival. What then are some of the issues that might contribute to an accelerated maturity in the race, and how might those factors be explored and hastened?

The five scenarios I have examined that could contribute to a quantum leap in human consciousness are:

1. Benevolent control
2. Planetary invasion
3. Genetic mutation
4. Extraterrestrial or intraterrestrial intervention
5. Intervention from the future

Benevolent Control

In this scenario the human race discovers a method or technique that would eliminate the need for contentious behavior without emasculating the vitality of the race.

This is the conventional area of hope for most of us in contemporary technological societies. Since the European Renaissance we have put our energies behind a rational worldview, which has permeated our efforts to understand and come to grips with the chaos that seems to surround us.

We have come to look for answers mainly from technology, and there are some very promising signs: communication systems, for instance, that are drawing us into a global village, or the growth of an awareness of the fragility of the planet, or new models of physics that include transcendent consciousness. The latter two both contain the elements that, if allowed to flower, might be able to weld us into one cohesive race with a mutual sense of purpose. However promising these models might be, they are up against the seeds of self-destruction that appear to be lodged in the very same roots of the culture that developed them. Just the capacities that drew us down out of trees and onto the plains are turning out to be promoters of the wanton destructiveness that characterizes so much of "civilized" life.

Until recently in the West, we have allowed ourselves to become somewhat myopic about other worldviews that encourage a more integrated approach to the evolution of consciousness. For instance, the Eastern religious systems, which on the whole tend to favor the balance of the very forces that have erupted in opposition to one another in our culture, have only very recently started to create an impact on Western cultural outlooks. The Western equivalent, alchemical mysticism, seems to have had only a peripheral impact on the general tendency of technological progress.

Our dualities, whether they are war/peace, young/old, high-tech/art, or dependency/independence, appear by definition to be in opposition to one another. Consequently, in the tumble to occupy the "good" side of the duality, we miss the potential for the creative tension between the two sides, which can amplify the evolution of consciousness. And, by placing an overemphasis on the "acceptable" aspect of this duality, the unacceptable or negative side is repressed so that it pervades our society and causes "dealing with evil" to be one of our major social preoccupations. Imagine the money and energy we expend yearly as a race, "dealing with evil" in one way or another!

Benevolent control, therefore, whatever its sources, would have to constructively incorporate ambiguity. To function effectively, this benign worldview would have to provide a healthy balance of technology and a philosophical belief system that integrates the duality of the human condition into a creative energy source. As an example of a rather unusual approach to benevolent control and its impact of the future, I should also include the bulk of Jacques Vallee's theories about UFO manifestations. He hypothesizes that the UFO phenomenon is a control device manipulated by either a top-secret government organizations using psychotronic devices or occult groups following highly developed esoteric systems of image and thought control.

Dr. Vallee concludes that the "reason" for this sort of manipulation (whether intraterrestrial or extraterrestrial in origin) is to create a grassroots change in worldview, moving us away from philosophical geocentricism to a broader universal cosmology. This would therefore fall into the category of benevolent control, with a deliberately camouflaged source point.

Planetary Invasion

This traditional science fiction scenario presumes our tendency as a race to draw together in the face of hostile intentions. If this did occur, and assuming that extraterrestrial entities arrived from another solar system or possibly galaxy, common sense indicates that from the technological capabilities of the aliens, this period of planetary cooperation might unfortunately last only as long as the invasion.

Aggressive beings from technological races, whatever their motive for invasion, would surely defeat the human race, since their technology by definition would be superior to ours. The invaders might, of course, ultimately fall victim to earthly diseases, but if they are sufficiently intelligent they would presumably have done their homework before invading.

I have limited this category to aggressive extraterrestrials, which in itself could well be merely a paranoid projection of our own destructive instincts. If a technologically advanced race had indeed evolved without going through an aggressive adolescent period (as perhaps the whales and dolphins have here on Earth) or more probably had learned how to deal with their negative, destructive energies, then it would be unlikely that they would approach us so invasively. In a sense, just knowing that it is possible to transcend aggression might be example enough for the human race to leave contentiousness behind.

Other possible invaders might include a life-form that is outside our range of communication, but by its actions makes it obvious that it/they desire to occupy the planet. An intelligent virus, a nonphysical intelligence (Fred Hoyle's Black Cloud, for example), a "hive mind" of some sort, could all come under this category. Dependent on the virulence or intentionality of the initial attack and how long it lasted, the existing power structures would likely pull together under one leadership for a period. This could possibly resolve in extended planetary cooperation, whether we banished the invaders or negotiated a peaceful coexistence.

Genetic Mutation

Not to be confused with recombinant DNA manipulation (a late-starter in terms of its potential impact on the overall world crisis), this would include mutations wrought by natural or man-made genetic changes.

There are three overall categories of speculation: a broad-based mutation, a DNA answer, and the catchall category.

A Broad-Based Mutation

Some prominent and adventurous biologists are eyeing the growing number of "wonder children" and asking if the emergence of these special paranormal powers in the young might be signifying the start of an overall mutation in the human nervous system. Much more important, for instance, than whether Uri Geller is a fraud or not, are the inevitable reports of children mimicking his televised examples of spoon bending.

In relation to this specific mutation, the biologist Lyall Watson infers the emergence of a "contingent system," a matrix of consciousness in which everything is in contact with everything else, that lies encoded in the mitochondria of human reproductive cells. We can only assume what factors might be signaling this mutation, but if this tendency can be understood and encouraged rather than feared, then the race might indeed start to possess the necessary powers to right our imbalances.

A DNA Answer

Timothy Leary proposes, in a perhaps more imaginative scenario, that our DNA coding has only reached the four "terrestrial neurogenic circuits" and that there are four coded extraterrestrial circuits in the human brain as yet untriggered.

The fifth circuit—and the first one of the extraterrestrial circuits—can be precipitated by a whole number of preeminently end-of-the-twentieth-century features like rapid change, exposure to TV, the exhilaration of traveling at high speeds, the use of psychoactive drugs, and the chaos resultant from the failure of long-standing belief systems, to name only a few. He suggests that these can emulate or mimic the effects of the body leaving Earth's gravitational field, an obvious historical point if the theory is correct; the DNA could be expected to kick in the next neurological capability.

In partial demonstration of his point, he notes that a disproportionately high number of astronauts claimed to have had some form of transformative paranormal experience.

The Catchall Category

This is largely a hodgepodge of speculations and hysterical fantasies, but through all the individual examples runs a thread that, if even remotely true, might accumulatively cause the required radical changes in our approach to reality—for all purposes, radical enough to cause a mutation. Here, in short, are just a few examples.

Mutagenic Radiation

Whether by nuclear power plants, through holes in the ozone, atmospheric testing, X rays, microwave generators of "toxic" wavelengths, whatever the source, radiation certainly yielded some preconceptual and postnatal genetic changes in animals. Radiation at many of these wavelengths surrounds us and must undoubtedly be affecting our bodies in ways about which we have no real understanding.

Day-to-Day Life in Technological Cultures

We know that preservatives, food additives, mass-marketing techniques, pollution of all sorts, psychological strain, overcrowding, and many other aspects of modern civilization examined in isolation can cause profound psychological and physical stress. Might this be mutagenic?

The Worldwide Rise in the Use of Mood-Altering and Psychoactive Drugs

We know something of the effects of these drugs on individuals but have little understanding of their impact on society.

Extraterrestrial or Intraterrestrial Intervention

Assuming that the intervention is benign, it could take a direct or indirect form.

Direct Intervention

After the initial impact of the first encounter sends its ripples through our belief systems, our religious structures, and our geocentric chauvinism in general, we would hopefully use the example—that of another technological race having solved its growing problems without self-destructing—to resolve our own crisis. Given the seriousness of the situation and our capability to destroy the planet, it is likely that a benevolent force, assuming they have a wider span of intelligence, would have intervened already unless:

(a) They cannot intervene without creating destructive effects on themselves or on us.

(b) They're not allowed to intervene. This would imply external rules inherent in cross-species relationships or the possible existence of an external authority structure (Galactic Federation or whatever).

(c) Their "plan" involves us sorting out our own problems.

(d) They are planning to intervene at some future point.

(e) They have already directly or indirectly intervened, and we are not aware of it.

Indirect Intervention

I am using this heading to cover either covert intervention without our knowledge or entities acting through human intermediaries, with or without their knowledge or permission.

An example of this form of intervention might be found in Robert Anton Wilson's suggestion that the UFO experience is a form of electromagnetic disturbance program designed to inculcate the cosmic philosophy of "we are not alone" deep into the human psyche. However spurious the claims of UFO sightings might be, there are by now at least twenty million Americans who undeniably "think" they have seen UFOs. Wilson's approach does not depend on the objective veracity of UFOs, but on the subjective effect of a "sighting" on the consciousness of the contactee.

The sources of indirect intervention can be broken down into three broad categories:

Extraterrestrial Intervention

Calculations based on Sagan and Drake's formula indicate that the chances of a technically advanced race within one hundred to twenty thousand light years of our planet is unlikely. At the one-hundred-light-year end of the spectrum, the figure of likely civilizations in the Milky Way alone would be five million, which in itself would considerably lessen the importance of the human race as something needing preserving. The other extreme, calculated using the pessimistically realistic figure of fifty years as the probable life expectancy of an adolescent technological society, indicates that there might be only five advanced civilizations in our galaxy.

Either way, it would seem unlikely that they would intervene unless we postulate a Galactic Federation Task Force that shepherds teething high-tech races through their fumbling first moves into space. And if that is the case, it is either surprising, indifferent, or downright cruel of them not to have intervened and obviated the terrible suffering engendered in this century alone. It is also possible, of course, that extraterrestrials may have observed our race at some point in our history and have decided not to have anything to do with us. Whether that speaks of a "superior" intelligence or not, we can only guess.

Intraterrestrial (or Interdimensional) Intervention

This category seems to attract some of the more weird and wonderful concepts. I include three of them because they appear to have had an extremely powerful effect on the psyche of large numbers of people.

The Old Ones Scenario

Throughout the history of human mythology we see the reoccurrence of highly potent and magical belief systems that place our recent history in the context of four previous racial genotypes. Each race, so the theory goes, has been destroyed or has destroyed itself or—as in the case of the Old Ones, beings of elemental power who lived in the Second Epoch—has placed itself in an uneasy state of suspended animation deep within the earth.

This "reality" has underpinned much of European esoteric and metaphysical thinking in the nineteenth and twentieth centuries and has most recently surfaced in the German metaphysician Hoerbiger's writings, which motivated many of Hitler's Hollow Earth theories. If this approach does have a basis in objective reality, then the massive infusion of psychic energy and the blood sacrifices of the Second World War might well have contributed to waking the Old Ones out of their sleep.

It has also been suggested that the Old Ones create subterranean influences that may be manifesting through the proliferation of denial-oriented hypnotic cults, with their capacity to dominate people's psyches on the deepest levels.

The Walk-In Scenario

Ruth Montgomery, a generally reliable observer of the psychic arena, writes of an increasing number of exchanges, called Walk-Ins, taking place between spirits in physical form (us) and more advanced spirits not currently using bodies. Doris Lessing, in her remarkable work *Shikasta,* also suggests a somewhat similar scenario.

Unless Montgomery's scenario is a complete fabrication, she has been contacted by a number of people claiming to be Walk-Ins, who say they are gathering into group minds and are working diligently for a reconciliation of our present world crisis. The motivating force behind these exchanges appears to be that this, the consensual level of physical reality, is needed as a testing ground for evolving spirits, and if we do destroy ourselves and render the surface of the planet uninhabitable, then these spirits will no longer have a physical domain in which to evolve. In the Walk-In scenario, this current crisis seems to provide a splendid opportunity for adventurous spirits to work off some karma.

The Multiple Worlds Scenario

This theory propounded most recently by Professor DeWitt and Dr. David Deutsch draws its basis from an interpretation of classical quantum mechanics. It postulates that there are an infinite number of universes coexistent with each other.

For our purposes here, the theory does not go as far as to demonstrate any direct interaction between these separate universes in a way that can be detected. This can be circumvented, however, if we remember that if these multiple universes are seen in sufficient microscopic detail, they can be perceived as part of larger "sets of universes." And interaction between these larger "sets" is in all probability much more observable. This approach would obviously become relevant if some way of "sidestepping" from universe to universe was possible.

Some recent theoretical discussions stimulated by Dr. David Böhm's implicate order approach also suggest that modern physics may be on

the verge of postulating a unified field theory. If this can be well sub-
stantiated, the implications inherent in a theory that argues that all
things are essentially contingent will permeate our approach to reality much in the same way as Einsteinian physics pervaded twentieth-
century scientific, artistic, and social thought. My own experimentation
with this scenario has tentatively indicated that these parallel universes are much more available to us than we previously thought
possible.

Intervention from the Future

If we assume the reality of serial time and put aside for a moment some
of the paradoxes contained in our approach to space and time as being
the result of our own restricted thinking, then we can reason along the
following lines:

(a) If we survive this next twenty to forty years, we can assume that
the race will have a future.

(b) With the little information currently available about time travel,
we can assume that it will be a practical proposition within the
relatively near future, say the next two thousand years.

(c) If time travel proves possible, we can assume that this particular
sixty-year period will be the focus of considerable attention from
the future.

(d) With the level of expertise available to the future, we can assume
that the crisis has been, is being, or will be resolved by intervention
from the very future that the successful intervention guarantees.

It seems extremely difficult, looking at the current ongoing world crisis, to appreciate exactly what our value might be to future generations,
assuming they exist. One answer that circumvents this issue is that the
future needs us as a gene pool and that solid physical roots are of continuing importance. Therefore, speculating that future generations will need
physical bodies as a base from which to develop, the rough and tumble of
the geopolitical situation could be viewed as some form of holographic
movie designed to keep us occupied and in possession of a sense of control
over our own destiny.

I am postulating that within this scenario, the overall decisions regarding our future have already been made, but that we need to go through the motions of resolving the crisis ourselves because the upheavals that inevitably lie ahead of us will only mature and strengthen the quality of the gene pool.

Appendix B

The Sacred Use of Entheogens, Power Plants, and Sacred Chemistry

The use of entheogens is mentioned several times over the course of these adventures, and because these substances have become so misunderstood and demonized by the authorities in much of the Western world, I feel it's necessary to briefly explain why I believe entheogens have such value for the examined life.

Rather than calling these substances "psychedelics" or "psychomimetics," both terms placing the emphasis on the "psyche" rather than their spiritual aspect, I use R. Gordon Wasson's word *entheogen,* from the Greek and meaning "becoming Divine within." An entheogen is defined in the dictionary as, "A chemical substance, typically of plant origin, that is ingested to produce a non-ordinary state of consciousness for religious or spiritual purposes."

Common sense dictates that entheogens are not for everybody. I'm certainly not recommending their indiscriminate use by people completely unprepared for the raw psychic power of the entheogenic experience. It was a great tragedy when Timothy Leary chose to ignore Aldous Huxley's advice not to make a public spectacle of LSD. The unintended consequences of Leary's misguided irresponsibility crippled scientific research into entheogens for fifty years, led to the imprisonment of hundreds of thousands, and labeled serious truth seekers as criminals.

Yet working with entheogens is an ancient and valuable shamanic and spiritual tool, practiced throughout history in virtually every culture. There will always be people—generally reincarnates—whose inner guidance leads them to explore these substances. It's been pointed out by others how closely parallel are Albert Hofmann's development of LSD-25 and the Manhattan Project's creation of the atomic bomb. How neatly they counterbalance one another: the one delivering death in unimaginable profusion, the other delivering glimpses of life in its deepest aspect.

Entheogens used as tools to access alternative states of consciousness demand the uttermost respect. They are a serious business. Used wisely, entheogens can open us up to the hidden elements of life and the workings of the Multiverse. They are also one of the few remaining ways in our materialistic society by which a person may have a direct *experience* of the Divine.

I was fortunate to have stumbled on LSD in 1960, well before it became illegal. With the advantage of a purity guaranteed by Sandoz Laboratories and a lack of the paranoia generated later by its criminalization, I was able to explore the spiritual dimensions revealed by the substance, given a supportive set and setting. I also had the privilege in 1963 of working with a professor of organic chemistry at London University, investigating and testing a number of plant and synthesized entheogens, including ibogaine, DMT, and DET.

These early experiences with entheogens triggered my lifelong interest in nonhuman intelligences and allowed me to understand how a shift in the way our senses are calibrated can produce access to different frequency-domains. More recently, Terence McKenna's work with psilocybin and DMT and Dr. John C. Lilly's exploration of ketamine both speak to these different frequency-domains and the beings that inhabit them.

As I write in 2010 there appears to be something of a revival of interest in entheogens as spiritual tools. Martin W. Ball, for example, writes openly and courageously of his personal experiences of Divinity through his use of 5-MeO-DMT in his 2008 book, *The Entheogenic Evolution: Psychedelics, Consciousness and Awakening the Human Spirit.* James Oroc's 2009 book, *Tryptamine Palace: 5-MeO-DMT and the Sonoran Desert Toad,* while he is not as obviously enthusiastic as Martin Ball about this powerful natural chemical found in the glands of the humble toad, is both a rich vein of hitherto hidden information and a passionate plea for the restoration of experiential mystical spirituality to Western civilization.

As is true of much literature currently emerging on entheogens, both James Oroc and Martin Ball's books are the hard-won result of many years of personal investigation. These aren't dry, dusty tomes by scientists who wouldn't want to compromise their objectivity by actually experiencing entheogens. Both Oroc and Ball are authors who gain their gnosis by bravely throwing themselves into the entheogenic mystery, to return with information that will become vitally important as the years pass.

There are also a number of serious scientific research projects currently under way investigating the various properties of entheogens, picking up from some of the breakthroughs made before psychedelics were outlawed. Dr. Rick Strassman's research into DMT at the University of New Mexico in 1990 was the first officially sanctioned examination of an entheogen's ability to draw out mystical states of consciousness. Dr. Strassman's primary interest is the presence of DMT in all human bodies, which he believes is made in the pineal gland, a tiny organ situated in the center of our brains.

Summarizing his research in 2001, in his book, *DMT The Spirit Molecule: A Doctor's Revolutionary Research into the Biology of Near-Death and Mystical Experiences,* Strassman confirms many of Terence McKenna and others' insights as to DMT's capacity to introduce the subject to different frequency-domains. In it Dr. Strassman writes, "Even more impressive was the apprehension of *human and 'alien' figures that seemed to be aware of and interacting with the volunteers.* Non-human entities might be recognizable: 'spiders,' 'mantises,' 'reptiles,' and 'something like a saguaro cactus'" (my emphasis added).[1]

One of the doyens of entheogenic research, the brilliant pharmacologist Sasha Shulgin, who co-wrote *PIHKAL: A Chemical Love Story* with his wife Ann, expresses beautifully in the introduction to *PIHKAL* what so many of us have come to feel. "I deem myself blessed, in that I have experienced [with entheogens], however briefly, the existence of God. I have felt a sacred oneness with creation and its Creator, and—most precious of all—I have touched the core of my soul."[2]

It may well turn out that the easing of restrictions prohibiting research into entheogens has occurred at a time when the substances can be used in beneficial ways. MDMA, for example, although technically an empathogen, and psilocybin, an entheogen, are currently emerging as extremely effective treatments for soldiers returning from war with post-traumatic stress disorder. Having been born in a war myself, with some traumatic repressed memories of bombs exploding all around, my early experiences with LSD were invaluable in revealing the severity of those imprints, as well as suggesting a way of releasing the trauma.

The medical and psychological benefits of entheogens have been known for a long time, and with a more thoughtful approach to their social impact, the value of these ineffable substances could restore to Western culture an opportunity for people to experience something of the hidden dimensions of life. If it is so that "people die of lack of vision," we might well look back at our age and be amazed that we hadn't availed ourselves of these perfectly natural plant medicines to reinvigorate the psychological and spiritual well-being of our people.

I'm grateful to entheogens for breaking open my head so many years ago. They prepared me well for some of the more unusual events and encounters I've had over the course of these adventures. Since it appears that most if not all alien intelligences, whether BVF or extraterrestrial, inhabit different frequency-domains, a facility for moving through alternate states of consciousness will become increasingly important as we rejoin the galactic community. More importantly, those who have some practical knowledge of operating in higher frequency-domains will find it increasingly helpful as our world moves more fully into the Great Transformation.

Appendix C

The Spiritual Underpinnings of the Multiverse as a Cosmic Hologram

My interest in the holographic hypothesis has always been purely practical. I wanted to find a way of accounting for what I've experienced, and this model comes closest to describing the underlying structure of the Multiverse.

My training in architecture included a certain amount of engineering and science, enough anyway to grasp the basic principles of some of the key technological advances of the past one hundred years. Since my near-death experience in 1973 my primary interest has been in the spiritual nature of life, and I've always been intrigued to see which current scientific hypothesis most matches or explains my personal experiences in the subtle realms.

Becoming friends with the brilliant Czech engineer and mystic Itzhak (Ben) Bentov back in the 1970s was, for me, an early introduction to his holographic model of reality. Ben's hypothesis, which he developed in his book, *Stalking the Wild Pendulum,* was the first to account for the shifting frequency-domains I'd experienced in my entheogenic explorations. When, some years later, the psychologist and neurosurgeon Karl Pribram collaborated with theoretical physicist and philosopher David Böhm to introduce their holonomic model of brain function, I wondered if they were providing (albeit unknowingly) a scientific basis for Ben's intuitive leaps of understanding.

Although there continues to be disagreement among scientists as to how the brain might decode a "cosmic hologram," the holonomic model, well-described in Michael Talbot's *The Holographic Universe* appears to account for a number of anomalous paranormal phenomena. Telepathy, synchronicity, nonhuman intelligences, precognition, even mystical experiences, all matters I've written about in some depth in my three linked books, are now starting to move out of the metaphysical shadows, to be taken more seriously by the scientific community.

In these days of Wikipedia, when the intricacies of holography are easily researched, I should emphasize the model I'm describing here is my own. It is drawn from personal revelatory experiences, my metaphysical studies, the holonomic concepts of Bentov, Böhm, and Pribram, and what I'm learning about the nature and structure of the Multiverse from *The Urantia Book.*

I should lay out the basic principles of holography as I understand them before I propose how they might be applied to the way the Urantia communicants describe the Multiverse. The simplest hologram to visualize is the optical—of photons moving in a highly focused coherent stream, splitting into a reference beam and a working beam (sometimes called the illumination beam), and then being brought together to create an interference pattern on a recording medium (a photographic plate, for example). After the working beam has illuminated the object to be reproduced, the light striking the photographic plate is called the object beam. Whenever the plate is illuminated later by a coherent light source, the object will then appear as a three-dimensional "virtual object" hanging in space.

It's important to know that these optical holograms are not truly three-dimensional—unless the object is originally photographed from a series of different angles—but merely appear so from the way light is distributed slightly differently to each eye. Strictly speaking, a hologram isn't an image, but, according to Wikipedia, is "an encoding system which enables the scattered light field to be reconstructed. Images can then be formed from any point in the reconstructed beam either with a camera or eye."

Salvador Dali was the first world-class artist to use holography artistically in a 1972 exhibition; 3-D optical holograms have been around since the late '70s. The advent of cheap solid-state lasers put holograms in DVD machines, recording devices, and supermarket checkout stations. Flat holograms have since become ubiquitous on credit cards and are even printed on some national currencies. There are many other applications of holography, but all holograms are created in essentially the same manner.

There are some intriguing aspects to a hologram that have particular relevance when applied in a metaphysical context. If an object is captured on a photographic plate and the plate is shattered, each shard, when illuminated by the original light source, will recreate the entire virtual object. The smaller the shard, the fuzzier the virtual object becomes, but unlike the torn-up pieces of a photograph, a piece of a hologram will always show the entire virtual object.

The second peculiarity results when the interference pattern on the photographic plate is lit by a light source that is not as coherent as the original reference beam: the virtual object will still be discernible, but increasingly fuzzy the less coherent the illumination. One further strangeness of a hologram, which everyone will have encountered from the picture on their credit cards, is that the image, unlike a normal photograph, will be slightly different when viewed from different directions.

While Böhm and Pribram's holonomic model is far more complicated than needs to be described here, if their hypothesis is correct, they speak of each sense as being a "lens," each of which refocuses wave patterns, to quote Wikipedia, "by perceiving a specific pattern or context as swirls, or by discerning *discrete grains or quantum units*" (my emphasis added).[1]

Since it's been known for some time that brains transform the incoming signals received from the environment into the electrochemical signals the brain then interprets as reality, the holonomic model suggests how this might occur. Pribram argues that the cells of the primary visual cortex, like those of the auditory system, are tuned to different wave frequencies. Taking that concept one step farther, Pribram and others also contend that a similar tuning must happen in the somatosensory cortex. This area of the brain is also known more intriguingly as the sensory homunculus—the "little man in the brain"—and can be thought of as a map of sensory space that places and processes the sense of touch.

The implication that our brains contain what Pribram calls "a multidimensional holographic-like process" is profound, since it suggests it is a similar process that allows us to decode and order the particles and waveforms we perceive as composing the Multiverse. Given this holonomic/holographic model of reality I suggest research will finally show all the cells of the body are tuned, or tunable, to different wave frequencies, so that our entire physical vehicle can be understood as one unified and integrated sensory lens.

Turning now to how all this might apply to metaphysics and more particularly to the cosmology advocated by *The Urantia Book*, what quickly springs out upon reading the book (although never directly stated) is that the communicants appear to be speaking about a holographic Multiverse. The book was completed some years before the Hungarian physicist Dennis Gabor developed electron-holography in 1947, so the terms used by the communicants are, of necessity, spiritual or religious. Yet, all the hints are there.

If the Multiverse is indeed a massive hologram, the first thing we can expect to find will be an original coherent energy source, which then splits into a reference beam that maintains the original coherence and a working beam that descends directly into the Creation. Turning to *The Urantia Book* we find that the communicants speak of a "Central Universe" as the original Creation and as being eternal, perfectly formed, and the location of the Creator. It's from this Central Universe that the material "Universes of Time and Space" are projected and energetically downstepped to manifest as the seven vast Superuniverses and the four "Outer Space Levels." Thus, we have an original source in that the Central Universe is a "perfect and eternal nucleus," which, due to its perfection, can also be understood as coherent. Then, we have a secondary creation in the Superuniverses, which we can think of as the cosmic recording medium.

I'm abridging and simplifying a thoroughly complex narrative here to explore the holographic possibilities. A far fuller account of how the angels describe the structure the Universe can be found on page 129 of *The Urantia Book*. As I touched on earlier in this book, the Urantia communicants claim that the Creator manifests in three distinct personified aspects that echo the Christian Trinity, but with one important difference. The Eternal Son, the second person of the Urantia Trinity, is a split-being, which they call the Mother/Son, thus restoring what has been lost in the patriarchal takeover of Christianity.

They go on to tell us that while the Trinity stay within the Central Universe, their direct progeny, the Creator Sons (the Michaelsons) and their co-creators, the Mother Spirits, seven hundred thousand of each, modulate the energy coming from the Central Universe and create the life-forms that exist within their Local Universes. If we regard the energy coming from the Central Universe as coherent, this can be thought of as the reference beam of holography. This beam would then be split at the point of each individual Michaelson and his Holy Mother Spirit. Since the Michaelson is a direct reflection of the Creator God, he also can be identified with the reference beam. The working beam in this model is the Mother Spirit, the clue being lodged in her name: from the latin *mater*, matter. The Spirit in the matter of the Multiverse is the working beam, or perhaps calling it the illumination beam at this stage is more appropriate, since the objects being illuminated are matter in all its forms.

For the last stage of this cosmic hologram we need a lens, something like Karl Pribram's multidimensional holographic-like process, which can decipher and make sense of the interference pattern created by the inter-action of the reference beam and object beam.

Switching now from the material to the spiritual, we find the Urantia communicants assuring us that we are indwelt by the Father Spirit, or to put it in holographic terms, we possess the coherent energy of the reference beam. If Böhm and Pribram prove correct and our brains act to decode the interference patterns created by the energy scattered off the surrounding environment, the resultant holographic image can be said to be in constant process of being created by the Father Spirit as a reference beam, interacting with the Mother Spirit as present in matter.

It's in the nature of a hologram that if its recording medium is broken and scattered, each piece will replicate the entire image with different degrees of clarity. Applying the holographic model I suggest that any aggregation of matter, whether it's a molecule, ant, lion, human, tree, mountain, planet, or star, represents a piece of the whole, each with its varying degree of clarity. This clarity will depend on the size and function of the piece of aggregated matter and its level of consciousness, and this, as Ben Bentov proposes, is broadly dependent on its needs and its capacity to decipher the hologram. An ant's consciousness will be shaped by its genome, by the Mother Spirit's presence in the matter of its body, and by the needs and requirements imposed on it by its environment. It will thus interpret the hologram according to its capacity and needs.

Bringing it back to a human level of consciousness and remembering this is a feature of the hologram, each of us will perceive the hologram— the world around us—in our own idiosyncratic way. We may have more developed decoding abilities and a far greater freedom of choice than the ant, but the deeper issue suggested by this model is that each one of us is a direct participant in co-creating the hologram of the Multiverse. The quality of our lenses, as individuals, their clarity or their distortions, will dictate how we perceive the world around us. The key here is the understanding that on the most basic of levels, when we perceive something external to us with our senses, we are in actuality co-creating what we perceive.

It's also evident from altered states of consciousness that this lens is highly mutable and capable of revealing different dimensions and frequency-domains, just as in everyday life a hungry person will tend to notice the food shops more readily than someone with a full stomach. Any distortion in the lens will produce a distorted perception of the hologram. The implication of this—the metaphysical concept that each of us "co-creates our own reality"—becomes far more accessible in the holographic model.

And it *is* only a model, just as string or M-brane theories are only mathematical models. A complex three-dimensional hologram allows for a multiplicity of dimensions and habitable frequency-domains in a way not suggested by the mathematical models. The Multiverse hologram might not yet be able to be mathematically described, but it is relatively straightforward to visualize. *The Urantia Book* tells us the Universe of Time and Space (i.e., the Multiverse) is shaped like a slightly flattened torus, the Central Universe being the hole in the middle of the doughnut. The volume of the torus can be visualized as a series of layers or zones containing matter aggregated into the superuniverses, all of which orbit the center.

At the moment, the Multiverse as a cosmic hologram is more of a great idea than a demonstrable fact, but some recent surprises resulting from an inexplicable "noise" plaguing a German research project attempting to accurately measure gravitational waves have opened up an important clue.

According to Craig Hogan, now director of Fermilab's Center for Particle Physics, in the January 15, 2009, issue of *New Scientist,* "the GEO600 experiment has stumbled upon the fundamental limit of space/time—the point where space/time stops behaving like the smooth continuum Einstein described and instead dissolves into 'grains, . . .' It looks like GEO600 is being buffeted by the microscopic quantum convulsions of space/time."[2]

These grains are described as tiny units like pixels, but a hundred billion billion times smaller than a proton, at a Planck length so far beyond the reach of any current experiment that up to now the possible graininess of the Universe has been formally discounted. The suggestion that space-time, the material Universes of space and time, is granular and appears to have a limit, becomes profoundly significant in the light of the holographic model. We have Böhm and Pribram speaking of our senses being lenses, each of which refocuses wave patterns by discerning *discrete grains or quantum units.* *The Urantia Book* describes all space-time as being composed of particles called "ultimatons," so tiny they can be thought of as quantum events occurring at a Planck length, a particle, if you like, of the smallest possible size. And we have prominent scientists speculating that if the "noise" turns out to be caused by granular quantum events, then we'll be one step closer to understanding the Multiverse as a cosmic hologram.

Yet, in the final analysis, Dr. John Lilly's reminder to regard any belief system as a rung in the ladder of self-awareness encourages me to remain open to the far deeper discoveries and revelations to come.

Appendix D

Three Unusual Personal Experiences Suggesting Optimism

I'm including these three personal incidents because each one empirically demonstrated for me both the existence and the accessibility of other intelligent beings in the Multiverse.

THE CONSCIOUSNESS AMPLIFICATION DEVICE

I've understood through the course of my experimentation with altered states of consciousness that the power for change has to be with the individual if it is to have any deep meaning. I was very excited by Itzhak Bentov's work on a holographic model of consciousness, which, of course, due to the peculiarity of the hologram, potentially allows an individual unit of consciousness to have a direct relationship with, and influence over, the whole field of consciousness.

The first of the experiences occurred as a result of exploring the Walk-In scenario. I was interested to see whether there was any way of consciously precipitating the phenomenon, of inviting another more effective entity to take over my body. I was at a stage in my life when I felt I'd completed what I needed to do in this lifetime, and I sincerely wished to offer up my physical vehicle for the good of all. So, working with the entheogen ketamine hydrochloride, this is what occurred.

I entered a meditative state with the stated intention to offer my body to any being who felt more fitted for the tasks ahead than I, but on two conditions: that the being also offer over this vehicle when its function draws to a close in the same way as I was doing, and that a conscious part of me would be able to share in the experience.

Deeply into the meditation I found myself surrounded by an all-pervading white light and a vast confluence of benign nonmaterial entities. I soon became a funnel for them. Rather than just one being, one after another was coming down through the funnel of light, entering me and then immediately turning my body over to another entity. I'd have burst out laughing if I was in control of the body and not merely a speck of consciousness observing these strange shenanigans. Of course, I asked for this, but not all at once, please. There was something deliciously humorous about this, the way each being (and I've come to understand they were angels) offered to turn the vehicle over so selflessly and without any hesitation.

My consciousness and awareness seemed to expand exponentially as larger and more profound beings flowed down and through me. I was still me, a point of consciousness, yet I was everything else as well. At that point I realized I'd stumbled inadvertently onto a consciousness amplification device. Whatever was happening, I felt progressively more of an active participant in the living Multiverse. This process accelerated until I entered into a whole new realm of peace and gnosis.

While in this transcendent state, I experienced the presence of another entity fall around me. I felt as if someone was using my assemblage of atoms to transmit a wholly different message. The manifestation was clear enough for my girlfriend, acting as ground control, to draw the entity overlighting my body.

Apparently he was from many years into our own future—a scientist who deliberately interacted with me because I'd intentionally opened myself to the possibility. I don't believe he spoke, and my girlfriend told me later she thought he was telepathic. I have an intuitive sense he has embedded information in my physical vehicle somewhere below my conscious reach. The experience itself lasted for about half an hour.

Although I'm cautious of information received mediumistically and make sure to thoroughly reality-check it, this was an event of a totally different order. It was an overlighting powerful enough to be captured in a drawing. The incident happened. That was undeniable to both my girlfriend and myself.

This entity from our distant future has never made a reappearance that I've been aware of since that one time. Yet it had a profound effect on my life, and although I have no desire to build a belief system around the manifestation, I feel reassured by the evident existence of a future for the human race.

BACKWARD SERIAL REINCARNATION

I first met R. T. in 1980, and after several months he trusted me sufficiently to confide that he believed himself to be an anthropologist from the forty-third century in the future. He told me he has been working his way back to the late twentieth century through what he calls backward serial reincarnation. Apparently, this is a system designed to soften the cultural and neurological shock of entering a distant time and place, as well as aiding a future-mutated consciousness to interface with a twentieth-century central nervous system.

After initially being skeptical I came to know the man well enough to understand he wasn't deluding himself. Rather, he was bravely exploring a personality, or an aspect of his personality, as an intuitive experience. This was familiar territory for me, having spent many years marshaling my own subpersonalities, so in R. T.'s case I chose to suspend judgment.

Over the time I knew him I saw his confidence in this futique (to use Dr. Leary's word) personality grow. He told me he was making field notes for his research into life on the planet at this key point in human history. He spoke of a short paper he was going to write when he returned to his own century and for which he was collecting data. When I got a glimpse of a few of his notes I was astonished not only at their clarity and the brilliance of the insights, but also by their extraordinary brevity, with a whole world of information compressed into a mere four or eight lines.

I could see there was a very fine intelligence at work, which was seeking to challenge the more conventional approaches to self-awareness. R. T. was the most unassuming of men and appears to have made no effort to capitalize on his futique identity apart from continuing to keep his superbly condensed fieldnotes. He showed no desire to intervene with the present, beyond living what appeared to be a perfectly normal life. When I raised the usual objection to time travel, generally posed as the "grandfather paradox," he assured me this was avoided by the system of backward serial reincarnation, since he was essentially a normal twentieth-century person. Any action of his, he explained, that might be likely to substantially influence the future, was taken as a twentieth-century person and therefore would be integrated into the regular timeline.

Over the couple of years I knew R. T. he showed no signs of any mental imbalance, nor was he pathologically delusional, in that he was quite prepared to consider delusion as a reasonable conclusion. I don't think either of us made a big deal out of who, or what, he might be. I had no sense from him that we were facing any imminent discontinuity in human history, no apocalypse or 2012. I found the experience of knowing R. T. personally helpful in that it expanded my acceptance level as well as providing me, as in the previous example, with the reassurance that a human future might indeed exist.

It was in the fall of 2009 that I met R. T. again and had the chance to ask him for a brief comment on his current state of mind.

The conversations Timothy Wyllie refers to occurred in 1980 and 1981. Nearly 30 years later—I am writing in early 2010—I still find myself interested in the topic of time travel, but far less certain of my own origins.

Perhaps some analogue of the Tibetan Buddhist bardos is applicable here. One of these realms might be my home base, so to speak, in some inter-incarnational dimension that serves as the starting and end point of "voyages" into $(n + or, - x)$ –dimensional space. This would be where I maintain my (as it were) "permanent" abode. Each "voyage" would be a discrete lifetime. One can only theorize about these things during this lifetime.

As the old spiritual goes: "Further along we'll know more about it/Further along we'll understand why. . . ."

MEETING AN ARCTURIAN

In 1996 I was living in New Mexico in the small village of Monte Alto, while I was building a house out in the desert. I'd return at the end of the working day and enjoy relaxing my bones in a tub on a late summer's afternoon. The pleasure of a long bath is one of the particularly English foibles I brought with me to my adopted home.

So it was one sunny evening, with the leaves on the elm tree outside my bathroom shivering in the breeze, the light in the room still bright although shaded from the sun, and myself in the tub facing the window, relaxed yet quite awake. I gradually became aware of two distinct forms standing against the far wall in between the window and the door. I wasn't frightened, but I could feel my heart beating faster. I consciously relaxed while keeping my eyes on the two forms, who seemed to be resolving into material reality.

The light coming in the window prevented me from seeing them with great clarity, but they were definitely there: one a remarkably tall female figure, the other, perhaps three or four feet tall, but looking even smaller in comparison to the figure next to it. I could discern long black hair against an unnaturally white face on the tall female, and I believe, although I can't be sure because of the shadow in the corner of the room, she was wearing an indigo-blue, or blue-violet, close-fitting garment.

In spite of the woman's obvious beauty it was the small form that grabbed my attention. It was slim and rather finely formed, and I couldn't quite see if it had legs or whether it was floating, since it seemed to bob gently up and down. I do remember the eyes, large and slightly slanted and strangely blank. The entity's color was hard to make out, but it seemed to be a dull greenish-white. I wondered if it was a robot at first, it seemed more angular and crystalline than organic, yet somehow I knew it was sentient and friendly.

I was surprised I wasn't afraid and didn't want whatever was happening to stop. It was then I heard a clear female voice, resonant and without a discernible accent, that I believed at first I was hearing with my ears until the voice explained she was speaking to me telepathically.

There followed what must have been a twenty-minute conversation before the two figures faded and I scrambled out of my bath to try to capture in my journal something of what I learned. I find that typically I'm unable to recreate dialogue since telepathic communication tends to be difficult to retain unless I'm writing it down in the moment, so I'm simply passing along some of what I learned.

I can't be absolutely sure because of the female voice, but I believe it was the small one who was actually doing the telepathic talking. She informed me she was from a star we'd call Arcturus. When I queried how they could come from a star, she explained that they lived in a higher dimension on a planet that appeared to us as a star.

She claimed they existed in the fifth dimension and had to descend through the fourth to reach the third dimension. She described the earth's vibrations as being "very harsh." When I asked her about the purpose of the third dimension she told me it was to learn how to synchronize our physical, emotional, mental, and spiritual bodies. She said the vibrations of the earth would be rising and that would reveal all sorts of weaknesses in the emotional and physical states of being. This will give us the chance to work on these vulnerabilities.

She claimed humanity is soon due to enter the fifth dimension and we needed to find what she called "a new state of ecstasy" if we are going to move to a higher frequency. She emphasized, too, the importance of developing what she called a "telepathic state of mind" and also "listening to our hearts."

Then, she really surprised me by calling me "Artor," or at least that is what it sounded like, and told me she knew me from a lifetime I'd had on Arcturus. Apparently I was one of those souls who volunteered to return to Earth for this time of transition. I must have looked confused because she added quickly that she was almost four hundred years old.

She warned me about the times ahead, because as the planetary vibrations increase those individuals who are letting go of their negative emotions will start separating themselves from those still embedded in their anger and fear. This will create conflicts, she told me, between both individuals and groups. She anticipated more and more people reaching for higher states of consciousness and said this will precipitate even more clashes.

She referred to Earth as "a training ground," and when I asked about the fifth dimension she astonished me by saying it was the same dimension as that of the fairies. She said that the fourth dimension was more like a dream state, a dimension in which everything exists simultaneously. In fact, she said, we had agreed to meet in the dream state—although I have no conscious memory of this.

Finally, she gave me another clue as to why I might have relocated to the high desert of New Mexico. My house nestles in the foothills of the Manzano mountains, which are a continuation of the Rockies, given that the mountains run south through New Mexico. My Arcturian friend told me they came from a large Arcturian ship parked in the fifth dimension over the Manzanos. (See plate 8.)

When I expressed my surprise at this, since it's deep within bunkers tunneled into the Manzanos that the United States stores much of its most dangerous thermonuclear weaponry, she became almost wistful. I don't recall how she put it, but the sense I got was that the Arcturians felt far closer and had more in common with normal folk than with the military mind and had little time for governments.

There was much more that I didn't have a chance to jot down, but what encouraged me was how much of what she talked about I'd already thought out for myself regarding dimensions and frequency-domains. Of course, since she was talking telepathically, she was doubtless using my vocabulary. Finally, she told me that the reason that the Arcturians are present on the planet right now is because they themselves, a couple of thousand years ago, had experienced the transformation that Earth and her inhabitants are currently going through, and they feel a responsibility to help out wherever possible. She claimed most of their work involved balancing out the electromagnetic energy currents, but they were also making some individual contacts with people with whom they had a natural affinity.

I found the contact basically heartening in that I didn't believe the Arcturians would bother to come here if the planet were going to go down in flames. To know that another planetary race of intelligent beings had successfully made this transformation of consciousness, and her emphasis *was* on consciousness, suggests, once again, that the Multiverse is an extremely well-organized place. Such an important event as a planetary transformation is clearly not being left to chance.

It was a couple of years later that I came across a remarkable book, *We, The Arcturians (A True Experience)* by Dr. Norma J. Milanovich, with

Betty Rice and Cynthia Ploski, which confirmed much of what my strange visitors had told me, including a reference to the Arcturian "starship" over the Manzano mountains.

Dr. Milanovich evidently has a serious academic background and was living and teaching in Albuquerque, at the University of New Mexico, when she became unexpectedly psychic following an automobile accident. The book is essentially a series of transmissions received from a group of Arcturians and recorded by Dr. Milanovich and her two friends. Her book goes into far more detail about planetary transformation and the Arcturian belief system than I was able to pick up from my brief conversation, and I thoroughly recommend it for an intriguing off-planet viewpoint.

Glossary

Many valuable insights in books have contributed to the themes and fundamental questions that *The Return of the Rebel Angels* seeks to explore, but the most reliable and comprehensive exposition of God, the Universe, and Everything that I have come across remains, after thirty years, *The Urantia Book*. A number of the concepts and words below are drawn from it and marked (UB), but the definitions are the author's.

Angel: a general term for any order of being who administers within a Local Universe.

Astral Energy/Astral Realm: a slightly shifted frequency-domain, accessible in dreams and out-of-body experiences, in which humans have an astral counterpart—an astral body.

Atman, Indwelling Spirit, Thought Adjuster (UB): an essence of the Creator that indwells all mortal beings, human and extraterrestrial.

Avonal Sons (UB): a descending order of high sons who accompany a Magisterial Son (UB) on his mission. While the Magisterial Son appears in a material body, the seventy accompanying Avonals remain in a contiguous frequency-domain.

Caligastia (UB): a Secondary Lanonandek Son who served as Planetary Prince of this world and who aligned himself with Lucifer.

Celestial Being (UB): a generic name for a high angel.

Creator Sons (UB): co-creators—each having a female complement, the

433

Mother Spirit (UB)—of each of the seven hundred thousand Local Universes (UB).

Daligastia (UB): a Secondary Lanonandek Son who served as Caligastia's right-hand aide.

Decimal Planets (UB): on every tenth inhabited planet the Life Carriers (UB) are permitted to experiment with the initial seeding of biological life by applying what they have learned from the previous nine implantations. Earth is a decimal planet.

Demons: negative thoughtforms.

Devas: the coordinating spirits of the natural world. All living organisms are cared for by devas (or nature spirits). In the human being the deva is that which coordinates and synchronizes the immense amount of physical and biochemical information that keeps our bodies alive.

Etheric Realms/Etheric Body: collective terms for the higher frequency-domains and the beings that exist within those realms. Many observed UFOs are etheric craft. The human subtle energy systems are also referred to as etheric bodies.

Extraterrestrial: mortal beings such as ourselves who hail from more developed worlds with access to our frequency-domain.

Frequency-Domain: the spectrum of frequencies that support the life-forms whose senses are tuned to that specific spectrum.

God: in *my* personal experience, God is both the Creator and the totality of creation, manifest and unmanifest, immanent and transcendent.

Guardian (Companion) **Angels** (UB): function in pairs to ensure their mortal wards grow in spirit over the course of their lifetimes.

Indwelling Spirit, Atman, Thought Adjuster (UB): an essence of the Creator that indwells all mortal beings, human and extraterrestrial.

Intraterrestrial or Ultraterrestrial Beings: the beings who inhabit our neighboring frequency-domain, and whom *The Urantia Book* calls the midwayers or midway creatures.

Jesus Christ: the Michaelson (UB) of our Local Universe (UB) who incarnated as Jesus Christ in the physical body of Joshua ben Joseph; he is also known as Michael of Nebadon (UB).

Lanaforge (UB): a primary Lanonandek Son who succeeded Lucifer as System Sovereign.

Life Carriers (UB): the celestial order responsible for the development and seeding of organic life on all inhabited planets.

Local System (UB): our Local System, named Satania (UB) is believed to currently possess between 600 and 650 inhabited planets. Earth is numbered 606 in this sequence (UB).

Local System HQ Planet (UB): the political and social center of the Satania System.

Local Universe (UB): a political grouping of inhabited worlds comprised of ten million inhabited planets.

Lucifer (UB): deposed System Sovereign and primary protagonist in the rebellion among the angels.

Machiventa Melchizedek (UB): the particular Melchizedek brother who served on this planet four thousand years ago and created a missionary school at Salem, in Palestine.

Magisterial Son (UB): a celestial being of the Avonal Order who appears as a material being of the realm to adjudicate a dispensation prior to entering a new one.

Master Universe (UB): the Multiverse that contains the seven Superuniverses (UB).

Melchizedek Sons (UB): a high order of Local Universe sons devoted primarily to education and who function as planetary administrators in emergencies.

Michaelsons (UB): a generic term for the spiritual ruler of any given Local Universe. Our Michaelson is Jesus Christ, who incarnated in the physical body of Joshua ben Joseph.

Midwayers or Midway Creatures (UB): intelligent beings who exist in a contiguous frequency-domain and serve as the permanent planetary citizens.

Mortals (UB): intelligent beings who emerge as a result of biological evolutionary processes on a planet. Souls are born to their immortal lives as mortals, whose physical bodies live and die before they are given the choice to continue their Multiverse career.

Mortal Ascension Scheme (UB): the process by which all mortal beings who live and die on the material worlds of the Local Systems pass up through the seven subsequent levels to the System's capital planet as they embark on their universe career.

Multiverse: the entire range of frequency-domains, on every level of the Master Universe (UB).

Nebadon (UB): the name of our Local Universe.

Outer Space Levels (UB): four great bands of matter in very early stages of organization that encircle the seven Superuniverses (UB) from four hundred thousand to fifty million light-years toward the edge of the Master Universe (UB).

Paradise Trinity (UB): Father, Mother/Son (split being), and Holy Spirit. The Trinity locates itself in the Central Universe (UB), the original Creation from which the Master Universe (UB) is energetically downstepped.

Satan (UB): Lucifer's right-hand aide who co-instigated the angelic rebellion 203,000 years ago.

Settled in Light and Life (UB): a phrase used to indicate that a global population has reached a level of overall spiritual harmony, social equity, and peaceful and creative cooperation.

Supernaphim (UB): the highest order of Central Universe ministering spirits.

Superuniverse (UB): a universe that contains one hundred thousand Local Universes (UB).

Supreme Deity (UB): a God in the making; an experiential Divinity derived from the spiritual experience of all sentient beings, material or celestial.

System of Planets (UB): a grouping of planets consisting of one thousand inhabited, or to be inhabited, planets.

System Sovereign (UB): the administrative angel, together with an assistant of the same rank, who is in overall authority of a Local System. Lucifer and Satan were the pair in charge of this System of planets.

Thoughtforms: quasi-life-forms existing in the astral regions, drawing their limited power from strong emotional thoughts projected out from human mentation, both conscious and unconscious. Thoughtforms can be negative or positive. Localized negative ones are referred to as fear-impacted thoughtforms.

Ultimatons (UB): subelectronic particles; the smallest possible quanta of matter, possibly the hypothetical Planck particle.

Ultraterrestrial or Intraterrestrial Beings: the beings who inhabit our neighboring frequency-domain and whom *The Urantia Book* calls the midwayers or midway creatures.

Universe Broadcast Circuits (UB): instantaneous transmission systems that interconnect all realms and worlds with developed intelligent life, with the exception of those planets under quarantine.

Universe Career (UB): a mortal's destiny, unless chosen otherwise, to rise through the many hundreds of levels of the Multiverse to finally encounter the Creator.

Universe(s) of Time and Space (UB): a synonym for the Master Universe to describe the manifest Multiverse.

Violet Blood (UB): the infusion of a slightly higher frequency for genetic endowment, which results in more acute senses and a deeper spiritual awareness and responsiveness.

Walk-In: an extraterrestrial being who, by prior arrangement with a specific human, takes over the physical vehicle, often at, or just before, the moment of the premature death of the original occupant.

Notes

CHAPTER 1. TRAVELS OUT OF BODY

1. Don Elkins, James Allen McCarty, and Carla Rueckert, *The Ra Material: An Ancient Astronaut Speaks* (Virginia Beach, Va.: Donning Company Publishers, 1984), 224.

CHAPTER 2. THE EMERGENCE OF THE SACRED

1. Benjamin Creme, *Maitreya's Mission* (London: Share International Foundation, 1993).
2. http://en.wikipedia.org/wiki/Panentheism.
3. Byron Belitsos, *The Call to Co-Create: The Omega Project, Radical Wisdom, and the Magisterial Mission* (n.p.: RomancingTheUniverse.net, 2011).

CHAPTER 5. INTIMATIONS OF A NEW VISION

1. John Ballou Newbrough, *Oahspe: A New Bible in the Words of Jehovih and His Angel* (Boston: Kosmon Press, 1882).
2. *The Urantia Book* (Chicago, Ill.: The Urantia Foundation, 1955), 736.
3. Ibid.
4. Ibid.

CHAPTER 9. RE-ENCHANTING THE PLANET

1. William Blake, *Jerusalem: The Illuminated Books of William Blake,* vol. 1 (Princeton, N.J.: Princeton University Press, 1997).

CHAPTER 11. THE EXTRATERRESTRIAL ENIGMA

1. The UFO Resource Center, November 27, 2000. Currently archived and available at www.uforc.com.
2. Dr. Jacques Vallee, "Five Arguments against the Extraterrestrial Origin of Flying Objects," *Journal of Scientific Exploration* (1990).

CHAPTER 12. THE ANGELIC CONSPIRACY AND THE GLOBAL TRANSFORMATION

1. *The Urantia Book* (Chicago, Ill.: The Urantia Foundation, 1955), 604D.
2. A. S. J. Tessimond, *The Collected Poems of A. S. J. Tessimond* (Reading, England: Whiteknights Press, 1985).

APPENDIX B. THE SACRED USE OF ENTHEOGENS, POWER PLANTS, AND SACRED CHEMISTRY

1. Rick Strassman, *DMT: The Spirit Molecule—A Doctor's Revolutionary Research into the Biology of Near-Death and Mystical Experiences* (Rochester, Vt.: Park Street Press, 2001), 147.
2. Alexander Shulgin, with Ann Shulgin. *PIHKAL: A Chemical Love Story* (Berkeley, Calif.: Transform Press, 1991), xx.

APPENDIX C. THE SPIRITUAL UNDERPINNINGS OF THE MULTIVERSE AS A COSMIC HOLOGRAM

1. http://en.wikipedia.org/wiki/Holonomic_brain_theory.
2. Craig Hogan, *New Scientist* (January 15, 2009).

Recommended
Reading

Argüelles, Jose. *The Mayan Factor: Path beyond Technology.* Santa Fe, N. Mex.: Bear & Company, 1987.

Ball, Martin W. *The Entheogenic Evolution: Psychedelics, Consciousness and Awakening the Human Spirit.* Portland, Ore.: Kyandara Publishing, 2008.

Barnard, George Mathieu. *The Search for 11:11.* Mt. Shasta, Calif.: Celestia/11:11 Publishers, 2003.

Belitsos, Byron. *The Call to Co-Create: The Omega Project, Radical Wisdom, and the Magisterial Mission.* n.p.: RomancingTheUniverse.net, 2011.

Bentov, Itzhak. *Stalking the Wild Pendulum: On the Mechanics of Consciousness.* New York: P. Dutton, 1977.

Böhm, David. *Wholeness and the Implicate Order.* London: Ark, 1983.

Bucke, Richard Maurice. *Cosmic Consciousness: A Study in the Evolution of the Human Mind.* New York: Penguin Books, 1991.

Burnham, Sophy. *A Book of Angels: Reflections on Angels Past and Present, and True Stories of How They Touch Our Lives.* New York: Ballantine Books, 2004.

Charon, Jean. *The Unknown Spirit: The Unity of Matter and Spirit in Space and Time.* London: Coventure Ltd., 1983.

Corazza, Ornella. *Near-Death Experiences: Exploring the Mind-Body Connection.* New York: Routledge, 2008.

Creme, Benjamin. *Maitreya's Mission*. London: Share International Foundation, 1993.

———. *The Reappearance of the Christ and the Masters of Wisdom*. London: Tara Press, 1981.

Crowley, Aleister. *The Confessions of Aleister Crowley: An Hagiography*. London: Mandrake Press, 1929.

Davidson, Gustav. *A Dictionary of Angels*. New York: The Free Press, 1967.

Denaerde, Stefan, with Wendelle C. Stevens. *UFO . . . Contact from Planet IARGA*. Tucson, Ariz.: UFO Photo Archives, 1982.

Dewey, Barbara. *Consciousness and Quantum Behavior: The Theory of Laminated Space-Time Reexamined*. Inverness, Calif.: Bartholomew Books, 1993.

Drury, Nevill. *The Visionary Human: Mystical Consciousness and Paranormal Perspectives*. Shaftesbury, U.K.: Element, 1991.

Eadie, Betty J. *Embraced by the Light*. Placerville, Calif.: Gold Leaf Press, 1992.

Eisner, Bruce. *Ecstasy: The MDMA Story*. Berkeley, Calif.: Ronin Publishing, 1989.

Elders, Lee J., Brit Nilsson-Elders, Thomas K. Welch, and Wendelle C. Stevens (supervising editor). *UFO Contact from The Pleiades*. Vol. 1. Phoenix, Ariz.: Genesis 111 Productions Ltd., 1979.

Elkins, Don, James Allen McCarty, and Carla Rueckert. *The Ra Material: An Ancient Astronaut Speaks*. Virginia Beach, Va.: Donning Company Publishers, 1984.

Farrell, Joseph P. *The Cosmic War: Interplanetary Warfare, Modern Physics and Ancient Texts*. Kempton, Ill.: Adventures Unlimited Press, 2007.

———. *The Philosophers' Stone: Alchemy and the Secret Research for Exotic Matter*. Port Townsend, Wash.: Feral House, 2009.

Ferguson, Marilyn. *The Aquarian Conspiracy: Personal and Social Transformation in the 1980s*. New York: Tarcher Publishing, 1980.

Fowler, Raymond E. *The Andreasson Affair: The Documented Investigation of a Woman's Abduction aboard a UFO*. Englewood Cliffs, N.J.: Prentice-Hall, 1979.

Friedman, Stanton T. *Top Secret/Majic*. New York: Marlowe & Company, 1996.

Fuller, John G. *Incident at Exeter: Unidentified Flying Objects over America Now.* New York: G. P. Putnam's Sons, 1966.

———. *The Interrupted Journey: Two Lost Hours "Aboard a Flying Saucer."* New York: The Dial Press, 1966.

Gardner, Martin. *Urantia: The Great Cult Mystery.* Amherst, N.Y.: Prometheus Books, 1995.

Garrett, Eileen J. *Telepathy: In Search of a Lost Faculty.* New York: Helix Press, 1968.

Gerber, Richard. *Vibrational Medicine: New Choices for Healing Ourselves.* Santa Fe, N. Mex.: Bear & Company, 1988.

Godwin, Malcolm. *Angels: An Endangered Species.* London: Simon and Schuster, 1990.

Gray, John. *Men Are from Mars, Women Are from Venus.* San Francisco, Calif.: HarperCollins, 1992.

Greer, Steven M. *Disclosure: Military and Government Witnesses Reveal the Greatest Secrets in Modern History.* Charlottesville, Va.: Carden Jennings Publishing Co., 2001.

Guirdham, Arthur. *The Great Heresy.* London: C. W. Daniel Company Ltd., 1993.

Heim, Michael. *The Metaphysics of Virtual Reality.* Oxford, U.K.: Oxford University Press, 1993.

Hoagland, Richard C., and Mike Barra. *Dark Mission: The Secret History of NASA.* Port Townsend, Wash.: Feral House, 2007.

Hofmann, Albert. *LSD: My Problem Child: Reflections on Sacred Drugs, Mysticism, and Science.* New York: Tarcher/Penguin Publishing, 1983.

Hurtak, James J. *The Book of Knowledge: The Keys of Enoch.* Los Gatos, Calif.: Academy of Future Science, 1987.

James, William. *The Varieties of Religious Experience: A Study in Human Nature.* New York: Routledge, 2002.

Jansen, Karl. *Ketamine: Dreams and Realities.* Santa Cruz, Calif.: MAPS, 2004.

Jaynes, Julian. *The Origins of Consciousness in the Breakdown of the Bicameral Mind.* Boston: Mifflin Company, 1977.

Kaczynski, Theodore J. *Technological Slavery: The Collected Writings of Theodore J. Kaczynski.* Port Townsend, Wash.: Feral House, 2010.

Kinder, Gary. *Light Years: An Investigation into the Extraterrestrial Experiences of Eduard Meier.* New York: Atlantic Monthly Press, 1987.

Krapf, Phillip H. *The Challenge of Contact*. Novato, Calif.: Origin Press, 2002.

———. *The Contact Has Begun: The True Story of a Journalist's Encounter with Alien Beings*. Novato, Calif.: Origin Press, 1998.

———. *Meetings with Paul: An Atheist Discovers His Guardian Angel*. Novato, Calif.: Origin Press, 2008.

LaViolette, Paul A. *Genesis of the Cosmos: The Ancient Science of Continuous Creation*. Rochester, Vt.: Bear & Company, 1995.

Leadbeater, Charles Webster, with Annie Besant. *Thought-Forms*. IndoEuropeanpublishing.com, 2010 (first published 1901).

Lehrman, Fredric. *The Sacred Landscape*. Berkeley, Calif.: Celestial Arts Publishing, 1988.

Leigh, Richard, Henry Lincoln, and Michael Baigent. *Holy Blood, Holy Grail*. New York: Delacorte Press, 1982.

Leslie, Desmond, and George Adamski. *Flying Saucers Have Landed*. London: TBS Ltd.—The Book Service, 1970 (Revised edition).

Lilly, John C. *The Mind of the Dolphin*. New York: Doubleday, 1967.

———. *The Scientist: A Novel Autobiography*. Philadelphia, Pa.: Lippincott Publishing, 1978.

———. *Simulations of God: The Science of Belief*. New York: Simon and Schuster, 1975.

Mack, John E. *Abduction: Human Encounters with Aliens*. New York: Scribner, 2007.

MacLaine, Shirley. *Out on a Limb*. New York: Bantam, 1986.

Mallasz, Gitta. *Talking with Angels*. Einsiedeln, Switzerland.: Daimon Verlag, 1989.

Masters, R. E. L., and Jean Houston. *The Varieties of Psychedelic Experience*. New York: Holt, Rinehart, and Winston, 1966.

McKenna, Terence. *The Archaic Revival: Speculations on Psychedelic Mushrooms, the Amazon, the Rebirth of the Goddess, and the End of History*. San Francisco, Calif.: HarperCollins, 1992.

———. *Food of the Gods: The Search for the Original Tree of Knowledge*. New York: Bantam Books, 1993.

Michell, John F. *The New View over Atlantis*. London: Thames & Hudson, 2001.

Milanovich, Norma J., with Betty Rice and Cynthia Ploski. *We, The Arcturians (A True Experience)*. Scottsdale, Ariz.: Athena Publishing, 1990.

Monroe, Robert A. *Far Journeys*. New York: Main Street Books, 1985.

———. *Journeys Out of the Body*. New York: Doubleday Anchor, 1972.

Montgomery, Ruth. *Strangers among Us*. New York: Fawcett Books, 1984.

Moolenburgh, H. C. *A Handbook of Angels*. Essex, U.K.: C. W. Daniel Co., 1984.

Newbrough, John Ballou. *Oahspe: A New Bible in the Words of Jehovih and His Angel*. Boston: Kosmon Press, 1882.

Oroc, James. *Tryptamine Palace: 5-MeO-DMT and the Sonoran Desert Toad*. Rochester, Vt.: Park Street Press, 2009.

Pallmann, Ludwig F., with Wendelle Stevens. *UFO Contact from ITIBI-RA*. Tucson, Ariz.: UFO Photo Archives, 1986.

Puharich, Andrija. *The Sacred Mushroom: Key to the Door of Eternity*. Garden City, N.Y.: Doubleday & Comany, 1974.

Ramer, Andrew. *Angel Answers: Creating Heaven on Earth*. New York: Simon & Schuster Pocket Books, 1995.

———. *Little Pictures: Fiction for a New Age*. New York: Ballantine Books, 1987.

Randles, Jenny. *The UFO Conspiracy: The First Forty Years*. New York: Barnes & Noble, 1987.

Regis, Edward Jr. (editor). *Extraterrestrials: Science and Alien Intelligence*. London: Cambridge University Press, 1985.

Royal, Lyssa, and Keith Priest. *The Prism of Lyra: An Exploration of Human Galactic Heritage*. Scottsdale, Ariz.: Royal Priest Research Press, 1989.

———. *Visitors from Within*. Scottsdale, Ariz.: Royal Priest Research Press, 1992.

Russell, Peter. *The Global Brain Awakens: Our Next Evolutionary Leap*. Palo Alto, Calif.: Global Brain Inc., 1995.

———. *Waking Up in Time: Find Inner Peace in Times of Accelerating Change*. Novato, Calif.: Origin Press, 1992.

Salla, Michael E. *Exopolitics: Political Implications of Extraterrestrial Presence*. Tempe, Ariz.: Dandelion Books, 2004.

Schucman, Helen. *A Course in Miracles*. Omaha, Neb.: Course in Miracles Society, 2007.

Shearer, Tony. *Lord of the Dawn: Quetzalcoatl and the Tree of Life*. Happy Camp, Calif.: Naturegraph Publishing, 1971.

Sheldrake, Rubert. *A New Science of Life: The Hypothesis of Formative Causation.* London: Paladin Grafton Books, 1983.

Shulgin, Alexander, with Ann Shulgin. *PIHKAL: A Chemical Love Story.* Berkeley, Calif.: Transform Press, 1991.

Smith, Huston. *Cleansing the Doors of Perception: The Religious Significance of Entheogenic Plants and Chemicals.* New York: Tarcher/Putnam, 2000.

Strassman, Rick. *DMT: The Spirit Molecule: A Doctor's Revolutionary Research into the Biology of Near-Death and Mystical Experiences.* Rochester, Vt.: Park Street Press, 2001.

Strassman, Rick, Slawek Wojtowicz, Luis Edwardo Luna, and Ede Frecska. *Inner Paths to Outer Space: Journeys to Alien Worlds through Psychedelics and Other Spiritual Technologies.* Rochester, Vt.: Park Street Press, 2008.

Swimme, Brian. *The Universe Is a Green Dragon: A Cosmic Creation Story.* Santa Fe, N. Mex.: Bear & Company, 1984.

Talbot, Michael. *The Holographic Universe.* New York: HarperCollins, 1992.

Taylor, Scott. *Souls in the Sea: Dolphins, Whales, and Human Destiny.* Berkeley, Calif.: Frog Ltd., 2003.

Temple, Robert. *The Sirius Mystery: New Scientific Evidence of Alien Contact 5,000 Years Ago.* Rochester, Vt.: Destiny Books, 1998.

Trench, Brinsley Le Poer. *The Sky People.* London: Saucerian Books, 1960.

Urantia Foundation. *The Urantia Book.* Chicago, Ill.: The Urantia Foundation, 1955.

Vallee, Jacques. "Five Arguments against the Extraterrestrial Origin of Flying Objects." *Journal of Scientific Exploration,* 1990.

———. *Messengers of Deception: UFO Contact and Cults.* Berkeley, Calif.: Ronin Publishing, 1979.

Wasson, Gordon R. *Soma: Divine Mushroom of Immortality.* New York: Harcourt Brace Jovanovich, 1968.

Wasson, Gordon R., Albert Hofmann, et al. *The Road to Eleusis: Unveiling the Secret of the Mysteries.* New York: Harcourt, 1978.

Wilber, Ken (editor). *The Holographic Paradigm and Other Paradoxes: Exploring the Leading Edge of Science.* Boulder, Colo.: Shambhala, 1982.

Wyllie, Timothy. *Adventures among Spiritual Intelligences: Angels, Aliens, Dolphins & Shamans.* Novato, Calif.: Origin Press, 2001.

———. *Dolphins, ETs & Angels.* Santa Fe, N. Mex.: Bear & Company, 1993.

———. *The Helianx Proposition, or, The Return of the Rainbow Serpent.* Daynal Institute Press, 2011.

———. *Love Sex Fear Death: The Inside Story of the Process Church of the Final Judgment.* Port Townsend, Wash.: Feral House, 2009.

Wyllie, Timothy, Alma Daniel, and Andrew Ramer. *Ask Your Angels: A Practical Guide to Working with the Messengers of Heaven to Empower and Enrich your Life.* New York: Ballantine Books, 1992.

Index

Abraham, 30, 35, 111

acceleration of consciousness under way, 220

Adamski, George, 322, 323

Ahuru Mazda, 128

Albigensians, 112

  Catholic genocide of, 103, 280

Alexandria library, 112

alien/hybrid children, 336

angelic conspiracy, 391

angels, 7, 10, 12, 65, 106, 107, 108, 193, 309, 316, 350, 387

  Abigrael, 351

  artist's depictions of, 314

  disguised as humans, 395

  dismissed as childish delusions, 387

  Enlightenment, 132

  fallen, 392

  guardian, 4

  guidance, 144

  of light, 335

  predict gentle transition to year 2012, xvi

Zadkiel, 351

Zophiel, 351

ants, 319

apartheid collapse, 160

apocalypse, 7

Apollo, 189, 208

  Temple of, 193

Aramaic culture, 44

Area 51, 371, 385

Arcturus, plate 8, 6, 317, 430

Argüelles, José, 301

Argüelles, Lloydine, 302

Armageddon, 97

Arnold, Kenneth, 14

ascension into the fifth dimension, 384

Ask Your Angels, 301

astral thoughtforms, 135

astronauts transformation, 407

atheism, 83

Atlantian black magicians, 396

Atkin, Juno, 306

Atlantis, 40

Atman, 168
atomic weapons, 403
Attila, 88
Avonals, 90
ayahuasca, 382
Aztecs, 302

Ba'al, 111
Baigent, Michael, 114, 269
Bailey, Elise, 372
Ball, Martin W., 415, 416
Baltonborough, 259
Bambridge, Elli, 365
Barnard, George, 245
Battistero, 153–56
Battle of Britain, 11
Beatea, 132
Bedouins, 111
Begin, Israeli Prime Minister, 33
BVF (Beings of the Violet Flame),
    318, 333, 339, 346, 371, 372,
    392, 394, 417
Belitsos, Byron, 91
Benjamin, Walter, 10
Bentov, Itzhak, 324, 418
Big Show, 380
Blake, William, 258
Blavatsky, Madame, 77
Blood Spring, 74
Böhm, David, 323, 411, 418, 420,
    424
Book of Enoch, 43, 44n
Book of Revelation, 383
Brookings report, 331
Brown, Dan, 270
Brown, Jerry, 38

Buddha, 85, 166
Buddhism, 81–82
Burnham, Sophie, 310

Cain, 44
Caligastia, 28n, 40, 41, 42n, 87,
    104, 107–9, 111, 112, 198,
    210, 342n, 390
  God of Urantia, 198
  God of the world, 390
Cape de la Hague, 261
  Atomic reactor, 265
Carter, Jimmy, 360
Castle, Christopher, 60-62, 128
Cathars, 102–6, 112, 159, 255,
    265, 269, 270, 378, 397
  Catholic slaughter of, 103, 280
Catholic church, 133
  aversion to, 134
  shackles of Mother Church, 152
Cayce, Edgar, 383
Celtic mythology, 71
Central Universe, 89, 166
Chagal, Marc, 139
Chalice Well, 63
Cherubim Order, 129n
Chief of Archangels, 164
Chief of Seraphim, 164
Christ, xv, 4n, 26, 28, 29, 42, 65,
    87, 88, 103, 134, 157, 166, 181,
    183, 267, 345, 354, 357, 378,
    392
  crucifixion of, 63
Christ Michael, plate 1, xv n, 30, 87,
    88, 89, 130, 163, 165, 166, 167,
    342. See also Christ

Christianity, 31
  death-oriented religion, 31
  hypocrisy and priestcraft, 88
CND (Campaign for Nuclear
    Disarmament), 17
Cocteau, Jean, 114
Cold War, 1, 17, 292, 330
coming superwave, 384
Conferences-in-Spirit, 51
Confucius, 88
conventional Christianity, 183
Cortez as god, 302
cosmic consciousness, 178
cosmic wake-up call, 347
Creator Sons, 89
Cree Native Americans, 83
Creighton, Gordon, 329, 332, 333
Creme, Benjamin, 54–56, 59, 78,
    79, 86, 90
Crete, 211
crop circles, 7, 238
Crowley, Aleister, 254–56, 322

Da Vinci Code, 270
Dalai Lama, 122, 124
Dali, Salvador, 419
Daligastia, 40, 108–9
Daniel, Alma, 5, 295–315, 360
Darwinian paradigm, 83
Dawkins, Richard, 74, 159, 354
Dead Sea Scrolls, 29
deep minds, 136
Delphi, 182–85, 208
Delphic Oracle, plate 4
Demons, 60, 370
Denaerde, Stephan, 243, 339, 346

DET, 415
Deutch, David, 411
Devil, 112
  as adversary, 142
DeWitt, Bryce, 323
discarnate intelligences, 91
Disclosure Project, 348
Divine experience, 83
Divine Mother, 28
Djinn, 332–33, 346, 372
DMT, 415, 416
DNA, 151, 375, 382, 383, 407
dolphins, 3, 113, 129, 163, 169,
    182–83, 208–9, 213, 349, 373
Dolphins, ETs & Angels, 239
doodlebugs, 12
Dostoevski, 183
dragons, 156–57
Drake, Frank, 409
Draypal Rinpoche, 18
dreams, 135
druids, 63

Earth, 383, 389
earth energies, 70
Earth quarantined from
    Multiverse, 5
Egypt, 128
Eisenhower, Dwight, 106, 330
Einstein, Albert, 424
Elkins, Don, 44
Ely, Carolina, 369
Enoch, 45
entheogens, 13, 19, 88, 195, 260,
    370, 414
  direct experience of the divine, 415

ineffable substances, 417
sacred oneness with creation, 416
environmental pollution, 5
Erhard, Werner, 361
ethylene, 190
ETs. *See* extraterrestrials
Euripides, 203
Everett, Hugh, 323
evolving deity, 177
Exopolitics, 348
extraterrestrials, xiv, 2, 3, 5, 7, 8, 14,
    15, 18, 44, 68, 106–7, 113, 327,
    348, 371, 372, 374, 381, 384,
    385, 417
  benign intervention, 408
  extraterrestrial intelligence, 387
  extraterrestrial races, 6
  Greys, 33
  Nordics, 330

fall of Communism, 160
Faust, Danny, 24
Faust, Robert, 24
feminine energy, 170
Ferguson, Marilyn, 258–59, 301
floatation tanks, 296
futique, 427
Future Alternatives, 21
Future Studies Research Group, 19,
    21–24

Gabor, Dennis, 421
Gaia, 129, 190
Galactic Federation, 384
Gandhi, 88
Gardener, Martin, 353

Geller, Uri, 407
genetics, 385
  mutation, 406
GEO 600 experiment, 423–24
  Einstein continuum disintegrates,
    424
geomantic creations, 128
German reunification, 160
Giorgias, 185–89, 207
Glastonbury, plate 3, 61–68, 71,
    125, 254–56
global village, 404
Gnostics, 105, 112, 378
God, 81–85, 128, 168–69, 220,
    245, 389, 390, 391
  concept of, 84–85
  early gods, extreme emotions of,
    111
  God as best friend, 220
  God of our hearts, 111
  Indwelling God, xiii
  in impersonal form, 168
  Living God, 220
  See also Goddess(es)
Goddess, 95
goddesses, 40, 45, 129, 189,
    190–92, 203, 240, 241,
    332–33, 386
  bad behavior of, 386–87
godhead, 397
god-kings, 45
  bad behavior of, 386–87
Gospel of Thomas, 114
grail legend, 63
Grand Multiverse, 198
Gray, John, 176

Grays, 383
Great Lamasery, Lhasa, Tibet, 50
Great Network, 132
Great Spirit, 391
Great Transformation, 417
green power, 380
Greer, Steven, 348
group-mind, 123

Hafez al-Assad, 33
Harmonic Convergence, 303–17
Hathor, Egyptian goddess, 62
Hawkings, Stephen, 387
Helianx Proposition, 228
hell, 380
Hellenism, 190
Hildegard of Bingen, 88
Hill, Betty, 18
Hinduism, 82
Hiroshima, 310
Hitchens, Christopher, 84, 159, 354
Hitler, Adolf, 398
Hitler's Germany, 35
Hoerbiger, 410
Hofmann, Albert, 415
Hogan, Craig, 423
Hollow Earth, 410
Holy Blood, Holy Grail, 269
Holy Grail, 49
Hopi prophesies, 92, 383
Hoyle, Fred, 406
Huron Native Americans, 83
Hurtak, James, 165
Huxley, Aldous, 414
Hynek, Allen, 336

Iarga, 340–41
ibogaine, 415
Icarus, 239
icaros songs, 383
ICBM silos, 7
Ichazo, Oscar, 361
immortality, 110
Inez (hurricane), 329
international terrorism, 5
Internet, 115, 247
intraterrestrial craft, 320
Iran hostage rescue plan, 360
    White House rejection, 362
Iroquois Native Americans, 83
Isis, 179
Islamic thought, 157
Israel, 225–31

Jacob, 136
Jaynes, Julian, 240–41
Jehovah, 110–11
Jerusalem, 30–31
Jesse, 263–84
Jesus, 180
Jesus Christ, xv, 83, 87–89, 114, 157, 164, 180, 183, 267, 342
    transfiguration of, 26
Jesus and dolphins, 183
Joseph of Arimathea, 62, 72
Joshua ben Joseph, 165-66, 342
Judeo-Christian culture, xiv
    dogma, 84
    tradition, 356
Judgment Day, 380
Jung, Carl, 62

Kali Yuga, xv
Keel, John, 333
Kellogg, Wilfred Custer, 353
ketamine hydrochloride, 415,
   425–26
King Arthur, 61, 63, 72
Knights Templar, 114
Koch, Laura, 93
   artist, occult astrologer, 96
Koch, Raymond Bret, 93, 121, 265
   Cathar history and ethos, 102–3
   Cocteau's death in his arms, 114
Koran, 335
Krapf, Phillip, 343–44
Krishnamurti, 70
Kundalini yoga, 14, 50

Lao-tze, 88, 116, 166
Last Supper, 74
Lavaldieu, 272, 273
LaViolette, Paul, 381, 382, 384
Layne, Meade, 335
Leadbeater, C. W., 77
Leary, Timothy, 407, 414, 427
Lehrman, Fredric, 259
Leigh, Richard, 269
Lemuria, 40
Leonardo da Vinci, 88
Leslie, Desmond, 322
Lessing, Doris, 129, 411
Leviathan, 67
Life Carriers, 166–67
Lilly, John C., 297, 349, 415, 424
Lincoln, Henry, 269
Local Universe, 89
LSD-25, 415, 417

Lucifer, 41–42, 81, 104, 107, 110,
   112, 389–90, 392, 393–94
   Declaration of Liberty, 356
   Invisible God denied, 390
   manifesto, 112
   Rebellion, 4, 5, 42–43, 87, 98,
      104–5, 108, 113, 132, 160, 167,
      198, 245, 246, 269, 316, 346,
      350, 355–56, 358, 364, 377, 378,
      390, 391, 394, 398
   rhetoric, 356
   scenario, 355–56

Macchu Piccu, 50
Mack, John, 336
MacLaine, Shirley, 294
Magdalene, Mary, 270
Magisterial Son, 87, 90
Magocsi, Oscar, 129
Maitreya, xv, 54–56, 60, 77, 85,
   87, 92
Maltwood, Katharine, 63
Manfredonia, 173–74
Manhattan Project, 415
Manicheans, 112
Marie-Louise, 160
Maya, 316, 342
Mayan calendar, 92, 301, 383
   end date, 302
McCarty, James Allen, 44
McKenna, Terence, 415
MDMA, 195, 306, 307, 417
Melchizedek, 28–30, 35, 88, 111,
   162, 169, 342n, 355, 378
   Brotherhood, 164
   Covenant of Faith, 30, 169

Divine Being in Dead Sea Scrolls, 29
lack of compassion, 355
servant of the Most High, 29
Melinda, 19–25, 45–53, 65, 75,
    86–93, 114, 119, 130–33, 139,
    159–73, 203, 230–35, 377
Merkaba, 384
Messenger, Stanley, 286, 288
Messiah, xv, 58, 92, 372
Michael, 87, 378
Michell, John, 128, 291–92
    hacked into CIA, 292
microdot acid, 195
midwayers, xvi, 43, 65n, 108, 192,
    199, 218, 228, 235–39, 243
    described in detail, 244
    facilitated Christ's miracles, 354
    rebel midwayers, 202
Milanovich, Norma, 431
Milky Way, 409
mirror universe, 335
Mohammed, 88, 166
Monjoronson, 91
Monroe, Robert, 323, 329
Montgomery, Ruth, 411
Moolenbegh, H. C., 350
Mormons, 30
Moses, 88
Mother Gaia, 175
Mother Spirits, xv n, 391
multiple words scenario, 411
Multiverse, xvii, 3, 5, 28, 42, 43, 87,
    106, 108, 113, 130, 132, 166, 169,
    175, 177, 198, 317, 318, 320, 326,
    351, 387, 389, 390, 400, 420, 421
    Authorities, 197, 205

presumed benign, 330–31
co-creating a New Reality, 224
cosmic hologram, 418
living Multiverse, 400
multilayered nature of, 319
torus shaped, 423
Multiverse of Spirit, 158
mutagenic radiation, 408

Nablus, 231
Naboteans, 163
Navajo Native Americans, 83
Nazi death camps, 310
near-death experience (NDE), 2–3,
    164, 252, 320, 360
Nechung Rinpoche, 18
Nephilim, 43, 45
Network of Light, 178, 308
New Mexico, 367–68
new physics, 404
Newbrough, John Ballou, 164
Nice, 136
Nietzsche, Friedrich, 138
Nixon, Richard, 360
NORAD, 385
Nostradamus, 383
Notre Dame Cathedral, 127, 130,
    191

Odin, 111
Old Ones, 410
Old Power, 175
OOBE. See out-of-body experience
Oracle of Delphi, 191
Oreibasius, 189
Orion, 44

Oroc, James, 415, 416

Orwell, George, 292

Osiris, 179

Ouroboros, 67

Ouspenski, P. D., 335

out-of-body experience, 14, 18, 19

P-scope, 324

PLO, 37

Palestine, 35–37, 229–30

Palestine/Israeli stalemate, 227

pantheism, 82–83

Paradise, 10

Paris, 122

   Nazi occupation of, 123

Parma, 152–54

Pentagon, 385

Persian Gulf civilization, 198

Peru, 128

phencyclidine, 195, 196

Philo, xii

PIHKAL, 416

Pistis Sophia, 105

Planet IARGA, 339–40

   contact reported, 340

planetary cooperation, 404

planetary evacuation, 381

planetary invasion, 406

Planetary Princes, 107, 108

Planetary Seraphic Government, 169

planetary transformation, xiii

Plato, 88

Pleiades, 317

Ploski, Cynthia, 43

Plutarch, 190

Pogo, 143

Pope Benedict, 385

Pope Innocent III, 103

Posnnakoff, Yanni, 295, 313

pre-Adamic men, 335

Premaratma, Baba, 58-59, 70, 76, 87

President Obama, 385

Pribram, Karl, 323, 418, 420, 424

Prieure de Sion, 114

prison worlds, 392

priestesses of Apollo, 190

Process Church, 17

PROCESS magazine, 16

prophecies, 383

   inherently unreliable, 9

psilocybin, 415

psychoactive drugs, 408

pyramid of Cheops, 20, 38, 44, 46, 48

Pythia, 190

Quetzalcoatal, plate 6, xv, 302–7

Quist, Roberta, 373

Ra Material, 44

Rainbow Serpent, 62

Ramana Maharshi, 101

Ramer, Andrew, 5, 308–15

Raphael, 88

Rapture, 380

Ravenna, 161

Reagan, Ronald, 97, 292

Rebecca, 167

Rejoining the galactic community, 417

remembering the future, 427–28
   Tibetan Buddhist analogue, 428
Rennes-le-Château, 271
Rice, Betty, 432
Roberts, Tony, 62, 128
Roman Catholic misogyny, 159
Roswell incident, 14, 339, 370
   film "restoration," 339
Rueckert, Carla, 44
Russell, Peter, 258
Rwanda, 347

Sacred Circle, Central Park, 306
Sadat, Anwar, 27, 33
Sadler, William, 352
Sagan, Carl, 403, 409
Sagittarius, 76
Saint George legends, 156
Saint Michael, 72
Salla, Michael, 241
Sandoz laboratories, 415
Satan, 41, 103, 107, 112, 364
Selva di Fasano, 180
seraphim, 132
Serpent People, 16
Seth, 44
SETI, 322, 387
Shandron, 358
Shearer, Tony, 302
Shulgin, Sasha, 416
Siddhartha Gautama, 88
singularity, 92
Sirius, 317
sixties dreams shattered, 293
space migration, 21
spark of Creator in all, 222

Steel, John, 259
Stevens, Wendelle C., 339
Stewart Rod, 120
Stirling, Peter, 106, 382
Stonehenge, plate 5
Strassman, Rick, 416
Streiber, Whitley, 243
Superuniverses, 421
Supreme Being, 177

Talbot, Michael, 419
Templars, 70
Temple of Athena Pronaia, 202
Teresa of Avila, 88
Tessimond, S. J., 379
Theosophy, 77
Thom, Alexander, 64
thoughtforms, 124, 147, 325
   the coming of the True Age, 149
   the New Vision, 149
Three Mile Island, 309
time travel, 412
transformation of planet Earth, xvii
Trench, Brinsley Le Poer, 16, 110,
   329–30

UFOs, 3, 7, 14, 15, 62, 132, 243,
   304, 310, 322, 330–37, 370,
   371, 387, 405, 409
Ultimatons, 196
ultraterrestrials, 333
Universe Broadcast Circuits, 129
Universe Careers, 391n
Universe Circuits, 207
unlimited energy, 21
untriggered brain circuits, 407

Urantia Book, xv, 4, 28, 29, 30, 40, 41, 43, 45, 87, 104, 105, 112, 128, 129, 136, 163, 166–68, 204, 206, 210, 239, 241, 246, 304, 333, 336, 338, 341, 346, 347, 351, 359, 364, 377, 378, 380, 389, 390, 393, 396

   cosmology, 197

   Kellogg family role, 352

   origins and influence, 4n

   Seventh Day Adventist links alleged, 353

   skeptics dismiss as mass delusion, 353

Urantia, the Great Cult Mystery, 353

Urantia Trinity, 89

Ursa Major, 317

V-1 bombs, 11

V-2 bombs, 12

Vallee, Jacques, 244, 337–38, 405

Vedas, 168

Vence Cathedral, 139

Verdants, plate 7, 341, 343–48

   star cruiser, 345

Vimanas, 242

Walk-Ins, 44n, 411, 425

war in heaven, 356

Wasson, R. Gordon, 414

Watergate, 360

Watson, Lyall, 407

White House, 362

Wilcocks, David, 385

Wilson, Robert Anton, 409

women, 157

   subjugation of, 158

wonder children emerging, 407

Woodruff, Cheryl, 310

world mind, 53

world population growth, 5

Wyllie, Diana, 55, 254, 287–88

Xavier, Francois, 131–32

Yaldabaoth, 106

Year 2012, xvi, 383, 384, 401

   angelic reassurance, xvi

   Big Show at End of Time, 342

   gentle dimensional shift, 401

   global cataclysm, 401

   global threat, 386

   long cycle ends, 304

   more to be revealed after 2012, 349

   superwave, 386

Yom Kippur 1973 war, 33

Zen gesture, 49

zero-point energy, 317

Zeta Reticuli, 106, 349, 382, 383

Zetas, 386

Zeus, 111

Zionist extremists, 36

Zodiac of Glastonbury, 63

Zodiac of Dendara, Egypt, 64

Zophiel, xvi

Zoroastrian Saoshyant, xv

Zunis, 369

About the Author

Photo by June Atkin

Timothy Wyllie chose to be born in London in 1940 at the height of the Battle of Britain. Surviving an English Public School education unbroken, he studied architecture, qualifying in 1964 and practicing in London and the Bahamas. During this time he also worked with two others to create a Mystery School, which came to be known as the Process Church, and subsequently traveled with the community throughout Europe and America. He became art director of *PROCESS* magazine, designing a series of magazines in the 1960s and '70s that have recently become recognized as among the prime progenitors of psychedelic magazine design.

In 1975 Wyllie became the director of the New York headquarters, organized a series of conferences and seminars on such unorthodox issues as out-of-body travel, extraterrestrial encounters, alternative cancer therapies, and Tibetan Buddhism. After some fractious and fundamental disagreements with his colleagues in the community, he left to start a new life in 1977. The record of Wyllie's fifteen years in the Mystery School of the Process Church and the true account of this eccentric spiritual community appears in his book *Love, Sex, Fear, Death: The Inside Story of The Process Church of the Final Judgement,* which was published by Feral House in 2009. It is slowly becoming a cult classic.

A profound near-death experience in 1973 confirmed for Wyllie the reality of other levels of existence and instigated what has become a lifetime exploration of nonhuman intelligences. Having created his intention, the Multiverse opened in a trail of synchronicities that led to his swimming with a coastal pod of wild dolphins, two extraterrestrial encounters—during one of which he was able to question the ET mouthpiece as to some of the ways of the inhabited Multiverse—and finally to an extended dialogue with a group of angels speaking through a light-trance medium in Toronto, Canada.

Wyllie's first phase of spiritual exploration was published as *The DETA Factor: Dolphins, Extraterrestrials & Angels* by Coleman Press in 1984 and republished by Bear & Company as *Dolphins, ETs & Angels* in 1993.

His second book, *Dolphins, Telepathy & Underwater Birthing,* published by Bear & Company in 1993, was republished by Wisdom Editions in 2001 under the title *Adventures Among Spiritual Intelligences: Angels, Aliens, Dolphins & Shamans.* In this book Wyllie continues his travels exploring Balinese shamanic healing; Australian Aboriginal cosmology; human underwater birthing; dolphins, death, and sexuality; entheogenic spirituality; the gathering alien presence on the planet; and his travels with a Walk-In, along with much else.

Wyllie's work with the angels through the 1980s resulted in the book *Ask Your Angels: A Practical Guide to Working with Your Messengers of Heaven to Empower and Enrich Your Life,* written with Alma Daniel and Andrew Ramer and published by Ballantine Books in 1992. After spending time at the top of the *New York Times* religious bestsellers, *Ask Your Angels* went on to become an international success in eleven translations.

The Return of the Rebel Angels continues the series he began with *Dolphins, ETs & Angels* and *Adventures Among Spiritual Intelligences,* presenting further in-depth intuitive explorations of nonhuman intelligences. It draws together the many meaningful strands of Wyllie's thirty-year voyage of discovery into unknown, and long taboo, territories into a coherent and remarkably optimistic picture for the immediate future of the human species, with the inconspicuous help of a benign and richly inhabited living Multiverse.

The Helianx Proposition or The Return of the Rainbow Serpent, also thirty years in the making, is Wyllie's illustrated mythic exploration of an ancient extraterrestrial personality and its occult influence on life in this world. Published by Daynal Institute Press in 2010, it includes two DVDs and two CDs of associated material. The CDs contain 19 tracks of the author's visionary observations augmented by Emmy-winning musician Jim Wilson, master of digital sonic manipulation.

Wyllie is currently continuing his work on *The Autobiography of an Angel,* a multivolume personal exploration of the angelic realms over the past half a million years of their presence on the planet, which will be published over the years in a serialized form on eBooks.

Wyllie lives in a house of his own design at the foot of a mesa somewhere in the wilds of the New Mexico high desert, where he can hear the subtle whispers of the unseen realms.

BOOKS BY TIMOTHY WYLLIE

The DETA Factor: Dolphins, Extraterrestrials & Angels, 1984 (currently in print as *Dolphins, ETs & Angels,* 1993).

Ask Your Angels: A Practical Guide to Working with the Messengers of Heaven to Empower and Enrich Your Life, 1992 (cowritten with Alma Daniel and Andrew Ramer).

Dolphins, Telepathy, & Underwater Birthing, 1993 (currently in print as *Adventures Among Spiritual Intelligences: Angels, Aliens, Dolphins & Shamans,* 2001).

Contacting Your Angels Through Movement, Meditation & Music, 1995 (with Elli Bambridge).

Love, Sex, Fear, Death: The Inside Story of the Process Church of the Final Judgment, 2009 (editor, with Adam Parfrey).

The Helianx Proposition or the Return of the Rainbow Serpent, 2010.

The Return of the Rebel Angels, 2011.

BOOKS OF RELATED INTEREST

Dolphins, ETs & Angels
Adventures Among Spiritual Intelligences
by Timothy Wyllie

Bringers of the Dawn
Teachings from the Pleiadians
by Barbara Marciniak

Family of Light
Pleiadian Tales and Lessons in Living
by Barbara Marciniak

Earth
Pleiadian Keys to the Living Library
by Barbara Marciniak

The Pleiadian Workbook
Awakening Your Divine Ka
by Amorah Quan Yin

The Secret History of Extraterrestrials
Advanced Technology and the Coming New Race
by Len Kasten

Grey Aliens and the Harvesting of Souls
The Conspiracy to Genetically Tamper with Humanity
by Nigel Kerner

The Pleiadian Agenda
A New Cosmology for the Age of Light
by Barbara Hand Clow

INNER TRADITIONS • BEAR & COMPANY
P.O. Box 388
Rochester, VT 05767
1-800-246-8648
www.InnerTraditions.com

Or contact your local bookseller